Family Planning and Pregnancy Counselling Projects
for Young People

The Policy Studies Institute (PSI) is Britain's leading independent research organisation undertaking studies of economic, industrial and social policy, and the workings of political institutions.

PSI is a registered charity, run on a non-profit basis, and is not associated with any political party, pressure group or commercial interest.

PSI attaches great importance to covering a wide range of subject areas with its multi-disciplinary approach. The Institute's 30+ researchers are organised in teams which currently cover the following programmes:

Family Finances and Social Security
Health Studies and Social Care
Innovation and New Technology
Quality of Life and the Environment
Social Justice and Social Order
Employment Studies
Arts and the Cultural Industries
Information Policy
Education

This publication arises from the Health Studies and Social Care programme and is one of over 30 publications made available by the Institute each year.

Information about the work of PSI, and a catalogue of available books can be obtained from:

Marketing Department, PSI
100 Park Village East, London NW1 3SR

Family Planning and Pregnancy Counselling Projects for Young People

Isobel Allen

POLICY STUDIES INSTITUTE
100 PARK VILLAGE EAST, LONDON NW1 3SR

**The publishing imprint of the independent
POLICY STUDIES INSTITUTE
100 Park Village East, London NW1 3SR
Telephone: 071-387 2171; Fax: 071-388 0914**

ISBN 0 85374 489 0

A CIP catalogue record of this book is available from the British Library.

1 2 3 4 5 6 7 8 9

How to obtain PSI publications
All book shop and individual orders should be sent to PSI's distributors:

BEBC Ltd
9 Albion Close, Parkstone, Poole, Dorset, BH12 3LL

Books will normally be despatched in 24 hours. Cheques should be made payable to
BEBC Ltd.

Credit card and telephone/fax orders may be placed on the following freephone
numbers:

FREEPHONE: 0800 262260 FREEFAX: 0800 262266

Booktrade Representation (UK & Eire)
Book Representation Ltd
P O Box 17, Canvey Island, Essex SS8 8HZ

PSI Subscriptions
PSI Publications are available on subscription.
Further information from PSI's subscription agent:
Carfax Publishing Company Ltd
Abingdon Science Park, P O Box 25, Abingdon OX10 3UE

Laserset by Policy Studies Institute
Printed in Great Britain by BPCC Wheatons Ltd, Exeter

Acknowledgements

This study was initiated and funded by the Department of Health. Several members of staff at the Department gave their support and guidance at various stages of the research. Their help and encouragement were much appreciated by the author.

The study was designed and directed by Isobel Allen, who wrote the report. Catherina Pharoah was responsible for the ongoing collection of data, liaison with the project teams, organisation of interviewing and much of the coding and analysis of questionnaires, activity sheets and other factual data presented in the Appendices. Lynda Clarke was responsible for collecting, analysing and writing up the demographic data presented in Appendix I.

Philip Kestelman coded and collated the returns from the young people's clinics and drop-in centres, and provided advice on demographic data. Annette Walling provided valuable assistance with data analysis and interviewing. Ian Christie was closely involved in the initial stages of the evaluation, particularly in the design of research instruments and negotiation with the project teams. Hilary Gellman, Maureen Farish and Sandra Williams helped with interviewing, and Pat Gay helped with coding questionnaires. Karen MacKinnon was responsible for the computing and preparation of tables and her help was much appreciated in the computer analysis of the data.

We are grateful to all the professionals in the three areas who spared the time to be interviewed by us. In particular, we should like to thank the members of the three project teams and staff of Brook Advisory Centres for their cooperation during the monitoring period. The report draws attention to the problems encountered by teams brought together to set up 'demonstration' projects which are expected to provide a model for others to follow, and yet are operating under tight time constraints and the close scrutiny of external evaluators.

Finally we should like to thank the young people we interviewed in the three areas. Services for young people are too often designed without listening closely to the voice of the consumer. We hope that those providing and commissioning services for young people will take careful note of the views and experience of the young people reported in this study. There is a vital need for sympathetic and appropriate services for all young people, and much can be learnt from the interviews conducted in this evaluation.

Contents

vi

Tables

Appendices

Chapter 1
Introduction

The three young people's projects described in this report were set up with funding from the Department of Health with the aim of reducing the risk of unwanted pregnancy among young people and encouraging them to seek advice early if they suspected they were pregnant. The health authorities responsible for running them put in bids in response to an invitation from the Department of Health in July 1986 for interested health authorities to submit proposals for projects to provide a family planning and pregnancy counselling service specifically for young people under 25. The proposals from City and Hackney, Milton Keynes and South Sefton health authorities were selected as being particularly suitable for the Department's purposes.

The projects themselves were intended originally to have funding for three years, starting at the beginning of 1987, but, in the event, the government funding ran for an eighteen-month period from October 1987 to March 1989. During this time, the projects were monitored and evaluated by Policy Studies Institute.

Background to the project
The Department of Health set up these projects because research funded by the Department (RCOG, 1984, Allen, 1985, Simms and Smith, 1985) had suggested that the needs of younger people were not being adequately met by existing provision for family planning and abortion. In particular, the Department thought that the relatively high incidence of late abortions among young people could be reduced if better facilities were available, for example, more youth advisory centres offering counselling services more closely geared to the needs of the young. The Department stressed that its own policy for many years had been to encourage health authorities to consider establishing separate facilities for the young. Evidence at the time suggested that possibly only 50 per cent of health authorities actually had such facilities (FPA, 1985). When the funding for the projects was announced in July 1986, the then Minister for Health said he hoped the

1

findings of the evaluation would help authorities generally in providing services appropriate to this age group.

Aims and purpose of young people's projects

The aim of the projects, as described by the Department of Health in its original briefing paper, was 'to establish a service providing advice and information for young people, both to those women at risk of becoming unintentionally pregnant, or those who have become so (and their partners), in such a way as to attract and reach as great a number of the target population (under 25s in the above group) as possible'.

The purpose of the projects, and their evaluation, was to see what effect these models of service had on various indicators, for example, target population reached, proportion of late abortions, abortion rate, conception rate, proportion of NHS versus non-NHS abortions, etc.. The Department also considered that it would be helpful if the evaluation measured consumers' attitudes towards the service provided by the projects.

It is perhaps useful to summarise the content of the projects as envisaged by the Department. The Department was keen to look at three different models of service in similar areas, in that it was thought the lessons learnt from a number of different models might be of more practical benefit to the NHS than simply looking at one type of model in different areas. It did not want to lay down rules about the detailed content and structure of the projects, but said that a common aim would be to provide a confidential and friendly atmosphere in which the user could confide in an independent professional person, for example a trained counsellor, family planning doctor or nurse, and discuss their worries about becoming pregnant or what to do once pregnant. The projects would provide advice and information about contraception, refer people to clinics or GPs where appropriate, and perhaps either provide contraceptive treatment on site or make available the means of contraception.

The Department did not give precise guidelines on the way in which such a service might be provided. It suggested that it could be peripatetic or centre-based, specialist family planning or dealing with more general health problems, and that it could be a new venture or could build on existing activities. It did, however, stress the importance of the need for the projects to liaise with other services, particularly with family practitioner and health education services, but also with the education service and social services. It also stressed that it was of paramount importance that the project was not seen as, in any way, undermining family stability or parents' relationships with their children.

The projects
Services provided
In all three areas, the projects were set up to provide both a direct contraception and pregnancy counselling service to young people and to develop outreach work with young people and other professionals and agencies. The direct services are described in more detail in Chapter 2 to 4, and the outreach work is discussed in Chapters 10 to 13, but a brief summary here will set the scene.

In Milton Keynes and South Sefton, the projects provided a direct service to young people at their project base through a daily drop-in service and a weekly clinic session with a doctor present. Both projects aimed to develop outreach work with young people and other professionals and agencies from their project base. The same staff were responsible for both the direct service and the outreach work, with the additional help of a clinic doctor only for the clinic sessions.

The Milton Keynes project (You 2) was based in two rooms in The Bakehouse, a building used for other community purposes in Wolverton, in the north of Milton Keynes. The You 2 premises had a separate entrance at the back of the building. For the first six months of the project, a drop-in session was provided once a week at a Neighbourhood House in Netherfield, a district of Milton Keynes. In the last twelve months of the project this session was transferred to the Barnhouse, a youth centre in Central Milton Keynes.

The South Sefton project (PACE) was based in three tiny rooms with an additional Portakabin built on to one of the rooms in the King George VI Centre, a community centre in Bootle, which was used for other community purposes, including old people's clubs and youth clubs. It had no separate entrance.

In City and Hackney, the direct service to young people was provided by the Brook Advisory Centres at three clinic sessions based in the Shoreditch Health Centre on two evenings a week and on a Saturday morning. The outreach work with young people and professionals was provided by the City and Hackney Young People's Project (CHYPP) team, from the project base in the City and Hackney community health headquarters, located near the Shoreditch Health Centre.

Staffing
City and Hackney was set up with a coordinator who was a health authority employee, who had helped to prepare the proposal to the Department of Health and who had experience both of the health authority and of women's

health projects. She had responsibility for the budget, for managing the CHYPP project on a day-to-day basis and for the liaison with Brook. There were three other development workers, one full-time and the other two part-time. Two of these were experienced in community work, and one had considerable experience in related projects with young people, with particular skills in developing outreach work. Two of the development workers left and were replaced seven months before the end of the project. There was also a change in the clerical and administrative support staff.

Five of the six CHYPP team members (coordinator and development workers) had worked with young people before working on the young people's project, none of them had worked in a family planning clinic, three had been involved in pregnancy counselling, three had experience in sex education and four of the six had had some training in counselling.

The Brook clinic staff was usually made up of an administrator, a doctor, a nurse and a lay counsellor at each session. Brook had a considerable number of changes of administrator during the eighteen months of the monitoring period. It retained a small core of medical and nursing staff during this time, but locum doctors and nurses were frequently used. The counsellor remained in post throughout the project period. All staff had had previous experience with young people, in family planning clinics and in counselling.

In Milton Keynes, four health workers were appointed initially on an equal level, two of whom had previously worked for the Women's Health Group in the Bakehouse. Both worked part-time, and one had trained as a teacher. One of the new staff was male and medically qualified, but not working as a doctor, while the other had community experience. The need for a team 'leader' soon became apparent, and the male health worker was appointed to this position. There were several changes of staff in the monitoring period, although three of the four original health workers were still in post at the end of the project. There was a change in clinic doctor when the original doctor was off sick and when she had maternity leave. Both clinic doctors were local GPs. There was no nurse as such, although one of the health workers who was employed for several months in 1988 had a nursing background. Administrative and clerical support was provided by two part-timers, both of whom left and were replaced during the monitoring period.

Five of the six You 2 health workers had worked with young people before, none had ever worked in a family planning clinic, three had experience of pregnancy counselling, three had done some sex education and five had had some counselling training.

In South Sefton, one of the two health workers was a social worker who was appointed as health promotion officer, while the other was a health visitor, appointed for this expertise. Both had experience of working with young people, working in family planning clinics and had done some pregnancy counselling. One had counselling training, but neither had experience in sex education. The third member of the team provided administrative and clerical support. No project coordinator was appointed as such, although the health promotion officer took this role unofficially. All three members of the team were still in post at the end of the monitoring period. The clinic doctor was a GP in Liverpool. Locums were used for the clinic doctor when she was on prolonged sick leave.

The majority of the staff in all three projects were in their thirties or early forties. Only one project team member and one doctor were under the age of 30. Only one male worker was employed in any of the projects, although Brook sometimes employed male doctors in City and Hackney.

Management and steering groups

The management of the projects varied. In City and Hackney, the District Medical Officer was initially responsible for the project within the district. The project coordinator had responsibility for the day-to-day running of the project and had an additional role of managing and developing the work of the project within the health authority.

In Milton Keynes, the Specialist in Community Medicine in the health authority was responsible for the project within the district. The District Health Education Officer had day-to-day management responsibility, and the project coordinator reported to him.

In South Sefton, the Unit General Manager, Priority and Community Care, had responsibility for the project within the district. The District Health Promotion Officer had day-to-day management responsibility for the project. One of the two health workers was the de facto project coordinator, although not appointed as such. The three members of the team had different line managers, in health promotion, nursing and administration.

In City and Hackney and Milton Keynes, steering groups were set up at the beginning of the projects, with representatives from the health authority, education authority and other interested parties, such as BPAS and social services in Milton Keynes, and Brook and representatives of groups working with young people in City and Hackney. In South Sefton there was an internal steering group made up only of senior health authority staff.

The Milton Keynes steering group met regularly until the end of the monitoring period. The City and Hackney steering group met irregularly to begin with, but no meetings were held in the last few months of the project. In South Sefton meetings of the steering group became more sporadic during the monitoring period.

Funding

The projects were funded by a grant from the Department of Health. Over the period 1987-89, City and Hackney DHA received £130,000, Milton Keynes DHA received £119,000, and South Sefton DHA received £76,000. The money received by City and Hackney covered both the CHYPP activities and the Brook Advisory Centres clinics. The bulk of the expenditure in all three areas was devoted to salaries.

The evaluation

At the same time as the Department invited proposals from health authorities for running the projects, it also invited proposals from reseachers for evaluating the projects. Policy Studies Institute was asked to carry out the evaluation. In our proposal to the Department of Health, we pointed out certain factors which should be taken into account in evaluating projects of this kind. These are discussed here in some detail since they have an important bearing on the following report.

There were three main problems in evaluating these projects. The first was the selection by the Department of three areas with broadly similar characteristics which had put forward proposals for differing models of service provision. The Department recognised the problems this presented to the evaluator, but thought that the benefits to other health authorities of this approach outweighed the methodological disadvantages to researchers. It was, however, concerned that the projects should be capable of satisfactory evaluation and comparison one with another.

The second problem was that of satisfying the Department's wish to see what effect the models of service established by the three projects had on various indicators such as target population reached, abortion rates, proportion of late abortions, conception rate and so on.

The third problem was how to evaluate what might be described as the 'softer' indicators of success, such as the effect the projects had on the knowledge and behaviour of young people, or the extent to which they affected the attitudes or practice of professionals working with young people. A number of such factors were implicit or explicit in the aims of all three projects.

Differing models of service provision

Evaluating three projects with differing models of service provision poses problems in that is difficult to conduct a 'controlled' study if all the participants are trying to achieve their objectives by different means, and may, indeed, have different sets of objectives. It is particularly difficult to make any comparison across the projects, for example, in trying to attribute success or failure in reaching young people to one factor or set of factors rather than others, if each project does not employ the same means.

But it could be argued that an evaluation of services of this kind does not lend itself to such an approach in any case. Even if three projects set up services which attempted to provide identical models of service delivery for the same amount of funding, it would still be difficult to attribute differences in outcome to specific factors, even if the outcome measures themselves were clearly defined. There are far too many differences of a local nature which could affect service success or failure, such as historical provision of services, as well as demographic, social and economic factors, not to mention differences in the organisation, structure and management of the projects. It is not easy to design a 'tidy' intervention in such an untidy field.

In accepting the Department's desire to demonstrate as many models of good practice as possible, we stressed that it would be preferable if the selected projects could all provide at least a common 'core' of services, so that some comparison could be made across the districts. If none of the projects used any methods in common it would have been difficult to make any comparison at all. In the event, all three projects provided a clinic service to young people and all three developed outreach work. Two of the projects provided a drop-in service to young people.

The main problems in the evaluation, however, did not lie in whether the three projects offered different models of service, but in the outcome measures which were to be used. How could the projects be assessed as successful or not successful? By what criteria were they to be judged?

The indicators of success suggested by the Department of Health

The Department of Health suggested that the effect of the projects on various indicators, such as the target population reached, birth-rate, abortion rate, proportion of NHS/non-NHS abortions, proportions of late abortions and so on, could be used as measures of success.

We agreed that it was necessary to measure the target population reached, but pointed out that this in itself was a fairly crude measure, in that it could not indicate whether those using the services were people who had never used services before, or were dissatisfied customers of other services, or were clients moving between services. It could not show, in the short term, whether people were using the service only once, and it could not indicate whether there was anything special about the project that attracted people who would not otherwise have used a service. We concluded that the collection of routine data on the 'target population' reached was an inadequate measure on its own of the impact and effectiveness of the projects.

We pointed out four main problems in using birth, conception and abortion rates as indicators, particularly in the short-term;

(i) the services were likely to build up a clientele over time, so that the impact would probably be gradual rather than immediate;

(ii) there is a time-lag with both births and abortions, so that even if there were an immediate widespread take-up of services or increase in the efficient use of contraception which affected birth or abortion rates, it would not show up in the figures for some months;

(iii)there are fluctuations in the birth rate and abortion rate at a local and national level from year to year in any case and the figures for one or two years are insufficient to show any reliable trend;

(iv)there is a time-lag in the collation and publication of statistics on births and abortions which makes any regional or national comparisons in the short-term very difficult.

We argued that the use of these indicators to measure the impact of the projects in the short-term, ie at the end of a two or even three year period, was very limited. In the longer term it would certainly be possible to measure the trends, but even so, given a short-term intervention of eighteen months, it is difficult to say how much weight could be given to any upward or downward movement in any of the figures. We present the relevant statistics on birth rates and abortion rates in the 1980s for the three districts and for England and Wales in Appendix I, together with a commentary. As the tables show, little can be discerned from an analysis of separate years.

We added that extraneous local or national factors operating totally independently of the projects could have considerable effects on outcome measures of this kind. For example, at a local level, the retirement of a consultant gynaecologist who performed very few terminations of pregnancy and his replacement by one with a very 'liberal' policy might

8

have a marked impact on the number and proportions of NHS abortions, or on the number and proportion of 'late' abortions. Changes of policy at a local level had undoubtedly had some effect in the districts in previous years. Probably the most noticeable was in Milton Keynes, where the proportion of terminations of pregnancy on NHS premises plummeted from 1986 to 1988, because the health authority entered into an agency agreement with BPAS by which terminations paid for by the authority were carried out on non-NHS premises in another Regional Health Authority. As the tables in Appendix I show, this completely altered the proportion of NHS:non-NHS abortions over a two-year period.

The 'softer' indicators of success

Given the limitations of basing the evaluation of the projects solely on examining the numbers of the target population reached and birth and abortion rates, particularly in the short-term, we felt it necessary to put forward supplementary methods of measuring both the effects and the effectiveness of the projects.

'Outcome measures' are notoriously difficult to develop for projects of this kind. Some of the services offered by the projects were rather intangible and difficult to measure both in terms of 'input' and 'outcome'. It is easy to count the number of pill prescriptions or pregnancy tests, but much more difficult to measure 'advice' and 'counselling'. All three projects studied laid stress on 'health education' and 'information', but the nature of this is difficult to quantify and it is certainly difficult to assess, particularly in the short-term.

We had to develop methods of assessing the services offered by the projects which could be written up fairly quickly after the monitoring period had ended. The Department of Health had suggested that some kind of consumer survey could be carried out in order to measure users' attitudes towards the services offered by the projects, and, indeed, consumer satisfaction was one of the main criteria of success suggested by project team members, their managers and other professionals interviewed in connection with this study.

We agreed that it was important to hear the voice of the consumer, but we also thought it important to hear the views of young people who had not used the services. We considered that it was necessary to measure more than satisfaction with services, which can be a misleading indicator. We thought it important to explore, both with users and non-users of the services, the practice and attitudes of young people towards a number of factors affecting take-up of services and use of reliable methods of contraception. Many people speak on behalf of young people, and the projects were set up and designed by professionals and managers who thought they knew what was needed, but we wanted to hear what the young people themselves had to say.

In addition, we thought it important to seek the views of other professionals, both on the achievements of the projects and on services of this kind for young people. Such professionals are often in a key position to refer or inform young people about services aimed specifically at them, and, of course, many young people currently use the services and advice they provide, and will continue to do so.

Finally, we wanted to hear the views and assessment of the project teams and their managers and advisers. Their experience in trying to implement the aims of the Department of Health was of great importance to the evaluation, particularly in demonstrating to other health authorities and agencies how they attempted to overcome the acknowledged difficulties in setting up and running services of this kind for young people.

Methodology used by PSI in evaluation

We used a variety of methods in this evaluation. These are summarised briefly here:

Baseline statistical information

We collected data for the 1980s on 'target' population, births and abortions for the three districts and England and Wales (see Appendix I).

We collected information on the use of existing family planning services by GPs and family planning clinics in the districts. These figures had a different basis of collection and were of limited value. The age-groups used for the clinic figures did not distinguish clients under the age of 25. We collected details of numbers, times and locations of family planning clinics in the districts.

The figures on GP services give no age breakdown of patients, and are only based on returns for women prescribed the pill or fitted with an IUD. No other family planning or pregnancy counselling services provided by GPs are measured, and no indication is given of frequency of consultation. There were additional problems in assessing the GP service provision in these areas, since the health authorities were not coterminous with the Family Practitioner Committee boundaries. It was suggested to us that we might select a sample of GPs to try and establish a baseline of services offered to young people under 25, but we felt that the response rate might be too low and feared that the results would be biased towards the more active GPs. It would not have been a simple exercise for even the most cooperative of GP practices and we considered that the results would be too unreliable to justify undertaking it.

We collected information on abortion services within the NHS and in private and charitable facilities. Apart from the close link between the Milton Keynes project and BPAS, which carried out abortions on an agency basis for the health authority, there was little or no contact between the projects and consultant gynaecologists, hospitals or clinics.

Monitoring of the projects
(i) Organisation of the projects
We collected details for each project of staffing, management, premises, costs, hours available to members of the public, type of 'direct' services offered, 'outreach' work, extent and type of liaison with other relevant professionals and agencies and publicity arrangements.

(ii) Clients of the projects
We designed forms in conjunction with managers and project team members before the beginning of the monitoring period to record basic information about the users of the clinic and drop-in services of the projects. These record cards were completed by the project team members. They covered information on age, sex, marital status, occupation, ethnic origin, parity; reasons for attendance; source of referral or how client came to project; how client heard of project's services; other contraceptive methods and services ever used; previous terminations of pregnancy; dates of each visit; outcome of each consultation. The record card for drop-in clients was rather shorter, but also included information on where the project referred the client. Chapters 2 to 4 of the report give a detailed analysis and discussion of this information.

(iii) 'Outreach' activities of the project teams
We designed 'activity' forms in conjunction with the project teams to monitor their outreach activities. These forms were completed by the team members on a daily basis and returned to PSI for coding. They gave details of the location, type, purpose and content of each contact with a professional, agency or group of professionals and each outreach contact with a young person or group of young people. The analysis of these activity sheets is given in Appendix II.

(iv) Telephone enquiries

We designed forms in conjunction with the project teams to monitor telephone enquiries to the projects from professionals, other agencies and young people. The forms included details of the age of young people, the job or status of the professionals or other enquirers, and the nature and topic of the telephone call or enquiry. The analysis of these telephone enquiry forms is given in Appendix III.

(v) Self-completion questionnaires filled in by under-25s using family planning clinics and BPAS

Short forms were designed for self-completion by women under 25 who attended family planning clinics in Milton Keynes and South Sefton for the first time during the monitoring period. The forms were distributed by the clinic staff to women on their first attendance at all six of the Milton Keynes clinics and at the eight South Sefton family planning clinics within the vicinity of Bootle. (Two of the South Sefton clinics only held monthly clinic sessions and did not return any information.) In addition, forms were distributed to young women under 25 attending BPAS in Milton Keynes for counselling in connection with a termination of pregnancy. City and Hackney family planning clinics did not take part in the exercise because the health authority considered that it would be too onerous a duty for the staff of the clinics.

The purpose of the forms was to establish the extent and source of knowledge of the projects among young people using family planning clinics and BPAS for the first time, to elicit reasons for attending these clinics, and to see to what extent any knowledge of the existence of the projects had influenced the young people in their decision to attend other clinics or BPAS. The analysis of these self-completion forms is given in Appendix IV.

Interviewing

Personal interviews were carried out with respondents from the following four groups. Details of sampling, selection and numbers are given in the relevant chapters and in Appendix V. All interviews were carried out by members of PSI staff or by two experienced interviewers, using semi-structured questionnaires. All respondents were asked the same questions in the same order, but a number of questions were 'open-ended', allowing for full answers to be recorded verbatim. A code-frame was constructed for the analysis of these answers, but this technique allows for the extensive use of quotations from interviews used in this report.

(i) The project teams, their managers and advisers

All members of the project teams and their principal managers and advisers were interviewed when the projects had been running for about three months or when they joined the team, and again immediately after the end of the 18-month monitoring period. A detailed account of these interviews is given in Chapters 12 and 13 of this report.

(ii) Professionals

Interviews were carried out towards the end of the monitoring period with a variety of professionals working with young people in the districts. Family planning clinic doctors, family planning clinic nurses and health visitors were selected at random from lists supplied by the health authorities. The AIDS coordinators in each district and four staff from BPAS in Milton Keynes were interviewed because of their special relevance to the projects. The other professionals were selected from the contacts made by the project teams, and were usually those with whom the teams had had most contact. 110 professionals were interviewed in the three areas. A detailed account of these interviews is given in Chapters 10 and 11.

(iii) Young people using the projects' services

Interviews took place at the project premises in Milton Keynes and South Sefton and at the Shoreditch Brook clinic in City and Hackney, with 142 young people using the projects' services. Interviewing started at the beginning of November 1988, five months before the end of the monitoring period. We aimed to interview 50 young people in each district, but only achieved 42 interviews in South Sefton by the end of the monitoring period. In City and Hackney, all 50 interviews were with women; 49 women and 1 man were interviewed in Milton Keynes and 37 women and 5 men in South Sefton. A detailed account of these interviews is given in Chapters 5, 6, 7 and 9.

(iv) Young people who had not used the projects' services

Interviews took place with 31 young women, the majority of whom had had unwanted pregnancies or who had become pregnant while teenagers. They were selected from young women attending a teenage ante-natal clinic, young mothers' groups, a schoolgirl mothers' support centre and young women seeking termination of pregnancy. Although they were interviewed as non-users of the projects, three of them had in fact used the projects' services, two for pregnancy testing and one for a smear. Details

13

of the interviews and selection of respondents are given in Chapters 8 and 9.

The nature of the report

This report is an evaluation of three projects set up and funded for a limited time period of eighteen months. The activities of the project were monitored only during this period, although much of the final interviewing with the project teams and their advisers and managers took place after the end of the monitoring period.

The report therefore presents a snapshot of what happened during a defined period. Things have moved on since then, and the projects themselves have changed in size, scope and nature, as well as in the source of their funding. The object of this evaluation, however, was to present a picture of how three centrally-funded 'demonstration' projects went about achieving the aims of the Department of Health. The report describes the processes by which they set about providing models of service for others who might wish to provide young people's services for family planning and pregnancy counselling, and it discusses in detail the reactions of both young people and professionals to the activities of the projects.

The structure of the report

The report is divided into five main sections. Section 1 (Chapters 2 to 4) describes in detail the use made of the direct services the projects provided to young people. The chapters provide an important background for understanding the impact the projects made on the target population. They contain a number of tables, but the text can be read without reference to the tables. These chapters, however, contain a lot of detailed information which may not be of interest to every reader. A summary of the most important information, together with a discussion of the relevance of the information is given in Chapter 14 – Discussion of Findings. Readers who wish to concentrate on the way in which the projects worked, and their impact on young people and professionals in the areas, may wish to use Chapters 2 to 4 for reference only and to move on to Chapter 5 and subsequent chapters.

Section 2 (Chapters 5 to 9) covers the experience and views of young people, both users and non-users of the projects' services. Section 3 (Chapters 10 and 11) looks at the liaison between the projects and professionals and other agencies involved in working with young people, and examines the views and experience of these professionals and other agencies in relation to the work of the projects. Section 4 (Chapters 12 and

14

13) analyses the views and experience of the project team members, as well as their managers and advisers.

In Section 5, Chapter 14 is a discussion of the findings of the research which was so wide-ranging and identified so many issues of fundamental importance for those planning and providing services for young people. Chapter 15 brings together the conclusions from the findings and makes recommendations based on the findings. The aim throughout this report is to be constructive and to point out the lessons which can be learnt from the experience of these 'demonstration projects'.

Chapter 2
What did the projects provide and who used them?

The three projects were set up with the aim of reducing the risk of unwanted pregnancy among young people and encouraging them to seek advice early if they suspected they were pregnant. The projects approached this aim in different ways by providing different types of services directly to clients. The first part of this chapter summarises this direct service provision, since a clear understanding of what was being provided by the different projects is essential as a background to the tables and discussion presented in the following chapters.

Service provision to young people

In City and Hackney, three clinic sessions a week were provided in the Shoreditch Health Centre by the Brook Advisory Centres on Monday and Thursday evenings and on Saturday mornings. The Monday evening clinic was an existing Brook clinic which continued to function from the beginning of October 1987 when the monitoring period began. There had been a young people's clinic at Shoreditch run by the City and Hackney health authority on a Thursday evening, but this had had poor attendance figures and was discontinued when the project began. The Brook Thursday evening and Saturday morning clinics started at the beginning of November 1987.

The service to clinic clients in City and Hackney was the direct responsibility of Brook, who ran the Shoreditch clinic sessions independently of the CHYPP staff in the same way as they ran their other clinics. It was known as a Brook clinic, and this undoubtedly had implications in terms of its usage. The staff were employed and paid by Brook, using the Department of Health project money allotted by City and Hackney for the two new sessions and DHA money for the continuing Monday session, and were made up of doctors, nurses, a counsellor and an administrator for each session. (There were considerable staff changes during the monitoring period.) The Shoreditch clinic was used for other health service purposes at other times, and was equipped accordingly.

Apart from the Brook clinic, no other services were provided by the City and Hackney project directly to young people, other than on an outreach basis. The CHYPP offices were not intended to provide a counselling service to young people either in person or by telephone, and the CHYPP staff only provided services directly to young people outside their own base.

In Milton Keynes, one clinic session a week was provided at the You 2 base at the Bakehouse from the beginning of the project in October 1987. It was available on a Thursday afternoon from 2 to 4 pm until December 1988 when the clinic was changed to a Friday afternoon when there was a change of doctor. No nurse was employed, and the project staff provided reception and counselling services as required during the clinic session. One of the two rooms at the Bakehouse was equipped with a couch and running water, but its clinical facilities were limited. During the clinic session, only one other room was available for all the other activities of the project staff.

The You 2 project provided a drop-in service at the Bakehouse five days a week and on a Saturday morning. This was initially set up to be available only at certain times during the day, but the staff found that young people did not necessarily know or care about opening hours, and, in practice, a drop-in service was available whenever health workers were on the premises. The clerical and reception staff were present every weekday during working hours, and it was usual for at least one health worker to be available.

In addition, a drop-in service one afternoon a week was made available from the beginning of the project at the Neighbourhood Centre in Netherfield, a district of Milton Keynes. It had no clients in the six months that it was available, and in April 1988, the service was transferred to the Barnhouse, a youth centre in Central Milton Keynes, again available one afternoon a week. This drop-in service was only marginally more successful than that at Netherfield, in spite of the fact that the centre was used by young people. Very few clients were recorded as using the You 2 service at the Barnhouse.

In South Sefton, the PACE team had no premises of their own until mid-January 1988, when they moved into the King George VI Centre, where they had three small rooms available. From April 1988, they also had the use of a Portakabin which was built onto one of the rooms and used for clinic sessions. It had limited clinical facilities. One clinic session a week was held on a Wednesday afternoon from the beginning of February 1988. During the absence of the regular clinic doctor on sick leave, locum doctors were used from April to the beginning of June 1988. The project staff provided reception and counselling facilities during clinic sessions as in Milton Keynes. No clinic nurse was employed, but one of the health workers was a trained health visitor.

Drop-in facilities were available every week-day at the King George VI Centre. There was usually a member of staff in the PACE offices to offer counselling or pregnancy testing.

Who used the services?
This chapter is concerned with an analysis of the use of the two types of direct service provision – the clinic service in all three areas and the drop-in service in Milton Keynes and South Sefton. The actual nature of the services received at these two types of service is analysed and discussed in Chapters 3 and 4.

Before the monitoring period began, it was agreed with all three projects that information on users of the services would be recorded by the staff on the same forms in all three areas. These forms were designed in conjunction with senior staff in the areas and with the project staff who were in post in the months before the monitoring began. The clinic form covered rather more information than the drop-in form, but both were designed to collect information on the age, sex, marital status, number of children, occupation and area of residence of the client. In addition, the clinic form was designed to establish the ethnic origin of the client.

The analysis of the users of the projects by the type of service they used proved to be a complicated exercise. In City and Hackney, it was relatively straightforward. The users of the projects used only the clinic service, as this was the only service available. It has therefore been possible to construct a simple set of tables, showing the characteristics of the users of the clinic as outlined above.

With the other two areas, however, the analysis of the profile of users was much less straightforward. It proved fairly simple to construct a profile of the users of the project as a whole by most of the characteristics outlined above, since data was collected both from those using the clinic services and from those using the drop-in services. But this in itself is not enough. Two very different types of services were being offered in each of these projects – a clinic service once a week with a doctor in attendance and a drop-in service every day staffed by non-medical personnel.

We felt it necessary to analyse who went to the two different types of service, and to see who used the clinic services and who used the drop-in services. We were particularly interested to establish whether there were any differences between those whose *first* visit to the project was to the drop-in service and those whose first visit was to the clinic service. The first crossing of the threshold of services of this kind may well determine whether a young person continues with a service or not, and may have a major impact on their subsequent use of contraception and family planning services. We wanted to see whether people went first to one service provided by the projects rather than the other because they required a different kind of service. It is almost impossible to establish true motivation from figures of the kind we collected, but we had data on the nature of the type of service given at the consultations, and this is analysed in the next chapter.

The analysis would have been fairly straightforward if users had used *either* the drop-in service *or* the clinic service only. A high proportion of users in both areas did so, but a significant minority used both services, which made the construction of the profile of users of the Milton Keynes and South Sefton projects more complicated than in the City and Hackney project.

The information on the characteristics of users was collected at their first visit to one or the other service. If they used both services, the data was collected at each first visit. The records were kept in the same file and the same number was allocated to them, with a distinguishing code given for the type of service used on each visit. The data collected on characteristics of those using each of the services for the first time forms the basis of the tables and discussion in this chapter.

Who used which service?
We have designed the tables for the three projects to allow the maximum amount of information to be presented in the simplest possible way. The tables always show the three projects analysed separately and never give figures for the total number of people or visits for the three projects as a whole, since there is no methodological justification for doing so.

Table 2.1 shows how many people used each project and which services they used, and Table 2.2 gives the same information by the sex of those using the projects. These two tables give numbers as well as percentages, so that the reader can see at a glance the actual numbers using each project as well as the quite considerable differences in size between the projects. The rest of the tables describing people in this report use percentages for simplicity of presentation, but always give the base of the numbers of people involved. Tables describing visits usually give the numbers of visits only.

Tables 2.1 and 2.2 show that 883 people used the City and Hackney project services, of whom 876 (99 per cent) were female and 7 (1 per cent) were male, 711 people used the Milton Keynes project, of whom 701 (99 per cent) were female and 10 (1 per cent) were male, and 360 people used the South Sefton project, of whom 210 (58 per cent) were female and 150 (42 per cent) were male.

There were marked differences between the projects in terms of use of services, both in total numbers and percentages and also in terms of use by sex. The most striking difference was, of course, between City and Hackney and the other two, in that all the visits by both sexes in the former project were to the clinic.

Looking at the other two projects in more detail, it can be seen from Table 2.1 that in Milton Keynes, 82 per cent of the users made drop-in visits only, compared with 63 per cent in South Sefton. Table 2.2 shows that if these figures are analysed by sex, 82 per cent of Milton Keynes women made drop-in visits only, compared with 50 per cent of the South Sefton women. The proportion of South Sefton men using only the drop-in service was much higher, at 81 per cent, which is not surprising. It is, in fact, surprising that as many as 19 per cent of the South Sefton men used the clinic at all.

Six per cent of the Milton Keynes women made clinic visits only, compared with 21 per cent of the South Sefton women, while 13 per cent of the Milton Keynes women used both services, compared with as many as 28 per cent of the South Sefton women. Again, it is surprising that as many as nine men in South Sefton used *only* the clinic service, but the nature of the service in South Sefton was such that, initially at least, men or boys who requested condoms on more than one occasion were very strongly encouraged to see the clinic doctor, particularly if they happened to attend on the afternoon when the clinic was being held.

We analysed the data on those who used both services in terms of which service they used first. In both areas, the majority of the women using both services went first to the drop-in service. There were a variety of reasons for this which will be analysed in more depth in the next chapter. Clearly, greater frequency of availability of service was a factor. However, it should be noted that since the overwhelming majority of first attendances at the drop-in service at Milton Keynes were for a pregnancy test, the main reason for attending the clinic after using the drop-in service first was in connection with an unwanted pregnancy, usually to request a termination of pregancy. The pattern among women in South Sefton was rather different, as will be seen. The number of men in South Sefton using both services was small, and it appeared that those who used the clinic service first were either accompanying a girlfriend or happened by chance to go to the centre on the afternoon that the clinic was open.

We looked at those who ever used one or the other service at all. (This included those who had used only the particular service concerned *plus* those who had used both.) We found that 94 per cent of the Milton Keynes women project users had ever used the drop-in service, while only 18 per cent of the women project users had ever used the clinic service. In South Sefton, the pattern was quite different, with 79 per cent of the women project users having used the drop-in service and 50 per cent of the women project users having used the clinic service. The figures for men in Milton Keynes were really too small for any meaningful comparison to made with the South Sefton men. Over 90 per cent of the South Sefton men had ever used the drop-in service, and 19 per cent had ever used the clinic service.

Number of visits made to the services

Tables 2.3 and 2.4 show the number of visits made by the users of the three projects to each service, and give the average number of visits made by the users over the eighteen month period of monitoring. The question of average number of visits to the projects must be treated with caution, since the projects were acquiring new clients throughout the eighteen month period. A client attending in the last month of monitoring (March 1989) was clearly less likely to have attended more than once than a client attending first in October 1987.

These tables show that both the City and Hackney and South Sefton projects were used rather more often by individuals on average than the Milton Keynes project. Again, the nature of the reason for attending and the actual service provided by the projects is probably the key to this, in that such a high proportion of visits to Milton Keynes were for pregnancy tests, after which, in a substantial number of cases, no service was sought from the project.

The tables are perhaps most useful in giving some indication of the workload of the projects. In three sessions a week, the Brook clinic in City and Hackney dealt with 1958 visits in the 18-month monitoring period, all of them to the clinic. In one session a week each, the Milton Keynes clinic

21

dealt with 204 visits and the South Sefton clinic dealt with 223, having started four months after the other two clinics. The workload was rather different of course, in that the South Sefton clinic had 39 visits from men, compared with 21 in City and Hackney and one in Milton Keynes.

Assuming that equivalent numbers might have attended City and Hackney if there had only been one clinic a week, it can be seen that the Brook clinic was relatively much more popular than the other two, in that over 650 visits in the eighteen month period might have been expected from one session a week.

The average number of visits to the drop-in service was rather lower among Milton Keynes women than in South Sefton. It should be noted that in South Sefton, as Table 2.5. shows, very frequent and intensive counselling was offered to a small number of women which undoubtedly affected the average number of visits to the drop-in service.

Among the South Sefton men, the average number of visits was higher than for women, and one obvious reason for this was that the majority of the visits by men were to collect condoms. Collection of contraceptive supplies only was an infrequent reason for women visiting either drop-in service.

The number of visits to the different services made by the clients of the services give a rather different dimension to the analysis, as Table 2.5 shows. There were big differences between the projects. In City and Hackney, people only used the clinic service, and it can be seen that 45 per cent made one visit to the clinic during the monitoring period, 24 per cent came twice and 16 per cent came three times. 15 per cent came four or more times. The need for some form of ongoing support for a small number of women was demonstrated by the fact that 3 per cent of clinic users came seven or more times.

The figures for Milton Keynes show that over 70 per cent of women came once only to the project and a further 17 per cent came twice. 13 per cent came three or more times. Looking at the drop-in service alone, 79 per cent of the women came once only, while 70 per cent of those attending the clinic came once only. The use of Milton Keynes as a pregnancy testing centre is underlined by the high incidence of one-off visits to the drop-in service. Less than a handful of women came seven or more times.

In South Sefton, 58 per cent of women used the project once only, 17 per cent used it twice, while 25 per cent used it three or more times. 68 per cent of the women using the drop-in service attended once only and 63 per cent of clinic users attended once only. South Sefton was characterised by a small number of women who made repeated visits to the project, as can be seen by the fact that ten women made seven or more visits to the project over the monitoring period, representing around 6 per cent of visitors.

Profile of users of the projects

The projects were intended to provide a service for young people under the age of 25. No mention was made in the original brief from the Department of Health on the marital status of the young people, and no lower age limit was given. Although the brief stated that the aim of the projects was 'to establish a service providing advice and information for young people', it went on to say '...both to those women at risk of becoming unintentionally pregnant, or those who have become so, in such a way as to attract and reach as great a number of the target population (the under 25s) as possible'. This could be interpreted as an implicit assumption that the services would be aimed only or mainly at women, but this was never made explicit, and all the projects made clear their intention to provide services for both sexes.

Age

Since the aim of the projects was to provide a service for young people under the age of 25, it was important to see whether this was, in fact, what they achieved.

Table 2.6 shows the use of the projects by the age of the users. This table covers the use of all services offered by the projects and therefore in Milton Keynes and South Sefton it does not distinguish between those who used the drop-in service only, those who used the clinic service only and those who used both services. It simply shows the ages of those who came to the project at all. The following tables analyse the use of the different services by age. In City and Hackney, of course, Table 2.6 shows the age profile of those using the clinic service, and therefore the project service.

There were quite striking differences between the projects in terms of the ages of those using them. In Milton Keynes, 11 per cent of the women users were 25 or over, in City and Hackney, this proportion was 20 per cent, while in South Sefton, as many as 36 per cent were 25 or over. The numbers of women using the City and Hackney and Milton Keynes projects were considerably greater than those using the South Sefton project, and they used the services for rather different reasons, as will be seen, but nevertheless it must be asked why a service aimed at people under 25 was used so much by women over 25 in South Sefton. It was not as though the women were only just over 25. 15 per cent of the female users in South Sefton were over the age of 40.

23

The numbers of men using the City and Hackney and Milton Keynes projects were very small, and only one man (in City and Hackney) was over 25. In South Sefton, the appeal of the project to young men was much more striking than among the women, with only 7 per cent of the men aged 25 or over. The South Sefton men using the project were much younger than the women, with 21 per cent of the males being under the age of 16, and 80 per cent being 19 or under. Indeed, the majority of the men using the South Sefton project were boys of 14, 15 and 16 who accounted for 57 per cent of the male users. They came predominantly for condoms.

Looking at the use of services by younger women, only 4 per cent of the City and Hackney female users were under the age of 16, compared with 7 per cent in Milton Keynes and 15 per cent in South Sefton. The biggest single age-group of women using the City and Hackney and Milton Keynes projects was the 20-24-year olds, accounting for nearly 50 per cent of female users in both areas, while in South Sefton the proportion of women in this age-group was less than 20 per cent.

It might be assumed that the age-groups that the Department of Health thought would be the most likely to use young people's services of this kind would be 16-24 year old women. In Milton Keynes, 82 per cent of the women users fell into this age-group, in City and Hackney the proportion was 76 per cent, while in South Sefton, the proportion was only 49 per cent – less than half the women users of the project's services. As we have seen, this was largely accounted for by that project's appeal to older women and its greater proportionate appeal to the under-16s, although, in terms of *numbers* of under-16 year old girls, both the Milton Keynes and the City and Hackney project saw more (46 and 34 respectively, compared with 31 seen in South Sefton).

Further analysis of the figures show that 32 per cent of the City and Hackney women and 28 per cent of the Milton Keynes women were aged between 22 and 24, compared with 9 per cent in South Sefton. There can be little doubt that both the City and Hackney and Milton Keynes services appealed to women in their early twenties rather more than to the younger age-groups who might be thought to be at most risk from an unwanted pregnancy. In Milton Keynes, given the fact that the vast majority of visits were for pregnancy tests, in many cases in connection with *wanted* pregnancies, this finding was not particularly surprising. In City and Hackney, the age profile of the Brook clinic users suggested that the project was not getting through to the younger age-group in the numbers that might have been expected, given that it was a project aimed specifically at young people.

What kind of project services were the users in Milton Keynes and South Sefton using? Was there any indication that younger users might tend to go to a drop-in service rather than a clinic service? Much stress was laid by the staff in all three projects on the need for a non-clinical, informal approach. To what extent did potential users discriminate between the clinic service and the drop-in service?

The figures in themselves can only offer a guide to the reasons for what was happening. The fact that the drop-in service was open five or more days a week, while the clinic service was only available on one afternoon a week, might have had far more effect on the use of the services than the question of whether a service was 'clinical' or not. Much, of course, depended on what people wanted when they came through the door for the first time, and that is discussed in Chapter 3.

Table 2.7 shows the proportions of women in the various age-groups who used the different services in Milton Keynes and South Sefton. It can be seen that there were marked differences between the two projects, and that in both projects there were marked differences between the age-groups.

Looking at the youngest age-group first, it can be seen that they were much less likely in Milton Keynes to have used only the drop-in service than the older women. The staff clearly tried very hard to get these younger girls to the clinic to see the doctor if at all possible, and this can be seen by the fact that over half the under-16s attending the Milton Keynes project went to the clinic, compared with around a quarter of the 16-19 year olds and only 10 per cent of the 20-24 year olds.

However, the ease of access to the drop-in service is underlined by the fact that nearly 90 per cent of the under-16s used it, and over 90 per cent of the other age-groups did so.

In South Sefton, the picture was rather different. In general, the women users of the services were less likely than those in Milton Keynes to have only used the drop-in service, apart from those in the under-16 age-group, where nearly 60 per cent used only the drop-in service compared with less than 50 per cent in Milton Keynes. The South Sefton women were rather more likely to use the clinic than the women in Milton Keynes, and this was particularly marked among those of 20 and over. The numbers in each age-group in South Sefton were small, and the tables should be treated with some caution. However, in comparison with Milton Keynes, there was a clear tendency for women over 16, and particularly those over 20, to use the clinic service offered by the project.

There can be little doubt that the women over 25 who accounted for over a third of the South Sefton project's users were predominantly going there for the clinic service, and the reasons for this require scrutiny. They may reflect an unmet need for well-woman and family planning clinic services for older women in the area in which the project was operating. It must be queried whether the best way of identifying this need is through central government funding for a young people's project.

The use of services by the young men in City and Hackney and Milton Keynes does not merit a detailed breakdown. In South Sefton, the use of the different services by age did not differ much from the overall pattern presented in Table 2.2, which showed that 19 per cent of all the male users attended the clinic at least once. An analysis by age showed that this was true of those aged 19 and under, but since these accounted for 80 per cent of the males attending the South Sefton project, this was to be expected.

Was there any difference among the age-groups in who went where first? It might be thought that older women might use the projects for the contraceptive service it offered, and that they might feel that this was more readily available at the clinic, since the main female methods of contraception – the pill, cap and the IUD – all require a doctor's services.

Tables 2.8 and 2.9 show the data on the age profiles of the women using the services in a different form from that shown in Table 2.7. This format is used for some further tables in this chapter and needs to be explained. The City and Hackney figures reflect the profile of women attending the clinic at their first attendance at the clinic. The figures for the other two projects are presented in three different ways. The first column shows the age of those whose *first* visit to the project was either to the clinic (Table 2.8) or to the drop-in service (Table 2.9). The bases of these first columns from the two tables taken together add up to the total number of people attending the projects. For example, 701 women used the Milton Keynes project, of whom 45 used the clinic first (or *only* used the clinic) and 656 used the drop-in service first (or *only* used the drop-in service.) However, some people attended both services and this is reflected in the second column in each table which shows the age of those who attended one service having attended the other service first. The final column shows the ages of those who attended the relevant service at all, ie those who ever used the drop-in or the clinic service. (This clearly adds to more than the total users, but is given to show the age profile of those using that particular service).

This may appear to be a rather complicated way of presenting the data, but, in fact, is the clearest way of presenting in tabular form the various categories of people. As the following discussion shows, they demonstrate some interesting differences in the use of the services. Tables will be given for each of the relevant characteristics of the users, but the discussion concentrates on age since this was one of the most important elements in this study.

Tables 2.8. and 2.9 should be looked at together. The City and Hackney figures show the age profile of the clinic users as shown in Table 2.6, and are presented to demonstrate the considerable difference between the pattern of clinic usage by age in City and Hackney compared with the other two projects. This is obscured by Table 2.6, which looks only at use of the projects as a whole.

Table 2.8 shows quite clearly that female clinic users in Milton Keynes, whether they attended the clinic first or whether they attended the clinic having been to the drop-in first, were considerably younger than those using the clinic in either City or Hackney or South Sefton. Over three-quarters of those attending the clinic on their first visit to the project were 19 or under, compared with a quarter of the same age-group in South Sefton and just under a third in City and Hackney. Over 70 per cent of the Milton Keynes women who ever used the clinic were in this age-group compared with 38 per cent of the similar group in South Sefton. This was largely accounted for by the fact that over 40 per cent of the South Sefton clinic users were over 25, and as many as 56 per cent of the women whose first visit to the project was to the clinic were over 25.

The most striking difference between City and Hackney and the other two projects was that nearly half (48 per cent) of their women users were between 20 and 24, while only a quarter of the Milton Keynes women clinic users and just over a fifth of the South Sefton women clinic users were in this age-group.

However, the age profile of the drop-in service users shows that nearly 50 per cent of women whose first visit to the Milton Keynes project was to the drop-in service were aged between 20 and 24. Since so few women went first to the clinic and then to the drop-in service in that area, this proportion is also shown among ever users of the drop-in service. The pattern for South Sefton is quite different, with the 16-19 year-olds accounting for the largest single age-group of drop-in users, both at first visit or having used it at all. Again, the older age profile of the users in South Sefton accounts for the main difference between the two projects, but it is quite striking that only 18 per cent of those who ever used the drop-in service were aged between 20 and 24 while the comparable figure for Milton Keynes was 48 per cent.

Comparing the figures for clinic and drop-in service usage within the projects, it can be seen that the clinic users in Milton Keynes were younger than the drop-in users, whether at first visit or in terms of having used the service at all. Over 70 per cent of those who ever used the Milton Keynes clinic were under 20, compared with 40 per cent of the drop-in users. (It must be remembered that there is duplication within these figures, since a proportion of 'ever' users used both services.) But looking at the ages of those visiting the clinic or drop-in service on their first visit to the Milton Keynes project, (where there is no duplication), it can be seen that 76 per cent of those who went first to the clinic were under 20 compared with 40 per cent whose first visit was to the drop-in service. The drop-in users in Milton Keynes bunched in the 20-24 age-group, where they accounted for nearly half those using this particular service.

In South Sefton, the teenagers were more likely to have used the drop-in service first rather than go to the clinic first, while the over-25s were much more likely to have gone to the clinic first. But the age profile of users of the South Sefton service is dominated by the fact that over 40 per cent of the clinic users and a third of the drop-in users were over the age of 25.

There was also a considerable difference between City and Hackney and the other two projects in terms of use of the clinic by girls under 16. They accounted for only 4 per cent of the City and Hackney clinic users, compared with 19 per cent in Milton Keynes and 13 per cent in South Sefton.

Marital status

Services aimed at providing family planning and pregnancy counselling specifically for young people under the age of 25 might be expected to attract a high proportion of unmarried young people, although a substantial proportion of women are married by the age of 25.

Table 2.10 shows that the overwhelming majority of the City and Hackney project users were unmarried. Only 4 per cent were currently married, although a further 8 per cent said they were living as married. In Milton Keynes, 29 per cent were currently married, with 16 per cent living as married, and in South Sefton, 27 per cent were currently married, with 4 per cent living as married. In South Sefton, the women over 25, who accounted for a relatively high proportion of project users, were usually married, and if they were excluded from the table, the proportion of unmarried women using the South Sefton project would be much greater.

The clear message from Table 2.10 is that all three projects were predominantly used by unmarried women and men. It is interesting to remember that it was only in the early 1970s that the Family Planning Association opened its doors officially to single women, even if unofficial policy had allowed them to use clinics before then in some areas. The picture in the late 1980s was quite different, and the profile of the users of these projects reflected considerable changes in society and living patterns over the past twenty years.

Table 2.11 shows the different use made of the services by the marital status of the users. The pattern which emerges is that the single women in Milton Keynes were much more likely to have used the clinic than the other groups in that area. This largely reflects the greater use of the Milton Keynes clinic by teenagers. Married women and those living as married were much more likely to have used only the drop-in service, reflecting the predominant use of the Milton Keynes project as a pregnancy testing service, often to confirm a wanted pregnancy. Indeed, 100 per cent of the married women and 99 per cent of those living as married had used the drop-in service in Milton Keynes.

In South Sefton the distinction was not as clear, with higher proportions of all groups using the clinic or both services than in Milton Keynes. The married women were less likely to use the drop-in service than the other groups in South Sefton, and much less likely to use it than their counterparts in Milton Keynes, reflecting the fact that the over-25s in South Sefton were often using the project's service as a well-woman or family planning clinic service.

Tables 2.12 and 2.13 confirm the expected pattern. The Milton Keynes clinic users were much more likely to be single than those using the drop-in service. This was particularly true of those using the clinic as their first contact with the project, nearly all of whom were single. Indeed only 5 per cent of those who ever used the clinic were married. The drop-in service in Milton Keynes was much more likely to be used by married women or those living as married.

The married women in South Sefton were more likely than other groups to use the clinic as their first point of contact with the project, while the single women were more likely to use the drop-in service first.

Number of children

The number of children of the users of the projects was not necessarily related to marital status, which is not surprising considering the proportion of babies now born to single mothers. This cannot be directly deduced from Table 2.14, except in South Sefton where 62 per cent of the women were single and 56 per cent of the women had no children. In the other two areas, detailed analysis showed that childlessness was not necessarily related to singleness.

However, there were differences between the projects, with over three-quarters of the City and Hackney women having no children, compared with 61 per cent in Milton Keynes and 56 per cent in South Sefton. The South Sefton women had bigger families, with 25 per cent having two or more children, compared with 15 per cent in Milton Keynes and 8 per cent in City and Hackney. This again reflects the older age profile of the South Sefton women. The vast majority of the men in all three areas had no children.

Table 2.15 shows what might be expected from the age profile of the users of the projects. In Milton Keynes, the women with no children were rather less likely to use the drop-in service and were more likely to use the clinic than those with children. In South Sefton, the opposite was true, with women with children being more likely to use the clinic and less likely to use the drop-in service than those without children.

As might be expected, nearly 90 per cent of those who used the Milton Keynes clinic as their first contact with the project had no children, compared with under 60 per cent of those who used the drop-in service first. In South Sefton, women with children were more likely to use the clinic service as their first contact and women with no children were more likely to use the drop-in service first.

Comparisons between the two projects were complicated by the fact that fewer women in South Sefton were childless. However, around 60 per cent of those who ever used the drop-in service were childless in both areas, while 81 per cent of the Milton Keynes clinic users were childless in comparison with 49 per cent of the South Sefton clinic users.

Social class and occupation

The data on occupation was collected only about the project users themselves. We decided from the beginning not to attempt to collect occupational data about the 'head of household' for a number of reasons, not least the difficulty of trying to establish who the head of household might be, and in attempting to draw any meaningful conclusions from data where schoolgirls' fathers might be compared with married women's husbands and with single women head of households. We therefore attributed social classification solely on the basis of the user's own occupational status.

Table 2.16 shows clear differences between the projects in terms of social class and occupation. In City and Hackney, the largest single group of women users – 31 per cent – were mainly office workers in the skilled non-manual group, while nearly a quarter were students or schoolgirls. Only 6 per cent described themselves as housewives or mothers. The proportion in semi-skilled and unskilled occupations was 6 per cent, while 12 per cent were in managerial or professional jobs.

In Milton Keynes, nearly 30 per cent were housewives or mothers, while less than 20 per cent were in skilled non-manual occupations. 15 per cent were students or schoolgirls, and only 4 per cent were in managerial or professional occupations. On the other hand, 17 per cent were in semi-skilled or unskilled occupations.

The South Sefton female clients were different again, with only 12 per cent in skilled non-manual jobs. The biggest single group were students or schoolgirls (27 per cent), with a fifth of the users describing themselves as housewives or mothers. Nearly 10 per cent were on an MSC scheme or were YTS trainees – a category hardly encountered in the other two areas. Only 5 per cent were in professional or managerial jobs and 10 per cent were in semi-skilled or unskilled jobs.

In all three areas the proportion of women who said they were unemployed was around 12 per cent.

The differing age profiles of the users of the three projects clearly accounted for some of the differences in the occupations of those using them, but it cannot account for all of it. For example, the City and Hackney project, with rather older users among the under-25s than the other projects, nevertheless attracted quite a high proportion of students and schoolgirls. And in spite of its substantial number of women clients in their early twenties it hardly attracted any housewives and mothers, while Milton Keynes, with a rather lower proportion in their early twenties, attracted a good number of housewives and mothers, but a rather low proportion of students and schoolgirls. Again this was probably related to the fact the Milton Keynes project was used so much as a pregnancy testing service. The low attendance by housewives and mothers at the City and Hackney clinic could also reflect the unsuitability of the timing of early evening and Saturday morning clinics for people with family responsibilities.

South Sefton had a much lower proportion of women clients who were actually in paid work (excluding government schemes) than the other two projects – 28 per cent, compared with 42 per cent in Milton Keynes and 52 per cent in City and Hackney. Nearly half the women clients were students or housewives, as might be expected from the ages of those using the South Sefton project, with its greater representation of the oldest and youngest age-groups of women.

The numbers of men using City and Hackney and Milton Keynes were too small for any analysis of occupations to be meaningful. The most striking finding from the South Sefton figures on occupations of male users was the high proportion of students or schoolboys (52 per cent) and those on MSC/YTS schemes (15 per cent), many of whom were actually working at the King George VI Centre. 11 per cent of the male users were unemployed, and, in fact, only 14 per cent of the male users were in paid employment (excluding government schemes).

The proportion of South Sefton users who were not in paid work reflects the high proportion of unemployed young people in that area, a fact that was commented on by virtually every professional respondent interviewed in South Sefton.

An analysis of the proportion in each social class who used the various services offered by the Milton Keynes and South Sefton projects confirmed that students in Milton Keynes were more likely to use clinic services than other groups. It also confirmed the marked difference between the two projects, in that only 8 per cent of the housewives or mothers who used the Milton Keynes project ever used the clinic, compared with over half the comparable group in South Sefton. The services were clearly being used for different reasons in the two areas by specific groups of women.

Ethnic origin

The question of whether we should ask about the ethnic origin of users arose at an early stage. We felt that it was necessary to establish whether these special services designed for young people were being used by young people from ethnic minority groups in the areas. If they were not, they were clearly not fulfilling the objective of reaching as many young people as possible.

The information on ethnic origin was only recorded for those using clinics. The amount of information recorded on those using the drop-in services was thought by those collecting it to be as much as they could reasonably establish in the short time often available at a drop-in visit, and there was no doubt that some of those collecting the data felt uncomfortable about asking about ethnic origin. We did not want the person filling in the form to make a guess at people's ethnic origin, so we agreed that this information should not be requested at drop-in visits.

We designed a short form to be filled in by users themselves at the Brook clinics. This contained some of the information which the clinic administrators felt reluctant to ask – on marital status, number of children and ethnic origin. We asked people of which ethnic group they considered themselves to be a member. This procedure, using a self-completion form for some of the information, was not felt to be necessary in the other two areas. However, as can be seen from Table 2.17, the information was not always obtained from the City and Hackney users at the Brook clinic, and information on ethnic origin was not recorded for 12 per cent of the female clients.

Table 2.17 shows that the overwhelming majority of the women using the clinics in Milton Keynes and South Sefton were white British. Only one woman, in South Sefton, said she was of Irish origin, although in a community like Bootle, there were undoubtedly more whose grandparents had come from Ireland. Three per cent of the Milton Keynes women were Black British or of West Indian origin and 2 per cent were of African origin. Less than one per cent were from the Indian sub-continent and a tiny handful of women came from other European countries or the Commonwealth. In South Sefton, all those for whom there was any information – 98 per cent – were white British or Irish.

In City and Hackney, the picture was rather different, reflecting the different ethnic mix of the population, both of the area itself and the surrounding areas from which so many clients were drawn. 55 per cent of the women were British or Irish (51 per cent British, 4 per cent Irish). Eighteen per cent of them described themselves as Black British or of West Indian origin, with a further 3 per cent African and 3 per cent from the Indian sub-continent. One per cent were Turkish, Greek or Cypriot and less than one per cent were Chinese or Vietnamese. Seven per cent were from other countries in the world, reflecting the cosmopolitan population of London.

It is difficult to draw too many conclusions from the evidence on ethnic origin in City and Hackney, since the information is unavailable for 12 per cent of the clients, and it is impossible to say how the various ethnic groups were represented among them. However, it is possible to say that nearly a quarter of the users of the service were from black or brown ethnic minority groups.

Table 2.1   All users of projects by project and type of service used

numbers and percentages

	City & Hackney	Milton Keynes	South Sefton
People who made drop-in visits only	-	581 (82%)	227 (63%)
People who made clinic visits only	883 (100%)	41 (6%)	54 (15%)
People who made drop-in *and* clinic visits	-	89 (13%)	79 (22%)
Of whom: first visit was to drop-in	-	84 (12%)	54 (15%)
first visit was to clinic	-	5 (1%)	25 (7%)
People who made drop-in visits *at all*	-	670 (94%)	306 (85%)
People who made clinic visits *at all*	883 (100%)	130 (18%)	133 (37%)
Base: all project users	*(883)*	*(711)*	*(360)*

Table 2.3   Visits made to the projects by type of service, and average number of visits per user

numbers

	City & Hackney	Milton Keynes	South Sefton
Total no. of drop-in visits	-	890	575
Average no. of drop-in visits per user	-	1.3	1.9
Total no. of clinic visits	1958	204	223
Average no. of clinic visits per user	2.2	1.6	1.7
Total no. of visits to project	1958	1094	798
Average no. of visits to project per user	2.2	1.5	2.2

Table 2.2   All users of projects by sex and type of service used

numbers and percentages

		Females			Males	
	C&H	MK	SS	C&H	MK	SS
People who made drop-in visits only	-	572 (82%)	106 (50%)	-	9 (90%)	121 (81%)
People who made clinic visits only	876 (100%)	40 (6%)	45 (21%)	7 (100%)	1 (10%)	9 (6%)
People who made drop-in *and* clinic visits	-	89 (13%)	59 (28%)	-	-	20 (13%)
Of whom: first visit was to drop-in	-	84 (12%)	44 (21%)	-	-	10 (7%)
first visit was to clinic	-	5 (1%)	15 (7%)	-	-	10 (7%)
People who made drop-in visits *at all*	-	661 (94%)	165 (79%)	-	9 (90%)	141 (94%)
People who made clinic visits *at all*	876 (100%)	129 (18%)	104 (50%)	7 (100%)	1 (10%)	29 (19%)
Base: all project users	*(876)*	*(701)*	*(210)*	*(7)*	*(10)*	*(150)*

Table 2.4   Visits made to the projects by sex of user and type of service, and average number of visits per user

numbers

		Females			Males	
	C&H	MK	SS	C&H	MK	SS
Total no. of drop-in visits	-	880	298	-	10	277
Average no. of drop-in visits per user	-	1.3	1.8	-	1.1	2.0
Total no. of clinic visits	1937	203	184	21	1	39
Average no. of clinic visits per user	2.2	1.6	1.8	3.0	1.0	1.3
Total no. of visits to project	1937	1083	482	21	11	316
Average no. of visits to project per user	2.2	1.5	2.3	3.0	1.1	2.1

35

Tables 2. 5   Number of visits to projects by type of service

column percentages

	City & Hackney Clinic/ Project	Milton Keynes			South Sefton		
		Clinic	Drop-in	Project	Clinic	Drop-in	Project
One	45	70	79	71	63	68	58
Two	24	15	15	17	16	19	17
Three	16	7	4	7	11	7	9
Four	7	7	2	3	6	2	5
Five	3	–	*	2	–	1	3
Six	2	<1	*	1	2	1	2
Seven plus	3	–	*	<1	2	1	6
Base: all women users of relevant service	*(876)*	*(129)*	*(661)*	*(701)*	*(104)*	*(164)*	*(209)*

Table 2.6   Use of projects by age and sex of users

column percentages

	Females			Males		
	City & Hackney	Milton Keynes	South Sefton	City & Hackney	Milton Keynes	South Sefton
Age						
11-15	4	7	15	14	40	21
16-19	28	36	32	14	50	59
20-24	48	46	17	57	10	13
25-29	15	8	16	14	-	1
30-39	4	3	5	-	-	1
40 plus	<1	<1	15	-	-	5
Base: all project users	*(876)*	*(701)*	*(210)*	*(7)*	*(10)*	*(150)*

Table 2.7   Service used by age of females using (Milton Keynes and South Sefton only)

column percentages

	11-15		16-19		20-24		25-29		30-39		40+	
	Milton Keynes	South Sefton	Milton Keynes	South Sefton	Milton Keynes	South Sefton	Milton Keynes	South Sefton	Milton Keynes	South Sefton	Milton Keynes	South Sefton
Type of service used												
Drop-in only	46	58	73	61	90	37	93	41	100	40	67	47
Clinic only*	13	16	9	13	3	17	-	38	-	40	33	25
Drop-in *and* clinic	41	26	18	25	7	46	7	21	-	20	-	28
- 1st to drop in	37	26	16	24	7	31	7	9	-	10	-	16
- 1st to clinic	4	-	1	1	-	14	-	12	-	10	-	13
Drop in at all	87	84	91	87	97	83	100	62	100	60	67	75
Clinic at all*	54	42	27	39	10	63	7	59	-	60	33	53
Base: all women users of project	(46)	(31)	(251)	(67)	(24)	(35)	(58)	(34)	(19)	(10)	(3)	(32)

*   Relative figures for City & Hackney would be 100 per cent in each age-group for clinic only and clinic at all.

37

Table 2.8   Age of female clinic users at first visit to clinic

column percentages

	Ever users of clinic	Users of clinic who used clinic first or only		Users of clinic who used drop-in first		Ever users of clinic	
	C&H	MK	SS	MK	SS	MK	SS
Age							
11-15	4	18	8	20	18	19	13
16-19	28	58	17	49	36	52	25
20-24	48	22	18	26	25	25	21
25-29	15	-	28	5	7	3	19
30-39	4	-	8	-	2	-	6
40 plus	<1	2	20	-	11	1	16
Base: all women users at first visit to clinic	*(876)*	*(45)*	*(60)*	*(84)*	*(44)*	*(129)*	*(104)*

Table 2.9   Age of female drop-in users at first visit to drop-in service (Milton Keynes and South Sefton)

column percentages

	Users of drop-in who used drop-in first or only		Users of drop-in who used clinic first		Ever users of drop-in	
	MK	SS	MK	SS	MK	SS
Age						
11-15	6	17	40	-	6	16
16-19	34	38	60	7	34	35
20-24	48	16	-	33	48	18
25-29	9	11	-	27	9	13
30-39	3	3	-	7	3	4
40 plus	<1	13	-	27	<1	15
Base: all women users at first visit to drop-in	*(656)*	*(150)*	*(5)*	*(15)*	*(661)*	*(165)*

Table 2.10 Use of projects by marital status and sex of users

column percentages

	Females			Males		
	City & Hackney	Milton Keynes	South Sefton	City & Hackney	Milton Keynes	South Sefton
Marital status						
Single	75	50	62	57	100	90
Married	4	29	27	-	-	8
Living as married	8	16	4	-	-	1
Divorced/separated	3	5	7	-	-	1
DK/NA	10	<1	<1	43	-	-
Base: all project users	*(876)*	*(701)*	*(210)*	*(7)*	*(10)*	*(150)*

Table 2.12 Marital status of female clinic users at first clinic visit

column percentages

	Ever users of clinic	Users of clinic who used clinic first or only		Users of clinic who used drop-in first		Ever users of clinic	
	C&H	MK	SS	MK	SS	MK	SS
Marital status							
Single	75	96	42	82	75	87	56
Married	4	2	43	6	16	5	32
Living as married	8	2	3	2	2	2	3
Divorced/separated	3	-	12	10	7	6	10
NA/DK	10	-	-	-	-	-	-
Base: all women users at first visit to clinic	*(876)*	*(45)*	*(60)*	*(84)*	*(44)*	*(129)*	*(104)*

Table 2.11 Service used by marital status of females using (Milton Keynes and South Sefton only)

column percentages

	Single		Married		Living as married		Divorced/separated		DK/NA	
	Milton Keynes	South Sefton	Milton Keynes	South Sefton	Milton Keynes	South Sefton	Milton Keynes	South Sefton	Milton Keynes	South Sefton
Type of service used										
Drop-in only	68	56	97	41	97	63	78	29	100	100
Clinic only	11	17	1	32	1	13	-	29	-	-
Drop-in *and* clinic	21	27	3	27	2	25	22	43	-	-
- 1st drop-in	20	25	3	13	2	13	22	21	-	-
- 1st to clinic	1	2	-	14	-	13	-	21	-	-
Drop-in at all	89	83	100	68	99	88	100	71	100	100
Clinic at all	32	44	3	59	3	38	22	71	-	-
Base: all women users of project	(351)	(131)	(200)	(56)	(111)	(8)	(37)	(14)	(2)	(1)

Table 2.13 Marital status of female drop-in users at first drop-in visit

column percentages

	Users of drop-in who used drop-in first or only		Users of drop-in who used clinic first		Ever users of drop-in	
	MK	SS	MK	SS	MK	SS
Marital status						
Single	47	71	100	20	47	66
Married	30	20	-	53	30	23
Living as married	17	4	-	7	17	4
Divorced/separated	6	5	-	20	6	6
NA/DK	<1	1	-	-	<1	<1
Base: all women users at first visit to drop-in	*(656)*	*(150)*	*(5)*	*(15)*	*(661)*	*(165)*

Table 2.14 Use of projects by number of children and sex of users

column percentages

	Females			Males		
	City & Hackney	Milton Keynes	South Sefton	City & Hackney	Milton Keynes	South Sefton
No. of children						
None	76	61	56	43	100	89
One	10	24	16	-	-	3
Two	6	11	15	-	-	4
Three or more	2	4	10	-	-	3
DK/NA	7	<1	3	57	-	1
Base: all project users	*(876)*	*(701)*	*(210)*	*(7)*	*(10)*	*(150)*

Table 2.15 Service used by number of children of females using (Milton Keynes and South Sefton only)

column percentages

	Number of children of females									
	None		One		Two		Three or more		DK/NA	
	Milton Keynes	South Sefton	Milton Keynes	South Sefton	Milton Keynes	South Sefton	Milton Keynes	South Sefton	Milton Keynes	South Sefton
Type of service used										
Drop-in only	76	57	92	56	89	32	89	24	100	83
Clinic only	8	17	2	18	1	35	4	38	-	-
Drop-in *and* clinic	16	26	6	26	9	32	7	38	-	17
- 1st to drop-in	15	25	6	18	9	19	7	10	-	17
- 1st to clinic	1	2	-	9	-	13	-	29	-	-
Drop-in at all	92	83	98	82	99	65	96	62	100	100
Clinic at all	24	43	8	44	11	68	11	76	-	17
Base: all women users of project	(429)	(118)	(165)	(34)	(76)	(31)	(28)	(21)	(3)	(6)

42

Table 2.16 Use of projects by social class/occupation of users

column percentages

	Females			Males		
	City & Hackney	Milton Keynes	South Sefton	City & Hackney	Milton Keynes	South Sefton
Social class/occupation						
I	1	-	-	-	-	-
II	11	4	5	-	-	2
IIIN	31	18	12	14	10	3
IIIM	3	3	1	-	-	5
IV	5	16	9	-	10	3
V	1	1	1	-	-	1
Unemployed	12	11	12	43	10	11
Housewife/mother	6	29	20	-	-	-
Student/at school	23	15	27	29	40	52
MSC/YTS trainee	1	1	9	-	20	15
DK/NA	5	3	4	14	10	8
Base: all project users	*(876)*	*(701)*	*(210)*	*(7)*	*(10)*	*(150)*

Table 2.17 Ethnic origin of female clinic users

column percentages

	City & Hackney	Milton Keynes	South Sefton
Ethnic origin			
White British and Irish	55	94	98
West Indian/Black British	18	3	-
African	3	2	-
Indian/Pakistani/Bangladeshi	3	<1	-
Chinese/Vietnamese	<1	-	-
Turkish/Greek/Cypriot	1	-	-
All others	7	<1	-
Mixed	1	-	-
DK/NA	12	-	2
Base: all women clinic users	*(876)*	*(129)*	*(104)*

Chapter 3
What services did people receive at the projects?

We have seen that there were quite striking differences between the three projects in terms of the characteristics of their users, but there were also differences within the Milton Keynes and South Sefton projects themselves between those using the clinic services and those using the drop-in services. There were further differences between those using one service or the other as their first contact with the projects.

These differences have important implications for service provision for young people. It cannot be assumed that setting up a young people's service will automatically attract a homogeneous bunch of young people. Indeed, as the South Sefton experience showed, it cannot be assumed that a young people's service will necessarily attract only young people. The effect of setting up services of this kind cannot be evaluated without some understanding of the areas in which they are set up, some analysis of the services already in existence in those areas and some assessment of the needs which these services were designed to satisfy. None of these projects were set up in a vacuum, and some of the results were perhaps not quite what was expected.

It was clear that the differences in the profile of people using the three projects could not be accounted for only in terms of the types of services offered. Indeed, the Milton Keynes and South Sefton projects, on the face of it, offered very similar types of service, with daily drop-in facilities and a weekly afternoon clinic. South Sefton had fewer staff, but the actual service provision to individual clients was designed in much the same way as in Milton Keynes.

And yet the South Sefton project attracted a high proportion of women over the age of 25, particularly to the clinic service. The South Sefton women were also more likely than those in Milton Keynes to have used the clinic service offered by the project, while Milton Keynes women were more likely than those in South Sefton to have used only the drop-in service. The female clinic users in Milton Keynes were much younger on the whole than those in either South Sefton or City and Hackney.

In City and Hackney, nearly half the women clinic users were in the 20-24 age-group and were less likely to be married or to have children than the users of the other projects, although the difference was not so marked between the City and Hackney and Milton Keynes clinic users, mainly because of the greater youth of the Milton Keynes clinic users.

Different types of people were obviously going for rather different reasons to the different projects, and this chapter looks in detail at why people used the projects and what kinds of services and methods they received when they went there.

What services did users receive on their visits to the projects?

The projects collected data for us on the main service received on the first visits, and on subsequent visits, to both the clinic and to the drop-in service. Rather fewer services were provided at the drop-in service than at the clinic, mainly because the non-medical staff could not provide the medical methods of contraception available from a clinic through a doctor.

Although we wanted to establish *why* people were using the projects, we found it almost impossible to devise a way of having this recorded on a standard form by the project staff. It is very difficult to record an accurate reason for visiting a project without allowing a subjective element to enter the recording. We therefore agreed that the staff would record the main service which was provided on each visit, and that only one service would be recorded as the *main* visit. Separate information was recorded about other services received, contraceptive methods chosen, pregnancy testing and smears. We felt it important that we should get as near as we could to establishing the reasons for the visit, and we considered that the recording of the main service was the most neutral way of doing this. The following discussion looks in detail at what happened at the *first visits* to the projects and to the different services provided by the projects, since it is on the first visit that the main reason for attending is most likely to be found.

Tables 3.1 and 3.2 should be looked at together. They show the main service received at the first clinic visits and at the first drop-in visits, and follow the same pattern established in the previous chapter. There is only one column for City and Hackney, showing the service received at the first visit to the clinic. For the other two projects, the first column in both tables shows the service received at the first clinic or drop-in visit by those for whom this was their first visit to the project. (This represents the total

45

number of people who went to the projects, in that everyone went first to one or the other service.) The second column shows what was received by those who had been to the other service first, and the last column shows what those who *ever* used that service received.

First clinic visits

The traditional role of a family planning clinic is to provide contraceptive advice and supplies. This was why they were originally set up, and this remains, for the large part, their main role. To what extent were these clinics, aimed at young people under the age of 25, performing this function?

We distinguished three main types of service offered in connection with contraception – a contraceptive method only, contraceptive advice only and contraceptive advice and supplies. It was clear from the outset that different doctors were likely to record what they did in different ways, and, in the event, we found that there was a blurring between the first and third categories. Some doctors thought they always gave advice when they prescribed a method or gave supplies, while others did not. The two categories could easily be merged for statistical purposes in that there is no duplication in the counting.

Taking the three categories together, it can be seen from Table 3.1 that 38 per cent of the City and Hackney women received contraception as the main service on their first visit to the clinic, in comparison with 72 per cent of the Milton Keynes women and 41 per cent of the South Sefton women whose first visit to the project was to the clinic.

There was therefore a striking difference between Milton Keynes and the other two projects in the proportion of women attending for contraception on their first visit. But if around 60 per cent of women were attending with the main aim of getting something other than a contraceptive service why were they going? The figures show that 42 per cent of the women on their first visit to the City and Hackney Brook clinic had a pregnancy test, a further 3 per cent had pregnancy counselling with or without a referral for termination of pregnancy and 9 per cent had post-coital contraception. This meant that more than half the women at their first visit to the City and Hackney clinic were pregnant or thought they might be pregnant.

The comparable figures for the other two projects were very different. Only 11 per cent in Milton Keynes and 14 per cent in South Sefton had a pregnancy test or pregnancy counselling on their first visit to the clinic if this was the first time they used the project. Eleven per cent in Milton Keynes and 3 per cent in South Sefton had post-coital contraception.

So, if well under half the South Sefton women were going for contraception or post-coital contraception and only 14 per cent were going for a pregnancy test or pregnancy counselling, what were the others using the clinic for? The big difference between South Sefton and the other projects was the proportion who received only a smear or received treatment, advice or diagnosis in connection with some gynaecological problem – accounting for one third of the first visits. These users, combined with the 7 per cent of South Sefton clinic users who received general advice and counselling only, accounted for 40 per cent of those using the clinic on their first visit to the project. The majority of them were over 25 and confirms the finding that some older women were using the South Sefton clinic as a well-woman clinic. Very few women used the clinics in the other areas in this way, particularly on their first visit.

What about those who went to the drop-in service first and then went to the clinic? There was certainly a difference in the nature of the service they received on their first clinic visit, but again there were differences between Milton Keynes and South Sefton, and much of this is related to why people used the projects in the first place.

In Milton Keynes, nearly 50 per cent of the clinic users who had been to the drop-in first received a pregnancy test or pregnancy counselling on their first clinic visit, and nearly three-quarters of these received a referral for termination of pregnancy (see Table 3.1). This pattern was quite different from those Milton Keynes users who went first to the clinic and was much more like that of the City and Hackney clinic users. The main difference between these Milton Keynes clinic users and those in City and Hackney was that very few of them actually had a pregnancy test at the clinic. This reflected the fact that most of them had had a test at the drop-in service first.

The South Sefton women attending the clinic who had used the drop-in service first were different again. Over half of them went for contraception, the vast majority of them aged under 25, perhaps showing the success of the drop-in service in encouraging younger women and teenagers to use the clinic. Only 13 per cent had a pregnancy test or pregnancy counselling, which confirmed that the South Sefton clinic was not being used to any great extent as a pregnancy counselling service. It was, however, being used as a well-woman service, in that 21 per cent of those who had first been to the drop-in service used the clinic either for a smear only or for a gynaecological or other health problem.

The final column shows what happened on their first visit to the women who used the clinic at all, whichever service they used first. Nearly 60 per cent of all first visits to the Milton Keynes clinic were for contraception, but over a third were in connection with a pregnancy test or pregnancy counselling. The comparable figures for City and Hackney were 38 per cent for contraception and 45 per cent in connection with a pregnancy test or counselling, compared with 46 per cent in South Sefton for contraception and only 14 per cent for a pregnancy test or counselling. 27 per cent of all first clinic visits in South Sefton were for a smear only or for a women's health or gynaecological problem.

It should be noted that the relatively high proportion of women over 25 attending the City and Hackney clinic can largely be accounted for by the fact that the policy of London Brook Advisory Centres is to provide a contraceptive and counselling service for all young people up to and including 25 years of age, but for those facing an unwanted pregnancy there is no age limit. The majority of clients over 25 attending the City and Hackney clinic were pregnant.

First drop-in service visits
Table 3.1 on first visits to clinic services must be looked at in conjunction with Table 3.2 on drop-in services. We have already seen that the Milton Keynes drop-in service was providing the pregnancy testing that was being provided in City and Hackney by the clinic service. It is also by looking at the tables together that the great difference between the Milton Keynes and South Sefton projects can be seen.

88 per cent of those who first went to the drop-in service in Milton Keynes went for a pregnancy test and a further 5 per cent went for pregnancy advice of some kind. The comparable figures in South Sefton were 27 per cent for a pregnancy test and 11 per cent for pregnancy advice. Only a tiny proportion of women first visited the Milton Keynes drop-in service for any other reason, but in South Sefton 36 per cent of first visits to the drop-in service received contraceptive advice, while 13 per cent received general health or gynaecological advice.

The numbers of women who went first to the clinic and then attended the drop-in service was very small in both areas, so that very little can be deduced from the second column of Table 3.2. The final column simply confirms the rest of the table. The Milton Keynes drop-in service was essentially a pregnancy testing service, while the South Sefton Service was a more broadly-based service – for women at least.

Subsequent clinic and drop-in visits

If the first visits to the projects indicated why people went in the first place, what can we learn from looking at the repeat visits? We know that the majority of people in both Milton Keynes and South Sefton used the clinic or the drop-in service only once, but that in City and Hackney more than half the clinic attenders used the clinic more than once. But for what reason did people return? And most important, were there any indications that they returned to the clinic for contraception after a positive or negative pregnancy test or after a termination of pregnancy? To what extent are women motivated to use reliable methods of contraception after a pregnancy 'scare'?

Table 3.3 shows the main service received at all repeat clinic visits, ie all those visits subsequent to a *first* visit to the clinic, whether this was the first visit to the project or not.

The table only shows aggregated data, so that it is not possible to follow individual cases. What it shows is that the pattern of usage of clinics by those who returned after the first visit conforms much more to what might be expected from a family planning clinic, in that over half the repeat consultations were for contraceptive advice and supplies in City and Hackney and South Sefton, as were nearly 70 per cent of the repeat visits in Milton Keynes.

However, nearly a fifth of the repeat consultations in both City and Hackney and South Sefton were in connection with a pregnancy test or counselling. Some of these were clearly follow-up consultations concerning the pregnancy discussed on the first visit, but some were pregnancies which had occurred after the first visit.

In City and Hackney, 7 per cent of repeat visits were for counselling following a termination of pregnancy, as were 8 per cent in Milton Keynes. It is also striking that 14 per cent of the repeat visits in City and Hackney were for advice and counselling only. There can be little doubt that the general advice and counselling service offered by the Brook clinics and their employment of trained non-medical counsellors was a service valued and used by women.

The main difference between South Sefton and the other two areas was shown again in this table by the fact that 24 per cent of the repeat clinic visits were for a smear only or for treatment, advice or diagnosis of a gynaecological problem.

It might have been thought that repeat visits to the drop-in services would show a rather different pattern from that of the first visits. For example, it might have been thought that women in Milton Keynes who had had a pregnancy test on their first drop-in visit might have had a different service if they returned. However, this was not the case, since 86 per cent of second and subsequent visits in Milton Keynes were also for pregnancy tests. From the figures, it looks very much as though women with negative pregnancy tests were advised to return for a second test. There are few other deductions which can be made from the figures which show that 88 per cent of first drop-in visits were for pregnancy tests and 86 per cent of repeat drop-in visits were for pregnancy tests. Certainly 6 per cent of repeat visits were for pregnancy advice, but it cannot be deduced from the figures what had happened at the first consultation. What is clear from the figures is that only a tiny proportion of repeat visits to the Milton Keynes drop-in service were in connection with contraceptive advice, reflecting the pattern of the first visits.

In South Sefton, repeat visits to the drop-in service show a relative increase in the proportion of visits involving pregnancy advice as opposed to pregnancy tests. It appears that some women were encouraged to return to the drop-in service for pregnancy counselling after having a pregnancy test, whether positive or negative. It must be asked whether this might have contributed to any delay in seeking early termination of pregnancy when this was the desired outcome. Evidence suggests that prolonged 'counselling' may not be in the interests of women seeking termination of pregnancy. Other repeat visits to South Sefton which were classifed as 'pregnancy advice' offered intensive ongoing support to women continuing with a pregnancy. A tiny number of women made frequent visits to the project and, again, the use of the young people's project for this purpose should perhaps be queried.

The repeat visits to the South Sefton drop-in service show a lower proportion of contraceptive advice than on first visits, indicating that women were either satisfied with the advice or went to the clinic as a result of the advice. However, as many as a fifth of the repeat visits by women to the drop-in service were about contraception. The main difference between Milton Keynes and South Sefton was again in the proportion of women who went for general health and gynaecological problems. Nearly one fifth of the repeat South Sefton drop-in consultations were for these reasons.

Services received at all clinic and drop-in visits

Although it is important to distinguish between what happened at the first visits and subsequent visits, particularly at the clinic, it is also useful to look at what happened at all visits to the services offered by the projects. This gives some idea of the actual workload of the projects in terms of the main services provided.

Table 3.5 shows what might be expected from the previous discussion. Less that half the consultations by women with the clinic doctors in City and Hackney and South Sefton were mainly to do with contraception. (It must be remembered that contraception was sometimes given as an *additional* service, for example to people whose *main* reason for attending was in connection with an unwanted pregnancy. This was particularly true in City and Hackney.) However, in Milton Keynes over 60 per cent of all consultations at the clinic were mainly to do with contraception.

Over a quarter of all the consultations over the 18-month period at the clinics in City and Hackney and Milton Keynes were in connection with a pregnancy test or pregnancy counselling or a referral for termination of pregnancy, compared with 15 per cent of the clinic consultations in South Sefton.

The City and Hackney and South Sefton clinics were more likely than the Milton Keynes clinic to be used for general advice and counselling only, while South Sefton was much more likely than the other two clinics to be used as a well-woman clinic in treating and advising on gynaecological or women's health problems or in providing smears only. Indeed, a quarter of all consultations at the South Sefton clinic were for these reasons.

Table 3.5 shows that the majority of the men who used the City and Hackney clinic received advice and counselling only, while the majority of men using the South Sefton clinic received contraceptive supplies or advice. Some indication of the extent to which the young men attended the clinic with their girlfriends and were then counted as a client can be seen by the proportion who are recorded as having received a service in connection with pregnancies. It is unlikely that young men accompanying women are counted as clients by most clinics.

Table 3.6 shows the workload of the drop-in services, and confirms the fact that the Milton Keynes drop-in service was mainly a pregnancy testing service. Nearly 90 per cent of the visits by women were for a pregnancy test and 5 per cent were for pregnancy counselling. The comparable figures in South Sefton were 21 per cent and 18 per cent respectively. Over a quarter of the South Sefton visits were for contraceptive advice and around one fifth were for general advice or counselling or in connection with women's health matters.

Very few men attended the Milton Keynes drop-in service, but there were 277 visits by men to the South Sefton drop-in service. The vast majority (84 per cent) of these visits were for condoms, with a further 9 per cent for contraceptive advice. The question of whether a free condom-providing service is a good use of a young people's family planning and pregnancy counselling service is a matter for some discussion, but the fact remains that this was what the South Sefton project provided. It brought in 150 young men and boys, and family planning staff and health educators alike know how difficult it is to attract men to any kind of contraceptive or family planning service.

The provision of AIDS advice and counselling was not a specific task which the projects were charged with providing. They were, however, opened at a time shortly after the government had mounted a major campaign to make people aware of the dangers of AIDS. In the event, only two people were recorded by the projects as having received AIDS counselling advice as the main service provided at any visit, whether first or repeat visit – one man and one woman – both in South Sefton. AIDS advice and counselling might have been provided as an additional service in the projects, but it was almost never recorded.

Pregnancy counselling and pregnancy tests
One of the aims which the Department of Health had laid down for the projects was that young people should be encouraged to seek advice early if they suspected they were pregnant. One of the reasons for this was the general concern felt about the numbers of late abortions, a relatively high proportion of which were performed on very young women who had not sought advice early (RCOG, 1984). But it could be argued that early advice for young women who suspect they are pregnant is not only desirable to avoid late terminations of pregnancy. There are indications that young unsupported women who proceed with pregnancies may be at risk in many ways, and a pregnancy counselling service may help people who wish to continue with their pregnancies as well as those who wish to terminate the pregnancy.

Pregnancy tests
It is clearly important for young women to establish at an early stage whether they are pregnant or not. All three projects offered pregnancy

testing as a routine part of their service, as do most family planning clinics. Free pregnancy testing has been a vexed issue for many years, and the pattern in family planning clinics in the country is very variable. The pregnancy advisory charities charge for pregnancy testing. Free pregnancy testing facilities have been set up in some areas, and in City and Hackney a free walk-in pregnancy testing service has been set up and was evaluated as part of the young people's project (Fleissig, Jessopp, Griffiths, 1989).

It is usually stressed that a pregnancy testing service without available pregnancy counselling is not a good idea, although many thousands of women buy home pregnancy testing kits every year to see for themselves without the benefit of counselling. Chemists also provide pregnancy testing, and it must be acknowledged that not every woman wants pregnancy counselling, either at the time of a pregnancy test or even at any other time (Allen, 1985).

Table 3.7 shows the enormous differences between the projects in the extent to which they were used as pregnancy testing services. The table shows what happened at the women's first visit to the project, and distinguishes between those who first went to the clinic and those who first went to the drop-in service in Milton Keynes and South Sefton. The figures add up to the total number of women using these projects. (It does not show what happened to those who made a subsequent 'first' visit to the other service.) One of the aims of this table is to show in very simple terms why women used these projects.

The Milton Keynes *drop-in service* was used essentially as a pregnancy testing service, with nearly 90 per cent of those using the drop-in service as their first contact with the project having a pregnancy test. The Milton Keynes *clinic* was used in a quite different way by people who went straight to the clinic service, with only 7 per cent of the first attenders at the clinic having a pregnancy test. As we have seen, a high proportion of those who went to the clinic having been to the drop-in service first had already had a test at the drop-in service.

It was also clear that the City and Hackney clinic was used as a pregnancy testing service to a much greater extent than might have been expected. 45 per cent of women users had a pregnancy test on their first visit to the clinic. But, of course, the subsequent decisions at that first visit meant that it was not used only as a pregnancy testing service in the way that the Milton Keynes project was.

South Sefton presented quite a different picture from the other two areas. Just over a quarter of those making their first project visit to the drop-in service had a pregnancy test, as did 10 per cent of those going to the clinic as their first project visit.

Why were the projects so different from one another? It is clearly vital to put the services into context, and this table demonstrates the danger in simply assuming that services of any kind can be set up without considering what has gone before and what other services are available in the area. The differences cannot be understood only by looking at the demographic profile of the areas.

In Milton Keynes, the You 2 project was established in the Bakehouse, a building which was used for a number of purposes, among which was a Women's Health Group. This group ran out of funding shortly before the young people's projects were set up. Two of the staff from the Women's Health Group (WHG) were taken on as two of the health workers on the young people's project without going through a formal competitive process, and a further two health workers from different backgrounds were appointed at a later date. Much of the work of the Women's Health Group had been pregnancy testing and the Bakehouse was well known in the area as offering a pregnancy testing service. The WHG continued in a more modest form during the project monitoring period without offering the widespread pregnancy testing which it had provided before. It was absolutely clear from the interviews carried out with professionals and clients that little distinction was made in the minds of many users between the Women's Health Group and the You 2 project. More important, if women came to the WHG for a pregnancy test, they were usually directed to the You 2 project, particularly if they were under 25.

The overwhelming demand at the beginning of the project for pregnancy testing at the You 2 project led initially to a ban being imposed on free pregnancy testing for those over the age of 20. This was then raised to a ban on free testing over the age of 25. It certainly seemed to deter many of those over 25, as can be seen by the figures, but nevertheless the image stuck for a variety of reasons, and the Milton Keynes drop-in service remained mainly a pregnancy testing service throughout the 18 months of the monitoring period.

The situation in City and Hackney was less straightforward. Women who had a pregnancy test when they came to the clinic were much less likely to be using it solely as a pregnancy testing service. In South Sefton, the use of the pregnancy testing service was different again.

The outcome of pregnancy tests

It might be assumed that women seeking a pregnancy test from a family planning clinic or from a young people's advisory service might be seeking confirmation of an unwanted pregnancy in order to proceed with a request for termination of pregnancy. It might be thought that women who wanted to be pregnant would seek confirmation of their pregnancy from a GP or even from a hospital. These assumptions might be wrong.

Table 3.8 shows the results of the pregnancy tests carried out at the first visits to the projects and it also shows the outcome. There was a marked difference between the projects in the proportion of pregnancy tests which were positive. This in itself is a finding which can be open to a number of different interpretations.

In City and Hackney, 78 per cent of the tests were positive, at the Milton Keynes drop-in service, 48 per cent were positive, and at the South Sefton drop-in service, 34 per cent were positive. (The actual numbers of people having tests at the clinic sessions in these two areas were so small that no meaningful analysis can be made.)

One of the most probable explanations of this big difference between the projects is that the women attending the City and Hackney clinic were more likely than those going to the drop-in centres in the other areas to have already had a pregnancy test and to know that they were pregnant before they went. In these cases the reasons for the test at the clinic appeared to be to confirm the pregnancy for the clinic's purposes.

It also appeared that the women who had positive pregnancy tests at the City and Hackney clinic were attending the clinic specifically for advice on how to get an abortion. 63 per cent of those who had pregnancy tests on their first visit to the City and Hackney clinic had a positive test and the outcome was a request and referral for termination of pregnancy. It should be noted that this was the outcome of 28 per cent of all the first visits by women to the City and Hackney clinic during the monitoring period.

The Brook clinics have traditionally considered that a pregnancy counselling service is part of their role, but it might be argued that for over a quarter of all first visits to the clinic to result in a referral for termination of pregnancy is a rather surprisingly high proportion.

Looking at the outcome of the pregnancy tests at the other two projects, marked differences can be seen between all three areas, although the relatively small number of tests involved in South Sefton indicate that caution should be exercised in comparing that area with the other two.

In Milton Keynes, although nearly half the pregnancy tests at the first drop-in visits were positive, the majority of these were to women who expected to continue with the pregnancy. One third of the women having pregnancy tests at the Milton Keynes project had positive tests and were having them to confirm a wanted pregnancy. A further ten per cent had negative pregnancy tests but were recorded as wanting to be pregnant. This meant that over 40 per cent of the women having pregnancy tests at their first drop-in visit to Milton Keynes wanted to know whether they were pregnant with a wanted pregnancy, and that, essentially, was all they required from the service. This proportion increased with age and, among the over-25 year-olds having pregnancy tests, over 50 per cent either had a positive test and were expected to continue with the pregnancy or had a negative test and wanted to be pregnant. In addition, it was not clear from the recording what proportion of the rest of those with negative pregnancy tests actually would have wanted to continue with the pregnancy if it had been confirmed.

In South Sefton the pattern was different again, although the number of tests was fairly small. Two thirds of the tests were negative and one third positive. Nearly 20 per cent were positive and the women expected to continue with the pregnancy and 8 per cent had negative tests but wanted to be pregnant. Again it is not clear how many of the others with negative tests might have wanted to be pregnant.

And so, again, the differences between the projects were apparent in the use made of the services by those having pregnancy tests at their first visit, who, as we have seen, accounted for the overwhelming majority of the Milton Keynes drop-in users and over half the City and Hackney clinic users. In City and Hackney nearly two-thirds of those having pregnancy tests requested referral for termination and only 3 per cent were expected to continue with the pregnancy. In Milton Keynes, one third of those having pregnancy tests were expected to continue with the pregnancy, and in less than ten per cent of cases was the likely outcome of the pregnancy test a request for termination referral. South Sefton was notable for the high proportion of negative pregnancy tests, the low proportion of termination requests and the fact that around one fifth of the women having tests had a positive pregnancy test confirming a wanted pregnancy.

Previous terminations of pregnancy

We were interested in the extent to which the projects were being used by women who had had previous terminations of pregnancy. If the projects could succeed in helping women who had had a termination of pregnancy adopt reliable methods of contraception they could be said to have achieved a desirable outcome. At the same time, it might be thought rather worrying if women who had already had terminations of pregnancy were using the service as a pregnancy testing service or as a referral service for further terminations of pregnancy. We therefore asked the projects to record the number of previous terminations of pregnancy of users at their first visit to the clinic or the drop-in service.

Table 3.9 shows the proportions of women visiting the projects who had had previous terminations of pregnancy. The figures show the status of the woman as recorded at her first visit to the project, whether to the clinic or drop-in service. It is perhaps surprising that nearly a quarter of those making a first visit to the City and Hackney clinic had had at least one previous termination of pregnancy, whereas in the other two areas the proportion was approximately 10 per cent, a figure which has been recorded in other family planning studies. Looking at those making a first project visit to the drop-in services, rather over 10 per cent in Milton Keynes and only 3 per cent in South Sefton were recorded as having had a previous termination of pregnancy.

It is difficult to assess whether the figures for clinic users are more accurate than those for drop-in users, in that the clinic information was sought and recorded by the doctor while the drop-in information was recorded by a non-medical project worker. It would have been possible for the figures to be underestimates in both cases.

It might be hoped that the experience of a previous termination of pregnancy would encourage the reliable use of contraception and help to prevent repeated unwanted pregnancies. We looked at those having pregnancy tests to see to what extent they had had previous terminations of pregnancy. Table 3.10 shows that the proportions of women having pregnancy tests at their first visit to both the City and Hackney clinic and the Milton Keynes drop-in service who had had previous terminations of pregnancy was an almost exact mirror of the profile for the attenders as a whole as shown in Table 3.9. Over a quarter of the City and Hackney women and over 10 per cent of the Milton Keynes drop-in attenders having pregnancy tests at their first visit to the project had had previous terminations of pregnancy.

The figures should be treated with some caution, in that, at least in Milton Keynes, a relatively high proportion of pregnancy tests were in connection with a pregnancy which the woman wanted to continue. However, this was not the case in City and Hackney, and there can be little doubt that these figures reflect the fact that some young women find it very difficult to control their fertility.

Smears

One of the reasons that young girls are said to be put off going to family planning clinics is that they are worried about having internal examinations. It is, of course, impossible to take a smear without having an internal, and we asked the doctors to record whether a smear was taken at the clinic visits.

There was clearly a difference between South Sefton and the other two areas in whether women had a smear taken at their first visit to the clinic, as Table 3.11 shows. Nearly 40 per cent of those who went first to the South Sefton clinic had a smear, compared with 7 per cent in both City and Hackney and Milton Keynes. Over a quarter of women who used the clinic at all in South Sefton had a smear on their first visit compared with 5 per cent in Milton Keynes.

There are a number of probable reasons for this. Perhaps the most important was the extent to which women using the South Sefton clinic were more likely to be older and were seeking advice on general health or gynaecological matters rather than contraception or pregnancies. There were also a number of women who went to the clinic only for a smear. In addition, the greater use of the clinics in City and Hackney by women who were pregnant probably also diminished the potential number of smears.

However, whatever the reasons for individual cases, it was quite clear that the clinic doctors in City and Hackney and Milton Keynes were considerably less likely to take smears than the doctors in South Sefton.

Contraceptive methods provided

Since family planning clinics are usually used to give advice and supplies of contraceptive methods, we asked the projects to record what methods were provided at the visits to the clinic.

Table 3.12 shows a pattern which might not have been expected from a young people's family planning clinic. However, given the services provided at first visits to these clinics which have already been described, it is not perhaps so surprising.

In City and Hackney and Milton Keynes, around 50 per cent of the women attending the clinic received oral contraception at their first visit. This was true of only around a quarter of the South Sefton clinic users.

Very few women were fitted with an IUD at City and Hackney or Milton Keynes, and none were fitted in South Sefton. The premises in Milton Keynes and South Sefton were simply thought to be unsuitable for IUD fitting. But similarly, only a tiny number of women were fitted with caps at any of the clinics. Caps were clearly not a popular method.

Injectable contraception or Depo-provera was a method used in Milton Keynes for as many as 6 per cent of the young women on their first visit to the clinic, but only 1 per cent in City and Hackney and none in South Sefton.

Sheaths were much more popular, but it should be noted that they were often given in addition to other methods and rarely on their own in City and Hackney and Milton Keynes. This was not true in South Sefton, where as many as a quarter of women received sheaths on their first visit to the clinic.

Post-coital contraception was given to 8 per cent of women in City and Hackney on their first visit, and to over 10 per cent of those using the Milton Keynes clinic as their first contact with the project.

Perhaps the most interesting figure is the proportion of women who received no contraceptive method at all on their first visit, ranging from just over 10 per cent of those using Milton Keynes clinic for their first contact with the project to 30 per cent of those who went to the Milton Keynes clinic having used the drop-in service first. In City and Hackney the proportion receiving no contraceptive method on their first visit was also 30 per cent while in South Sefton it was as many as 60 per cent of those using the clinic as their first contact with the project.

This reflects how the projects were used in such different ways by their clients. Around a third of the City and Hackney clinic users were pregnant on their first visit and seeking a termination of pregnancy. They were not usually given contraception. Similarly, this was true of nearly a third of the Milton Keynes women who had used the drop-in service before using the clinic. However, in South Sefton, women were much less likely to use the clinic service as a referral source for termination of pregnancy, and indeed, were much less likely to be pregnant than in the other two areas. The fact that over half those using the South Sefton clinic received no contraceptive method on their first visit reflected the extensive use made of the clinic there by women seeking advice on general health or gynaecological matters.

Table 3.13 shows that the vast majority of women attending the Milton Keynes drop-in service for the first time were not given a contraceptive method, which might have been expected, given the fact that most of the first visits were for a pregnancy test, and that a fairly high proportion of those having negative pregnancy tests wanted to be pregnant.

In South Sefton, where pregnancy testing was not nearly so common, nevertheless nearly three-quarters of the women attending the drop-in service for the first time left without a contraceptive method, in spite of the fact that around one third of them were recorded as receiving contraceptive advice as their main service on their first visit and a further 7 per cent were recorded as receiving sheaths as their main service.

Both drop-in services were, of course, limited in that they could only supply non-medical methods of contraception, but, even so, it was perhaps surprising that only just over a quarter of the South Sefton women left with contraception – usually sheaths. It might be thought that young women might have been given sheaths by a young people's service, just in case they did not return to the clinic or go to another doctor or clinic for contraception. However, it is likely that this reflects the use of the drop-in service in South Sefton for reasons other than contraception, as a well-woman service by older women and as a more general counselling service than the other two projects.

The overwhelming majority of men using the drop-in services, most of whom were in South Sefton, were given sheaths.

Table 3.1 Main service received by women at first visits to clinic

column percentages

	Ever users of clinic	Users of clinic who used clinic first or only		Users of clinic who used drop-in first		Ever users of clinic	
	City & Hackney	Milton Keynes	South Sefton	Milton Keynes	South Sefton	Milton Keynes	South Sefton
Main service received							
Contraceptive method only	19	27	12	13	16	18	13
Contraception advice only	2	7	2	6	9	6	5
Contraception advice and supplies	17	38	27	31	30	33	28
Post-coital contraception	9	11	3	-	-	4	2
Pregnancy test only	9	-	-	1	2	1	1
Pregnancy test and counselling	33	4	12	2	7	3	10
Pregnancy counselling only	1	-	2	14	2	9	2
Pregnancy counselling and TOP referral	2	7	-	31	2	22	1
TOP follow-up counselling	1	-	-	-	-	-	-
Advice/counselling only	4	4	7	-	7	2	7
Smear only	1	2	20	1	7	2	14
Diagnosis/treatment/ other gynae	1	-	13	-	14	-	13
Cap/IUD check	1	-	3	-	-	-	2
AIDS advice/coun- selling/supplies	-	-	-	-	2	-	1
Base: all women users at first visit to clinic	(876)	(45)	(60)	(84)	(44)	(129)	(104)

Table 3.2 **Main service received by women at first drop-in visit (Milton Keynes and South Sefton only)**

column percentages

	Users of drop-in who used drop-in first or only		Users of drop-in who used clinic first		Ever users of drop-in	
	Milton Keynes	South Sefton	Milton Keynes	South Sefton	Milton Keynes	South Sefton
Main service received						
Contraceptive advice	4	36	-	13	4	34
Post-coital advice	2	1	40	-	2	1
Pregnancy test	88	27	60	7	88	25
Pregnancy advice	5	11	-	7	5	11
Sheaths/cont. method	<1	5	-	27	<1	7
Info/leaflets	<1	3	-	-	<1	3
General advice/coun-selling	1	3	-	-	1	3
General health/gynae	-	13	-	47	-	16
AIDS/STD advice	-	-	-	-	-	-
Base: all women users at first visit to drop-in	*(656)*	*(150)*	*(5)*	*(15)*	*(661)*	*(165)*

Table 3.3   Main service received by women at repeat clinic visits*

column percentages

Main service received	City & Hackney	Milton Keynes	South Sefton
Contraceptive method only	27	32	18
Contraceptive advice only	3	5	3
Contraceptive advice & supplies	24	31	30
Post-coital contraception	3	1	1
Pregnancy test only	4	-	6
Pregnancy test and counselling	4	-	8
Pregnancy counselling only	7	4	3
Pregnancy counselling and TOP referral	1	4	1
TOP follow-up counselling	7	8	1
Advice/counselling only	14	1	6
Smear only	2	1	9
Diagnosis/treatment/other gynae	3	5	15
Cap/IUD check	2	4	-
AIDS advice/counselling/ supplies	-	-	-
Other	<1	1	-
Base: all repeat visits to clinic	*(1061)*	*(74)*	*(80)*

*   Repeat visits are all those subsequent to a first visit to the *clinic*, whether this was the first visit to the project or not.

Table 3.4   Main service received by women at repeat drop-in visits* (Milton Keynes and South Sefton only)

column percentages

	Milton Keynes	South Sefton
Main service received		
Contraceptive advice	4	20
Post-coital advice	-	1
Pregnancy test	86	17
Pregnancy advice	6	27
Smears/other cont. method	<1	8
Info/leaflets	-	4
General advice/counselling	3	5
General health/gynae	-	17
AIDS/STD advice	-	1
Base: all repeat drop-in visits	*(219)*	*(133)*

*   Repeat drop-in visits are all those subsequent to a *first* visit to the drop-in service – whether this was the first visit to the project or not.

Table 3.6   Main service received by men and women at *all* drop-in visits

column percentage

	Females		Males	
	Milton Keynes	South Sefton	Milton Keynes	South Sefton
Main service received				
Contraceptive advice	4	28	20	9
Post-coital advice	1	1	-	<1
Pregnancy test	87	21	-	<1
Pregnancy advice	5	18	10	2
Sheaths/other contraceptive method	<1	8	40	84
Info/leaflets	<1	3	-	2
General advice/counselling	2	4	30	1
General health/gynae	-	17	-	1
AIDS/STD advice	-	<1	-	<1
Base: all drop-in visits	*(880)*	*(298)*	*(10)*	*(277)*

Table 3.5 Main service received by men and women at *all* clinic visits

column percentages

	Females			Males		
	City & Hackney	Milton Keynes	South Sefton	City & Hackney	Milton Keynes	South Sefton
Main service received						
Contraceptive method only	23	23	15	10	-	44
Contraceptive advice only	2	6	4	-	-	3
Contraceptive advice and supplies	21	33	29	5	100	36
Post-coital contraception	6	3	2	-	-	-
Pregnancy test only	6	<1	3	-	-	-
Pregnancy test & counselling	17	2	9	-	-	5
Pregnancy counselling only	4	7	2	-	-	3
Pregnancy counselling & TOP referral	1	16	1	-	-	3
TOP follow-up counselling	4	3	1	-	-	-
Advice/counselling only	10	1	7	81	-	3
Smear only	1	1	12	-	-	-
Diagnosis/treatment/ other gynae	2	2	14	-	-	-
Vasectomy request/ advice	-	-	-	5	-	-
Cap/IUD check	1	1	1	-	-	-
AIDS advice/coun- selling/supplies	-	-	-	-	-	1
Base: all clinic visits	*(1937)*	*(203)*	*(184)*	*(21)*	*(1)*	*(39)*

Table 3.7   Pregnancy tests at first visit to projects (women only)

column percentages

	At first clinic visit*			At first drop-in visit*	
	City & Hackney	Milton Keynes	South Sefton	Milton Keynes	South Sefton
Pregnancy test	45	7	10	89	27
No pregnancy test	55	93	90	11	73
Base: all women project users	*(876)*	*(45)*	*(60)*	*(656)*	*(150)*

*   When this visit was the first visit to the project.
The totals together add to the total number of women attending the projects.

Table 3.8   Pregnancy tests and their outcome

column percentages

	At first clinic visit*			At first drop-in visit*	
	City & Hackney	Milton Keynes	South Sefton	Milton Keynes	South Sefton
Result of test and action					
PT positive - outcome undecided	12	-	-	7	8
PT positive - TOP request and referral	63	67	-	8	8
PT positive - expected to continue	3	-	17	33	18
PT negative - wanted to be pregnant	-	-	-	10	8
PT negative - given contraception	8	-	-	-	-
PT negative - referral to FPC or GP	-	-	-	27	50
PT negative - no action/no need	14	33	83	17	10
Base: all those having pregnancy test	*(392)*	*(3)*	*(6)*	*(581)*	*(40)*

*   When this visit was the first visit to the project.

Table 3.9   Number of previous TOPs

	At first clinic visit*			At first drop-in visit*	
	City & Hackney	Milton Keynes	South Sefton	Milton Keynes	South Sefton
None	71	87	88	87	93
One	20	11	10	11	3
Two	3	-	-	<1	1
Three +	<1	-	-	-	-
DK/NA	6	2	2	1	3
Base: all women project users	*(876)*	*(45)*	*(60)*	*(656)*	*(150)*

*   When this visit was the first visit to the project.

Table 3.10   Proportion of those having pregnancy tests by number of previous TOPs

column percentages

	At first clinic visit*			At first drop-in visit*	
	City & Hackney	Milton Keynes	South Sefton	Milton Keynes	South Sefton
No. of previous TOPs					
None	70	33	100	87	95
One	24	67	-	11	3
Two	3	-	-	<1	-
Three +	<1	-	-	-	-
DK/NA	3	-	-	<1	3
Base: all women users having PT at first visit to project	*(392)*	*(3)*	*(6)*	*(581)*	*(40)*

*   When this visit was the first visit to the project.

Table 3.11 **Proportion of women clinic users having smear taken at first clinic visit**

column percentages

| | | Users of clinic who used clinic first or only | | Users of clinic who had used drop-in first | | Ever users of clinic | |
	C&H	MK	SS	MK	SS	MK	SS
Yes	7	7	38	4	11	5	27
No	93	93	62	96	89	95	73
Base: all women clinic users	*(876)*	*(45)*	*(60)*	*(84)*	*(44)*	*(129)*	*(104)*

Table 3.12 **Contraceptive method provided to women at first visit to clinic**

column percentages

| | Ever users of clinic | Users of clinic who used clinic first or only | | Users of clinic who had used drop-in first | | Ever users of clinic | |
	C&H	MK	SS	MK	SS	MK	SS
Contraceptive method							
Pill - OCP	50	49	20	55	27	53	23
Pill - POP	1	4	2	1	-	2	1
IUD	2	4	-	1	-	2	-
Cap	4	4	-	1	5	2	2
Injectable	1	7	-	6	-	6	-
Chemical/foam etc.	3	-	2	1	2	1	2
Sheath	10	16	25	17	20	16	23
Female sterilisation	<1	-	-	-	-	-	-
Post-coital pill	7	11	3	-	-	4	2
Post-coital IUD	<1	-	-	-	-	-	-
None	29	13	57	29	48	30	53
Not stated	<1	2	-	2	-	2	-
Base: all women clinic users	*(876)*	*(45)*	*(60)*	*(84)*	*(44)*	*(129)*	*(104)*

Table 3.13 Contraceptive method provided to women at first visit to drop-in

column percentages

	Users of drop-in who used drop-in first or only		Users of drop-in who used clinic first		Ever users of drop-in	
	MK	SS	MK	SS	MK	SS
None	89	72	80	67	89	72
Sheaths	10	25	20	33	10	26
Sponge	-	5	-	7	-	5
Spermicides	1	6	-	7	1	6
Not stated	1	1	-	-	1	1
Base: all women drop-in users	*(656)*	*(150)*	*(5)*	*(15)*	*(661)*	*(165)*

Chapter 4
Why people used the projects and what happened

There was a generally accepted view among project team members and their managers and advisers that the projects would appeal to young people who had not used contraceptive methods or services before. Interviews at the beginning of the projects suggested that there was a big pool of young people who had not used existing family planning or counselling services, often because they were inappropriate to their needs. All three projects aimed their services at young people who were unlikely to have used GPs or family planning clinics.

Previous and current use of contraception
It was to be hoped that services designed specifically for young people would attract young people who had not used contraception before. The clinic doctors asked the women what methods of contraception they had used before their first visit to the young people's clinic.

There was a clear difference between the clinic users in City and Hackney and those in the other two areas. Two-thirds of the London women had used oral contraception before they first visited the City and Hackney clinic compared with less than half of those in both Milton Keynes and South Sefton who used the clinic as their first visit to the project, and fewer of those who had been to the drop-in service first in both areas.

The IUD had been used by 7 per cent of the City and Hackney users, hardly at all in Milton Keynes, but by over 10 per cent of the South Sefton women who used the clinic as their first visit to the project. This undoubtedly reflected the use of the clinic in South Sefton by older women.

Nearly 40 per cent of the City and Hackney clinic users said they had previously used the sheath, compared with around half the Milton Keynes users, but only a quarter of the South Sefton clinic users. The cap had not been a popular method, although nearly ten per cent of the City and Hackney women had used it at some time. Other methods had rarely been used. It is probable that the use of the 'safe period' is considerably under-reported in this table, and it was also clear that women were not being asked about their use of withdrawal as a method of contraception.

There was again a difference between City and Hackney and the other two projects in the proportion of those who were recorded as never having used a contraceptive method. Only 11 per cent in City and Hackney had never used contraception before attending the clinic, compared with just under a quarter of those who used the Milton Keynes and South Sefton clinics as their first contact with the projects. It was interesting that nearly a third of those using the South Sefton clinic after using the drop-in centre first had never used contraception. The majority of these were teenagers, nearly half of them under 16, and even though the numbers were very small, it is some indication of the success of the South Sefton drop-in centre staff in encouraging young girls to go to the clinic.

The information gathered on previous use of contraception is not only useful as an indicator of the extent to which the women using these projects had used medical methods of contraception before, but it also shows that just because women have used contraception it does not necessarily mean that they will not have unwanted pregnancies, considering how many of the women, particularly in City and Hackney, sought help from the clinics in obtaining a termination of pregnancy. As other studies have demonstrated, the fact that women use contraception does not mean that they will not become pregnant.

The women using the drop-in services were asked about their current method of contraception. In view of the fact that so many of the Milton Keynes drop-in users came for a pregnancy test, it is not surprising that nearly 60 per cent said that they were not using a contraceptive method at the time. However, this was also true of nearly 60 per cent of the South Sefton drop-in users. This again demonstrated the difference between the two drop-in services. As Table 3.2 showed, the South Sefton drop-in users were much more likely to be seeking contraceptive advice or general health advice than the Milton Keynes users, and much less likely to be seeking a pregnancy test. The fact that the same proportion in both areas were not using a current method of contraception can be interpreted in completely different ways. In Milton Keynes it can be accounted for by the fact that so many were pregnant or wanting to be pregnant, while in South Sefton, it was accounted for by the fact that so many teenagers using the drop-in service for the first time were not using contraception – 85 per cent of the under-16s and over two-thirds of the 16-19 year-olds. Some of them were pregnant, but in nothing like the proportions in Milton Keynes.

In Milton Keynes, over a fifth of the women said they were currently using the pill, although this, of course, included some women seeking a pregnancy test, while in South Sefton the proportion using the pill was 12 per cent. Information was not available for over 10 per cent of the South Sefton women which made true comparisions between the projects rather difficult. Rather more than ten per cent in each area said they were currently using the sheath.

Previous use of family planning services

One of the aims of the projects was to attract young people who had never used family planning services before. We therefore asked the projects to record what family planning services the women had used before they came to the clinics. They did not ask this question of those using the drop-in centres.

Unfortunately, as Table 4.3 shows, the recording of this information was rather haphazard, and it is incomplete for all three projects. In Milton Keynes and South Sefton it was not recorded at all for over 40 per cent of clinic users.

However, incomplete as the data is, it does show that around one third of those using the City and Hackney and South Sefton clinics had been to their GPs for family planning help. Over a quarter of the City and Hackney women had used a family planning clinic and one third had previously used a Brook clinic. Only 6 per cent in Milton Keynes and 13 per cent in South Sefton were recorded as having used a family planning clinic and only one person – in South Sefton – had used a Brook clinic. As might have been expected, older women were more likely to have used family planning services than the teenagers, but it is impossible to say to what extent the proportions are under-recorded.

Very few people were recorded as never having used a family planning service, but it is, of course, unclear what, if any, services were used by those for whom no information was recorded.

This information is presented in its incomplete form to show that a not insignificant proportion of women had used family planning services – usually their GPs in Milton Keynes and South Sefton – before going to the projects' clinics. This could have been deduced from Table 4.1 showing previous contraceptive use, which showed that the pill had been used by around 40 per cent of those using the Milton Keynes and South Sefton clinics and 66 per cent of the City and Hackney clinic users.

The question to be asked is whether the people who had used other family planning services had found them satisfactory, or whether they found the services offered by the young people's clinic more suitable for them, and, if so, in what way. These themes could not be answered by an analysis of the data recorded by the projects, but they will be explored in more depth in Chapters 5 and 6 which look at young people's views and experience of the three projects.

How did the users get to know about the projects?

The projects were set up to appeal to young people, but clearly they had a great deal to do in a short period of time. The Milton Keynes and South Sefton projects were starting from scratch, while the City and Hackney project was building on an existing Brook clinic in Shoreditch, which had previously been open one night a week.

It is well known that word of mouth is an important factor in attracting young people to use services of any kind. But this is true of older women as well and previous research has shown the importance of 'friends' in encouraging women to use family planning clinics.

However, the projects had to make themselves known in order to attract users who could tell their friends about the services. They used various methods of publicising their services. We asked the staff to record the source through which the clients came to the clinic and to the drop-in service. We were interested in seeing whether word of mouth was as important in projects like these, which had resources to publicise their services, as in more conventionally funded services.

Table 4.4 shows the big difference between the City and Hackney project and the other two in that one-fifth of the clinic users said they came because they were already using one of the young people's clinic sessions held at the Shoreditch clinic, either by Brook on a Monday evening or by the Health Authority on a Thursday evening. The City and Hackney clinic had a solid base of users on which to build, which was not shared by the other two projects.

The importance of friends and other users of the clinics as a source of information about the clinics can be seen in all three projects. We had tried to separate out friends from other users, but as the table indicates, the project staff found it difficult to differentiate. Over a quarter of the City and Hackney women came to the clinic because of a friend or other user, but this proportion was higher for both Milton Keynes and South Sefton, accounting for around 40 per cent of those who came to the clinic on their first visit to the project. It accounted for nearly two-thirds of the under-16s in both areas.

One of the most striking features of the City and Hackney clinic was the proportion who came because the Brook central office in London had told them about the Shoreditch clinic. These clients, representing 14 per cent of the women clinic users, did not necessarily live locally, but simply wanted to attend a Brook clinic. Their need was sometimes urgent, as illustrated by the proportion who were pregnant, and it often appeared that they went to any Brook clinic where they could get an appointment. Whatever the reason, the link and referral source was Brook rather than the City and Hackney Young People's Project (CHYPP).

Relatives were a more important referral source outside London, and indeed a quarter of the Milton Keynes women came through a relative, with as many as 13 per cent of the Milton Keynes women coming to the clinic through their mothers. Most of these were single 16-19 year-olds, some of whom were pregnant.

Publicity was only rarely recorded in City and Hackney as a reason for attending the clinic, although local newspaper or magazine articles about Brook attracted around 5 per cent. It certainly played a larger role in the other two projects, with around 20 per cent of the clients coming to the clinic as their first visit to the project saying they came through publicity of some kind in both Milton Keynes and South Sefton.

The activities of the project staff both at the project centre and outside it brought some people to the clinic for the first time, but their main function was clearly to encourage people to come to the clinic who had been to the drop-in centre first, as can be seen by the very high proportion in both areas of those who came to the clinic for this reason after going to the drop-in centre.

It was perhaps surprising on the face of it that relatively few people said they came to the clinics as a result of talking to professionals of any kind. Given the activities of the project staff in schools and with teachers, it was disappointing that no-one in Milton Keynes or South Sefton was recorded as coming to the clinic through a teacher or through hearing a speaker at school or college, and that the same was true of less than one per cent in City and Hackney.

Only a tiny number came to the clinic in City and Hackney and South Sefton because of a recommendation by a GP or other health professional, and no-one was recorded in Milton Keynes as coming through these sources. In all three areas around 2 per cent came through social services or a social worker and a similar proportion came through another welfare agency or through the CAB. Telephone directories were used by 4 per cent in City and Hackney, usually to look up Brook in the telephone directory, since the booking for Brook clinics was made by the central London office. And finally, a small proportion of women came to all three clinics through the recommendation of other clinics or pregnancy advisory services.

Table 4.5 shows that friends and other users of drop-in services were as important in getting people to the drop-in service as to the clinic, with just under 40 per cent in both Milton Keynes and South Sefton coming to the drop-in service through this source. However, it was the most important source for the under-16s, with nearly two-thirds of this age-group in both areas saying they came because of a friend or other user. Relatives were rarely mentioned by any age-group, which was perhaps surprising, considering the rather higher proportion who went to the clinic because of a relative.

It is notable that nearly two-thirds of the men going to the South Sefton drop-in service went because of a friend or another user. This was particularly marked among the under 16-year-olds, where over 80 per cent came to the drop-in service through this source, and the 16-19-year old age group, of whom three-quarters came for this reason. The older male drop-in users were more likely to be working at the King George VI Centre and to come to the drop-in service through chatting to the PACE staff at the centre.

One of the most interesting figures in this table on sources of referral is the 20 per cent who went to the drop-in service in Milton Keynes because their GP suggested it. There can be little doubt that in the vast majority of cases this was a straight referral to You 2 as a pregnancy testing service, and for no other reason. Most of those who came at their GP's suggestion were over 20 and a fifth of them were over 25. It would be completely misleading to interpret this relatively high proportion of 'referrals' from GPs as an indication of close liaison between the GPs and the Milton Keynes drop-in service. There was certainly little evidence of liaison between GPs and the clinic service, as Table 4.4 showed and as the activity sheets completed by the project staff indicate (see Appendix II).

The comparable proportion in South Sefton of referrals from GPs to the drop-in centre was one per cent, and there was no indication at all in South Sefton of close liaison between GPs and the PACE project, either in referrals to the clinic or to the drop-in centre.

One of the most important sources of referral to the South Sefton drop-in service was through the PACE project staff talking to people at the King George VI Centre outside their own offices. This source accounted for one fifth of those coming to the drop-in service, and suggests that placing the service in a community centre of this kind had some success in encouraging people to attend. In Milton Keynes, the situation was rather different in that the You 2 staff did not spend much time in the rest of the Bakehouse, since their premises were rather more separated than in South Sefton. However, 16 per cent of their drop-in referrals came from other staff at the Bakehouse. In the majority of cases, this appeared to have been through the Women's Health Group staff telling women under 25 seeking pregnancy tests that they could obtain a free test at the You 2 drop-in service.

The effect of publicity appeared greater in South Sefton than in Milton Keynes, with over 10 per cent saying that this brought them to the drop-in centre. The efforts of project staff outside the centres brought in only small numbers of people, and, again a very low proportion of people came to the drop-in service in either area because of hearing about it at school, college or through a teacher. Other health professionals were rarely cited as referral sources, and social workers or other welfare agencies were also mentioned very little, although 4 per cent of those attending the South Sefton drop-in service came through a social worker.

It is possible that professional referrals to the clinic and to the drop-in services in these two areas were under-recorded, and that young people might prefer to say that they came through a friend or other user rather than through a professional source. Certainly there was absolutely no indication of any young people of either sex coming through a drug counsellor or other drugs worker in South Sefton, and yet the project staff there spoke of their close liaison with the drug service, and said that the project services were often used by drug users who had been referred by professionals working with them.

It should be emphasised that the data analysed for the tables in Chapter 2, 3 and 4 was based on records kept and collected by the project staff. The project staff were perhaps in a better position to record the referral source more accurately than outsiders. It is possible that young people might have been reluctant to tell outside interviewers of their reasons for coming to the projects, although this did not appear to have been a problem in the interviews we conducted for this study. However, whichever way the data was collected, very few professional referrals to these projects were recorded.

If there was an under-reporting of professional referrals by project staff, it is a matter of some concern, since it is important that there should have been an accurate representation of sources of referral in a monitoring exercise of this kind. If, on the other hand, the data is accurately recorded, and referrals from professionals were as limited as they appear to have been, it is also a matter of concern. Special services of this kind for young people should be used and trusted by other professionals. We collected information on the liaison between the projects and other professionals through interviews both with the project staff and with samples of professional workers in both areas, as well as through the activity sheets completed by the project staff. This is discussed in detail in Chapters 10 to 13 and in Appendix II.

Where did the drop-in service refer clients?

What happened as a result of the drop-in visits? It might be assumed that people attending the clinics might continue to attend them for contraception or pregnancy counselling, and that clinics of this kind could offer all or most of the services that young people wanted. However, this might not necessarily be true of the drop-in services which were staffed by non-medical personnel. We therefore asked the staff at the drop-in services to record to whom they referred clients.

Table 4.6 has to be considered in conjunction with the services received by the women at their visits to the drop-in centres. As Table 3.2 indicated, nearly 90 per cent of those attending the Milton Keynes drop-in centre for the first time had pregnancy tests, compared with just over a quarter of women in South Sefton. South Sefton drop-in clients were more likely to come for contraceptive advice or for general health advice.

There was a difference between the two projects, which can be largely accounted for by the reasons for attending. Nearly 70 per cent of the women in Milton Keynes were referred to their GP after their first drop-in visit, compared with only 12 per cent in South Sefton. In over a quarter (27 per cent) of all Milton Keynes drop-in clients, women were referred to their GPs specifically for ante-natal care after their first visit. It must be presumed that most, if not all, of these women had had a positive pregnancy test at the drop-in service and had confirmed a wanted pregnancy. A further 37 per cent of *all* Milton Keynes drop-in clients were recorded as having been referred to their GP, with no reason being given, while only 3 per cent were referred to their GPs specifically for advice on a termination of pregnancy.

At first sight, the very high proportion of referrals to GPs by the Milton Keynes drop-in service might appear to indicate good liaison between the You 2 project and GPs. The explanation is undoubtedly much more functional. The overwhelming majority of women used the drop-in service as a pregnancy testing service. Those with positive tests who wanted to be

77

pregnant would usually naturally continue with their pregnancies under their GPs' care. A proportion of those who did not want to continue with their pregnancies might seek a termination of pregnancy with the help of their GPs, while others might wish to discuss the situation further with their own GPs before making a decision. Among those with negative pregnancy tests there was a fairly high proportion who wished to be pregnant who might reasonably want to go to or return to their GPs. Given the nature of the drop-in service as a pregnancy testing service, it is perhaps not so surprising that so many women were referred to their GPs.

In South Sefton nearly 40 per cent of drop-in users were referred to the project's clinic, compared with 25 per cent of the drop-in users in Milton Keynes. It appeared that the majority of these cases in both areas were in connection with contraception, although a certain proportion in both areas were referred for help with getting a termination of pregnancy. Older women were more likely than teenagers to be referred to the clinic in South Sefton.

There was a big difference between the two areas in the proportion who were advised to return to the drop-in service after their first visit – 45 per cent in South Sefton and 18 per cent in Milton Keynes. In Milton Keynes, there was no doubt that a relatively high proportion of these were women with negative pregnancy tests who were advised to have a second test. In South Sefton, there was clearly a tendency for the project staff to suggest to teenagers that they should return to the drop-in service for further discussion, whether in connection with contraception or pregnancy.

The drop-in staff made very few referrals to other agencies or professionals. This fact can be interpreted in a number of different ways. The implication is that the majority of people using the drop-in service came in connection with contraception or pregnancy, and wished to be referred to a service which would help them with this. This would be a completely reasonable outcome. However, project staff often stressed that many of their clients had a number of problems which required help other than contraceptive services or pregnancy counselling. It looks as though the project staff either tried to help these clients themselves or that they referred them to either the GP or the young people's clinic in connection with these problems. Given that so many of the professionals we interviewed thought young people needed advice, counselling and help in a number of areas of their lives, it is perhaps surprising that more referrals were not made to other agencies. In Milton Keynes, the picture was undoubtedly distorted by the fact that so many of the drop-in clients were pregnant or wanted to be pregnant. Even so, it might be thought that some of these women might have had problems which might have been helped by professionals other than GPs or clinics.

The evidence on referrals to and from the young people's projects suggests that there was not much liaison between the projects and other professionals. This evidence was certainly borne out by the interviews we conducted with the project staff and other professionals working in the areas. The fact that one fifth of the Milton Keynes drop-in clients came at the suggestion of their GPs and that nearly 70 per cent were referred back to their GPs is accounted for largely by the fact that so many of the women users of the drop-in service were pregnant or wanting to be pregnant. It cannot be taken as evidence of liaison for any other reason.

Table 4.1   Contraceptive method previously used by clinic users

column percentages

Contraceptive method	Ever users of clinic City & Hackney	Users of clinic who used clinic first or only Milton Keynes	South Sefton	Users of clinic who used drop-in first Milton Keynes	South Sefton	Ever users of clinic Milton Keynes	South Sefton
Pill - OCP	66	47	47	42	30	43	39
Pill - POP	3	2	3	4	-	3	2
IUD	7	-	13	2	2	2	9
Cap	9	4	5	1	5	2	5
Injectable	1	-	-	2	-	2	-
Chemical/foam etc.	2	-	-	-	-	-	-
Sheath	39	51	23	49	30	50	26
Safe period	1	-	-	-	-	-	-
Female sterilisation	<1	-	3	-	2	-	3
Post-coital pill	2	-	-	-	-	-	-
Post-coital IUD	<1	-	2	1	-	1	1
None	11	24	23	20	32	22	27
Not stated	5	4	7	4	7	4	7
Base: all women clinic users	(876)	(45)	(60)	(84)	(44)	(129)	(104)

Table 4.2   Current contraceptive method of women at first drop-in visit (Milton Keynes and South Sefton)

column percentages

Current contraceptive method	Users of drop-in who used drop-in first or only		Users of drop-in who used clinic first		Ever users of drop-in	
	MK	SS	MK	SS	MK	SS
None	59	58	40	20	59	55
Pill	22	12	20	7	22	12
IUD	2	1	-	13	2	2
Cap/Diaphragm	1	-	-	-	1	-
Chemical	<1	-	-	-	<1	-
Sheath	15	13	40	40	15	15
Rhythm	<1	1	-	-	<1	1
Sponge	<1	-	-	-	<1	-
Injectable	<1	-	-	-	<1	-
Sterilised	<1	2	-	13	<1	3
DK/NA	1	12	-	7	1	12
Base: all women drop-in users	*(656)*	*(150)*	*(5)*	*(15)*	*(661)*	*(165)*

Table 4.3   Family planning service ever used by women clinic users

column percentages

FP service used	City & Hackney	Ever users of clinic Milton Keynes	South Sefton
GP	32	42	34
Family Planning Clinic	26	6	13
Brook	33	-	1
Other Youth Advisory Clinic	4	-	-
BPAS/Other Pregnancy Advisory Clinic	6	2	-
Other	2	-	-
None	5	9	14
Not stated	22	47	42
Base: all women clinic users	*(876)*	*(129)*	*(104)*

Table 4.4 **Referral source to clinic of women on first visit**

column percentages

	Ever users of clinic	Users of clinic who used clinic first or only		Users of clinic who used drop-in first		Ever users of clinic	
	C&H	MK	SS	MK	SS	MK	SS
Referral source							
Already using clinic	20	-	-	-	-	-	-
Self-referral	8	9	2	1	-	4	1
Friend	24	36	5	7	-	17	3
Other user (this proj.)	3	4	37	1	5	2	23
Relative (unspec.)	1	4	2	1	-	2	1
Sister	1	7	3	-	-	2	2
Boyfriend	<1	-	-	-	-	-	-
Mother	1	13	-	-	-	5	-
Publicity (unspec.)	1	2	2	-	-	1	1
Project publicity at other org.	4	16	18	4	-	8	11
Local newspaper/ mag	5	-	-	-	-	-	-
Project staff	<1	2	5	77	95	51	43
Project staff outside centre	<1	4	8	1	-	2	5
Other staff at project centre	1	2	8	1	-	2	5
School/coll. outside speaker	<1	-	-	-	-	-	-
Teacher	1	-	-	-	-	-	-
GP	2	-	2	2	-	2	1
Other health prof.	2	-	2	-	-	-	1
Brook	14	-	3	-	-	-	2
Hosp. professional	3	-	-	-	-	-	-
STD clinic	<1	-	-	-	-	-	-
Social worker/social services	1	2	2	1	-	2	1
Other welfare/CAB	2	2	3	2	-	2	2
Telephone dirs	4	-	-	-	-	-	-
Other FPC/BPAS/ PAS/YAC	6	4	5	-	-	2	3
Base: all women clinic users	*(876)*	*(45)*	*(60)*	*(84)*	*(44)*	*(129)*	*(104)*

Table 4.5 Referral source/how came to drop-in service for first visit (Milton Keynes and South Sefton, women only)

column percentages

Referral source	Users of drop-in who used drop-in first or only		Users of drop-in who used clinic first		Ever users of drop-in	
	MK	SS	MK	SS	MK	SS
Already project user	-	-	80	100	1	9
Self-referral/walking by	9	6	-	-	9	5
Friend	25	1	-	-	24	1
Other user (this project)	14	37	20	-	14	33
Relative (unspecified)	4	1	-	-	4	1
Sister	2	-	-	-	2	-
Boyfriend	1	-	-	-	1	-
Mother	2	2	-	-	2	2
Publicity (unspecified)	5	11	-	-	5	10
Project staff at centre	1	19	-	-	1	18
Project staff outside centre	1	5	-	-	1	4
Other staff at project centre (inc. WHG)	16	5	-	-	16	4
School/coll./outside speaker	1	1	-	-	1	1
Teacher	1	3	-	-	1	2
GP	20	1	-	-	20	1
Other health professional	3	3	-	-	3	3
Other FPC	1	3	-	-	1	2
Hospital professional	-	1	-	-	-	1
Social worker/social services	1	4	-	-	1	4
CAB/welfare rights	1	1	-	-	1	1
Rape crisis	<1	-	-	-	<1	-
DK/NA	1	-	-	-	1	-
Base: all women drop-in users	*(656)*	*(150)*	*(5)*	*(15)*	*(661)*	*(165)*

Table 4.6   To whom women referred by drop-in service at first visit

column percentages

	Ever users of drop-in services	
	Milton Keynes	South Sefton
To whom referred		
GP ante-natal	27	5
GP for TOP referral	3	1
GP	37	7
FP clinic	3	1
STD/AIDS counsellor	<1	-
BPAS/other PAS	2	2
Other counsellor	<1	-
YPP clinic/doctor	25	35
National Childbirth Trust	<1	-
Teenage Pregnancy clinic	-	1
Return to YPP drop-in	18	44
PT/chemist/home test	<1	1
Housing	1	1
Social services	<1	-
CAB/welfare rights	2	1
Well-women/Women's Health Group	<1	-
Rape crisis	<1	-
Young mothers' group	<1	-
Hospital consultant	<1	1
None necessary/requested	4	8
Base: all women drop-in users	*(661)*	*(165)*

Chapter 5
Young people's experience and views of the projects' services

Many assumptions are made about what young people want and about why they do or do not use contraceptive and pregnancy counselling services. These projects were set up by the Department of Health because there was thought to be a need for special services for young people. This view was supported in the areas in which the projects were set up. Interviews with senior health service staff and professionals in the three districts indicated strongly that young people needed special services to help them with their use of contraception and with pregnancy counselling. There was a consensus of opinion among professionals that the way in which other services are delivered was not appropriate for young people, and that sex education programmes in the schools were inadequate.

We will look at the views of professionals and the project staff in later chapters, but, having described the characteristics of the young people who used the projects in the last three chapters, we thought it useful to give an account of their views and experience, not only of the services offered by the projects, but also of other services offering contraception or pregnancy counselling that they might have used. We wanted to know what they thought of the sex education they had received at school or elsewhere, and we asked them why young people might find it difficult to use the contraceptive and pregnancy counselling services on offer generally. We were particularly concerned to seek their recommendations on the best way to deliver services to young people. After all, they are the consumers, and those wishing to design the most appropriate services for the needs of young people should listen carefully to what they have to say.

Interviewing the young people
We decided to aim at interviewing 50 young people using the project's services in each of the three areas, giving us a total sample size of 150

interviews. The intention was to interview the young people as they attended the projects towards the end of the monitoring period, at a time when the projects had had time to build up a clientele and the project staff had had time to establish the kind of service they wished to offer. The sample size was relatively small, but, given the numbers of young people attending the projects, we knew that it would be difficult to achieve more interviews with users of the projects.

We had originally intended to interview young people in the last three months of the monitoring period, but it became clear that we might have difficulty in achieving our sample size by the end of March 1989 if we waited until January 1989 before we started interviewing. We also realised that we had to rationalise the interviewing. In both Milton Keynes and South Sefton, days could pass without any clients visiting the projects, or with only one or two clients.

We therefore started interviewing in all three areas at the beginning of November 1988. We knew from the attendance figures that we would complete our sample of 50 interviews much more quickly in City and Hackney than in the other two areas, but we thought it best to have a common starting date. We also decided to restrict our interviewing in Milton Keynes and South Sefton to the days on which clinics were held. We knew that this would give us a rather more homogeneous sample overall, in that City and Hackney were only providing a clinic service, and, of course, we could not afford to spend days achieving only one interview. Even with this strategy we only managed to achieve 42 interviews in South Sefton in the five-month period November 1988 to March 1989, and we only just managed to achieve our quota of 50 interviews in Milton Keynes. In City and Hackney, all 50 interviews took place with women, in Milton Keynes, 49 women and 1 man were interviewed, while in South Sefton, interviews took place with 37 women and 5 men.

Although we interviewed on days on which clinics were held in Milton Keynes and South Sefton, over a fifth of the Milton Keynes respondents and over a third of the South Sefton female respondents did not see the clinic doctor, and were seen only by the non-medical project staff. The young people interviewed therefore included those who did not go to the projects specifically for the clinic services offered. The sample was too small to differentiate their views overall from those of the clinic attenders.

Profile of the young people interviewed

There is one important reservation which must be made about the sample of those interviewed, particularly in South Sefton, and to a lesser extent, in

City and Hackney. As Table 5.1 shows, 46 per cent of the women interviewed in South Sefton were aged 25 or over, and indeed 19 per cent were aged 30 or over. It is doubtful whether their views can really represent the views of young people. We included them in the sample, because they were the people using the South Sefton service. As we saw in Chapter 2, 41 per cent of the total women using the South Sefton clinic service were 25 or over, so that our sample reflects the profile of those using the project's services. If we had restricted our sampling only to those under 25, we would have achieved interviews with only 20 women in South Sefton in the last five months of the monitoring period. Where the views of the South Sefton women differ significantly from those in the other two areas, we draw attention to it.

It should also be noted that 18 per cent of the City and Hackney sample were aged between 25 and 29, compared with only 2 per cent of the Milton Keynes sample. This again reflects the ages of the clinic clientele in both areas. The samples of those interviewed in South Sefton and City and Hackney therefore cannot be said to represent only the views of young people under 25, but we present the material with this proviso. Much of the analysis was restricted to the experience of those under 25. We always give particular stress to the ages of the people making comments, and the vast majority of quotes are taken from young people under the age of 25. Only a tiny number of men were interviewed, and we have not included them in any tables used. All six of them were aged between 16 and 19.

The marital status of the young people interviewed reflected the marital status of those using the clinics in the three areas (Table 5.2). Only 4 per cent of the women interviewed in City and Hackney and 6 per cent in Milton Keynes were married, compared with 19 per cent in South Sefton. Nearly 15 per cent of those interviewed in South Sefton were widowed, separated and divorced, compared with only a handful of women in the other two areas. Over 90 per cent of those interviewed in City and Hackney and Milton Keynes were single or cohabiting, compared with two-thirds of those interviewed in South Sefton. All the men interviewed were single.

As might be expected, 90 per cent in City and Hackney and 80 per cent in Milton Keynes had no children compared with just over half those interviewed in South Sefton. Indeed nearly a third of the South Sefton women had two or more children compared with only one woman in the other two areas combined. None of the men had any children.

The social class and occupation of those interviewed broadly reflected that of the clinic users in the three areas (Table 5.4), although in City and

Hackney, there was a higher proportion of interviews with women in white collar occupations than their numbers overall would have indicated, but the differences were not great enough to cause any concern. There was no evidence that women from any particular class or occupation were more likely to refuse than others. Four of the men were unemployed, one was a schoolboy and the other was in a clerical job.

The ethnic origin of those interviewed reflected the profile of those using the clinics. In South Sefton, everyone was white British, in Milton Keynes, only 2 per cent were non-white and in City and Hackney, 24 per cent of those interviewed were of West Indian or African ethnic origin and 2 per cent were from the Indian sub-continent, closely reflecting the overall profile of clinic users. All the men interviewed were white British.

How young people got to know about the project

If young people are to use reliable methods of contraception, they need to have access to services which supply them with these methods and help them use them. But to have access to services, they need to know that they exist and they have to feel able to use them. We wanted to know how the people we interviewed had first got to know about the projects and what had appealed to them about the idea of using them. We were particularly interested in the extent to which they had been influenced by informal or formal contacts and we wanted to know if they had seen any publicity and whether they had been influenced by that.

We started by asking how often they had been to the project. We have seen that quite a number of women attended these services only once, and we wondered whether we would pick up a lot of new users in these interviews. In the event, the profile was more or less what might be expected. One third of those interviewed in City and Hackney were making their first visit, compared with 51 per cent in Milton Keynes and 46 per cent in South Sefton, reflecting the rather better established Brook services in City and Hackney. It also reflected the fact that the Milton Keynes service was mainly a pregnancy testing service and thus dominated by one-off visits while South Sefton had been much slower to get off the ground than the other two services.

Overall, around a fifth were making a second visit in City and Hackney and South Sefton, compared with over a quarter in Milton Keynes. Around one-sixth in all three areas were making their third visit. In City and Hackney, nearly 30 per cent had been four or more times, compared with over 20 per cent in South Sefton and just over 10 per cent in Milton Keynes. Three of the men had been before, two of them four or more times.

The projects were quite different from one another, in that one-third of the repeat attenders interviewed in City and Hackney had first attended the clinic before the start of the projects in October 1987. They were women who had been to the Brook clinic before the projects had started, and were simply continuing to attend the clinics. They accounted for over a fifth of those interviewed in City and Hackney, so it was perhaps not surprising that the women in City and Hackney had made rather more visits than those in the other two areas.

Over 60 per cent of the repeat attenders in the other two areas had first come since July 1988, and half the Milton Keynes repeat attenders had first come since September 1988. The fairly slow build-up of anything approaching a regular clientele in both Milton Keynes and South Sefton is reflected in these figures.

Over 60 per cent of the under 16s were making their first visit, compared with under 40 per cent of the other age-groups. This can, of course, be interpreted in two ways. It could be argued that the under-16s were unlikely to attend more than once or it might be that they were only beginning to come near the end of the monitoring period as they got to know about the projects. There were suggestions that the latter was true, but the numbers were too small in this interview survey to draw hard conclusions from the evidence on age.

Publicity

How did the young people get to know about the projects? We realised at a very early stage that there would be a problem in City and Hackney in establishing whether young people used the clinic because it was a Brook clinic which they would have used in any case, whether or not there had been a City and Hackney Young People's project. We therefore asked a specific question in City and Hackney about whether the respondents had ever seen or heard anything about CHYPP (the City and Hackney Young People's Project). None of those interviewed at Shoreditch Brook had ever heard of CHYPP. This will be discussed later.

We then asked whether they had ever seen any publicity or read anything about Shoreditch Brook, deliberately distinguishing it from Brook Clinics as a whole. In the other two areas we asked the same question about You 2 and PACE.

We found that only one fifth of those interviewed in City and Hackney had seen any publicity or read anything about Shoreditch Brook, while around 50 per cent in the other two areas had seen publicity or read about

You 2 and PACE. The under-16s in all three areas were rather less likely to have seen or read any publicity than other age-groups, and the women over 30, all of whom were in South Sefton, were more likely to have done so than other age-groups.

So what had they heard or seen? The projects went to some lengths to try and ensure that they extended their publicity as widely as possible, although CHYPP in particular laid more emphasis on making themselves known to professionals rather than directly to young people. Nevertheless all three projects had 'launch' days and they tried to get local press coverage. You 2 and PACE made extensive use of posters, leaflets and cards. How much did this all get through? They were rarely given as reasons for coming to the projects according to the record card information. We made a point of asking the young people directly about publicity in our interviews.

Over two-thirds of those who had seen anything in Milton Keynes said they had seen a poster, a quarter said they had seen a leaflet and a handful said they had seen cards. In South Sefton, half of those who had seen anything had seen a poster, a third had seen leaflets and rather more had seen cards. The numbers in City and Hackney were so small that little could be deduced from their answers, although they were more likely than respondents in the other two areas to mention radio or television or local newspapers. It appeared that they were referring to Brook generally rather than Shoreditch Brook specifically.

We asked them where they had seen the publicity or from whom they had received it. The numbers were tiny, but it did appear that the siting of the projects had some impact, in that around a fifth of the respondents who had seen publicity in both Milton Keynes and South Sefton mentioned the Bakehouse or the King George VI Centre. It is often stressed that it is important to put publicity where young people go. Over a third of those in Milton Keynes who had seen publicity said it had been in a health centre or doctor's surgery, but this was hardly mentioned in the other two areas. Over 10 per cent of those who had seen publicity or read about the projects said it had been at school, with rather more mentioning it in Milton Keynes than in the other two areas. The workplace and the careers office were mentioned by a handful in South Sefton.

Were there any people who were instrumental in getting the publicity through to young people? Professional sources were rarely mentioned in this context, with one or two mentions each for project staff, teachers, outside speakers at school, a probation officer and the CAB. One of the few young people to mention a professional only found out by accident, it appeared, as this 23-year-old with two children pointed out:

> I saw some information lying on my probation officer's desk. It had her cup of tea on it. I thought I was pregnant and I saw this leaflet, so I had a good look. I got my probation officer to ring up...

It really did not appear that professional workers were taking much initiative in passing publicity on to young people. Perhaps they should be encouraged to distribute publicity about young people's services a bit more.

But did the publicity encourage people to come to the projects, and if so in what way? Just over half those who had seen any publicity said it had encouraged them to come. The fact that the services were for young people was thought to be important by some, while others mentioned that the publicity gave them confidence and came at the time that they needed it. Again this emphasises the need for continuing publicity about services of this kind. Young people, like older people, want to know about a service when they need it. If they do not need it, they often do not notice the publicity.

Although only a small number mentioned the attraction of the publicity in stating that the service was for young people, it did have an important impact on some, like this 19-year-old in Milton Keynes – 'The cards said it was the under-25s, so I thought they wouldn't look down on me...' This fear of being rejected or 'told off' came up many times in these interviews, and there can be no doubt that publicity which emphasises that the service is for young people may get through to those who might not use another service. Some of the cards were clearly handed around by friends, as this schoolgirl in South Sefton indicated – 'It said on the card, "A service for the youth". That made me come...'

Informal and formal referrals

Word of mouth recommendation is often said to be the most frequent reason for people using family planning services, and indeed this was found to be so when the record card information was analysed. We were interested to know how this word of mouth recommendation actually worked, and we also wanted to find out whether professionals were suggesting the use of the projects and what they were saying.

Over 80 per cent of those interviewed in all three areas said that someone had told them about the project. Word of mouth was particularly important in South Sefton, where nearly 90 per cent had heard about the project from someone else.

In the majority of cases, the respondents had heard about the projects from a friend, and this kind of recommendation was more frequently mentioned by teenagers. Relatives were mentioned much less frequently, although as many as one fifth of the Milton Keynes women who had heard of the project from someone else said it was their mother. A tiny number had heard from colleagues at work or neighbours.

We were interested to know how these informal contacts had got to know about the projects and whether they had ever used them. Not surprisingly, respondents often did not know how the contact had got to know about the projects, but a third said that they had heard from another friend. The importance of the 'grapevine' effect in disseminating information about services of this kind was recognised years ago by the Family Planning Association. It appears to be just as strong today. Over one in ten of those who had heard about the project through a friend or relative said this person had seen some publicity. It was interesting that less than three-quarters of these informal contacts had used the projects' services themselves. It appears that a good reputation can be spread without personal use of services.

Professional referrals were rarely mentioned. The most frequently mentioned was Brook itself, and it was clear that women rang the central London Brook office and were then told about Shoreditch Brook. This was how one third of the City and Hackney respondents who had spoken to anyone about the project had heard about it.

GPs were mentioned by only a handful of people, and then it appeared that most referrals were somewhat negative, as this woman in Milton Keynes indicated – 'I went to my GP for a pregnancy test. He refused and told me to come here instead..' – and this 27-year-old in South Sefton – 'I went to my GP for a smear test and he wouldn't do it, so he told me to come here. I didn't even know this place was here. I thought it was a social place for the old folks...'

GPs' receptionists were mentioned almost as often as GPs, usually in the same context of refusal to give a particular service or in connection with a pregnancy test. Only one woman, in Milton Keynes, had been referred by a family planning clinic doctor.

Two women mentioned a health visitor in South Sefton, one mentioned a hospital social worker, and one schoolgirl mentioned a school welfare officer, who had told her not to tell the school that she had referred her. No-one mentioned youth workers or any other professional working with young people.

There was clearly very little referral from professional workers to these projects, other than for pregnancy tests. This reinforces the evidence gathered from the record cards, and shows that young people's services of this type have a great deal to do in fostering good relationships with professional workers if they are to get through to people who need them.

Appeal of the projects

What appealed to the women about the projects? There was some difference in the areas. In City and Hackney and South Sefton, over a third of the women said they came because it was local and convenient, while this was mentioned by only just over 10 per cent in Milton Keynes. It should be noted that it was mentioned more often by the over-20-year-olds than by the teenagers. It should never be forgotten that most people have a rather functional view of services. It is not really surprising that older women used services which were local and convenient even if they were designed as young people's services. As long as they were prepared to welcome older women it was likely that they would be used by older women. This rather functional view was also expressed by some younger women, but often in a very specific context, like this 20-year-old seeking a pregnancy test – 'I work in Milton Keynes so it's convenient. They do the test on the spot, so I can get it done in my lunch hour...'

A quarter of the respondents in all areas said that the services appeared to be friendly and caring, and this view was reflected among respondents of all ages. This, combined with convenience, was what appealed to this 29-year-old with two children in South Sefton - 'The women from PACE who came to see us last Christmas at the playgroup just seemed so nice and easy to talk to. And it's handy for us because we all live locally...'

But younger women too were attracted by what they saw as the friendliness of the staff, especially when compared with their view of their doctors. This 15-year-old in South Sefton summarised the views of a number of schoolgirls – 'The people seemed so friendly and helpful. They are more understanding than doctors and try to do the best they can for you. I'd met them when I came with other girls...'

Nearly a third of the respondents in Milton Keynes and South Sefton stressed that what appealed to them about the projects was the confidentiality they offered. The question of confidentiality came up time and again in these interviews, and was clearly a very important factor, particularly for teenagers. Over half the under-16s mentioned that they had been attracted to the projects because they thought they would be confidential. In some cases it was because they did not want their parents to know that they were seeking contraceptive advice, while in other cases they were worried about confiding in their doctors who had known them since they were small.

Around 10 per cent of respondents said that they came to the young people's project because they did not want to go to a family planning clinic for a variety of reasons, while others stressed that the projects were not like a clinic or GP surgery. Around 10 per cent said they welcomed the opportunity to be able to get counselling or advice, and the fact that it was specifically for contraception and pregnancy counselling appealed to some. There was no doubt that the projects had attracted some women because they offered free and quick pregnancy testing. This was clearly a primary reason for using the Milton Keynes project, but it was also true in other areas, as this single 21-year-old with one child in South Sefton pointed out: 'My friend said I could get a pregnancy test. There's no charge, and the next place where there is no charge is in town and I didn't want to go all the way into town. It's very good here because I only live down the road...'

It was perhaps interesting that very few people said they were attracted by the idea of seeing a woman doctor, although a small number liked the idea of an 'all-female staff', even though this was only true of the South Sefton project. Only 5 per cent of respondents said that they were attracted by the fact that it was a young people's project. Given that some of the clients were not so young, this was perhaps not so surprising, but it was only mentioned by a small number of teenagers.

Why young people came to the projects

The analysis of the record cards gave us information about the service people received when they came to the projects, but did not tell us the reasons people had for using the young people's projects in the first place. We wanted to find out whether there was anything in particular that they were seeking from the projects' services which they could not find elsewhere.

We asked those who were making their first visit why they had come to the projects, and we asked those who were making a repeat visit why they had *first* come to the projects and why they had come on *this* occasion. As we have seen, around half the respondents in both Milton Keynes and South Sefton were attending for the first time, while in City and Hackney one-third were making their first visit.

Table 5.6 shows the reasons given for attending the projects. The bases are small, but the pattern reflects the general profile of the users of the projects indicated by the record card information. We present the material in percentage form for ease of comparison between the projects.

Nearly half those making a first visit to the City and Hackney Brook clinic were seeking a termination of pregnancy, although only one fifth of the repeat attenders said this was why they had come on their first visit. Repeat visitors to the City and Hackney project were much more likely to have come for contraceptive supplies or advice on their first visit than those attending for the first time on the day we interviewed them. It would be wrong to deduce too much from such small bases, but it is possible that those who come initially for contraceptive help may be more likely to turn into regular users than those who come initially for a TOP referral. On the other hand, 15 per cent of the repeat visitors in City and Hackney came for follow-up counselling after a termination of pregnancy. They usually received contraceptive supplies or advice as well.

One third of those coming to You 2 for the first time on the day we interviewed came for a pregnancy test, and nearly half of those making a repeat visit to You 2 had come the first time for a pregnancy test. It might have been assumed that the repeat visitors would be unlikely to come for a pregnancy test, but, in fact, a quarter of them said they came for that reason. It was not clear whether these were people who were coming for a repeat pregnancy test or whether they had come for something different on their first visit but were now having a pregnancy test.

The different use made of the South Sefton project was apparent, with the greater emphasis on advice, whether on contraception or on general problems. It was also notable that around one-sixth of those interviewed had come just for a smear, whether on their first visit or on a repeat visit, and more people had come in connection with a women's health problem than in the other two areas. This again reflects the use made of this project by older women.

In all three projects, people making repeat visits were more likely to have come for contraceptive supplies or advice than those making first visits. They were also more likely to have come for help with contraception on a repeat visit than on their own first visits. The numbers were very small when broken down in this way, but there did appear to be an indication that if people returned to the project, they did so for contraception. This is not particularly surprising, since they would be unlikely to come back for repeated pregnancy tests or termination requests over such a short period. What we do not know, however, is what happened to people who came once only, or, indeed, why they did not return.

Five of the men came for contraceptive supplies and one came for advice only.

What the young people felt about the project staff
The three projects were set up with the expressed intention of employing staff who were sympathetic to young people. It must be assumed that staff employed on these projects were motivated to provide a special service which would help young people and would have a particular interest in the problems of young people. We wanted to know how the young people felt about the staff, and how they compared them with any other services they had used.

(a) Doctors
Not everyone we interviewed saw a doctor on their visit. This was not surprising in Milton Keynes and South Sefton, since, although we interviewed on the clinic days, the clinics were held in the afternoons and we did manage to interview some people who came only to the drop-in sessions. In City and Hackney, 84 per cent of the women interviewed saw a doctor, in Milton Keynes the proportion was 78 per per cent and in South Sefton it was 65 per cent. The younger respondents were more likely to see a doctor, but this reflected the fact that the South Sefton respondents were generally older than the others. None of the men saw a doctor on the day that we interviewed them.

We asked the young people whether there was anything that they particularly liked or disliked about the service they got from the doctor. None of the women interviewed could think of anything they did not like about the doctor. The overwhelming response in all three areas was that what they liked was that the doctor was friendly and nice and relaxed. Over 70 per cent of the women in all the areas mentioned this.

Comments were often made about the friendliness of the project doctor compared either with their own doctor or their perception of what doctors were like. There can be no doubt that many of the young people interviewed had rather curious views of doctors. They certainly did not seem to find them very friendly, as this 16-year-old in Milton Keynes said when she explained what she liked about the clinic doctor – 'She was friendly. She didn't seem like a doctor. Doctors really lay into you – interrogate you...'

Nearly one-third of the women said that they liked the fact that the doctor was informative and helpful and explained things properly. This was often combined with a comment that the doctor was friendly, and it was important to the younger girls, as this 17-year-old in South Sefton who came for the pill said - 'She was really nice. I thought she might try and put me off or something, but she never. She was really friendly and explained to me in depth about how to use the pill...'

The use of the word 'friendly' in describing the project doctors was striking in these interviews. Two young women in different areas commented that the doctor spoke to them as though she knew them already, and it was clear that this kind of rapport and friendliness was found surprising by the young people, as this 23-year-old in City and Hackney commented – 'She's very caring. She actually sat there and listened...'

The informality of the clinics and the doctors was mentioned by a number of women as an added bonus to the friendliness of the doctors, as this unmarried 21-year-old with a child commented in Milton Keynes – 'She's cheerful, and it was informal. She didn't sit at a desk. I was expecting her to give me a hard time, but she didn't...'

There was certainly an image of doctors in general as being rather formal, unfriendly, wearing white coats and sitting behind desks which came through time and again in these interviews. The younger the girls the more frequently they presented an image of their own doctors as being forbidding and disapproving, as this 16-year-old in South Sefton indicated when she said what she liked about the clinic doctor – 'She didn't tell me what to do. She just advised me about what would be best for myself. And she never shouted at me. She never had a doctor's uniform on – a white coat. She looked comfortable...'

Nearly 20 per cent of the women mentioned that they liked the doctor for being non-judgmental and understanding, and again the younger girls were more likely to mention this, as this 15-year-old, who wanted to go on the pill but was too embarrassed to go to her GP, explained – 'She was very nice and very helpful. She didn't think that because of my age I shouldn't receive advice or anything...'

15 per cent of the women said they liked the time the doctor gave them, as this 15-year-old in South Sefton pointed out – 'She was very friendly and helpful, and sits down and really talks to you and tries to find out what's wrong. She's prepared to spend time with you...'

Very few women mentioned spontaneously that they liked seeing a woman doctor. They would have automatically seen a woman doctor in Milton Keynes and South Sefton, but not necessarily in City and Hackney. In fact, none of the respondents had seen a male doctor on the day we interviewed them. We asked all the women, whether they had seen a doctor or not, how much it mattered to them whether they saw a man or a woman doctor.

The women divided roughly into four main groups, each representing around a quarter of the total sample: the first group said they would much rather see a woman doctor, and might even refuse to see a man. This view was expressed by a third of those interviewed in South Sefton, but only one fifth of those interviewed in City and Hackney. The second group said that they would prefer to see a woman doctor, but would not refuse to see a man. This view was held by nearly one third of those in City and Hackney and Milton Keynes. A third group were less prepared to state categorically what they preferred, but commented that women doctors were more sympathetic or understanding, or that they were easier to talk to than men doctors. Nearly 10 per cent said that it depended what the consultation was for. The fourth group said that it did not matter whether they saw a man or a woman, with some adding the proviso that it was irrelevant as long as the doctor was good at his or her job and nice and friendly. Two per cent of those interviewed said they would prefer to see a male doctor.

There was very little difference in the ages, number of children, ethnic origin or occupation of those interviewed in their views on women doctors, but those who were living as married tended to express more preference for seeing a woman doctor. On the whole, however, it seemed to be a very individual thing.

There were some young women who were unhappy about seeing male doctors, among them a married 23-year-old with two children – 'A woman doctor is more sympathetic. A man just thinks you're a piece of meat...'

Among those who said they preferred to see a woman doctor, there was some stress on the idea that a woman doctor might have some shared experience with them which a man could not have. There was no doubt that women were seen as more approachable than men doctors by a lot of women like this 24-year-old married woman in Milton Keynes who had been sent to You 2 by her doctor for a pregnancy test – 'I always prefer a woman. It matters a lot. I feel more comfortable with a woman. Men have no understanding. They don't want to know...'

Her words were echoed by a 15-year-old from the same area, although she was less bothered by the sex of the doctor as long as they were nice – 'It doesn't matter which. It matters whether they make you feel comfortable when you're with them. That's all...'

There was an interesting distinction made by some women in preferring women for certain intimate consultations, and this view was repeated when they were asked about their own GPs. This was more often found among younger girls, particularly those who had not had children, as this 17-year-old in Milton Keynes explained – 'I wouldn't like an internal from a male doctor, but I don't mind going to a man for a method only...'

And one of the few comments from a male on this subject underlined this distinction, as this 16-year-old boy who had come for condoms explained. He had just started worrying about getting AIDS – 'It depends what you go for. For tests I'd rather see a woman doctor. You feel ashamed with a man...'

But, as we have seen, nearly one third of the women thought that it did not matter whether they saw a man or a woman, although not all were as relaxed as this 16-year-old in City and Hackney – 'It doesn't bother me. No-one of my age is bothered unless they're one of those shy girls...' – or as blunt as this 18-year-old in Milton Keynes – 'I'm not bothered. I'm not sexist...'

We asked women who had seen a doctor on the day we interviewed them whether it had mattered on that occasion whether they had seen a man or a woman doctor. We were interested in pursuing the possibility that women differentiated between male and female doctors for certain things, as the response to the general question had indicated.

61 per cent of women said it had mattered whether they saw a man or woman doctor on the day we interviewed them, while 39 per cent said it had not. Again, it had mattered more in South Sefton and Milton Keynes, where nearly 70 per cent said it was important, than in City and Hackney, where less than half the women thought it was. It mattered much more to the under 16s, of whom nearly nine out of ten wanted to see a woman doctor, than to older women, including the 16-19-year-olds, of whom just over half thought it mattered. And, as might be expected from the age profile, it mattered more to schoolgirls and students than to other occupational groups.

Why did it matter on this occasion in particular? The main reason given by all age-groups and in all three areas was that a woman doctor was considered to be more understanding and sympathetic and easier to talk to. This Milton Keynes 18-year-old YTS trainee did not think the sex of the doctor mattered in general, and she liked and trusted her GP. However, on this occasion she wanted to see a woman doctor:

'I wanted a woman's opinion. I asked her a lot more questions than I would have asked my GP, and I wanted to know how to deal with my boyfriend because I want him to wear sheaths but he refuses...'

The same was true of another 18-year-old in the same area – 'I came here because I knew it was a woman doctor. It's too embarrassing to discuss something like a termination with a man...'

And older women too, who were not very bothered in general by whether they saw a man or a woman, thought that for some things they preferred to see a woman, particularly if they wanted more discussion than they thought they would be able to have with a man. This 27-year-old had been attending her GP for seven years for the pill, but wanted to discuss different pills:

'If it had been a man here today I would have seen him, because I needed to, but you do feel more at ease with a woman. You expect women in places like this – I would have been taken aback if it had been a man here today. You can talk better to a woman. She experiences these things herself, so she understands better...'

The younger teenagers were often concerned about the fact that it was only their first or second visit to the clinic, as this 17-year-old in South Sefton explained – 'With it being my first visit, I felt a bit embarrassed coming anyway...' – and there was certainly worry about internal examinations among the under-16-year-olds, like this 15-year-old in South Sefton. She had never been to her GP because he was the family doctor and was male, and had never been to the family planning clinic because she thought they dealt with older people. She had first come to the clinic for advice on a relationship, and was coming for the pill and more advice on this occasion. She explained why it was important for her to see a woman doctor – 'Because I'm used to that doctor. I don't think half the girls would come here if it was a man doctor. A lot of girls are embarrassed for a man to examine them down below...'

Not all young women felt happy about male doctors. This 22-year-old single girl had been to her GP four years earlier for the pill, but he had disapproved because she was unmarried, so she had used condoms instead, not very successfully, it appeared, since she now had two children. She was very anxious to see a woman doctor – 'I get very embarrassed with men doctors... Women handle you more gently...'

And, of course, some of the younger teenagers were worried about men doctors being disapproving because they were under 16. This 15-year-old in City and Hackney had been to a family planning clinic six months before for a pregnancy test. It was negative so she had not been back. It had taken her six months to decide to come to Brook for the pill. It was important to her that she saw a woman doctor – 'Because I thought if I saw a man doctor he would be funny about it because I was so young. He could put across negative views about going on the pill...'

What about those who did not mind whether they saw a man or a woman doctor on this occasion? The main reason given by respondents was that that kind of thing did not worry them, with a typical response given by this 20-year-old in Milton Keynes – 'They're all doctors. They're all qualified. As long as they help me I don't mind who I see...'

The next most common response was that it did not matter on this occasion because the woman had come for the pill or on a routine visit, and not for an examination, reinforcing the clear distinction some of them had made between more intimate discussions or examinations and the more routine repeat prescription of the pill.

Women were often very clear in their assertion that niceness and friendliness in a doctor was much more important than the sex of the doctor, and one 18-year-old rooted her belief in the clinic itself – 'At Brook it's so different. It doesn't really matter...'

(b) Other staff at the project

We asked the respondents whether they had talked to any other staff at the project on that occasion. As we have seen, not everyone had seen a doctor. In City and Hackney, all those interviewed said they had talked to someone else. Nearly 90 per cent mentioned a nurse, one in five had seen a counsellor and one in six mentioned that they had talked to an administrator, although, of course, at Brook, they would all have been checked into the clinic by an administrator.

In Milton Keynes, two-thirds of those interviewed said they had only talked to the doctor, although, again, all of them would have seen a receptionist or health worker before seeing the doctor. One third of the respondents said they had spoken to one of the health workers, with roughly equal numbers for each of the women health workers, but only one of the respondents mentioning the male health worker on this occasion.

In South Sefton, just over half the respondents said they had only talked to the doctor, while just over one third had spoken to one of the health workers and one sixth had spoken to the other. Again, only two respondents mentioned speaking to the clerk-receptionist.

We asked them what kind of help they got from the other staff they spoke to. The most commonly mentioned help in Milton Keynes and South Sefton, perhaps not surprisingly, was a pregnancy test. In Milton Keynes well over half those who spoke to a member of staff other than the doctor had a pregnancy test, and most of these mentioned pregnancy counselling as well. Some indication of the way in which the help was given was expressed by this 21-year-old in Milton Keynes who was single, unemployed and already had one child. She had come for a pregnancy test, counselling and a referral for a termination of pregnancy. She described her encounter with the health worker – 'She made a coffee and I started talking and she listened and came back and responded. They'll sit and listen to you here. It's really nice...'

At the Brook clinic the most commonly mentioned help was advice and information on contraceptive methods, mainly given by the nurse, who was also said to have given routine medical checks, such as blood pressure and weight. Few other types of help were mentioned in any of the projects.

No-one had any particular dislikes about the help they got from staff other than doctors. The main thing that respondents liked was that the staff were nice and friendly and caring and easy to talk to. This was particularly true in Milton Keynes, where it was mentioned by almost all those who had talked to another member of staff. The City and Hackney women mentioned that the staff were thorough and helpful and explained things well. This probably reflected the fact that they were usually speaking about help given by nurses. But they too were struck by the type of help the nurses gave, as this 24-year-old said – 'She seems interested and is listening to you as a person. You're not just another person in the queue...' – while a 17-year-old on her first visit to Brook spoke of the nurse and other staff with warmth – 'She was very friendly and we had a laugh about the cap. Everyone's beautiful here...'

The stress on being treated 'as a person' was clearly very important to a lot of women when they described their experiences of health care of all kinds in these interviews. A 21-year-old in Milton Keynes spoke of her encounter with the health worker – 'She was very nice – interested – she treated me as an individual, not just another pregnancy test...'

The young teenagers again showed their fear of being 'told off' and their worry about being disapproved of. This 15-year-old spoke to two of the health workers in Milton Keynes. She had been to her GP three months previously to ask for the pill but he had insisted on her parents' permission. She had come for a referral for termination of pregnancy and had found the health workers reassuring – 'They were kind. They didn't shout, and they listened to me. They didn't say, "You shouldn't have done this"...'

The male health worker was found to be reassuring by the 17-year-old who saw him. She had one child already and was attending for a pregnancy test:

> He made me feel very at ease. I was nervous when I came in, and he
> explained to me about the pregnancy test and about the results because I
> was scared to look – and he told me about the project...

Sometimes the women felt they had got help from the health workers which they thought they would not have got from a doctor, as this 21-year-old who had had two positive pregnancy tests in Milton Keynes explained:

> She was friendly and down to earth. There's no way a doctor would have
> talked to me the way she did, and she explained things – like why I should
> give up smoking...

It was the practical approach which appealed to women in South Sefton as well, as this 17-year-old who came for advice on family problems explained – 'It was practical common sense. It just showed me how to put things into perspective...'

Some boys too appreciated the help they received in South Sefton – 'It was quick and private, and you didn't have to tell her your name if you didn't want to...' He was worried about AIDS, but his appreciation was not shared so deeply by another teenage boy, who was very puzzled by the question – 'I just came for the johnnies – nothing else...'

We asked everyone, whether they had seen anyone other than a doctor or not, how much it mattered whether other staff they spoke to were men or women in projects like this. The sex of other staff appeared to be less important than the sex of the doctor, with around 50 per cent of those interviewed in City and Hackney and Milton Keynes saying it did not matter. This view was only shared by a quarter of the South Sefton women, however.

Those who thought it mattered divided again, with rather over 10 per cent of the total sample thinking that it mattered very much and around a quarter saying that they would prefer to talk to a woman but would not refuse to see a man. The rest of the women said that women were more sympathetic and easier to talk to.

The reasons women gave for preferring women staff were very similar to their reasons for preferring women doctors, as this 21-year-old in Milton Keynes explained – 'I wouldn't have liked to come to a man here. I don't know – I'd be a bit put out. A man wouldn't understand the problems I've been having regarding how I got pregnant...'

Again, many women made a functional distinction between the reasons for the visit, as this woman in South Sefton explained – 'I think it depends what you're coming for. If it was for contraception, it wouldn't matter, but if it was for something more intimate, I'd prefer a woman...'

It must not be forgotten that some women are still very inhibited about talking to men about anything to do with sex, whether they are doctors or not, and we found this more frequently in South Sefton than in the other two areas. This inhibition cannot always be predicted from a woman's circumstances. This single mother of two was quite clear about her own feelings – 'If it had been a fellow here today that I'd had to ask for condoms, I'd have just walked right out without them...'

But, as we have seen, a high proportion of the women in Milton Keynes and City and Hackney were not at all worried about the sex of the other staff, as this single 24-year-old with one child said – 'It doesn't bother me. I've seen male and female counsellors here before. It depends on the person. The male counsellor was really nice...'

Had the sex of the staff mattered on this occasion? One third said it had mattered, but two-thirds said it had not mattered. It was more important to the women in South Sefton than in the other two areas. Again, it was the perceived sympathy of women and the ease of communication which was important to the women we interviewed. There was also an indication that the surroundings and specialist nature of the projects were important. A 21-year-old in City and Hackney said why it was important that the nurse was a woman. She had found the female GP in her practice very abrupt – 'In this case it was comforting speaking to a woman because I had to say why I was there. There's something funny about admitting you're sexually active...'

This comment was clearly a key indication in why some women find it difficult to use contraceptive services, and why it is only after a first pregnancy that they admit the need to use contraception. It underlines the need for GPs and others to treat even the most tentative approach by a woman about contraception with the greatest sensitivity. Not everyone is as robust as some of our respondents.

But, of course, there were other aspects of the services offered by the projects which were perhaps as important, if not more important than the sex of the doctors and the other staff, as a number of women pointed out, like this 17-year-old in City and Hackney – 'I don't know them, and they don't know my mum – so it doesn't matter...' And her view was reinforced by a 20-year-old in Milton Keynes – 'It doesn't matter as long as they keep it confidential...'

Anonymity, confidentiality, niceness and friendliness were the key factors in the minds of many of the women using the projects' services. If the staff could provide all these, then many women did not mind whether they were male or female. To others, the fact that they were likely to see female staff, who, in their minds, were more likely to be sympathetic and approachable, were very important factors in encouraging them to attend and to continue attending. The women were discussing things which were very intimate to them. There was a constant use of phrases about being made to feel 'comfortable' or being 'put at ease', which women used to describe their encounters with women doctors and staff employed in these projects.

Table 5.1   Age of young women interviewed

column percentages

	Total	City & Hackney	Milton Keynes	South Sefton
11-15	13	4	24	11
16-19	34	26	47	27
20-24	33	52	27	16
25-29	15	18	2	27
30-39	3	-	-	11
40+	2	-	-	8
Base: all women	*(136)*	*(50)*	*(49)*	*(37)*

Table 5.2   Marital status of young women interviewed

column percentages

	Total	City & Hackney	Milton Keynes	South Sefton
Single	72	72	82	59
Married	9	4	6	19
Living as married	13	22	8	8
Widowed/divorced/ separated	6	2	4	14
Base: all women	*(136)*	*(50)*	*(49)*	*(37)*

Table 5.3   Number of children of young women interviewed

column percentages

	Total	City & Hackney	Milton Keynes	South Sefton
None	76	90	80	54
One	15	10	18	16
Two	6	-	2	19
Three or more	3	-	-	11
Base: all women	*(136)*	*(50)*	*(49)*	*(37)*

Table 5.4   Social class/occupation of young women interviewed

column percentages

	Total	City & Hackney	Milton Keynes	South Sefton
I	1	2	-	-
II	10	24	-	5
IIIN	26	42	18	14
IIIM	11	6	10	19
IV	5	2	6	8
V	1	-	-	3
Unemployed	7	2	8	14
Housewife/mother	7	-	6	16
Student/schoolgirl	29	18	47	19
MSC/YTS trainee	3	4	2	3
NA	1	-	2	-
Base: all women	*(136)*	*(50)*	*(49)*	*(37)*

Table 5.5   Ethnic origin of young women interviewed

column percentages

	Total	City & Hackney	Milton Keynes	South Sefton
White British	82	58	94	100
White Irish	3	6	2	-
West Indian	8	22	-	-
African	1	2	-	-
Indian/Pakistani/Bangladeshi	1	2	2	-
Turkish/Greek/Cypriot	1	2	-	-
Other	3	6	2	-
Base: all women	*(136)*	*(50)*	*(49)*	*(37)*

Table 5.6   Why young people first came to the projects and why repeat visitors came on this occasion

column percentages

	Repeat visitors on first visit			First visitors			Repeat visitors on this occasion		
	C&H	MK	SS	C&H	MK	SS	C&H	MK	SS
Contraceptive method	52	42	40	24	36	29	70	58	55
Contraceptive adv.	24	13	5	12	12	24	12	4	5
Post-coital contraception	-	-	-	12	12	-	-	-	-
Pregnancy test	12	46	10	6	32	18	6	25	5
Pregnancy counselling	9	4	-	6	-	-	-	8	10
TOP referral	18	-	-	47	12	-	-	8	-
Advice/ counselling	-	-	25	6	-	29	3	-	20
Smear	-	-	15	6	4	18	9	4	15
Other gynae/ infection	9	-	10	-	-	18	9	4	5
IUD/cap check	3	-	-	-	-	-	6	-	5
TOP follow-up counselling	-	-	-	-	-	-	15	-	-
General chat	-	-	-	-	-	-	-	-	10
NA	-	4	-	-	8	6	-	4	-
Base: all women	*(33)*	*(24)*	*(20)*	*(17)*	*(25)*	*(17)*	*(33)*	*(24)*	*(20)*

Chapter 6
Young people and other family planning and counselling services

It would be wrong to assume that young people's services for contraception and pregnancy counselling are likely to be used only or even mainly by young people who have never used other family planning services. Services specifically for young people are fairly thin on the ground, and a lot of young people use family planning clinics or their GPs. Some will use them as a matter of course, while others will use them because there is no alternative. Many of the professionals interviewed were concerned that these services were not geared to the needs of young people, and that unhappy experiences or inappropriate treatment at such services could deter young people from using reliable methods of contraception and from discussing the anxieties about relationships which worry many young people.

Previous use of other young people's clinics
We had not expected many of the respondents to have used other young people's clinics before they came to the projects, mainly because there are so few of them. The lack of facilities in the particular areas was, of course, one of the reasons the projects were set up where they were. It should, however, be remembered that there was a Brook clinic already operating in City and Hackney at the Shoreditch clinic, and there was also another young people's clinic in the area run by the health authority. This was not true in Milton Keynes or South Sefton, where young people had to travel some way to find young people's services of this kind.

Ten per cent of the total sample of women interviewed had used another young people's clinic, but nearly half of these were over 25. Of those who had used another young people's clinic, nearly half had used the Brook Clinic in Central London, a quarter had used another London Brook clinic and nearly one third had used Liverpool Brook. Only one girl in Milton Keynes had used a young people's clinic in another area.

The numbers, of course, were tiny, but the interviews showed that most of those who had used another young people's clinic had done so for contraception, usually more than one year before they had come to the project. They had liked the clinics because the staff were friendly, understanding and sympathetic, but some had found the clinics inconvenient to get to, while others had found that they had to wait too long. They had usually stopped going either because they had moved house or changed job, or because they had found the young people's projects' services more convenient for their home or work.

The women who had used other young people's services were usually people who wanted contraception and wanted to use a young people's clinic which was convenient. Most of them had used a Brook clinic and had liked the service they received.

Previous use of family planning clinics

Family planning clinics were available in all three areas, and young people under 25 used these clinics, as the health authority statistics show. However, we were interested to see whether the young people attending the projects' services had used family planning clinics, and, if so, what they thought of them. We also wanted to find out why young people had not used family planning clinics.

The previous use of family planning clinics varied considerably between the areas, from 10 per cent in Milton Keynes to 30 per cent in City and Hackney to 41 per cent in South Sefton, where most of those who had used family planning clinics were over 25. Table 6.1 shows that previous use of family planning clinics among those under 25 was limited. One third of those between 20 and 24 had used a clinic but most of these were in City and Hackney. Only four (6 per cent) of the teenagers had ever used a family planning clinic. Again, the numbers were tiny, and it is difficult to generalise about the experience that they had had.

Rather higher proportions of older women had been to family planning clinics, and their experience there had often led them to seek advice from the young people's clinic. Some of their views may be of use to those planning services, but it must be stressed that this study was primarily interested in the views of the under-25-year-olds for whom these projects were designed. Considerable caution should be exercised before attaching too much weight to the views of older women when assessing services for young people.

Most of those who had used family planning clinics had attended one in the same health district as the project or in a neighbouring district. Most had been for contraceptive methods or advice, although a handful had been for pregnancy tests, including two of the four teenagers who had been to family planning clinics. The younger women had usually been to the clinics more recently than the older ones.

The older women were more likely than the younger women to have liked the family planning clinics, usually for the same reasons given by women for liking the young people's projects. They liked the friendliness and sympathy of the staff, and some stressed that they liked the all-female staff. None of the teenagers found anything they particularly liked about the clinic.

Although one third had no criticisms of the family planning clinics they had attended, there were quite strong criticisms among other users. Around a quarter found the clinics unfriendly, and a quarter thought they were too busy or crowded and that they had to wait too long. Nearly one fifth found them too formal and impersonal, while 10 per cent said they had been refused help of the kind they wanted.

There have been indications in the past that not all family planning clinic staff are happy dealing with women who request termination of pregnancy (Allen 1985). The young people under 25 who reported unhappy experiences with family planning clinics appeared to have encountered staff like this, as this 16-year-old schoolgirl who had been to a family planning clinic for a pregnancy test explained – 'They wouldn't see me. They said they couldn't deal with me and I would have to go somewhere else. She was all right until I told her my age. She just said she couldn't see me. I would have to go to my own area – so I just walked out...'

And this problem occurred with older women too, like this 27-year-old – 'They were very unsupportive. The doctor was against abortion and she wouldn't sign the green form – she sent me to the hospital. Why was she working in that place? She made me feel awful – terrible...'

So why had they stopped using the family planning clinic? One third of those interviewed said that the young people's project was more convenient and one fifth said they had moved house or changed job. Some of the older women had started using the GP's services instead, while others had stopped taking the pill. On the whole the reasons given were related to convenience among the 20-24-year-olds, while the teenagers had either been turned away, or had only used the clinics for pregnancy tests or post-coital contraception.

Reasons for not using family planning clinics

Nearly three-quarters of the women interviewed had never been to a family planning clinic. As we have seen, much higher proportions of those under 25 had never been and we were particularly interested in their reasons.

Nearly half of those who had never been said that they had never needed to, and this reason was given by over half the teenagers. This could be interpreted in a number of ways. Some of the young people said they had only just started having a sexual relationship, so they had never needed contraception before, while others said they had never needed to go to a family planning clinic because they were going to their GP or were using condoms. Some people who had 'never needed to' use a family planning clinic appeared to have been in need of some kind of ongoing help and support, like this unemployed 21-year-old single mother who had started going to her GP four years before for ante-natal services and then for the pill. She was still attending her GP for contraceptive services but could not get an appointment with him in the week we interviewed her. She had come to the You 2 project for a pregnancy test, counselling and a TOP referral. She said that she had never needed a family planning clinic because 'I've never been in this mess before...'

About one fifth of those who had never been to a family planning clinic could not think of any particular reason for never having been, but 10 per cent, mainly teenagers, said that they did not know anything about clinics or that it had never occurred to them to go, like this 18-year-old in Milton Keynes who had been to the GP a fortnight before for a pregnancy test – 'It never crossed my mind...'

There were worries that family planning clinics might not be confidential and there were worries about lack of privacy in a clinic. Not everyone liked what they had heard about clinics, like this 23-year-old with two children – 'They're too nosey. People who've been say they ask you all sorts of questions...'

There were indications that they were seen as places for 'older people', which often appeared to mean people over the age of 20. A 17-year-old in South Sefton who had been to Liverpool Brook for the pill but had found it too far and too long a wait, was quite clear about why she did not want to go to a family planning clinic:

> I went with my mum and there were lots of women with kids. I wouldn't be relaxed there and I might see someone I knew there. If I went somewhere specially for youth I wouldn't worry about bumping into my mum or being embarrassed by seeing other people I know...

Some teenagers, particularly the under-16s, were confused by the name, like this 14-year-old who said – 'I'm not planning a family...' – and other teenagers were worried and shy, like this 16-year-old schoolgirl in Milton Keynes – 'I made an appointment but cancelled it two days before. I was just so nervous, I couldn't go through with it. I was worried about the internals...'

Feelings of young people about family planning clinics

We thought the respondents might give us a different perspective if we asked them whether they thought young people in general were worried about going to an ordinary family planning clinic. People will often give more candid answers if asked about the feelings of 'other people'. Not all young people felt able to answer the question, however, like this single 24-year-old with one child who said, 'I don't know much about young people...'

Around 40 per cent in all three areas and of all ages thought young people were worried about going to ordinary family planning clinics. The main reason for their anxiety was thought to be that clinics were too public, not anonymous or not confidential. This fear was expressed more by the teenagers than older women, like this 14-year-old – 'Everyone would stare, thinking, "She's not married"...' But women in their twenties also thought that family planning clinics were off-putting, like this 22-year-old single woman with two children – 'Because you don't like everyone knowing what you're going for...' It was thought that GPs' surgeries were more anonymous and 'It's the other people in the clinic. They know why you're there. In a surgery it could be anything...' 'Other people' were clearly as worrying as the clinic staff or treatment, as this 21-year-old who had never been to a family planning clinic explained – 'There's women sat all around, staring at you, wondering why you're there...'

Young people were thought to be too shy or embarrassed to go to a family planning clinic, as this 19-year-old pointed out – 'The younger you are the worse it is – it's embarrassing. They might meet someone they know, or who knows their mother...'

There was plenty of evidence from teenagers that young people were worried about going to a clinic because they thought the staff would be unfriendly or disapproving, like this 16-year-old in City and Hackney – 'Because they're so young. They might feel people there were thinking young girls are tarts or they sleep around...' – and this 17-year-old in Milton Keynes – 'At You 2 it's an open and friendly atmosphere, but in an ordinary family planning clinic everyone is stern and they ask how old you are...'

111

This rather forbidding image of family planning clinics was endorsed by a 14-year-old in Milton Keynes – 'The main problem of under-age people is they think they'll be turned away, so they just don't bother in the first place...'

A more reflective view was given by a 21-year-old in City and Hackney who had been to a family planning clinic, which she had liked for the expertise of the women doctors, but had not liked waiting so long to be seen. She explained why teenagers might be worried about going to ordinary family planning clinics:

'If you've just started having sexual intercourse and you need to know more, you feel stupid asking basic questions of people who really know a lot. Having sex means you're an "adult" and you are very shy about this new role. Family planning clinics are "adult" places – and the name suggests you want to plan your family...'

Her view was endorsed by a 22-year-old in the same area – 'I thought clinics were for young mothers planning families and therefore not for young people...' – and it was quite clear that family planning clinics were often thought of as places mainly for women with children. Even young mothers did not necessarily like the idea, as this 21-year-old explained – 'A lot of people who go there have already had kids, so young people feel out of place...'

Teenagers certainly thought this might be so and some thought family planning clinics were the same as infant welfare clinics, like this 17-year-old in South Sefton – 'Family planning clinics are full of older women and their families. They're all sitting around looking at you. I've been to baby clinics with my mum and I thought it would be like that...'

Some had rather odd ideas of what family planning clinics were for, like this 17-year-old with one child in Milton Keynes – 'They're nervous about it because they don't really know what the clinics are about. They think it's something to do with divorce...' – and this 15-year-old in Milton Keynes – 'Family planning clinics are mainly for pregnant women rather than for discussing problems and giving advice...' – and this 16-year-old schoolgirl in the same area – 'They cater more for middle-aged women. It's easier to talk to someone who knows about your age range and can get on well with you...'

It should be emphasised that none of these respondents had actually been to a family planning clinic, but it does look as though clinics could brush up their image a bit if they are to attract more young people. Perhaps one of their main aims should be to inform teenagers about their role.

But nearly 50 per cent of those interviewed thought that young people were not worried about going to an ordinary family planning clinic, and again this view was found among all ages and in all three areas. Around a quarter of these respondents thought there was just no reason why young people should be worried – 'Not if they're planning a family...' – as a 14-year-old said. An 18-year-old in Milton Keynes thought young people were not worried about going to family planning clinics – 'It's just that there aren't any family planning clinics around here for them to go to...'

The main reason given for young people not being worried about going to family planning clinics was because they were seen as having expertise and offering a specialist service – the very reason why some girls were thought to be worried about them. This 16-year-old in Milton Keynes summarised the views of quite a number of teenagers:

> Well, a family planning clinic deals with that sort of thing specially. They're dealing with contraception all the time and it's more sort of "routine" than going to your own doctor for it, isn't it?

There was a feeling among respondents that family planning clinics were preferable to GPs because of this specialisation, as this 17-year-old in South Sefton explained – 'Because they're just for contraceptives and pregnancy tests, whereas doctors are for all kinds of things...'

The question of everyone else in the clinic waiting room knowing why others were there, which was a source of embarrassment to some, was seen as a positive thing by others – 'It's mainly girls who go and all the doctors are women and everyone is there for mainly the same thing...'

Clinics were thought to be anonymous and confidential by some – 'It seems to be more impersonal. They don't know as much about you as your own doctor does, and they don't know the whole family...'

It appeared that family planning clinics had very mixed images among young people, but it was rather more complicated than that. Some of the perceived characteristics of clinics were found attractive by some and not by others. There can be little doubt, however, that services aimed specifically at young people – however old they might be – could well be more attractive to teenagers and to women without children.

Previous use of GPs' services for contraception and related topics
We asked the women whether they had ever been to their GP for 'any kind of help with contraception or anything like that'. It was a difficult question to word, because we did not want to pick up all the consultations women might have had with GPs in connection with ante-natal care, but we did

113

want to pick up on pregnancy counselling in connection with an unwanted pregnancy. The question appeared to have been understood in the way we intended.

47 per cent of the women under 25 had used their GPs' services for contraception or related topics, compared with 70 per cent of those aged 25 or over. Among the teenagers, 20 girls (31 per cent) had used their GPs' services, compared with the four teenagers who had been to family planning clinics. There was a difference between the areas, with Milton Keynes having a much higher relative use of GPs' services than the other two areas in all the age groups under 25. A quarter of the under-16s in Milton Keynes had been to the GP, compared with none in the other two areas. Over half the 16-19-year-olds had been in Milton Keynes, compared with a quarter in City and Hackney and 10 per cent in South Sefton, and 85 per cent of the 20-24-year-olds had been to GPs in Milton Keynes compared with around two-thirds in the other two areas.

The GPs were mainly in the same area as the projects or in the surrounding area in both Milton Keynes and South Sefton, while in City and Hackney, the GPs were more often in other parts of London or outside London, partly reinforcing the evidence that the Shoreditch Brook clinic was often used by women from outside the area, and partly reflecting the mobility of the women clinic users in London.

The GPs were usually the women's own family doctors in Milton Keynes and South Sefton, but a quarter of the City and Hackney women had used other GPs' services, usually on a temporary resident basis while registered elsewhere, again reflecting the mobility of the London population. We had wondered whether women might go to a woman partner in the practice rather than to their own GP for specific contraceptive problems or pregnancy counselling, but this rarely appeared to be the case.

The majority of respondents said they had first been to their GP for contraceptive methods or advice, about ten per cent had been for a pregnancy test, and tiny numbers had been for pregnancy counselling, a referral for termination of pregnancy or for post-coital contraception.

The under-16s had all been within the last year, but the majority of all other age-groups had first been to the GP more than a year before we interviewed them. There was a small group of girls who had first been to the GP within the previous month, usually for a pregnancy test or with a request for termination of pregnancy.

The main reason given for first going to the GP of course covered a wide variety of circumstances. It might appear to be a rational choice leading to continued rational behaviour. In many cases, the interviews suggested it was no such thing, as this 20-year-old separated woman with one child, indicated. She had first been to the GP when she was 15 for a negative pregnancy test and the pill. She had stopped going several years ago because it was 'embarrassing' and she 'couldn't be bothered'. Her story reflected some of the less than orderly decision-making processes which we heard in other interviews:

> Mum is a worrier – she took me to the doctor. I missed a period and she thought I was pregnant. I was only a week late. I was drunk when I went because she'd tried the 'gin and tonic' remedy. The GP put me on the pill...

Two-thirds of the women said there was nothing they particularly liked about the service they received from their GP in connection with contraception and related topics, but around one quarter in all areas found their GPs helpful, friendly, nice and caring – the characteristics which have been found before in this study to give doctors a good name with women seeking contraceptive help or pregnancy counselling. Some doctors were liked for being 'good and competent', while others explained things well or were easy to talk to.

Unfortunately, not all doctors were regarded with such appreciation by their patients, and two-thirds of the women could think of things that they did not like about the service they had received from their GP in connection with contraception and related topics.

A quarter of the women had found their GP unpleasant or off-putting, and just under a quarter said that the doctor had no time to discuss or explain things. Often the two comments went together, particularly among the 20-24-year-olds, like this single woman with one child – 'Her attitude was indifferent. She wasn't interested. She wouldn't explain things to me or ask me questions about my health, and she didn't try to explore why the pill upset me...'

It was clear that some GPs felt uncomfortable when confronted with a request for termination of pregnancy, but this often seemed to affect later relationships with women, as this 22-year-old single mother of two illustrated:

> He was weird. He made me feel embarrassed. I wanted my first baby aborted but he was dead abrupt and wouldn't help me. And with the pill, I went through about eight different ones before I found one that suited me without side effects. You couldn't talk to him. I once went to him with a water infection and he told me to go to the venereal clinic – and all it was was a water infection...

Some teenagers found their GPs unsympathetic and disapproving, like this 17-year-old single mother in Milton Keynes – 'He's very abrupt and he doesn't like me I don't think. He was very rude to me when I got pregnant and very rude to me when he came to see me after the baby was born. It was more of a social call to my mother...'

A common complaint was that GPs were only interested in the pill, and this, combined with a perceived lack of time to discuss and an abrupt manner, often led to women to feel less than satisfied with their GPs' contraceptive services, like this 19-year-old in City and Hackney – 'He just gave me a prescription – no instructions or anything like that...' – and this 24-year-old single mother in Milton Keynes – 'He didn't seem to be bothered. He just wanted to put me on the pill. I wanted to know about all the different methods, but as far as he was concerned he just wanted me to take the pill...'

All the under-16s who had been to GPs had found them unsympathetic and disapproving, like this 14-year-old – 'He doesn't seem to want to know. He just said I couldn't go on the pill and that was it...'

We asked women why they had stopped going to their GPs for contraceptive services. Nearly a quarter said that they had not stopped, but had come to the project for a particular reason, with roughly equal numbers having come for a pregnancy test, post-coital contraception, a referral for termination of pregnancy, a smear or to see a woman doctor for advice or an examination. Some of those coming for a pregnancy test had been sent by their GPs. Other women came for the expertise they thought they would be offered at the young people's project, like this 18-year-old in Milton Keynes – 'I haven't stopped going to my GP, but I wanted a second opinion on the contraceptive injection. I wasn't sure whether to go back on the pill. I wanted a woman's opinion...'

Others had been sent to the project by their doctors for rather different reasons, as this 19-year-old in Milton Keynes explained – 'I haven't really stopped. He sent me here because he wouldn't prescribe the morning-after pill. He wasn't confident that it would work and he was worried that I would sue him if I got pregnant, had the baby and it was deformed...'

Around one third of the women had stopped going to their GPs because they did not like the advice or treatment they had received or the manner in which they had received it, like this 18-year-old single girl in City and Hackney – 'His whole manner. He's not very nice so I never went to him again for that sort of thing. He just said, "You can either have the baby or not," and he wouldn't give me any contraception for afterwards...'

It is possible that unhappy experiences with GPs when asking for contraceptive advice had contributed to some unwanted pregnancies. The GPs' perceived lack of interest in any method other than the pill was often a reason for stopping going to them for contraceptive advice, and other non-medical methods were not always found reliable.

Reasons for not using GPs' services for contraception and related topics

Rather over half the under-25-year-olds had not been to their GPs for contraceptive help or for help with related topics, and nearly 70 per cent of those under 20 had not been.

The main single reason for not going to the GP was because the doctor was male, but this reason was often combined with other factors, particularly among the teenagers. There was a very strong fear among some girls that the doctors might tell their parents, as this 17-year-old in South Sefton explained – 'He's male, and my mum's very friendly with him. She's seeing him a lot because she's needed a lot of treatment. They're very friendly and he knows all the family...'

Her views were echoed in City and Hackney by a 16-year-old – 'I don't trust him. He'd tell my mum. He's very close to my mum, especially since I had meningitis...' – and by a 17-year-old in Milton Keynes – 'He rings my mum every time I go near him...'

A quarter of the teenagers who had not been to their GPs were worried about confidentiality and this fear was repeated in many guises. Some girls also felt embarrassed about discussing contraception with their doctors who had known them since they were babies, while others simply did not like their doctors. The image of doctors being formal and unfriendly and sitting behind desks came through again in answer to this question. They were certainly seen by some girls as figures of authority dealing with illness, as this 16-year-old in Milton Keynes explained:

> I don't like him. GPs are stern as if they're going to have a go at you about things. You don't feel you can really tell them anything. Doctors are there for when you're ill. They don't want to listen to what you say...

Feelings of young people about using GPs' services for contraception and related topics

Over 80 per cent of the women interviewed thought that young people were worried about going to their GP for contraceptive help, and this view was held by well over 90 per cent of the teenagers interviewed.

117

The main worry was thought to be that the GP would tell the young person's parents. Nearly three-quarters of the under-16s and nearly half the 16-19-year-olds mentioned this, and older women too thought that young people would be worried by this. There was considerable anxiety about the widely-held view that GPs had to tell the parents of girls under the age of 16, as this 15-year-old in Milton Keynes explained – 'They're worried especially after there was that thing about doctors saying they'd tell parents if they were under 16 on the news about a year ago...'

The closeness of the 'family' doctor to the family was thought to endanger confidentiality – 'They don't think it will be kept quiet. I suppose it's a bit close to home...' – and a 17-year-old single mother gave reasons why others were worried about GPs – 'They don't want to talk to doctors. A lot of my friends don't, anyway. It's nerves, because their parents go to that practice and it might slip out even though the service is supposed to be confidential...'

A general feeling that the consultation might not be confidential was thought to worry young people, and again around half the teenagers mentioned this. Young people were also thought to be nervous about the possible reaction of the GPs to a request for contraception, as this 21-year-old explained – 'I was really scared. I so often went to my GP to ask for the pill and then didn't because I was too scared to come out with it...'

Again, there was an image of unfriendly and punitive doctors, as illustrated by an 18-year-old in South Sefton – 'I think they're nervous in case they are going to shout at them and say, "What do you need *that* for?"'

This nervousness was thought to be exacerbated by the lack of time that some GPs appeared to have, as another 21-year-old noted – 'It depends on the GP. A lot of them just don't have time and they don't realise how nervous you are. It might be just routine to them...'

The perceived lack of time for discussion, combined with a fear that the GP might disapprove or be unsympathetic, was thought to put young people off going to them for contraceptive help, as this 23-year-old explained – 'GPs talk down to you. When I first went I wanted advice but he just made the decision and put me on the pill. Young people need time, support and advice, which GPs are not prepared to give...'

The general image of GPs among these women interviewed was not very favourable, particularly in relation to these very intimate matters. Doctors were seen as good at dealing with illness, but there seemed to be a dearth of caring, friendly doctors who were prepared to discuss sensitive issues and to give time to uncertain teenage girls who might not necessarily want to go on the pill. This 17-year-old in Milton Keynes summarised a widely-held view:

> Young people have an image of an impersonal doctor who doesn't really care. Family planning is not the sort of thing that young people have experienced before, and they need time and understanding...

It was perhaps a relief that 10 per cent of the sample thought that young people were not worried about going to their GPs, and that this view was held by more than half the 20-24-year-olds interviewed. The main reason they thought young people were not worried was because discussion of contraception was more open 'nowadays', as this 21-year-old noted – 'It's publicised a lot more now with condom adverts, so they wouldn't be so embarrassed...'

Nevertheless, it was quite clear that GPs have a long way to go before they gain the trust of all young people and before young people feel comfortable in approaching them. Like family planning clinics, it does appear that they might need to try and change their image as far as young people are concerned. It is difficult to see how they can remove the gruff and grumpy image if that is how they are, but it often appeared that this was not always the real problem. They appear rushed to young people and they appear formal and they do not always appear interested. However, if they are concerned about preserving confidentiality, and they will not divulge information to girls' parents, there must be ways of making this known. If unwanted pregnancies among young girls are to be avoided, it seems essential that GPs should be perceived to be approachable and that they should be seen to be people who will preserve confidentiality.

Feelings of young people about attending the young people's projects' services

We knew that some of the young people might have felt worried about using family planning clinics and GPs' contraceptive services. We wanted to explore their feelings about coming to the young people's project's services. After all, here were services designed specifically for young people, which had been publicised, at least to some extent. If these services were to reach more young people, we thought it important to examine the views of those who had actually used them.

We asked them whether they had felt shy or embarrassed coming to the project's services for the first time. Overall, 40 per cent said they had. As might have been expected, the teenagers had been more apprehensive than the older age groups, with over 60 per cent of the under-16s and nearly half the 16-19-year-olds saying they had felt shy or embarrassed, compared with less than one third of the 20-24-year-olds.

The main reason for feeling nervous was lack of familiarity with the place or the procedure. The young people simply did not know what was going to happen to them and this worried them, as this 18-year-old in South Sefton explained – 'I felt nervous. You always feel nervous when you go to any place for the first time. I didn't know what would happen and what she'd say, and what I'd have to do...'

The worry and nervousness was by no means confined to young people who had never been to a GP or family planning clinic, as this woman in Milton Keynes illustrated – 'When I got up there I felt the atmosphere. They were all sitting there thinking, "What's she here for? How old is she?" I felt silly. I'm 20 years old and married with a child and I still felt silly...'

There was some indication in all the projects that they were felt to be too public, and the reception was thought to be a bit intimidating. In Milton Keynes and South Sefton there was little waiting space, and one 15-year-old was a bit alarmed by her reception – 'I walked in and there was a man and three women staring back at me. They looked at me as if to say, "I wonder what you're here for..."'

In City and Hackney, there was more apprehension about the possible reaction of the staff and worry about being pregnant and wanting an abortion, as this 16-year-old explained – 'Because I knew I was pregnant and I was embarrassed about telling people the first time. They might think I was sleeping around...'

It is often underestimated how nervous young women might be about going to a professional for contraceptive help or for pregnancy counselling. Even stressing the fact that the project's services were for young people did not necessarily help, as this 17-year-old said, 'I felt that I was a bit too young. I thought they might think I was too young to be here...'

And it should not be forgotten that men too can be shy or nervous about going to strange places, as this 19-year-old boy attending PACE for the second time, explained – 'I get embarrassed easily anyway. People say it's easy, but it wasn't easy the first time. But once you get to know them and talk to them it gets a lot easier...'

But nearly three-quarters of the 20-24 year-olds and over half the 16-19-year-olds had not felt shy or embarrassed about coming to the project for the first time, although the under-16-year-olds were more worried.

Women in their twenties often said that they were not shy people in any case – 'I've already had one child, and you don't feel shy or embarrassed once you've had a child...' – and their feelings were shared by younger respondents, like this 16-year-old boy in South Sefton, who found the question rather strange – 'I'm not a shy lad...'

Teenagers had often been assured by friends that there was no need to be shy about going to the projects. One fifth of the women under 25 said they were not embarrassed because the staff put them at ease. Among the younger girls, this was often combined with the fact that they had been to the project with friends before they used the services themselves. This 21-year-old had been too shy to go to a family planning clinic and had been to her GP four years before but had not liked him – 'I'd come down with a friend before when she had her test done and I saw what they were like here...'

The 'grapevine' effect was important in helping to overcome shyness among some of the teenagers, especially the under-16-year-olds. One 15-year-old explained why she was not shy or embarrassed about attending:

> Because I've talked to the women here before and knew there was no reason to be embarrassed. In school, a friend of mine thought she was pregnant and I told her to go and speak to the school welfare officer. She asked me to go with her and the welfare oficer advised her to come here, and I came with her, and that's how I knew the staff here. Also, another girl who was pregnant came here and I was with her when the lady told her she was pregnant. And another one came for the pill and asked me to come with her, so I'd been here four times with other girls before I came for myself and I knew them here and found them very friendly – and there was nothing to be embarrassed about...

Some of the women said that they were too concerned about their problem to be embarrassed, like this 17-year-old – 'I was just worried that I might be pregnant – that was the main thing...' – while others felt that the setting of the project was anonymous enough for them not to feel embarrassed, as this 17-year-old in South Sefton explained – 'It's a community centre here and if people see you they'll just think you've been playing bingo with the old fogies...'

It appeared that young women often found out quite a lot about the projects from friends before they actually approached them for help. There was undoubtedly a large reservoir of shyness and embarrassment about using services in connection with contraception or unwanted pregnancy. Even with services geared specifically for young people, it still took quite a lot of courage for many young women to make the first approach. There

121

can be little doubt that hearing about the good experiences of others was very encouraging for many of them. But this kind of 'grapevine' effect takes time to get established, and not everyone is on the grapevine. It seems clear that relying on the grapevine effect may well have led to a very slow build-up of a clientele in areas where there was thought to be a considerable need of services for young people.

Table 6.1   Previous use of family planning clinics by age of women

column percentages

	Age of women					
	11-15	16-19	20-24	25-29	30-39	40+
Yes	6	7	33	55	100	33
No	94	93	67	45	-	67
Base: all women	*(18)*	*(46)*	*(45)*	*(20)*	*(4)*	*(2)*

Table 6.2   Previous use of GP services for contraception by age of women

column percentages

	Age of women					
	11-15	16-19	20-24	25-29	30-39	40+
Yes	17	37	69	70	100	33
No	83	63	31	30	-	67
Base: all women	*(18)*	*(46)*	*(45)*	*(20)*	*(4)*	*(2)*

Chapter 7
Sex education and young people's service needs

There has been considerable debate over the past few years about the question of sex education at school. Certain groups claiming to speak for parents have brought strong pressure for sex education to be banned in schools. Such groups have claimed that sex education should be the responsibility of parents and that sex education at school can lead to increased experimentation and promiscuity. Research over the years has shown that this view is held only by a small minority of people, and that the vast majority of parents and children think there is a need for sex education to be given to children at school, not least because many parents find it difficult to speak to their children about very intimate subjects, and teenagers often find it embarrassing to talk to their parents about sex (Allen, 1987; Farrell, 1978).

Of course, much hinges around the question of what 'sex education' is. In the Policy Studies Institute research (Allen 1987), it was found necessary to define twelve topics which could be covered in 'sex education' at school. It could be taught in several subjects in the curriculum over several years. The idea that 'sex education' could be removed from the school curriculum at the stroke of a pen was clearly not feasible.

In the 1987 Education Act, responsibility for deciding on the form and content of sex education in schools was given to the governing bodies, along with a number of other new responsibilities. At the time that the young people's projects were set up in October 1987, there was some confusion in schools in many areas of the country about the exact nature of the governors' responsibilities as far as sex education was concerned. This was reflected in the areas where the projects were set up, and it was apparent from interviews with teachers and others involved in education that some school programmes in personal and social education had been affected by delays in decisions by governors on the exact nature and content of the sex education they wished to see in their schools.

All three projects were designed with a strong sex education component, both on an outreach basis and within the project premises. They all laid considerable stress on the need for young people to be well-informed about how their bodies worked, about contraception and about personal relationships. We thought it important to ask the young people themselves about the sex education they had received at school, from their parents and from other sources, and to assess their views on what it was like and how helpful it was.

Sex education at school

There is plenty of evidence that inadequate knowledge can lead to unwanted pregnancies. There is also evidence that knowledge alone is not enough, and that young people welcome discussion of issues surrounding sex, contraception and personal relationships in a structured environment with the help and guidance of a teacher or other responsible adult (Allen, 1987).

We were interested to know what kind of sex education the young people we interviewed had had at school and from other sources. Some of them were pregnant, others had clearly taken considerable risks of pregnancy before coming to the projects, while others had had unwanted pregnancies in the past. The nature of their sex education and their feelings about it could give important indications of the needs of young people in these areas.

65 per cent of the young people under 25 said they had had sex education at school. The proportion varied considerably among the three areas and among the age-groups. More than 80 per cent of the City and Hackney women under 25 had had sex education at school, compared with nearly 70 per cent in Milton Keynes and 60 per cent in South Sefton.

Only half the under-16-year-olds in South Sefton said they had had any sex education at school compared with two-thirds in Milton Keynes. Over 90 per cent of the City and Hackney 16-19-year-olds had had sex education compared with 60 per cent of the same age-group in South Sefton. The numbers were small, but the pattern was clear.

However, this pattern was not necessarily related to the educational policy in the areas, as we found out when we asked the respondents about their school. We were interested to know whether it was in the same District Health Authority area as the project and whether it was a Roman Catholic school.

Looking at the whole sample, including the older women, we found that 14 per cent were still at school in City and Hackney, compared with 40 per cent in Milton Keynes and 16 per cent in South Sefton. All but one of the girls in Milton Keynes were at school in the DHA area, compared with just over half in City and Hackney, and two-thirds in South Sefton, all of whom were at Catholic schools.

Among those who were not at school, the pattern was rather different. Around a quarter of the City and Hackney women had been at school in the DHA area, compared with over a third of the Milton Keynes women but as many as 80 per cent of those in South Sefton.

There was a striking difference in the proportion mentioning Roman Catholic schools. 40 per cent of those interviewed in South Sefton had attended or were still attending a Catholic school, compared with 20 per cent in City and Hackney and 4 per cent in Milton Keynes.

The schools to which the City and Hackney and Milton Keynes respondents were referring were drawn from a wide area, and it was therefore almost impossible to relate the experience and views of those interviewed to the schools in the district. In South Sefton a much higher proportion of respondents had been to local schools, but, given the small numbers, no specific conclusions could be drawn. However, the sample as a whole was big enough for us to examine what the project users felt about the sex education they had had at a variety of schools. We have generally restricted the analysis to age, except where there were major differences in response by area.

Views on sex education at school

We asked respondents who said they had had sex education at school what it had covered and what they had thought of it. Ten per cent said they had covered 'everything', with roughly equal proportions in each age-group under 25. Over 40 per cent of each age-group said they had covered puberty and biological functions of the body, over a quarter mentioned pregnancy and childbirth, 20 per cent mentioned reproduction and the same proportion mentioned contraception. Nearly 10 per cent mentioned animal reproduction and the same proportion mentioned information about sexually transmitted diseases and AIDS.

The question was left open rather than presenting the respondents with a list of topics, mainly because we knew that the amount of time these young women would be prepared to give us was limited. It is probable that a list would have prompted them to remember more topics, and that fewer of

125

them would have said they had had no sex education if animal and human reproduction had been included in a list. A quarter of them said that they had seen films or television programmes, but few mentioned discussions, reading books or listening to outside speakers.

We were more interested in their views on their sex education than on achieving a precise account of what it actually consisted of, but it was clear that our respondents had had very varied experiences of 'sex education'. Not everybody had benefited from the provision, like this 14-year-old in Milton Keynes – 'There *was* a lesson, but I didn't go. I was ill and I missed it...'

Nearly 30 per cent of those who had had sex education thought it had been good, interesting and thorough, while a further 30 per cent thought it had not gone into enough depth or detail. One fifth said that they had had very little and that it was boring or a 'waste of time', while around 10 per cent said that 'everyone had giggled'. Some teenagers said that it was too late, because they 'knew it all already', while others said it was too early because they were too young to understand at the time.

The enormous difficulty of getting sex education right for the majority of those in a class or age-group was highlighted by many of the comments from respondents. One 21-year-old in South Sefton who had been to a school in another district had had fairly comprehensive sex education but still had criticisms – 'We had everything. They had all films of what the penis does and what's the safe way, and they told you about the cycle and all that...I suppose it helped, but not that much. It didn't tell you enough about having babies...'

A 22-year-old in City and Hackney had been to school in another area. She had had '...Basic biology, contraceptives, diseases, also a bit on morality...It was good as far as it went, but it didn't bring in anything about sex as an expression of love between partners. There was no mention of keeping sex only within marriage. I think sex outside marriage debases it...'

Some found the manner in which the lessons were given to be off-putting. A 21-year-old student who had been at a London comprehensive said, 'We had two hours of a male biology teacher showing us his hairy chest to show that men get hairs, and a lot of embarrassed girls giggling. He got us to write our questions on a piece of paper, and everyone went silly... No way was I informed by it. I didn't gain anything whatsoever. In fact it made it all seem more hush-hush...'

Some of the women seemed to have had very limited sex education, like this 17-year-old in Milton Keynes who had been to a local school – 'We covered periods and reproduction... It wasn't enough. It was just a laugh...' – and a 21-year-old who had been to the same school – 'Not much. Just a woman talking about puberty and periods. They got us to write a word or a question on a piece of paper and then they wrote it and the answer on the board...There wasn't much detail – not like sex education on the telly...'

It is clearly difficult to know what kind of sex education to give teenagers and how to present it. Some were more robust than others and had wanted more detail, like this 22-year-old in South Sefton who had been to a local Catholic school:

> We didn't have much – just about what a man and a woman do. And they showed you how a woman has a baby, but they didn't show how bad it can be. I was in labour for 29 hours with my first. They didn't show anything like that... I think they should show single people too, not just what married couples do. I think they should show you about the diseases that you can get, which they didn't. I didn't think what they did show was any good at all. It wasn't realistic...

But too much reality had upset some respondents, like this 23-year-old in City and Hackney – 'In the first year biology lesson I fainted when they went into the gory details of pigs having breech births. It wasn't very well presented. We were only 11 years old. Some already knew everything and others weren't ready for it. It's particularly difficult to get the balance right in Cornwall...'

It was not only in Cornwall that it was difficult to get the balance right. A 22-year-old who had been to a Catholic school in City and Hackney had '...five minutes about rabbits – it was a waste of time...' She had been to the GP for the pill when she was 17 and was still using his services for contraception. She had attended the Brook clinic for a referral for termination of pregnancy and had come for counselling on the day we interviewed her.

A 15-year-old in Milton Keynes had been to her GP for the pill three months before we interviewed her. He had refused to give it to her without her parents' permission and she had come to You 2 for referral for a termination of pregnancy. She described her sex education – 'Films – the basics of contraception and how the body works. We didn't get much sex education. We did set topics. There were only four or five lessons and you were supposed to know everything. It didn't advance your knowledge much...'

The younger women had often had more than one lesson in various years at school, but there was evidence that many felt that this was inadequate. A 16-year-old in Milton Keynes described her sex education at a local school – 'It was pretty basic. They talked about AIDS. We had to design contraceptives. Even the boys did it, so that was good... It was pretty good because it got everyone thinking...'

In the Policy Studies Institute research (Allen, 1987) young people often stressed how much they valued the opportunity to discuss sex and personal relationships with members of the opposite sex in the context of a discussion group at school. There was little evidence from the interviews carried out among the users of these three projects that there had been much structured discussion of this kind in the schools they had attended. Most of them had had what they termed 'the basics', but, as a 19-year-old in Milton Keynes said, 'By the time they teach you though, you know everything already anyway...'

'Knowing everything already' had not, apparently, prevented some of the women we interviewed from becoming pregnant. We asked our respondents specifically whether they had had any education at school about contraception and what they had thought of it.

Education about contraception at school

Of the women under 25, 52 per cent said that they had had specific education at school about contraception, compared with the 65 per cent who said they had had sex education at school. Again, there was a difference between the areas, with around 50 per cent of the under-25-year-olds in City and Hackney and South Sefton saying they had education about contraception at school, compared with 60 per cent in Milton Keynes. It was interesting that, although the City and Hackney women had had more general sex education than the others, the proportion having specific education about contraception was rather lower, although they may have thought that it was covered in general sex education and not distinguished it separately.

We asked the women what kind of contraceptive education they had had and what they had thought of it. Around half said that they had covered 'everything', had been told about the different methods and had been shown examples. Around one third said that they had been given very little information or had been told only about some methods. Others just said that their education on contraception was part of the sex education programme.

Few of the women in South Sefton had received much education on contraception, but the numbers were small and it would be difficult to generalise from their experience. Some who had been to Catholic schools had had education on contraception, but like this 22-year-old with two children had found it inadequate – 'We didn't have much – just that there is a pill and a coil...They didn't go into depth or show you how to use it. They emphasised that you couldn't use it without your parents' consent. They didn't tell you about these clinics. I think if they did tell you about these clinics a lot of young girls wouldn't get pregnant...'

Some of the contraceptive education reported by women in City and Hackney seemed rather more comprehensive. This 16-year-old was at a local school and described her experience – 'All the different methods – which was safest, which might harm you. It was good. It helps you in later life to decide what contraception to have, so you don't go to a clinic with nothing in your head...'

It has always been clear that different people can be exposed to exactly the same teaching and retain different impressions and memories of it. It is therefore not surprising that education on something as potentially emotive and sensitive as sex and contraception might not have the same impact on everyone.

Three girls of 17 who had been to the same school in Milton Keynes described different experiences. The first stressed the need for discussion – 'Our science teacher showed us the methods and used plastic models of bodies. It was OK, but the tutorial sessions were the most interesting. Science lessons were so mechanical...' The second said that she had only covered reproduction in science. She had had contraceptive education in a tutorial group – 'The tutor showed us this and that – pictures of different contraceptives. It's silly because it's not done carefully. Everyone just giggles and mucks around...' She had clearly not profited greatly from her education since she was attending You 2 for a pregnancy test and a referral for termination of pregnancy. The third girl seemed to have had a different experience again – 'Only about the sheath. They never told us about the rest. It wasn't enough...'

Some of the girls in Milton Keynes described sessions run by the You 2 team. This 17-year-old was very enthusiastic about them – 'One of the women gave us a rundown on the basics of contraception and how it all works. The You 2 sessions were very good. What I liked best was that they were so open. You didn't need to hang back if you didn't know the correct terms – you could have a laugh...'

Others had been given talks by other outsiders but were not as impressed – 'A family planning expert gave us a talk on the different types of contraception – the pill and condoms mostly. She didn't go into much detail on anything and I don't think she talked about all the contraceptives, but it was OK as far as it went...' This girl was 20 and had been to the GP for the pill a year before. He had refused because she was unmarried. She had then gone to a family planning clinic but had come to You 2 because it was more convenient.

We asked the respondents how they would summarise their education on contraception, and again three main groups emerged. Around a third thought it was good, interesting and informative, while a further third said it was inadequate, often saying it was not detailed enough, while around a fifth said that it was adequate or 'all right'. Some felt it was too scientific while others found it funny. There can be no doubt that it is not easy to design good education on contraception which is detailed enough, well resourced, put over by teachers or others who are not embarrassed and who can conduct relevant and interesting discussions with mixed groups.

Assessment of adequacy of sex education at school
Less than a quarter of those under 25 in all three areas thought they had had enough sex education at school. The under-16-year-olds were least likely to think that they had enough and indeed only one in ten of them thought their sex education had been adequate.

What was it they wanted? Just under a third wanted more lessons, more detail, more depth and a more 'honest' approach to sex education – 'A bit more reality – everything was done with cartoons. It needs to be more realistic...' – was the view of a 21-year-old in Milton Keynes. A 16-year-old in Milton Keynes went further – 'We only had three lessons. You should have a lesson every week, and have it every year, especially as you get older. It's not a joke then. You need it in the fourth and fifth year...'

There was considerable stress on the need to discuss all aspects of sex and contraception. This 19-year-old Irish girl had had very little sex education – 'They should be more open and tell you about all the stages, and also about gay and lesbian people. People could grow up with hang-ups. Some grown-ups think no, it shouldn't be taught, but it's for the best. You could get pregnant...'

Nearly a third of the respondents wanted more education specifically on contraception. This was particularly true among teenagers in Milton Keynes like this 16-year-old – 'Let them know more about contraception and the problems that can come with not using it...' – and another 16-year-old who had come for a referral for termination of pregnancy – 'They should tell you where to go for contraception and where to go for help if you get pregnant...' – and a 17-year-old from the same school – 'There should be more to do with the dangers of getting pregnant and maybe even stories of young people who've got pregnant and how awful it can be...'

These views were shared in other areas, particularly by the under-16-year-olds, like this pregnant 15-year-old in South Sefton – 'They should cover everything. All they covered was a male and female and having a baby. They should have told us about contraception and what's the safest and how to use them...'

Over a fifth of the under-25-year-olds stressed that sex education should be a core subject and compulsory for everyone, as this 16-year-old explained:

> Someone should come in and talk to the children and let them know the risks. You could get AIDS or anything now, couldn't you? There should be more films about the use of contraceptives and all that. The only time we see anything like that is in the child care classes and there are only 30 out of 210 who take that class, and most of them are girls – there are just two lads...

There was considerable discussion about the best age or ages at which to give sex education. Not everyone held the same view. Some thought it should not start too young, like this 17-year-old in South Sefton – 'They should show videos. PACE staff should go round schools and talk to classes. At 14 you're too young because you're not having sex. They should talk to girls when they're 15 or 16...'

But for some girls that was too late, as this 17-year-old in Milton Keynes commented – 'They should bring it down to younger people – 12-13 years old. You start having sex when you're 13 or 14...'

There was again a strongly held view that it ought to be given in each year and adapted to each age group, as this 15-year-old in South Sefton explained – 'It shouldn't just be completed in the first year. It should be spread out over the five years that you have at school...'

Around one in six of the women thought there should be more discussion at school about emotions and relationships. Sometimes their views were relatively straightforward, like this 15-year-old in Milton Keynes – 'They could tell you more about the relationship side of things, and give you more advice...' – while in other cases the demands were perhaps more complicated – 'It should not just be "If you have sex it makes babies." They should say more about how it feels to make love to someone you love...'

Some respondents thought there should be more stress on the risks of sex – of getting pregnant, of contracting diseases or even AIDS. But a 17-year-old in South Sefton was concerned that this approach might be worrying and one-sided – 'If you're talking about junior age - 9 or 10-year-olds – all they hear about is rape and women getting attacked. They don't hear about the other side of sex. They should be told why people want to have sex – the good side of it...'

But one in six of the respondents thought there was no real need for improvements. As we have seen, some of them appeared to have had sex education which they regarded as good. Some had been to the same schools at the same time as other girls who had regarded their sex education as inadequate or poor. They may or may not have had the same experience, but the fact remains that people experience things in different ways. Some of the sex education at school was clearly woefully inadequate, but other sex education seems simply to have passed our respondents by.

The message which came through in these interviews time and again, however, was that there was a strong desire among young women using these projects for detailed and informative sex education, given in a manner which did not allow for embarrassment on the part of teacher or pupils, and which was reinforced and updated in an appropriate way in each year at school.

Sex education from parents
We were interested to know whether the women attending the projects had had any sex education from their parents. 50 per cent of those aged under 25 said they had. There were variations by area, with nearly 60 per cent of the Milton Keynes women having had sex education from their parents, compared with 50 per cent in South Sefton and just over 40 per cent in City and Hackney.

There were also differences by age, with two-thirds of the under-16s having had sex education from their parents, compared with nearly 60 per cent of the 16-19-year-olds and less than 40 per cent of the 20-24 year olds. This broad pattern in terms of age was found in all three areas, and can be interpreted in a number of ways. It could be argued that under-16-year-olds whose parent had talked to them about sex might be more prepared to seek contraceptive advice. Or it could be argued that those whose parents had given them sex education might be more likely to have sex. It should be remembered that some of the under-16s had not sought contraceptive advice, or had not been given it, and were pregnant when they first came to the projects. On the other hand it might simply be that their parents were more likely to be younger than those of the older women and were therefore more relaxed about giving sex education. The numbers were really too small to draw any firm conclusions but the pattern was interesting.

What kind of sex education had the women had from their parents and what did they think of it? A 23-year-old in City and Hackney spoke for a number of respondents whose parents had suggested that they should use contraception – 'I spoke to my mother at 16 when I wanted a sexual relationship. She put me on the pill. She said if I was mentally ready, go ahead. It was brilliant...'

Some of the frank and close relationships between the under-16-year-olds and their parents were summarised by this 15-year-old in South Sefton who had had no sex education at her Catholic school:

> They used to say, "Don't rush into things," and I used to say, "Don't be daft," and my mum would say, "You can fall in love overnight." She just told me the best ways of contraception and she said she's glad that I'm sensible enough to go on the pill, but she said I've also got to remember about things like AIDS and other diseases, and she's gone over all that with me too...

But really good relationships with parents and good sex education from home and school did not always mean that women did not get pregnant, as this 21-year-old in Milton Keynes who had just had a positive pregnancy test indicated – 'Mum and dad always answered my questions and completely covered everything. I was never worried about going to them – and I was very nosey. It was good. I could ask them anything at all...' Her experience was echoed by a 19-year-old in Milton Keynes who had been on the pill but was attending You 2 for post-coital contraception – 'They're open about it. Anything I wanted to know, I just asked. It was great. It stopped me being inhibited or embarrassed about it...'

Many of the girls whose parents told them 'everything' clearly had very relaxed relationships with them, like this 17-year-old who had had good sex education at school as well – 'They told me about periods, VD, everything – love. It just came up in general conversation. They didn't sort of sit down and tell me the facts of life...' Others also had good relationships with their parents but said their sex education had been rather more basic, as this 18-year-old explained – 'They told me about birds and bees – that was all. I thought, "What do we do now?" I figured it out for myself when I had a boyfriend...'

Some said their parents had told them about menstruation but little else, like this 17-year-old – 'Mum told me about periods and said go to the family planning clinic if I got up to anything...' – while over a quarter said their parents had told them to be careful, like this 16-year-old – 'Mum talked to me about it. She said if I got serious with anyone I should make sure I didn't get pregnant...' Unfortunately she had not followed her mother's advice since she was attending You 2 for a referral for termination of pregnancy.

Some parents had difficulty in speaking to their daughters about sex, but made a good attempt, again not always successfully, it appeared, as this 21-year-old with a child who was seeking a termination of pregnancy explained – 'Mum told us about contraception. She got a book and showed us about it, but she got very shy when she talked about the body. She got all shy but she was better than the school. Dad just left it to mum...'

Parents and teenagers in the Policy Studies Institute report (Allen 1987) often stressed that, however good and close the relationship between parents and children, there were certain areas which both found difficult to talk about. Parents often felt that they could give their children information but felt diffident about intruding on their children's emerging sexuality. Similarly, teenagers often felt embarrassed by discussions which impinged on their own sexuality or acknowledged, however obliquely, their parents' sexuality. This was one of the reasons for the overwhelming support by both parents and teenagers for sex education at school. This 16-year-old at a Catholic school in South Sefton was attending PACE for pregnancy counselling. She had a good and open relationship with her parents, but nevertheless had felt the need for more sex education:

> They said, "Be careful", and if I needed help I should go to them - if I wanted
> the pill or anything. They told me when I was young all about having babies.
> They could have told me more, but I think the school should do more,
> because you get embarrassed with your mum and dad...

There was clearly no hard and fast rule that good sex education from parents led to rational behaviour and regular and reliable use of contraception. But, of course, as we have seen, there is no guarantee that knowledge is always translated into behaviour. Many of the women we interviewed knew a great deal about sex and contraception, had had good sex education from both home and school and still found themselves with unwanted pregnancies, sometimes on more than one occasion.

Sex education from other sources

Schools and parents are not the only sources of sex education, and we thought it important to look more widely at how young people learned about sex and contraception from other sources, both formal and informal, such as youth clubs, youth training schemes, relatives, friends, television, books, leaflets and so on.

Successive reports have shown that much 'sex education' is picked up from friends and other sources which are not always particularly reliable. There are indications that young people are aware of the inaccuracy and unreliability of much of the information they receive from friends and acquaintances, but that they value the informality of a setting in which they can share their ignorance and doubts and can discuss feelings and emotions in a way which many find difficult, if not impossible, in a more formal setting or with a professional (Allen 1987). The problem arises, of course, when friends are misinformed themselves and provide the only source of education.

Two-thirds of the women said that they had had some education about sex and contraception from sources other than parents and school, and over 60 per cent of these said they had some education from friends. It is probable that a higher proportion of women had had at least some discussion with friends, but had not termed it as 'education'.

Around 60 per cent of all the under-25-year-olds said they had had some education on sex or contraception from friends, and a small number mentioned other relatives, such as brothers, sisters, aunts or grandmothers. Only four women spoke of any education from GPs or other professionals, and only one woman – who was over 25 – mentioned a youth club. The 16-24-year-olds were more likely than those under 16 to say that they had had some education on sex or contraception from books or magazines, with around 40 per cent mentioning these. Few women mentioned any other sources of education, but a handful mentioned television or leaflets.

Over half of those who had received education from other sources had found it useful or informative. Friends had often proved helpful, and had sometimes provided the only help of a very fundamental kind, as this 24-year-old explained. She had been to a Catholic school and had had no sex education from parents or from school – 'I had some from my friends and my sister. It helped at the time. I was in a state when my periods started. I didn't know what was happening...'

In other cases, women stressed that they had learned a lot from talking to friends, like this 24-year-old – 'I talked to friends who made mistakes. It made you realise you had to be more careful. Some girls at school were pregnant at 15. One girl couldn't take her exams because of having a baby...'

But many of the teenagers were very sceptical about the education they had received from friends – 'It was silly – the usual whispers...' – and often said that they were worried about the reliability of the information, like this 14-year-old in Milton Keynes, who said she had had no sex education from parents or school – 'You don't know whether to believe it if comes from a friend. You hear one story – then you hear something completely different from the next person...' Others struggled through, like this 15-year-old at the same school – 'It was a bit confusing. No-one really knows what they're talking about. You pick up bits and pieces and it doesn't always make sense. You find out eventually though...'

It often appeared that learning from friends was found a bit haphazard – '...just snippets of information – nothing specific...' – and that exchange of information was even more unreliable – 'We all used to discuss it together, but we didn't really know it. It was just what we heard...'

But even even those who had attempted to gain sex education more systematically from books or magazines had not always found reading adequate on its own. This 20-year-old had gathered information from books – 'But what I read wasn't the same as what happened. It didn't prepare me for the shock...' – although others had found books and magazines helpful and useful, like this 16-year-old schoolgirl who had had very little sex education from school or parents – 'The magazines showed me there were more contraceptives than I thought, and which was best, and how important it is to use it...'

There certainly seemed to be a need for schools to take a much more structured approach to sex education so that the 'whispers' and the 'snippets' and the 'bits and pieces' could be put into a context in which accurate information and support were available. As we have seen, accurate information alone is not enough. Education in sex and personal relationships is not simply a matter of passing on information and hoping that people will act on the information. Some people never hear it at all, others do not understand what they hear, while others select only what they want to hear. Others hear everything but do not act on what they hear. This fact is well known to health educators. The question remains of how best to help young people learn about sex and personal relationships so that they can enjoy their lives in a mature and responsible manner. Not everyone has a grandmother like this 17-year-old, who had had no sex education from parents or school – 'It was good because the way my nan comes out with it, she makes it sound friendly. She puts things really well...'

Sex education from the young people's projects

Since all three projects stressed their educative function, we were interested to know to what extent this had been communicated with the women using the projects. We asked them whether they had learnt anything at the projects that they had not learnt anywhere else. There was no reason why they should have answered in the affirmative, since many of them were simply using the projects as a source of contraception or were seeking termination of pregnancy without necessarily receiving new information.

Almost exactly 50 per cent of those under 25 said they had learnt something at the projects that they had not learnt elsewhere, but there was a marked difference between the projects. Nearly two-thirds of those under 25 in Milton Keynes said they had learnt something new, compared with 50 per cent in City and Hackney and less than one third in South Sefton. It was interesting that these proportions were reflected among the older age-groups too.

It was perhaps not surprising that the under-16s were more likely to have learnt something new than those aged 16-24, but it was a little surprising that as many as 60 per cent of the 25-29-year-old age-group had also learnt something new.

About a third of the women said they had learnt something new about contraception and the different methods, while a further third said they had learnt something new about the advantages and disadvantages of a specific method. The younger teenagers were more likely to have learnt about contraception in general, while the older women were more likely to have learnt something new about a specific method.

The remarks of some of the younger teenagers emphasised the need among many of these girls for the opportunity to ask questions and to discuss contraception and sex, as this 15-year-old in Milton Keynes illustrated – 'I learnt about the pills and about contraception. I think we could ask anything we wanted to know if we came back again...' – and her view was endorsed by another 15-year-old in the same area who had come for a referral for termination of pregnancy. She had learnt – '...to be more

137

careful and to try to involve my parents more in the relationships I do have...'

Around one in six of the respondents said they had learnt that the service they received at the project was confidential and helpful, like this 28-year-old at the Shoreditch Brook clinic – 'That there are people you can talk to in confidence about your problems knowing no-one will know about it...' Some stressed that the project offered help on matters related to sex and contraception which they had not been able to get elsewhere, as this 17-year-old in Milton Keynes said – 'I don't know how to explain this, but they don't tell you *what* to do. They give you guidelines instead – even family problems, not just contraception. They tell you how to go about things. You 2 needs to be much better known. It would prevent unwanted pregnancies...'

Some of the women said they had learnt more about their bodies, and had even been able to pass on the information, like this 22-year-old in City and Hackney who had been coming to Shoreditch Brook for some years – 'It was helpful, with explanations about how the pill works, and it was interesting to learn how my body works. I went home and told my mum...'

Others compared the information and service received at the projects with that received from other sources, particularly from their GPs. Sometimes the information was on more general women's health issues, but it was often on contraception and pregnancy. It was common for women to change from their GPs to another service because they felt they had not received enough explanation about the pill or had not been offered any alternative to the pill.

Some women had been impressed by the medical discussion at the projects, like this 17-year-old – 'I learnt about the more medical side of things – smears, blood pressure. It's not so simple really, is it?' – and this 21-year-old who had got the pill from her GP, found it did not suit her and was now seeking a termination of pregnancy – 'I learnt about not smoking. I never knew from my GP what smoking actually does to a baby, although he always told me to stop...'

Chapter 8
Young mothers, pregnant teenagers
and women seeking abortions

We thought it important to look at the views and experience of young people who were not using the projects' services to see if there were any differences between them and the project users. Resources were not available to conduct a large-scale survey of young people in the areas, but we felt that there could be some useful material gained from interviewing certain types of people who, on the face of it, might have benefited from using a contraceptive and counselling service aimed specifically at young people. We were particularly interested in young women who had had unwanted pregnancies or had become pregnant while teenagers. We wanted to hear about their views and experience of contraceptive methods or services, the extent and type of sex education they had had and what they thought was the best way of providing contraceptive and counselling services for young people.

Because of resource constraints we were not aiming at interviewing large numbers or in finding a representative sample, but in hearing the views of a variety of young people from the same age-group as the project users. We interviewed 25 young women under the age of 25 and six aged between 25 and 33. It should be stressed that the material gathered from these interviews, although analysed in as rigorous a way as the other data in this report, has to be regarded as more qualitative than the other data.

In City and Hackney we interviewed six young women attending the Teenage Ante-natal Clinic and three young women attending a Young Mothers' Group, all of whom were aged between 16 and 19. In Milton Keynes we interviewed five girls attending a centre providing support for schoolgirl mothers, of whom one was 14, one was 15 and three were 17. We also interviewed six young women attending BPAS seeking termination of pregnancy, of whom four were between 16 and 19 and two were between 20 and 24. (They were all women who would have had NHS

...ortions through the agency agreement the Milton Keynes health authority had with BPAS.) In South Sefton we interviewed 11 young women attending a young mothers' group, five of whom were between 20 and 24, and six of whom were between 25 and 33. The interviewing took place between February and May 1989, at the end of the monitoring period.

It would not be fair to say that all these young women had had unwanted pregnancies, particularly the young mothers in South Sefton, but it would be fair to say that the majority of the teenage mothers and those seeking terminations of pregnancy had had unintended pregnancies, even if they were not necessarily unwanted.

Knowledge or use of projects

Although we were aiming at young people who had not used the projects, we were interested to know whether any of those we interviewed had in fact used the project services, and, if not, whether they knew anything about the projects, which had, after all, been operating in the areas for around 18 months at the time that we interviewed.

The Milton Keynes project had been used by one of the schoolgirl mothers and one of the BPAS patients, both of whom had been to You 2 for a pregnancy test. The South Sefton project had been used by one of the young mothers under 25 who had been to PACE for a smear. The main aspects of the projects which had appealed to them were the on-the-spot pregnancy tests and the confidentiality.

None of those interviewed in City and Hackney had been to Shoreditch Brook, and indeed none of them had seen any publicity or heard anything about either CHYPP or Shoreditch Brook. This was perhaps surprising, since CHYPP had supported the Teenage Ante-natal Clinic a great deal towards the end of the monitoring period, and had had ongoing contact with the Young Mothers' Group. Nevertheless, the young women interviewed were quite adamant that they had never heard of any part of the City and Hackney project. Those attending the Teenage Ante-natal Clinic presumably knew one of the members of the CHYPP staff who worked closely with the Clinic, but they did not appear to connect her with the CHYPP project.

Three of the schoolgirl mothers but only one of the BPAS patients had seen any publicity about You 2, either at a Youth Club or in a GPs' surgery, and five of the young mothers in South Sefton had seen some publicity about PACE, either in the GPs' surgery, at a family planning clinic or in the King George VI Centre itself.

Two of the schoolgirl mothers had been told about You 2 by a friend, and three of the BPAS patients had been told about You 2 either by a friend, relation or by a GP receptionist who had suggested to one of them that she should go there for a pregnancy test. Three of the young mothers in South Sefton had been told about PACE by the coordinator of their group.

Use of family planning services

There has often been an assumption that women with unwanted pregnancies do not use contraceptive methods or services, and that if they had used them they would not have become pregnant. Successive studies (Allen, 1981; Allen, 1985; Farrell, Clarke, Beaumont, 1983; Bury, 1984) have shown that this is not so, but the idea still remains that if only women could somehow be plugged into the system all would be well.

There is clearly a lot more to avoiding unwanted pregnancies than simply using contraceptive methods or services at some time. People who avoid unwanted pregnancies use contraceptive methods and services regularly and consistently. There is plenty of evidence that many unwanted pregnancies occur when women do not use contraception even when they know about it, have used it in the past, but for one reason or another have not used it at the time they became pregnant. One of the great challenges for service providers is to design services that are attractive enough for women to use them regularly and consistently. It could be added that one of the great challenges for those wishing to lower the rate of unwanted pregnancies is to design a contraceptive method which has no drawbacks or side effects.

Use of young people's clinics

We found that only one respondent had used another young people's clinic or a Brook clinic. She had sought help in connection with an unwanted pregnancy over a year before we interviewed her. She had continued to use the service for contraception and only stopped when she had gone to her GP because he was nearer. She had nothing but praise for the confidential help and understanding she had received at the young people's clinic, and we give no more details so that she cannot possibly be identified.

Use of family planning clinics

Family planning clinics had been little used in City and Hackney or in Milton Keynes. One of the girls attending the Teenage Ante-natal Clinic had been to a family planning clinic for a pregnancy test, one of the BPAS patients in Milton Keynes had been for a TOP referral and one had been for contraception. In South Sefton, however, eight of the eleven young mothers interviewed had attended family planning clinics, all for contraception or smears.

On the whole, the women who had used family planning clinics were very positive about them, finding them convenient, the staff friendly and helpful, and appreciating the confidentiality. The main criticism was having to wait a long time. The women who had stopped going had either moved, or the clinic had shut, or they had wanted to have a baby or they had gone to their GP who was more convenient. The young mothers in South Sefton were particularly positive about the family planning clinics they had attended – 'It was very confidential and they had a nice caring attitude. They treat you like people...'

Those who had never been to a family planning clinic usually said that there was no particular reason why they had never been to one. It had clearly never occurred to most of them that they might have gone.

There was a fairly even division of opinion on whether young people were worried about going to an ordinary family planning clinic. There was a feeling that young people might think a family planning clinic was for older women with children, and there was also a fear that young people would be treated with disapproval. It was apparent in interviews with project users that family planning clinics had a rather forbidding image among some young people, whether they had been to one or not, and this image was also found among those who had not used the projects, particularly among the younger teenagers, like this teenage mother – 'You would feel uncomfortable. If you're under-age they make you feel you shouldn't be there. You will be discouraged – made to feel bad...'

It was not only the teenagers who felt this way. A 24-year-old in South Sefton summarised the views of some 'older women' – 'Young people don't feel it's for them. I think family planning clinics are for married women – not young teenagers...'

But others thought that young people were not worried about going to a family planning clinic, mainly because they thought they would see a woman doctor there and that the clinic would be more anonymous than going to their own GP.

Use of GPs' family planning services

There was a much higher usage of GPs' services in connection with 'contraception or anything like that', with over four-fifths of the respondents saying they had been to their GPs in this connection. However, this response had to be interpreted with caution. For example, all the schoolgirl mothers in Milton Keynes had seen their GPs for contraception, but in four cases this was after their babies had been born and in one case after she had become pregnant. Two of the girls said that their GP had visited them to prescribe the pill rather than the other way round. Four of the six BPAS patients had first been to a GP for a pregnancy test and a referral for termination of pregnancy. In City and Hackney, three of the six girls attending the Teenage Ante-natal Clinic and two of the young mothers had been to their GPs for contraception, while in South Sefton eight of the young mothers had been for contraception and one had been for a pregnancy test.

Their views of their GPs were very mixed, and reflected those held by women using the young people's projects. They liked their GPs when they were friendly, helpful, sympathetic and understanding and explained things well, and they did not like them when they refused to give them the pill or said they should tell their parents if they were under 16, or if they were abrupt or unfriendly, or if they did not discuss or explain the contraceptive methods.

Some of the girls said they became pregnant because they were refused the pill by their GPs or because they could not discuss their problems with their doctors. On the other hand, some of them reported friendly and supportive relationships with GPs, like this 18-year-old young mother in City and Hackney:

> I went to him when I was 15 because I didn't want to get pregnant while I was so young and I was at school, and he gave me the pill...He was just so good and understanding. He said I'd made a wise choice because some girls wouldn't bother to get anything... I came off the pill because I wanted to get pregnant, and now I've gone back to my GP for the pill...

She thought young people were worried about going to their GP for family planning help because – '...they don't want their parents to know. I was worried too, but then I told my parents I'd done it, and at first they were annoyed, but afterwards they were pleased because they didn't want me to get pregnant...'

Her views and experience were quite different from other girls in City and Hackney, like this 19-year-old who had been to her GP two years earlier for the pill – 'He asked too many questions – "Why do you want the pill? Do you think you're old enough? Don't you think you should be telling your mother?" I thought he *would* tell my mother, so I told him, "Forget it," and walked out...'

She thought that young people were worried about going to their GPs for family planning help – 'They're frightened of the doctor. Some of them are coarse. They don't know how to "handle up" and they ask too many questions...'

There was a strong undercurrent in interviews, both with project users and with non-users, of an embarrassment with some male doctors. It came through when women talked about their own experience with their GPs and it came through in comments about preferring women doctors. It was clear that some women had had unhappy experiences with particular male doctors which had coloured their feelings about male doctors in general. A 22-year-old young mother expressed some of the disquiet which she felt:

> He tries to insist that his patients go to him for contraception, but I don't like him and I asked at the family planning clinic if I had to, and they said no... I've never been because he's a male, he's too old and I feel embarrassed with him. I *hated* my post-natal with him – the internal. I'd never go back to him. He wasn't unpleasant, but I hated it, and I'm sure everyone can hear what he's saying. The walls of the surgery are so thin...

There was evidence in these interviews, as in the interviews with project users that many women felt more comfortable with male doctors after they had had a baby, not only because they had had more encounters with doctors but also because they had had more experience of internal examinations. Nevertheless there are still a number of women who much prefer to see women doctors and there is clearly quite a high proportion of women who prefer to see women doctors for intimate examinations and discussions, like this teenage mother – 'Before I was pregnant it would have mattered a lot whether it was a man or a woman doctor, but since I've had the baby it doesn't matter at all. Maybe for smears and things I still prefer a woman. In fact I put off my smear for five weeks because my doctor was male and then I discovered the female nurse had her own clinic for it, so I went to her...'

Virtually all those interviewed thought that young people were worried about going to their GPs for help with contraception, either because they were afraid that the GP would tell their parents, or because they thought they would not be able to discuss things 'properly' or ask questions, or that the GP would not be sympathetic. It should not be forgotten how much courage some of the teenagers said they had to pluck up to go their GPs. If they felt themselves to be rebuffed they often felt very wounded.

Their treatment could also affect their behaviour if they became pregnant, as in the case of this 17-year-old pregnant teenager. She had been told that her mother would have to 'sign something' before she could have the pill:

I just didn't bother. I didn't want my mum to find out...I went when I thought I was pregnant, on a Friday, and he said come back on Wednesday with a urine sample, but I didn't go, because I don't like him. He made me feel awful, so I just left it, but then I kept getting pains in my side and I went into hospital for three days, and they did a test there and it was positive...

On the other hand, there were teenagers whose GPs might have had cause for being a little less than sympathetic. This 18-year-old was seeking a termination of pregnancy. She had been to her GP first for the pill after a termination of pregnancy a year before. She had last seen her doctor in the previous week, and had not liked the experience – 'She did her job but that was all. She gave no support. She was really critical and I wondered whether she was Catholic. Normally she is warm and sympathetic towards me but not on this occasion...'

Sex education
Nearly 90 per cent of those interviewed said they had had sex education at school – a considerably higher proportion than among the project users. In general those who had had sex education seemed to have covered more topics than the project users and they rated it more highly. Around two-thirds of the respondents said they had had education about contraception, again a higher proportion than that found among the project users, and they also rated it highly.

This was perhaps a rather unexpected finding, since so many of them had had unwanted or at least unintended pregnancies. On the other hand, it should be remembered that a relatively high proportion of the project users were attending the projects for pregnancy tests or for referrals for termination of pregnancy, or reported previous unwanted pregnancies in the course of their interviews. It should not be assumed that just because they were using the projects their experience was necessarily very different from that of those who were not using the projects.

The girls attending the Teenage Ante-natal Clinic and the young mothers' group in City and Hackney had had very extensive sex education on the whole, like this pregnant 18-year-old – 'We had a lot – reproduction, everything. In the child development course we covered pregnancy and childbirth... It was good. It was really interesting to get to know all these things... They covered everything about contraception in child development...' This 18-year-old young mother described her sex education at a local school – 'How babies are made, how your body grows and changes... It was quite good. It helps you to know the meaning of life as you get older... At secondary school they showed us all the contraceptive methods and how to use them and what the methods do...'

Another young mother had had equally extensive education but was not quite as enthusiastic – 'We had the usual things – reproduction, periods, pregnancy, birth. We had them in the child development course and in science... They showed us all the different methods – the games teacher took the classes... It was interesting but not really helpful. At the time I didn't have a boyfriend so it didn't seem relevant to me...'

The sex education in Milton Keynes did not seem to have been as comprehensive as that in City and Hackney, although some of the comments indicated that some of the attempts made by teachers foundered, as this 17-year-old young mother explained – 'We were starting sex education in the third year. We had to role-play being agony aunts for a teenage paper. One person kept giggling so the teacher stopped and we never did it again...' But the school did not give up, and she had education on contraception – '...in the fifth year in science – they showed us creams, caps and condoms. The boys stole the condoms and blew them up. They explained what the methods did. There were loads. I didn't know there were so many... It was very helpful to know that there are alternatives to the pill. It was to be examined, but I missed the exam because of the pregnancy...'

We asked what improvements she could suggest in sex education, and her remarks illuminated the dilemma facing schools and others who try to design education in sex and personal relationships to suit everyone:

> The contraception was all right, but they didn't tell us about sex, and my parents told me nothing, not even about periods. There must be loads of young people like this. It would be good if you could talk about it at school... My sister told me about periods. I knew nothing until I was bleeding and then I went and told my sister. I was frightened and didn't know what to do...

In all three areas there was evidence that some people got too much too early while others got too little too late. Many of the comments reinforced those made by the young people's project users that there was a need for some education in sex and personal relationships to be given in each year in all secondary schools. It seemed to be too easy to miss crucial information and discussion, as this 14-year-old young mother pointed out – 'I didn't have sex education because I moved schools. The school I came from was going to do it in the next year and the school I went to had already done it... I think if I'd done it at school I wouldn't have had the baby. I would have gone on the pill before. I believed you needed your mum's permission to get the pill and I didn't want to ask my mum. But now I know I could have got the pill...'

But even if young people had extensive sex education it did not always appear to help them avoid unwanted pregnancies, as we have seen. This 16-year-old schoolgirl seeking a termination of pregnancy had had sex education of some kind in most years at school:

> In the last year in the middle school, and in the first year – just about reproduction and how your body works... You had to design your own form of contraception in the fourth year in the science lesson. It was quite good. It explained a lot of things...It would have been better if it had been discussed in a group. It's better to talk about things rather than just have a worksheet...

The majority of respondents using the young people's projects said that they had not had enough sex education at school and this view was shared by these young mothers and pregnant women who had not used the projects' services, in spite of the fact that they had received more education on sex and contraception than the others. There was a demand for more lessons in more depth on more topics more often, and there was felt to be a need for more information on contraception and how to avoid pregnancy, in spite of the fact that so many of them had had quite extensive education on contraception.

Not only had these young people had more extensive sex education at school than the project users, they also had had more extensive sex education from their parents. Three-quarters of them had had some sex education from their parents, and most of them had found it helpful, although it had not always been of much practical use, as this teenage mother in City and Hackney pointed out – 'My mum told me everything... It was not really useful. Look at my little baby! She told me everything but I didn't listen. I just took a chance...'

Her comments were echoed by a teenage mother in Milton Keynes – 'My mum talked to me about the pill and she offered to take me to the doctors because she knew I was in a serious relationship, but I refused. I was embarrassed...'

And a 16-year-old seeking termination of pregnancy had had rather directive sex education from her mother – 'My mother said I should go on the pill. She said it hundreds of times and now I wish I'd listened to her. She said you always think you know best, and you're wrong, and now you know it. Now I wish I'd listened to her. She used to go on a lot. I used to think it wouldn't happen to me. You just do. I got run over last year. I used to think that would never happen to me and it did...'

As we found with the young people's project users, there was plenty of evidence of close and frank relationships with mothers and other family members, as this pregnant teenager in City and Hackney explained – 'One evening one person would start and we'd have a big family discussion about it. It was nice the way it just happened and we weren't forced to talk about it. If I had questions they got answered...'

And her comments were echoed by an 18-year-old at BPAS in Milton Keynes – 'My parents were very open from an age when I could understand. They always answered my questions. It was one of their strong points. I can talk to my mum as if she was my sister...'

But good sex education from home and at school was not enough to help these women prevent unwanted pregnancies. More education and discussion was needed, in their view, and there was little doubt that they thought there was a need for different kinds of services for young people to help them use contraception more effectively, and to continue to use it.

Chapter 9
Young people's service needs

These projects were based on the assumption that there is a need for special young people's services to offer contraceptive help and advice and to provide pregnancy counselling. The health authority staff and most professionals interviewed thought there was such a need in the areas in which the projects were set up. What did the young people themselves think? Did they agree there was a need for a special young people's contraceptive and counselling service, and if so, what did they think it should be like? We asked them where it should be, who should staff it, when it should be open, and finally, if they could design an ideal service, what it would be like.

Virtually all those interviewed in all three areas thought there should be a special young people's contraceptive and counselling service. Only four women in the project users' sample and only three among the other groups of young women thought there was no need, generally because they thought that the existing services should be made more attractive to young people, as this woman in City and Hackney pointed out – 'There shouldn't really be a need for a special young people's service. Family planning clinics should be sympathetic to young people...'

One of the main recommendations among young people was that the services should be open more often or at more convenient times, for example, every day, at weekends or in the evenings, but there were some important differences between the areas. Over 50 per cent of those under 25 in both Milton Keynes and South Sefton said that it should be open in the evenings or weekends or after work or after school, while only 10 per cent said this in City and Hackney. Around half the respondents in South Sefton said the project or clinic should be open every day and should be available longer during the day, although this was mentioned only by one fifth in Milton Keynes and less than ten per cent in City and Hackney.

The projects in both Milton Keynes and South Sefton were usually open all day on each weekday, although they did not necessarily keep to regular opening hours, while the City and Hackney project only operated a direct service to young people through the Brook clinics. In Milton Keynes and South Sefton the clinics were held on only one day a week in the early afternoon, whereas the Brook clinics in City and Hackney were held in the early evening on two days a week and on a Saturday morning.

We have seen from the analysis of the record cards that the drop-in service at Milton Keynes was used mainly as a pregnancy testing service, while the drop-in service in South Sefton was used largely by older women and by boys picking up condoms. The request from our respondents for the projects to be open more frequently and at different times was a clear indication that the services in Milton Keynes and South Sefton were not necessarily available at the right time, and, perhaps more important, were not offering the clinic service as often as was needed or at the time that it was needed. This was an important finding and could well have contributed to the rather slow build-up of the clinic services offered by these two projects.

It should be stressed that many of those who said that the ideal young people's service should be open for longer periods or on different days were enthusiastic about the project's service. This was particularly true in Milton Keynes where 60 per cent of those questioned said the ideal young people's service should be like You 2, as this 15-year-old explained – 'It should be basically like this. It's homely – they put you at ease. It doesn't make you feel you're doing something wrong. It should be easy to get to, open after school hours and on Saturday and Sunday. I don't like missing school...'

It must be remembered that nearly half of those interviewed in Milton Keynes and one fifth of those in the other areas were students, with the majority of them still at school. They were mainly looking for a clinic service and it was clear that they could only attend clinics held in the early afternoon if they took time off school. It seems obvious that a young people's clinic which provides a service for schoolchildren should not be open only during school hours.

But it was not only the schoolgirls who found the timing of the clinics inconvenient in Milton Keynes and South Sefton. Young women who were working also found it difficult to get to the clinics, like this 17-year-old in South Sefton who had come to PACE because it was more convenient than the Liverpool Brook clinic – 'It should be aimed at young people – at Brook there were quite a few older women. It should be as widespread as possible.

Staffed by women – but perhaps a man for those who don't like going to a woman. Neither PACE nor Brook is open often enough. I'm coming here in work time. I've taken a half day off. Brook is packed in the session after work. It should be as natural as possible – clean, tidy and friendly...'

There was thought to be a need for more centres which were convenient to get to which were open more often. There was a plea for more local centres, as this 24-year-old explained – 'It should be in local areas, to be handy. If they're far away and you have to travel it puts people off. There should be little services dotted about – not one big central place. Some should be open weekends for people who are panicking, and some later nights – 6 to 7 pm...'

Younger teenagers certainly wanted more local clinics, as long as confidentiality could be guaranteed. This 16-year-old in South Sefton had never been to her GP because he might tell her parents. She described her ideal young people's service – 'There should be a few in every area, near a clinic. There should be understanding people who you can talk to and who smile and make you feel welcome when you come in. It should be open to 5pm, so that kids can come after school, or open from about 12 to 6pm. There'd have to be a lot of publicity so you'd know about it...'

A 17-year-old in Milton Keynes thought there should be more clinics in more places and agreed that confidentiality and the personalities of the staff were important – 'Some people don't like going to their doctor. They need somewhere confidential they can go to talk. It shouldn't always be in big centres – they're too anonymous. They should be based all over the place, even if they only visited each centre once or twice a week. They should be staffed by people with a knowledge of family planning, who are caring and understanding. They should open at least two clinics a week – one is too rigid...'

It was interesting how often the young people used words like 'discreet' to describe what kind of centre they wanted, like this 17-year-old boy in Milton Keynes – 'It should be very confidential – like this place. The staff should be outspoken, lively, friendly – no snobs. It should be open from 9am to 6pm for kids coming out of school, and it should be somewhere discreet – not in the town centre...' His words were echoed by a 21-year-old single mother who was seeking a referral for termination of pregnancy – 'It should be round the corner in a centre like this, but discreet so no-one can see you going in. I think it's great and I'm all for it. I can go home tonight and sleep and know that I'm getting help. I haven't been able to sleep before and it's going to make my life so much easier...'

Around a quarter of the under-25s in all areas said that the atmosphere should be non-clinical and informal and a similar proportion said that the staff should be friendly and non-judgmental. A 23-year-old in City and Hackney said – 'It should have a good environment. The counsellors should be as young as possible and down-to-earth – they must be non-judgmental. It should have sensible opening times as well. A non-clinical-looking place...' And her views were repeated in Milton Keynes by many young women, including this 16-year-old schoolgirl – 'It should be informal to encourage young people in – not like going to your doctor – someone you can talk to. It should be in town, easy to find, but not too conspicuous. There should be normal clinic staff but able to deal with anything that came up, like a social worker. It should be open every day – at least before and after school. Ideally it should be like You 2 but bigger...'

But although there was a stress on friendliness and informality, it was interesting that over a quarter of the respondents said that the staff should be well qualified and experienced. There was a clear desire for the staff to have expertise and to be professional. Friendliness was not seen to be enough, as this 22-year-old in South Sefton pointed out – 'There should be staff with the knowledge and a genuine desire to educate people...'

Over ten per cent of the respondents said that the staff should be young, and a further ten per cent said there should be staff of both sexes, while few of them said there should only be women staff. A 17-year-old in South Sefton talked about her ideal young people's service – 'Widespread, for the different areas. It should be modern with youngish doctors, male and female for both sexes. It should be sometimes open in the evening for people who are working, and during the day for people who have children. It should be friendly, but not artificially friendly. It should be in a community centre like this, where it can be inconspicuous...'

The stress on the need for the services to be confidential, discreet and inconspicuous ran through the interviews. There was also an emphasis on the need for the staff to be non-judgmental and to make the young people feel comfortable, which reflected the comments made by so many of them when they described what they liked about the young people's clinic doctors. Very few of the respondents said there should be 'no white coats' which was the phrase used so often by professionals when they talked about the kind of young people's service which should be run. It appeared that friendliness and a sympathetic manner were the most desirable characteristics that young people were seeking in the staff of these centres.

There was a feeling in all three areas that the services should be better publicised and some young people thought one of the best ways of achieving this was for the staff to go round the local schools, as this schoolgirl in South Sefton explained – 'It should be at a place you'd feel comfortable to come to and you wouldn't be scared. Like this place – a place where you feel at ease. I think a lady from here should come to schools to tell you all about it and what they can offer...' And girls sometimes felt that the boys should not be left out, like this 17-year-old in City and Hackney – 'There should be more clinics and they should visit schools so that the boys can join in...'

In the Policy Studies Institute study (Allen 1987) there was evidence that boys often received less sex education than the girls and were often worried that they might be missing something important. This 16-year-old boy in South Sefton certainly thought he might have been missing something, and made his recommendation – 'I'd have a special teacher in every school, like a lesson called 'sex education' or something like that. And I'd have something like this place for young people who aren't at school. Just like this. It's pretty organised – pretty helpful here...'

Although the main stress among respondents was on providing a clinic or contraceptive service for young people, some of them hinted at the need for more counselling services of a general nature, like this 14-year-old in Milton Keynes – 'It should be easy to find but hidden – staffed by trustworthy people, open Monday to Saturday, somewhere you could come and talk about your problems – just like this...' And her view was reinforced by a 24-year-old in City and Hackney – 'Although you get all the information from schools, you need somewhere for in-depth information and advice, and a counselling service for young people who can't talk at home...'

Few of the respondents talked specifically about the kind of premises in which the young people's service should be located, other than that it should be easy to find, discreet, inconspicuous, and in as many places as possible. Some said that it should be in a health centre or in a 'special part' of a health centre, but this view was not common, and some said specifically that it should not be in a health centre, like this 18-year-old in Milton Keynes – 'It's cold in a health centre. You don't want to sit down...'

It was perhaps surprising that very few of the respondents commented on the physical surroundings or furnishings of the services they wanted, although professionals thought this more important. Perhaps the respondents had low expectations of health service premises or perhaps the quality and nature of the staff was more important to them than the physical surroundings. Or perhaps some people were simply satisfied with what they got, like this 16-year-old in City and Hackney who was very clear about her ideal young people's service – 'It should be like Brook. My doctor would look down on me. Any girl who needs the pill should get it. They help so many girls here. It should be comfortable and modern – with settees – and I like the tea and coffee...'

We were interested to know whether the teenage mothers or pregnant girls or those seeking terminations felt that there was a need for a special kind of service that would help young people, and whether their views were different from those of women who were actually attending the projects. They were much less likely than the project attenders to mention opening hours or days, probably because they were usually talking about something rather more hypothetical than the project users, who were relating the question to their own experience at the projects. They were, however, much more likely than the project users to say that the staff should be friendly and non-judgmental. It did appear that some of them felt they had not been treated too well by professionals, like this 17-year-old schoolgirl mother. She thought a young people's service should be staffed by '...helpful people – not grumpy old bags who think you're too young. It should be somewhere easy to get to – somewhere people will know. There's lots of places you can never find – like the CAB...' And another schoolgirl mother in Milton Keynes felt the same – 'It should be somewhere that they'll give you a cup of coffee and sit you down and not say you shouldn't have done it. They should not tell your parents and should explain all the options...'

There was more support for informality and drop-in facilities among these young mothers and pregnant girls, often based, it appeared, on their appreciation of the service they were receiving, as this 18-year-old in City and Hackney attending a young mothers' group pointed out – 'There's more under-16s lately who are having sex and there should be something for them. Innocent babies are brought into the world and they end up in care or with the girls' mothers. There should be a special place for under-16s, where girls could pop in often to get a bit of support, like the Young Mums' Group. It's good – it gives you a break...' And a 17-year-old attending the Teenage Ante-natal Clinic in City and Hackney agreed – 'It's a good idea. It should be just like the Ante-natal Clinic – friendly and informal. You're not all herded together and queuing. It's much nicer here than up at the hospital...'

Chapter 10
Professionals' views of young people's needs and the projects' services

The three projects were set up in areas where there was thought to be a need for a special young people's contraceptive and counselling service. The original proposals submitted to the Department of Health from all three health authorities indicated that attention ought to be paid to education about sex, contraception and pregnancy. There was a clear implication that the services and education provided at the time of the submissions was thought to be inadequate for the needs of young people in the areas concerned, and that, given an injection of money from central government, services could be set up which would improve the situation.

We thought it important to seek the views of professionals who had been involved in the provision of contraceptive, counselling and sex education services to young people in the areas before the projects had been set up. We wanted to know what they had thought of the provision of services for young people before October 1988, and to what extent they thought the projects' services had improved things. We were interested in what they knew about the projects, how much contact they had had with the staff and what they, and the young people with whom they dealt, thought about the projects. We were keen to hear their views about the needs of young people in the area, and what they felt were the main messages from the projects when future services were being planned.

Professionals interviewed
Our intention was to interview a relatively small sample of key professional workers in each area, in that we wanted to explore some of the most important issues about young people's services with people who knew a lot about them and had contact with them. We aimed at achieving approximately half a dozen interviews in each area with family planning clinic doctors and about the same number with family planning nurses,

health visitors, teachers and youth workers. The exact numbers from each group are given in Appendix V. The numbers varied a little because of local factors, but we achieved our targets as far as possible. In addition, we interviewed small numbers of YTS managers, social workers, AIDS coordinators, special project workers, BPAS counsellors, a midwife and an educational welfare worker.

The family planning doctors and nurses and the health visitors were all selected at random from lists supplied by the health authorities. The AIDS coordinators (one from each authority) and the BPAS counsellors were interviewed because of their particular posts, whether or not they had any contact with the projects. All the other professionals were interviewed because the projects had had some contact with them at some time during the monitoring period.

We interviewed a total of 37 professionals in City and Hackney, 41 in Milton Keynes and 32 in South Sefton. It was not really possible to add them all together as an illustration of the views of professionals working with young people, except where there was a complete unanimity of opinion. The analysis was therefore carried out for each area separately, since, of course, the professionals were talking about quite different types of special young people's projects against a background of different types of service and educational provision.

Even within the areas, it was often misleading to talk about the professionals as a whole, since they were sampled in different ways and for different reasons. Some of them were selected at random from service providers while others were selected because they had had contact with the projects. Some caution must be exercised therefore in interpreting the results as an overall picture of what professionals in each area thought about provision for young people before and after the projects arrived on the scene. Nevertheless the comments of individuals and groups of professionals are illuminating, and provide important messages to practitioners and policy-makers alike about the difficulties of getting the right kind of service provision for young people.

Many of the questions we asked the professionals were the same as those we asked the project team staff and those associated with the management of the projects, for example about the existing services for young people, about the needs of young people in the area and about the achievements of the projects.

Professionals' knowledge about the projects
The main aims of the project
It was clearly important to establish whether the professionals knew why the projects had been set up, so we asked them what they thought were the main aims of the projects. There was quite a marked difference between City and Hackney and the other two areas. Around two-thirds of the professionals in both Milton Keynes and South Sefton thought one of the main aims was to provide a counselling service to young people on issues related to sex, pregnancy and contraception, while this aim was only mentioned by four (10 per cent) respondents in City and Hackney – two of whom were health visitors. About one in five of the respondents in Milton Keynes and South Sefton thought the main aim was to provide a young people's contraceptive clinic which was informal and sensitive to the needs of young people, but this was mentioned by only four respondents in City and Hackney, two of whom were family planning doctors and one of whom was a health visitor.

On the other hand, nearly one third of the City and Hackney professionals said that the main aim of the project was to educate young people about sex and contraception, with one fifth of respondents mentioning education in relationships and responsible attitudes and one fifth saying the main aim was to develop outreach forms of sex education. Around one in ten said that one of the aims was to train and support other people who worked with young people. These respondents mentioning the educational aims of the project were mainly teachers, youth workers, social workers and YTS managers, thus reflecting the views of the project team staff with whom they had had contact. There was no doubt that the CHYPP team felt very strongly that their main aims were educational rather than in the provision of services directly to young people, and this message had clearly been picked up by those with whom they were in contact, if not by the family planning staff and health visitors with whom they had had little or no contact.

Although educational aims were mentioned by a handful of professionals in the other two areas, none of the family planning staff or health visitors in Milton Keynes mentioned them at all. It was clear that the aims of the projects in these two areas were seen much more in service provision terms, both by those who had had contact with the project teams and those who had not.

One of the main aims of the Department of Health in setting up the projects was, of course, to reduce the risk of unwanted pregnancy among young people. This aim was mentioned by only about one in ten of the respondents in Milton Keynes, mostly teachers, by three people in City and Hackney, a family planning doctor, the AIDS coordinator and a teacher, and by two people in South Sefton, both family planning clinic staff.

It was interesting that such a specific aim was recognised by so few of the professionals interviewed. It reinforced the impression gathered from all sources throughout this research that the actual aims of the projects as set out by the Department of Health were not generally communicated either to the general public or to professionals, and that the teams themselves adapted the aims to their own operational framework. The idea of aiming to reduce unwanted pregnancies as such was, in fact, felt inappropriate by the City and Hackney team, as they stressed. The other teams, although recognising the general overall aim, nevertheless pursued their own aims in a functional way. Perhaps it is too difficult for people to look at the aims of services in conceptual terms or perhaps they found the concept too 'global'. Whatever the reason, the main aim of the Department in setting up these projects was not generally recognised by professionals until we told them about it towards the end of the interview.

Perhaps the most striking finding was the fact that a quarter of the professionals interviewed in City and Hackney said they did not know what the aims of the project were or that they did not know anything about the project at all. These included five of the six family planning nurses and one of the health visitors interviewed. These were all sampled at random and had not been mentioned by the project staff as having had contact with them. It could be argued that they should have known something about the project, in that they were employed by the health authority and were coordinated by staff based in the same building as the CHYPP team. In addition they were in close contact with young women who might have benefited from the projects' services, but their lack of knowledge of either CHYPP or Brook was quite apparent from their interviews. A handful of professionals who had had contact with the City and Hackney team were also unclear about the main aims of the project. Only one person in each of the other two areas, a health visitor and a family planning nurse, was unsure or did not know what the main aims of the project were.

How and when the professionals first heard of the project
We have already seen that young people rarely came to the project services at the instigation of a professional, and few mentioned other professionals as sources of information about the projects. However, it was clearly important for the projects to make themselves known to professionals in

touch with young people, so that they could get through to the clientele they were set up to attract.

Around a quarter of the professionals in each area had first heard of the projects through their publicity, and a similar proportion in City and Hackney and South Sefton had first heard of it through colleagues or at staff meetings. Over 40 per cent of the Milton Keynes professionals had first heard of it in this way, reflecting to a certain extent the rather more integrated health authority network of communication in that area, but also reflecting the fact that family planning staff in Milton Keynes had felt under-consulted about the setting up of the project at the beginning, and the matter had been widely discussed for this potentially negative reason.

Nearly one third of the professionals in South Sefton had first got to know about the project through a visit from a team member to their place of work, compared with about a fifth of the Milton Keynes respondents and less than ten per cent in City and Hackney. The South Sefton team had concentrated initially on getting themselves known to professionals, partly because they wanted to pursue this line of activity, but also because they had no premises from which to offer services to young people for the first few months of their existence.

Professionals also got to know about the projects through other organisations, particularly in City and Hackney, or through working in the same premises as the teams or through meeting the team members at other events.

Most of those interviewed had first heard of the projects before October 1987 or in the first six months of their operation. However, some of those interviewed only got to know about the projects when PSI wrote to them requesting an interview at the end of the monitoring period, while two-thirds of the family planning nurses in City and Hackney said they had never heard of the project before we approached them for interview.

Availability of services provided by the project
We wanted to know how much the professionals knew about the services provided by the projects, since oral communication is so important when informing young people about available services. We asked them if the project was providing any clinic sessions with a doctor present at the moment. It might be assumed that this would be one of the first things that professionals would know about a young people's pregnancy counselling and contraceptive service. However, nearly 60 per cent of the respondents in City and Hackney and Milton Keynes and nearly 40 per cent in South Sefton said they did not know whether the project was providing clinic

159

sessions or not, while a handful of respondents in each area said it was not providing clinic sessions.

It might be assumed that those respondents who had not been selected for having had contact with the projects might be less likely to know about any clinic service than those who had had contact, but this pattern was not found. The family planning doctors and nurses in City and Hackney and Milton Keynes were fairly evenly divided between those who knew there were clinic sessions and those who did not, while in South Sefton they were rather more likely to know than other groups. Health visitors in City and Hackney and South Sefton were also fairly equally divided, but in Milton Keynes, five of the six health visitors did not know whether a clinic service was provided by the project, which made it unlikely that they would refer any young person to the You 2 clinic.

Among other professionals there was a considerable lack of knowledge on clinic provision in City and Hackney, most strikingly among the people engaged in special projects with young people and among teachers. In the other areas, quite a number of professionals who had had contact with the projects did not know whether they provided a clinic session, and again, it was surprising to find such a lack of knowledge among teachers, even in Milton Keynes where a lot of work had been done in schools by the project team. Nearly half the teachers interviewed in Milton Keynes did not know whether the project provided clinic sessions with a doctor present.

It could be argued that CHYPP did not publicise the clinic sessions run by Brook, in that they felt their main aim to be educational. It was found surprising by some respondents, not least the Brook staff themselves, that the CHYPP team seemed to regard themselves as completely separate from the Brook clinic. We asked the professionals in City and Hackney who knew anything about the provision of clinic sessions whether the clinic sessions were provided by the project team staff or some other agency. There was considerable confusion on the part of respondents, as there was when we asked about the times when the clinic was open. Most knew that the clinic was run at the Shoreditch Health Centre, but only four respondents knew exactly when it was available, two mentioned Thursday evening only, which was when the health authority's young people's clinic had been open, two were clearly confusing the clinic with the health authority's present young people's clinic, while the others did not know at all. Three of the four professionals who knew when the Brook clinic was open were family planning clinic staff, while the fourth person was a YTS manager.

The position in the other two areas was little better, with four professionals in Milton Keynes and seven in South Sefton giving the correct answer about clinic times. Others gave incorrect information or said they had no idea or said they would ring up and find out if they wanted to know. It was perhaps comforting that the vast majority of those who knew that there was a clinic service knew where it was provided, but few professionals in any area knew whether the clinic placed any restrictions on whom it saw in terms of age or sex.

The main message which came through from the professionals in City and Hackney was that most knew nothing or very little about the availability of clinic sessions by the project, and that if they knew about the Brook clinic sessions, they did not connect them with the City and Hackney Young People's Project. Rather more was known about clinic sessions in the other two areas, but nevertheless, knowledge was very patchy and often appeared to have been based on chance or proximity rather than on a systematic approach to communicating such information to professionals.

If professionals were so vague and ill-informed about the provision of something as central to the success of a young people's project as the availability of a clinic session with a doctor present, it is hardly surprising that take-up by young people of the clinic provision was so poor in Milton Keynes and South Sefton and that the Brook clinic was successful mainly because of the Brook name rather than because of locally generated attendance.

We found considerable lack of knowledge of other services provided by the projects, with over a third of respondents in both City and Hackney and South Sefton and over a quarter in Milton Keynes having no idea what the projects were offering directly to young people. Again, this ignorance was by no means confined only to family planning staff and health visitors, but was found among those who were selected for having had direct contact with the projects.

Two thirds of the Milton Keynes and South Sefton respondents said the projects were providing a counselling or advice service, compared with one third of the City and Hackney respondents. Pregnancy testing was mentioned by one third of Milton Keynes professionals but few in the other two areas. Sex education was mentioned by around one third of respondents in Milton Keynes and City and Hackney and a quarter in South Sefton.

On the whole, the professionals who had had contact with the projects had a fair idea of what they were providing directly to young people, but a disquieting number had no idea. They were much better informed about

161

what the projects were providing to other professionals or workers in the field. Two thirds of the Milton Keynes and South Sefton professionals and 40 per cent of those in City and Hackney said the projects were providing a service to which other professionals could refer. In City and Hackney over 40 per cent said that the projects were providing training, help and support for other professionals, but this was mentioned by only a fifth in the other two areas. City and Hackney professionals were also more likely than those in the other areas to mention that the project team lent or advised on resources. In Milton Keynes and South Sefton a handful of professionals mentioned that the teams provided sex education sessions for their students, but this was not mentioned in City and Hackney.

The projects were set up at a time when there had been a lot of publicity about AIDS, and there was considerable Government interest in educating young people about the dangers of AIDS. Although the brief from the Department of Health had not specifically mentioned AIDS, we felt it important to ask both the teams themselves and professionals what the project was doing in relation to AIDS. Around 80 per cent of the professionals interviewed in all three areas had no idea. The AIDS coordinators in City and Hackney and South Sefton said that the teams were acquiring training and information about AIDS, while the Milton Keynes AIDS coordinator said the team was doing nothing because AIDS was not part of their brief. A handful of teachers and professionals in all three areas said that the teams were including some AIDS information in their general sex education or counselling advice, but basically, the majority of professionals knew nothing about the projects' activities as far as AIDS was concerned.

Adequacy of services for young people before the projects
Over half the respondents in each area said the provision of family planning and pregnancy counselling services had not been adequate for the needs of young people in the district before the project started. It was perhaps not surprising that family planning doctors and nurses were more likely to say that the provision had been adequate than other groups of professionals, but not all of them thought so, particularly in City and Hackney and Milton Keynes. Few of the health visitors in the area thought the provision had been adequate.

In South Sefton and Milton Keynes a number of teachers, YTS managers and others thought the provision for young people had been adequate. In City and Hackney, over a quarter of the professionals said they did not know what the services were like before the project started, reinforcing the impression noted before of a general haziness among professionals in this area about services of this kind. Otherwise, most professionals other than family planning clinic staff thought that services had been inadequate.

Family planning staff in general tended to say that the services had been adequate because there was such a wide choice of family planning services, as this doctor in City and Hackney explained – 'It should have been adequate because there are so many clinics and at all times of the day, so there shouldn't have been a problem – even for those at school. There's early evening, afternoon and lunchtime – and the doctors are very widespread...'

Doctors and nurses often said that the clinics were well attended by young people and some mentioned young teenagers, like this clinic nurse in South Sefton – 'I've dealt with plenty of young people in all the clinics I've done and they don't seem at all hesitant in coming to a family planning clinic. I saw three 15-year-olds last week. We told two of them about PACE, but they still preferred to come to us...'

The availability of clinics at all times of the day was stressed in each area, and the fact that GPs were also available was also mentioned, most particularly in Milton Keynes, as this woman family planning doctor said – 'I think I provide a good level of care. On the whole, GPs in the district are pretty good, and a lot of people get family planning from their doctors and the doctors have family planning certificates. We get a lot of young people at family planning clinics and I don't think young people are afraid of going...'

In South Sefton there was a little more hesitancy about GPs. One family planning doctor was also a GP – 'It depends on the GPs in the area. In our practice we're all young and open-minded and we see quite a lot of young girls, and we see them in the clinics. Older practices might not say the same. Some girls come to us because they're not happy with their GPs. I do my own pregnancy counselling, but not all the GPs in the area would have the confidence or the ability to do it. There are not a lot of young female GPs in Bootle. One or two older GPs have some very odd ideas...'

Some family planning staff, particularly in Milton Keynes, thought the services for young people were adequate, but, like this nurse, were worried about publicity and information about clinics not getting through to potential clients – 'I think the clinics we run are successful and would supply the service, but the publicity about the service is not enough. We have a lot of young people who come here instead of going to their GPs, but we need to sell ourselves more. The PR side is not good enough but the service is OK. If the PR side was better we would get more young people...'

Although most of the family planning nurses in City and Hackney thought the services for young people were adequate, the clinic doctors were less certain, like this woman doctor in her early thirties:

> I find I actually don't see many young people in my clinics. I guess they all go to Brook. I have done the (DHA) evening clinic for young people and then I *did* see lots of young people – they were all young. I very rarely see any girls under 16. I do seven clinics a week, and I reckon I've seen, over 18 months, only two under-16s. Either they're not going anywhere, or they're going somewhere else. I've never done a Brook clinic, so I don't know how many they see. I *hope* they're seeing them...

Her worries were shared by other doctors, and this nurse in her sixties was particularly concerned about the provision for young people – 'We only ever had one special young people's clinic in Richmond Road. I pestered them for years to set up three or four. It's not enough. We need them all over Hackney...'

Professionals who said that services for young people had been inadequate before the projects started mainly cited gaps in the existing services, in terms of times and places, or said that existing services were not directed at young people or well enough publicised to them.

The young people themselves had often said that services should be widely available in local clinics or in other local facilities. There was considerable emphasis by some of the professionals, particularly those with day to day contact with young people, like teachers and youth workers, that young people did not like travelling far to get to services, as this youth worker in City and Hackney explained – 'Young people round here don't know where to start looking for services. They have to be *local*. Transport around Hackney isn't easy and kids aren't motivated enough to go beyond their own little patch...'

And the same was said to be true in Milton Keynes and Bootle. This youth worker explained why the pregnancy counselling services were inadequate before PACE had been set up – 'There was no support service for young people. The nearest was BPAS in Liverpool. It's far too distant for these kids. For so many young women it's bad enough going to a place like that – never mind having to get the bus and finding it...' And a YTS trainer in the same area agreed – 'We take in girls from this area – Liverpool could be Singapore to them. It was no use telling them to go into Liverpool, but they know Knowsley Road where PACE is. This is on their doorstep...'

A picture was often painted by those working with young people of a curiously timid and parochial bunch, lacking confidence and certainly finding it difficult to find their way into unknown territory, whether it was on their doorstep or further afield. A youth worker in Milton Keynes summed up some of these views – 'It's not even adequate now, because You 2 is in Wolverton, and as far as young people are concerned that is another planet away. I would like a travelling service doing outreach work in youth clubs...'

The question of publicity was very important to some professionals, like this teacher in Milton Keynes – 'The services that were available were not advertised. As a form tutor I'd had difficulty finding out where young people in my care could go. Now You 2 advertise their services more widely, and through coming into school, the kids know better where to go...'

But concern about publicity was often linked to concern about the image of family planning clinics as being for older people, or for women with children. A BPAS counsellor said – 'There appears to be a crying need for someone, or an agency, to tell young people what's available. A lot of youngsters won't approach family planning clinics. They have an image of being available only to married folk...'

Health visitors in all areas were concerned about the image of family planning clinics possibly deterring young people, as this health visitor in South Sefton summarised – 'I think there was a gap in services for the younger clientele – that's young teenagers. We have got a large figure for teenage pregnancies, so it was evident that something was going awry somewhere along the line. I don't think they liked going somewhere where it was a known family planning clinic, where people would know what they were going in for, whereas at King George VI there are lots of things going on, so they could be seen going there for other reasons...'

Effect of projects on services for young people
Around one third of the professionals in City and Hackney and South Sefton thought that the project had improved the family planning and pregnancy counselling services offered to young people a lot, although only ten per cent of respondents in Milton Keynes were as enthusiastic about the You 2 project. About one fifth of respondents in City and Hackney and Milton Keynes thought that the projects had brought some improvement in services, a view expressed by over a third of respondents in South Sefton.

Nearly one fifth of professionals in Milton Keynes thought that services had been improved a little. A handful of respondents in all areas thought the services had not improved provision at all. However around half the respondents in both City and Hackney and Milton Keynes felt unable to comment on what difference the projects had made, compared with only ten per cent in South Sefton.

There was virtually no pattern to the response to this question, with individuals from each profession in each area judging the projects as having made a lot, some or little improvement to services. Family planning staff and health visitors were the most likely to feel unable to comment, but again even professionals who were selected as having had contact with the projects often found it impossible to make any comment on whether they had made any improvement to services for young people.

The main reason why professionals thought that services for young people had improved was because the projects were offering accessible and available services geared to the needs of young people.

Adequacy of sex education before the projects
Less than ten per cent of professionals in City and Hackney and South Sefton thought that the provision for education for young people about sex, contraception and pregnancy had been adequate in the district before the projects started, compared with nearly 20 per cent in Milton Keynes. One fifth of the City and Hackney respondents and over a quarter in the other two areas felt unable to comment on this.

Those who thought it was adequate included four of the nine Milton Keynes teachers and one from City and Hackney, and a handful of other professionals, including family planning nurses who thought the young women coming to clinics were well-informed at school. The teachers who thought it was adequate defended the sex education programmes for which they had been responsible before the projects appeared on the scene. Some said that these had been 'adequate but not good'.

Sex education in schools was mainly criticised for being too patchy, limited or variable or for being too little or too late. A number of professionals thought that schools should call more on outside experts to enhance their sex education programmes and to help integrate the approach across schools and across related topics. The variability of the provision was criticised by a Milton Keynes health visitor – 'The service is fragmented and if we're concentrating on young people they should draw in social services, health and education, and apply a team approach. If they targeted an age group and all the schools got together and pooled resources everyone would know what is happening, as opposed to each school doing their own thing...'

It was clear from the interviews with young people that there was a wide variety of sex education provision in the schools in the three areas. This was deplored by a number of professionals, like this teacher in Milton Keynes – 'It was very patchy and depended on the individual school. There has certainly been a reluctance in this school in the past to tackle sex education as an issue...' It was also felt that sex education was sometimes given only to certain groups of pupils, as this family planning nurse in South Sefton explained – 'Different schools have different approaches. Some children get more input into health education than others. The accent seems to be on achieving academic results at the expense of other things...'

The 'Gillick' ruling, which had been made in the year before the projects were set up, was thought to have had a major impact in South Sefton, where health visitors and family planning nurses had been active in schools before the case – 'As family planning nurses, we used to go into schools to give them advice, but since the Gillick thing and with the legal aspect of them being under 16 years, we're not allowed to now unless the parents have given permission to the schools...'

A quarter of the South Sefton professionals thought that sex education was inadequate in Catholic schools, and there was clearly a lot of concern among them, particularly with the dangers of HIV and AIDS. This health visitor was concerned about the general variability of sex education in schools and was particularly worried about the provision in Catholic schools, which she felt had deteriorated since the Gillick ruling – 'I think you need a uniform approach in every school of all denominations, and input from health visitors and/or family planning nurses. My workload is such that the first thing to go is schools – plus the head won't let me in anyway. It's a Catholic school and they won't have women talking to the boys. The talks now are only to the girls...'

Other professionals thought that sex education was difficult in any case, because it was still thought to be a taboo area or because teachers and others did not feel comfortable with it. There was considerable concern, particularly among some of those working closely with young people, like this youth worker – 'Adults don't seem to be able to cope with talking honestly and openly about feelings of sexuality. Our culture encourages it to be hidden away and not talked about. Adults are embarrassed to talk about it. Newspapers are using sex as a way of exploiting young people – their fears and their feelings of inadequateness. The AIDS advertising builds fear. We have a sick society in ways we don't want to come to terms with...'

Effect of projects on sex education

Well over half the professionals in Milton Keynes did not know whether the project had improved the provision of sex education in the area, compared with half the respondents in City and Hackney and one third in South Sefton. Again, although family planning staff and health visitors felt less able to comment than other professionals, there were still numbers of other professionals who had been selected for their contact with the projects who were surprisingly unable to talk about the effect of the projects on sex education, including nearly half the teachers in City and Hackney, four out of five of the youth workers in Milton Keynes and two-thirds of the YTS managers in South Sefton.

However, a quarter of the respondents in City and Hackney and a fifth of the respondents in South Sefton thought the projects had improved the provision of sex education a lot in their areas, compared with less than 10 per cent in Milton Keynes, where a quarter of respondents thought the projects had made some improvement to sex education, a view held by nearly a third of the South Sefton respondents and a fifth in City and Hackney. A handful of respondents thought the projects had made a little difference and a one or two in City and Hackney and South Sefton thought they had not improved sex education at all.

Again the views were held by very mixed groups of professionals and it was difficult to deduce a pattern. The teachers who felt able to comment usually said that there had been a lot or some improvement, but many added provisos. One teacher in City and Hackney was very enthusiastic about the personality of one of the workers and also the useful resources provided by the project – 'The materials are a lot more meaningful and applicable to young people. They don't have a moral standing – it's attractive to young people. They are open, and the discussions which we've had have been secure and comforting. They have a knack with young people and the young people listen to them...'

The resource material provided by the teams was found useful by teachers and others on the whole, although one teacher in Milton Keynes had some reservations about some of the resources – 'They were easy for the pupils to talk to, there were very informed and they brought in their resources. In the child development classes they actually gave them samples and some of us wondered if this was a good idea. The children didn't expect to get samples...'

Other teachers found that the team brought new ideas and techniques which were useful, as this Milton Keynes teacher pointed out – 'We are looking at the way we're trying to teach. It's so easy to romp through the programme you've done for years without looking to see whether it's appropriate. We've relied too much on videos, which is a very passive way. You can chuck so many facts at them, but you don't know whether they absorb it...'

Another Milton Keynes teacher thought the project team had widened the traditional approach of teachers – 'The project is trying to tackle a much broader issue than just contraceptive education. They're trying to broaden the programme so that the schools can include more about relationships and the pressure that might be on young people to have sex, so that if they find themselves in that situation they will be better prepared for it, and will make sure that whatever decision they make is the right one for them and is not made hastily...'

Several professionals who said the projects had improved the provision of sex education in the areas commented that they must have improved the provision simply by being there and having more time than others to provide help, like this youth worker in City and Hackney – 'It's important that CHYPP, or something like it, should be able to go into schools. With the new core curriculum there's going to be a lot less resources for this kind of work and for issues around women. And you can't rush these issues – you need several sessions. The young people do want to know. They eat up any leaflets...'

But professionals often found it difficult to make any general comments on whether the projects had improved the provision of sex education in areas. They usually related their views to their own contacts with the project teams which are discussed in more detail in Chapter 11. Several commented that the projects were only a 'drop in the ocean' when related to the real needs in terms of education, a view summarised by this youth worker in Milton Keynes – 'It has made a little improvement. Schools are finding it a resource, but still not enough time is spent on sex education in middle and secondary schools. It needs constant work – not a short-term project. If the Government is serious about trying to do something, we need more than short-term projects and then pulling the rug out from under their feet...'

Particular problems of young people in the districts

We asked the professionals the same question we asked the project teams and their steering or management groups about whether the young people in their districts had any particular problems which young people in other districts might not share. The project teams had not been able to do any 'market research' to see whether there were special needs to be met in their areas, and were thus very dependent on their own local knowledge, if they had any, and on the views of their steering groups. We wanted to see whether the projects as developed in these areas could be used as models for other areas, and in this respect we wanted to explore the extent to which they were attempting to deal with problems which they thought to be unique to their particular districts and whether this affected how they were developing services which might be transferable to other areas.

Two thirds of the professionals in City and Hackney and Milton Keynes and as many as 80 per cent of those in South Sefton thought there were particular problems for young people in their districts. We found a high degree of agreement between the professionals and the project teams and their steering groups on what these particular problems were.

In City and Hackney, over half the professionals who thought young people in the district had particular problems mentioned young people from ethnic minority groups. These young people were not mentioned at all by professionals in the other two areas. In Milton Keynes, over half the professionals citing particular problems mentioned young people from homes without extended family networks, who they felt suffered lack of support and rootlessness. This factor was mentioned by only one respondent in another area. In South Sefton, the main group cited by over half the professionals expressing concern about particular problems were young unemployed people. These were mentioned by a quarter of the respondents in City and Hackney, but hardly at all in Milton Keynes.

Young people suffering from multiple deprivation, inner-city problems or problems associated with low incomes and poorly resourced areas were mentioned by over half the professionals in City and Hackney and over one third in South Sefton, but by only one respondent in Milton Keynes. General concern was expressed about young people in single-parent families by a fifth of respondents in all areas, while one fifth of professionals in Milton Keynes were worried about young people in isolated areas who were cut off by poor transport facilities, and one fifth in South Sefton mentioned young people with drugs or alcohol problems.

It appeared that professionals were often answering the question in terms of particular problems of young people in the area rather than citing problems which young people in other areas did not share. However, in discussing the problems, they drew attention to the problems which young people in similar areas might have. The problems were often seen to be multidimensional, as this health visitor in City and Hackney pointed out:

There's a lot of family disharmony. Poverty, bad housing and unemployment affect the stability of family life. Young people round here don't see much future for themselves and don't have a positive attitude about themselves. With families there are often language difficulties, for the parents at least, so they're not aware of the services that are available – it must affect young people too. There's also conflict within families – especially over sex and contraception...'

The difficulties young people experienced in reconciling the culture of their homes with the culture of the society they were living in were discussed by professionals from all disciplines, like this teacher in City and Hackney – 'It's a very mixed culture. The girls are exposed to a lot of pressure. They've got to make sense of the culture at home and the different values around them. It's a great problem in this area...'

Her concern was shared by a family planning doctor – 'A lot come from mixed marriages, which causes problems because Turkish men regard a daughter who is pregnant and unmarried as a dreadful sin. Therefore mother and girl have to carry the burden by themselves. If their father is West Indian, Greek or Turkish they're petrified he'll find out...'

In Milton Keynes, the problems for young people were thought to be related to feelings of rootlessness, and, in spite of all the efforts of the planners, to a lack of a sense of community, as this health visitor summarised – 'Milton Keynes is a new city and has lots of problems. The main problems affect the parents' generation but this percolates down. There are no extended families, and there are lots of single parents in Milton Keynes, which makes a difference for adolescents. They suffer from stress because of isolation...'

Doctors cited emotional problems among schoolchildren with a lack of family support, and a family planning nurse was concerned about the way in which a combination of factors could combine to make young people unlikely to use services – 'There's a lot of mobility in this area, which might make it difficult to find out about services. There's also a lot of step-parenting in the area, and children may find it difficult to cope if they're not living with natural parents...'

In South Sefton there was considerable stress on unemployment among young people and a consequent hopelessness in their attitudes. Young women becoming pregnant as a way of getting away from home or to achieve some kind of status were cited by a number of professionals in the area, particularly by health visitors, like this one – 'I definitely think that in parts of this area you get girls getting pregnant deliberately so they can establish a home of their own. And then they have absolutely no idea about the reality of it all...'

The problem of drugs, although mentioned by most of the project team and management group, was mentioned by surprisingly few professionals – only the AIDS coordinator, a social worker and three of the youth workers. One said – 'Bootle is known as "Smack City" because of the drugs situation. There are areas where drugs are easily available. If people are desperate for drugs there are ways of getting the money – including sex...'

Factors preventing young people from using contraception or family planning services

Professionals were by no means in agreement on the main factors which prevented young people from using contraception or family planning services. Indeed, they gave a very broad range of answers to this question, with virtually no pattern being established, either within areas or among groups of professionals. Two main factors emerged as the most important, but even so, only around one third of professionals in each area mentioned each of them – young people were said to be prevented from using contraception or services by ignorance about existing facilities or ignorance about themselves and how their bodies worked. In addition, around one fifth of professionals in all areas thought that young people were prevented from using contraception or services because they took risks or took the view 'It can't happen to me...' Other factors mentioned included shyness and embarrassment, fears of parental anger, lack of social skills in seeking help, cultural barriers and fears of meeting older people or people they knew in ordinary family planning clinics.

It should be stressed that the inappropriateness or inadequacy of existing services, which was one of the key factors mentioned by project staff and their steering groups, was hardly mentioned at all by professionals in Milton Keynes, by less than one fifth of respondents in City and Hackney and by a quarter of respondents in South Sefton.

Family planning staff and teachers in Milton Keynes were most concerned about young people's ignorance of existing facilities, while teachers and health visitors in all areas were concerned about young people's ignorance about themselves and how their bodies worked. Youth workers in City and Hackney were particularly concerned about young people's ignorance both of existing facilities and about themselves and their bodies. Family planning staff in all areas thought young people often took risks, as this family planning doctor in Milton Keynes explained – 'The main reason is "It won't happen to me, especially the first time..." They think they'll make love for a week or two and then go to family planning. I think we're available and approachable, but do they know where we are? Advertising is a problem area...'

In City and Hackney, a family planning doctor summarised some of the anxieties of young people which she thought prevented them from using contraceptive methods or services – 'Feeling that they're too young to come along – uncertain of what reception they'll get. Feeling that they won't get pregnant the first time. Not accepting the fact that they're sexually active until it's too late. And a lack of knowledge about the facilities...'

A health visitor in City and Hackney summarised her views tersely – 'Not knowing where to go, not wanting their parents to know, and having a rather romantic view of sex...' – and a family planning doctor in the same area explored some of the reasons in more detail – 'I think it's the difficulty of going along to a clinic. A lot are put off because they think they're going to be examined internally straight away before they can get the pill. Some are frightened that if they're given forms of contraception their parents might find them. Some might worry about the side effects of the pill because they've read that you get side effects if you smoke or are overweight – which they are...'

Lack of social skills or skills in coping with boyfriends were mentioned by some respondents, like this family planning nurse – 'It's awkward to ask a casual boyfriend to use a condom...' – and risk-taking behaviour by boys, combined with a feeling that it was the girls' responsibility, was mentioned by some teachers and youth workers. There was clearly no general consensus among professionals in any of the areas on the main factors which prevented young people from using contraception or family planning services, and many of them mentioned a combination of factors.

Need for special young people's clinics

All three projects were set up with special clinic facilities for young people, offering a doctor's services in connection with contraception and pregnancy counselling. This meant that medical methods of contraception, like the pill, could be offered to young people, and that examination and medical counselling could be given in connection with contraception and unwanted pregnancies, with a referral for termination of pregnancy if appropriate. These were the essential factors distinguishing the clinic service from a counselling and advice service offered by non-medical staff, which could offer non-medical methods of contraception, pregnancy testing and counselling and information in connection with an unwanted pregnancy.

We asked both the professionals and the project teams and their steering groups whether they thought young people in their districts needed special family planning clinics offering contraception and pregnancy counselling separate from ordinary family planning clinics. Around 70 per cent of professionals in City and Hackney and Milton Keynes thought there was a need for special young people's clinics, around a fifth in both areas thought there was not, while a small number said they were not sure. In South Sefton, three-quarters of those interviewed said there was a need for such clinics and a quarter said there was not. The professionals least likely to think that there should be special young people's clinics were, perhaps not surprisingly, the family planning doctors and nurses, although overall they were fairly equally divided on the subject. Some saw a strong need for special clinics to attract young people into clinics, like this family planning nurse – 'I have worked in a family planning clinic which was purely for young people and I think it was excellent. It worked much better and the atmosphere was far more informal. It took away the stigma of an FPC. All their friends were there and the girls would come with their boyfriends. It all worked very well. I just think it took away the embarrassment. If you go to a normal FPC you see very few males, but at the young people's FPC it was equally divided...'

This stress on ordinary family planning clinics having the wrong image for young people was the main reason given by professionals for advocating special young people's clinics. There was a fear that family planning clinics were seen as suitable for older people or for women with children – a view which was so frequently found among the young people interviewed in this study. A youth worker in City and Hackney looked at some of the reasons – 'Because young people see their lives in terms of their local patch. It's a question of possession – a service that's theirs. All young people's services should be small and local so everyone has access. Family planning still implies "families", "mums and babies" – it should be more slick to appeal to young people. The approach still smacks of midwives and hospitals...'

And a health visitor in Milton Keynes agreed that young people needed something which they could feel they 'owned' – 'Young people have a particular need – to feel comfortable – which they wouldn't in the old clinic situation. The married woman feels she has a right to be there – for teenagers it takes a lot of guts. And there should be a place for boys – it should be a partners' clinic...'

A health visitor in South Sefton, who also worked in family planning clinics, like most of the health visitors in that area, agreed that special clinics were needed so that young people would use clinics. She thought that they were put off ordinary clinics because of an out-dated image of how they would be treated, and she echoed the view of so many of the young girls interviewed who were worried about the reactions of doctors – 'It's just the authority that they think doctors have. They think they are going to get told off. But I have to say, without exception, they are pleasantly surprised when they come to this clinic...'

Over a quarter of respondents said that young people needed a clinic service that was confidential and sensitive to their special needs. Brook came in for praise from some professionals, like this social worker in City and Hackney – 'I would put the stress on a resource which is particularly sensitive to young people. Young people can go to Brook in the knowledge that they'll meet someone skilled and sympathetic with young people...' – and this AIDS worker – 'I saw young people at Brook who wouldn't go anywhere else. There's very little understanding about the needs of young people. There's a feeling that "I have provided a service – now use it". Brook doesn't do this. It accommodates the needs of the clients and engenders trust...'

Some of those interviewed thought there should be special clinics for young people in the short term but that family planning clinics should adapt themselves more to the needs of all potential clients, as this AIDS worker commented – 'Yes, there should be special clinics if ordinary family planning clinics stay as they are – but the aim should be to get ordinary FPCs to change and to be more receptive...' And this view was shared by a teacher in Milton Keynes – 'In the short term there should be special clinics, but in the long term clinics should make themselves accessible to everyone...'

The need for special training and skills to work with and counsel young people was emphasised by some professionals who thought young people needed sensitive services, like this BPAS counsellor – 'It's a super idea to have separate clinics, because you could have people specifically trained to work with young people. It's not good enough to say, "I'm a mother and can deal with young people." It's not true – you need training...'

A family planning nurse in South Sefton agreed that young people needed help from people with special skills which were not necessarily found in ordinary family planning clinics – 'You don't have the time to talk to these children and they won't sit and wait around while adults are there. I think they need to be able to talk to people specially trained to deal with young people...'

The professionals who thought there was no need for special young people's clinics usually said that young people could and did use ordinary family planning clinics. Some family planning staff expressed concern that there was not enough publicity and information for young people about the availability and accessibility of ordinary family planning clinics. This nurse thought there should not be special clinics – 'No – so long as they could be made aware of what we are like. None of our 16-year-olds feel uncomfortable – they are satisfied. They just need to meet us – it would be nice for us to meet groups of young people. They are not sure of our relationship to GPs or whether we would tell their mothers...'

There was a general desire to integrate services rather than provide special services. It was thought by some that provision of more services in general would help to provide more local services for young people, while some youth workers thought there should be more link workers with young people to help attract them into ordinary clinics.

Views on young people's clinics provided by the projects
We asked the professionals how they would rate the young people's clinic service offered by the project. Three-quarters of the professionals in all three areas felt unable to give it a rating because they did not know anything about it. This lack of knowledge was found much more among those selected for having had contact with the projects than among the health authority staff selected at random. Indeed, in South Sefton, only one professional other than a family planning doctor, nurse or health visitor felt able to comment on the clinic service provided by the project. In City and Hackney, only three professionals who had had contact with the project felt able to comment, but in Milton Keynes one third of professionals other than health authority staff felt able to give the clinic a rating, whereas only two of the health authority staff could do so.

Because responses to this question were so limited it was difficult to draw any firm conclusions. Health authority staff in all three areas who felt able to comment usually rated the clinic service provided by the projects as very good, good or adequate, with only one doctor in Milton Keynes rating it as poor. The Brook clinic in City and Hackney was highly rated for its good facilities and accessibility, as this family planning doctor explained – 'The Shoreditch Brook is accessible because of the timing – evenings and Saturday mornings – and they've managed to improve the physical clinic area. It's now the nicest one in Hackney, with those red chairs and red curtains – it's more informal. All the others are grubby dark little rooms...'

The physical characteristics of the clinics in the other two areas were not favourably commented on, and some professionals in Milton Keynes thought the premises were unsuitable – 'It's not adequate because of the premises, but as we didn't have anything before it's better than nothing. The service they offer has to be tempered by the premises. It's cramped and up a flight of stairs. It's difficult if you have children in tow...'

A family planning doctor in Milton Keynes thought the clinic service was good with reservations – 'It's not so good from a doctor's point of view because there's no family planning nurse. If you had a lot of clients you wouldn't have time to explain to them how to use the pills etc... A nurse can do this. But it felt confidential and cosy...'

On the whole those rating the clinic services as good or adequate did so because they provided good, confidential or accessible services which met the needs of young people. Comments from professionals who had had contact with the projects were fairly limited, but those who did comment were usually enthusiastic, like this YTS manager in Milton Keynes – 'They have understanding doctors on a level with young people. The staff are friendly – young people can talk about anything without feeling stupid. When we've used it, it's been a very confidential, personal service...'

There were some reservations that there were not enough sessions available or that there was more need for publicity for the clinics. Given the striking lack of knowledge about the clinics among professionals, it was not perhaps surprising that young people had difficulty in getting to know about them, as this family planning doctor in South Sefton explained – 'It's good – the service is great. It's just that it's not known. The girls who come here just don't seem to know about it...'

Need for special young people's non-medical counselling and advisory service

As we have seen, over 70 per cent of professionals thought there was a need for special young people's clinics. There was even more support for special non-medical counselling and advisory services in connection with contraception and pregnancy. In City and Hackney, where this had not been built into the project, other than through the counsellors attached to the Brook clinics, there was overwhelming support for this idea, with over 90 per cent of professionals saying there should be such services. In Milton Keynes and South Sefton the need was supported by nearly 80 per cent of respondents.

The main reason for supporting non-medical counselling services for young people was that they needed to be able to discuss wider issues connected with contraception and pregnancy, such as relationships and sex, in a non-medical setting. This view was often combined with a comment that young people felt more comfortable talking to people who did not represent authority in the way that they felt doctors did. A youth worker in South Sefton echoed the views of a number of the young people interviewed for this study – 'A lot of youngsters are frightened of the medical profession. They don't like the white coats, and they like female staff...' A teacher in the same area thought that doctors sometimes missed the real needs of young people – 'A medical person talking to youngsters often does it very clinically without going into the emotional involvement that there actually is. Young people need advising on this...'

Some doctors, like this family planning doctor in City and Hackney, agreed with them – 'They need not so much a non-medical person, but someone in a non-medical role. People are afraid of doctors – they don't think doctors will respect their confidentiality. They don't fear this with other workers – maybe it's because doctors write things down. They also equate doctors with being in a hurry. They can't spend an hour with a doctor, but they can with a counsellor...'

It was perhaps this need to discuss problems at length which led professionals to think there was a need for a more generalised counselling provision for young people as well as a specific counselling service in connection with contraception and pregnancy, as this teacher in City and Hackney explained – 'They need somewhere that they could talk around issues and feelings. To go to the traditional facilities you need a specific purpose, such as thinking you're pregnant. You need somewhere to talk about doubts and fears...'

A BPAS counsellor explained why she thought there was a need for a non-medical counselling service, which did not assume automatically that the need was for contraception – 'I think a non-medical service is important because counsellors are more able to put things over in lay terms. Some of the situations surrounding whether to use contraception, or problems with the use of contraception, may be non-medical and it can be quite threatening to talk to a medic about things like that. They're mainly centred around feelings of guilt – for example, "Is it making me seem available? How do I feel about myself?" – and guilt about not telling parents. They're quite afraid to mention them to medical people because they seem silly. They're not, of course, but they're afraid they might get a bad reception...'

Some professionals thought that the Brook model, with its lay counsellors and medical advice available in one setting, was a good model, while some family planning nurses thought they already provided it in their own clinics, like this nurse in Milton Keynes – 'Part of our training is to provide counselling. It would take away part of our job if we channelled them to a counselling service...' Health visitors too thought that family planning nurses could provide this type of counselling in existing clinics.

Those who thought there should not be a separate non-medical counselling service agreed that these services should be provided within the existing services, and most thought they did this already. Some were worried about losing clients if they referred them elsewhere, like this family planning nurse – 'Here we do our own counselling rather than pushing them from one person to the next. If you push them on too many times they just don't go...' Others thought that underlying medical problems might be missed by non-medical counsellors while others, particularly family planning staff thought that misinformation on medical matters might be passed on by non-medical staff.

Views on non-medical counselling services provided by projects
Nearly 80 per cent of the professionals interviewed in City and Hackney and Milton Keynes felt unable to comment on the non-medical counselling services provided by the projects in their areas, compared with nearly 60 per cent in South Sefton. The majority of those who felt able to give the counselling services a rating thought they were good or very good, with less than a handful saying they were adequate or poor.

In City and Hackney and Milton Keynes only one member of the health authority staff felt able to comment on the non-medical counselling service offered by the project. None of the respondents in City and Hackney mentioned the Brook counselling service, and none of them really appeared to associate it with the project. The comments made by professionals who had had contact with the projects usually referred to the way in which members of the CHYPP team had conducted sessions with young people or schoolchildren. These are discussed in more detail in Chapter 11, but the general feeling was summarised by this teacher – 'They've provided sessions for the students that we didn't feel up to doing and they've demystified the subject for the staff. I'm going to have a go myself next year...' It must be remembered however, that only very few of those interviewed felt able to comment.

The same was true in Milton Keynes, but more than half the teachers felt able to comment. They all thought the non-medical counselling provided by the project team was good or very good, like this teacher – 'The sort of people working there are very approachable – the kids really open out to them...' – and another teacher in a different school – 'The personalities and openness of the people who do it here. They're the sort of people who've proved to me that they can get through to a group of young people who have never talked about these things to an adult. And I've been impressed by the seriousness with which they've done it...'

It should be noted that most of the teachers were commenting on the counselling they saw given in a group situation, and it was doubtful whether they were able to comment on the counselling service offered at the project base. This point was taken up by another professional in the area who had experience of the team – 'I'm a little concerned about some aspects of You 2. It's hard to understand how as counsellors you can have the strong aim of getting sex education into schools and counsel them on a one-to-one basis. The youngest person in the project is about 35-years-old. There is a need for younger counsellors – you need a cross-section of people. The staff are doing sex education in schools in a big way, but not so much on a one-to-one basis...'

The counselling service in South Sefton had very strong support from those who knew anything about it, like this YTS training officer – 'It's very good. If I ring them because I have someone with a problem they're interested and caring, and the feedback I've got from young people I've sent there is that they want to go back. The level of counselling and expertise appears to be excellent – young people can see through a facade straight away. They've all made other appointments. I know this because I have to give them time off work to go...'

But the main point to be made about the professionals' assessment of the non-medical counselling services provided by the projects, like the comments on their clinic services, was that the majority of professionals in all three areas, whether they had had contact with the project or not, did not feel able to comment. Although most of them thought there was a need for special young people's clinics and special counselling services for young people, even after these projects had been running for eighteen months, very few professionals could say anything about the services provided by the projects directly to young people in their areas which had been set up to fulfil those needs.

Chapter 11
Professionals' views of the achievements of the projects

An important part of the evaluation of these three projects was to find out what the professionals who worked with young people in the areas thought of the services provided by the projects. The last chapter showed that only a minority of professionals, whether they had had direct contact with the projects or not, felt able to comment on the services provided by the teams directly to young people. We wanted to establish the exact nature of their contact with the projects, and to explore in detail their views of the achievements of the projects and their recommendations on further developments of services for young people.

Professionals' own experience of working with young people
The professionals were all interviewed because they worked with young people and had experience of their needs, particularly in the areas surrounding contraception and pregnancy. We were interested to know how much direct contact they had with young people and how much time they spent talking to them about sex, contraception or related issues. We asked them how much time in an average week they spent working with young people under the age of 25, to reflect the age-group targeted by the projects, but we also asked them about the time they spent with young people under 20, in that these appeared to be perhaps more difficult to get through to than the 20-24 age-group.

The pattern in all three areas was similar among most professionals, so we looked at them together for the purposes of this analysis. Not surprisingly, the groups which spent most time with young people were teachers, social workers, youth workers, YTS managers and the special project workers. They all spent an average of 20 hours or more working with young people, both under 25 and under 20. Indeed, as might be expected, some groups worked solely with young people.

The family planning doctors, nurses and health visitors all spent a higher proportion of their time working with young people under 25 than with those under 20. The family planning doctors and health visitors spent an average of about 10½ hours a week in direct contact with young people under 25, while the family planning nurses averaged nearly 17 hours a week. Family planning doctors spent about 7 hours a week with young people under 20, while the health visitors spent about 5 hours a week. The family planning nurses spent 13 hours on average with young people under 20. The figures for family planning nurses were not really comparable between the areas, with the South Sefton nurses spending considerably more time with young people than those in Milton Keynes. This was mainly because of the other work they did.

As might have been expected, family planning doctors spent a fairly high proportion of their time with young people talking about sex, contraception and related issues – an average of 7 hours a week, about the same amount of time as the BPAS counsellors. Family planning nurses spent an average of 4 hours a week talking about these matters, although in South Sefton they averaged more than 6 hours and in Milton Keynes less than 2 hours. (It must be remembered that the Milton Keynes nurses tended to work fewer sessions than those in South Sefton.) No other groups of professionals spent more than 3½ hours a week on average talking to young people about sex, contraception or related issues, with health visitors and teachers averaging about 2½ hours a week.

These figures are, of course, averages, and can only present a rather rough guide to the amount of time spent by the individual professionals. It must be remembered too that not everyone was working full-time and that there were quite big individual differences. We left the question fairly open in allowing professionals to talk about 'related issues' which could cover a wide range of relationship problems which undoubtedly worry young people. Nevertheless they give a broad indication of the amount of time the professionals we interviewed spent in direct contact with young people and the amount of time taken up in discussing the issues of central concern to these projects.

Most of the professionals had been working with young people for some years. Just under 10 per cent in City and Hackney had been working with young people for less than five years, compared with 14 per cent in Milton Keynes and just over a fifth in South Sefton. Perhaps the most striking finding was what a long time some groups of professionals had been working with young people. 80 per cent of the teachers, 70 per cent of the youth workers and 70 per cent of the family planning nurses had been working with young people for more than 10 years. Indeed one third of the teachers had been working with young people for over 20 years, and all the BPAS counsellors had been working with them for more than 15 years. The family planning doctors had worked with young people for varying amounts of time, with one third working with them for more than 10 years. Among other groups there was a very broad spread, related, of course, to the age and length of experience of the professionals.

The main message from these findings was that most of the professionals interviewed had had considerable experience of the needs of young people, both in the amount of time they spent working with them each week and in the length of time they had been working with them.

Professionals' contact with the projects at the projects' base

We asked the professionals whether they had ever visited the project premises and, in City and Hackney, whether they had ever visited Shoreditch Brook, either with a young person or young people or for some other reason.

Visits to the projects with young people

Only six professionals had visited the project premises with young people – two in City and Hackney, one in Milton Keynes and three in South Sefton. In addition, six professionals had visited Shoreditch Brook, two of whom had also been to the project premises. Three of the six who had been to the project premises were YTS managers, while the others were a teacher, a special project worker and a youth worker. Those who had had been to Shoreditch Brook were drawn from six different professions.

Their main purposes had been to accompany young people to the clinic, either for contraception or a pregnancy test or to find out about the services available. Most had been once only, but some had been four times. One third had been before the project started, with the others going for the first time throughout 1988. Some stayed with the young people at the premises, while others introduced them and left. Two of the professionals saw displays or videos and explored the facilities with the young people they took to the project bases.

Visits to the projects for other reasons

Over 40 per cent of the professionals in City and Hackney and South Sefton had visited the project premises for other reasons, compared with just over one fifth in Milton Keynes. Three professionals had visited Shoreditch

Brook. The main purpose of the visits was to find out about the service the projects were offering and to look at or borrow resources. Some professionals went for help in planning sessions, preparing sex education sessions or for developing other services. Others attended the Open Day, some went to steering group meetings, and four of the six family planning doctors did locums at the projects.

The groups most likely to have been to the project premises were youth workers, special project workers and social workers. In these instances, more than half those interviewed had been for some reason. More than half the visitors had only been once or twice, but a number had been five or more times, with City and Hackney being particularly well used by a small number of professionals.

The visits had been spread over the monitoring period, with no indication that the numbers were increasing towards the end.

Visits with groups of young people

We had thought that professionals might organise visits to the project premises by groups of young people, but we found that no professional in Milton Keynes had done so, that two professionals had been to PACE with groups of young people – a youth worker and a YTS manager – and one professional – an AIDS coordinator – had been to Shoreditch Brook. The young people had been taken to find out about the services offered and had either had a talk by the project workers or seen a video and received leaflets and information. The two professionals in South Sefton had each been three times and the City and Hackney professional had been once.

Suggestions to young people to visit projects

We found striking differences between the areas when we asked the professionals whether they had ever suggested to young people that they might visit the projects. Nearly three-quarters of the South Sefton professionals had done so, compared with just over a quarter of the Milton Keynes professionals. In City and Hackney, one fifth had suggested to young people that they might visit CHYPP and 40 per cent had suggested that they should go to Shoreditch Brook.

One of the main reasons for the big difference between South Sefton and Milton Keynes was that no family planning doctor or health visitor and only one family planning nurse had suggested a visit to the project in Milton Keynes, compared with over half the family planning staff and two-thirds of the health visitors in South Sefton. Two-thirds of the teachers in Milton Keynes and four out of five of the teachers in South Sefton had suggested a visit to a young person. In City and Hackney, half the doctors and two-thirds of the family planning nurses and health visitors had suggested that young people visit Brook, but only one of the teachers had done so.

Among the other professionals, all the special project workers had suggested visits, but, perhaps surprisingly, only half the youth workers and YTS managers had done so. Overall around a fifth of professionals who had suggested a visit to a young person had done so only once, but nearly half had done so on five or more occasions. The professionals had usually suggested a visit to the clinic, but the drop-in services were also suggested, sometimes for contraceptive counselling, but sometimes for pregnancy tests or pregnancy counselling.

Just over half the professionals said that the young people had taken up their suggestion, but it was interesting that nearly half said they did not know whether the young people had done so or not.

Visits by project team to professionals' place of work
The project teams had certainly tried to get out and about even if the professionals had not come to them in large numbers. Nearly 60 per cent of the professionals in City and Hackney and South Sefton and nearly half those in Milton Keynes had had visits from members of the project team at their own place of work. Again, the family planning doctors, nurses and health visitors were the least likely to have had a visit, particularly in Milton Keynes and City and Hackney. In South Sefton, on the other hand, two-thirds of the health visitors and family planning nurses had had a visit.

The groups most likely to have been visited by the teams were those who had been selected for interview because they had had contact with the projects. The vast majority of teachers, YTS managers, youth workers and special project workers had had a visit from the teams in all areas. The team members had spread the visits relatively evenly between them, apart from City and Hackney, where one worker was mentioned far more often than the others, even though she had left the project some months before we interviewed.

Most of the first visits by all three project teams had taken place in the first nine months of the monitoring period. The South Sefton team had tended not to make as many visits as the other two teams, mainly because they had found it more difficult to get into the schools and develop sex education sessions.

The development or delivery of sex education sessions to young people at the professionals' place of work was said to be the main purpose of the team's visits in most cases, although some professionals thought it was to develop working relationships, and the family planning nurses in South Sefton said that a team member had come to them to develop her skills in family planning. The teams had worked with young people in about half the visits they made to the professionals' place of work. Not all the visits had been successful, as we shall see in more detail in the next section, and a number had been one-off visits with no follow-up.

Other contact by professionals with projects
Other contact reported by the professionals with the project teams was limited and sporadic, and ranged from informal contact, found mainly in City and Hackney, where the project team was based in the community health headquarters, to receiving advice and information on resources and services, attending conferences, specific meetings or open days. The amount of contact of this kind was perhaps surprisingly limited, given that so many of the staff interviewed were employed by the health authority. Again, it was particularly limited in Milton Keynes.

Professionals' views of contact with project team other than at their own place of work
The main aspects of the contact with the project teams which the professionals found useful were the availability of services to which they could refer and the resources available from the projects. The attitude of the staff was commented on favourably in South Sefton and Milton Keynes in particular, and help in training was referred to more in City and Hackney, where a sex education 'forum' came in for special praise, as this teacher said – 'The very professional way in which things were done. It was all very relevant and full – everyone liked it. It was one of the best courses I've been on...'

Some family planning staff in all three areas said they found nothing particularly useful in their contact with the project teams, and commented that they thought that they had been helping the teams rather than the other way round.

We asked them if there was anything they did not like about their contact with the project teams. The majority of professionals could not think of anything, and the main dislike was for the premises in both Milton Keynes and South Sefton. Otherwise the comments were mainly of an individual nature, ranging from a City and Hackney teacher's disappointment that so few pupils from her school were invited to the CHYPP Open Day, to a Milton Keynes family planning doctor's fear that the You 2 project team did not have enough counselling training or expertise and that they were suggesting to young people that they should go to their GPs rather than to family planning clinics.

A sense of competition between family planning clinics and the projects was evident in comments in both Milton Keynes and South Sefton throughout these interviews, and it looked as though a little more work could have been done by the health authority in introducing the projects, as this health visitor explained – 'It was a bit competitive. They thought they'd get more response than we do at our family planning clinics. I just thought the project was to pick people who don't come to our FPCs, but their idea seemed to be to take away our clients...' On the other hand, the family planning staff in City and Hackney knew remarkably little about the project at all, so that any sense of competition did not really arise.

We asked the professionals if there was anything the young people had liked about their contact with the project staff other than at their own base or school. Most of them could not comment on what the young people had thought, and it must be remembered that many did not even know whether the young people had gone when they suggested it. However, those who had been to actual sessions at the project premises were thought to have found it interesting, as this teacher in City and Hackney said – 'They liked going out and actually talking to the doctor and nurse. It made them feel grown up...'

A health visitor in City and Hackney had suggested a clinic visit to young people and had had good feedback – 'They thought it was a good idea. They'd all heard of Brook Advisory and the idea was acceptable to them. They like the separateness of the service from GPs and felt it was something positive for them to do which wasn't just adults telling them what to do...'

This emphasis on young people being treated as people in their own right was clearly something which impressed both the young people and the professionals working with them, as this YTS manager in South Sefton said – 'They liked the project team very much because they treated them as adults. Doctors don't treat them as adults, they say...' – and this view was reinforced by a health visitor in the same area – 'They said they could talk about anything and nobody was surprised at anything they were told. The attitude was that you have a right to be here and that it's the norm...'

Professionals had very few comments on the dislikes of young people, mainly because they had not been told and had not asked. A couple of people said the young people found the clinic too far away from their homes.

Professionals' views of contact with project team at their own place of work

The main aspect of the projects which the professionals liked at their own place of work were the skills, expertise and professionalism which they felt the team members brought with them. This was mentioned by over a third of the professionals who had had this kind of contact with the teams in Milton Keynes and by over a quarter of their counterparts in City and Hackney and South Sefton.

This was often combined with an appreciation of the resources which the teams brought with them and the help they gave the professionals in their own work. This was mentioned particularly in City and Hackney, where the team member most frequently cited was also thought to be especially good at getting through to the young people. A teacher summarised his experience – 'It was helpful. The children were much more tolerant about things related to sex – they didn't giggle so much. They could say what they wanted and ask anything. I liked the interaction between (the team member), myself and the kids. The children felt secure – they felt they could talk to her. The visual aids were great. The children could relate to it – it wasn't just words...'

And another teacher in the same area found the support and resources offered by a team which was local to be of help – 'There's a great value in having these local people with counselling skills and a knowledge of local services and personnel – but from *outside* the school – coming into the school in a supportive role. For teachers themselves the supportive role often conflicts with the authority role. And anyway, the teacher's main concern is with learning, not with pastoral care...'

Teachers and other workers in all three areas found that the teams gave them confidence in themselves and taught them to use certain techniques, as this YTS manager said – 'CHYPP could play into our way of working with young people – about them becoming more self-determined. Young people need more openness and honesty. We learned not to be clinical and use medical terminology, but to use language that people feel comfortable with. I felt on the same wavelength with them...'

The Milton Keynes team was particularly appreciated by teachers like this one – 'Their knowledge about resources was very useful, and their willingness to use themselves as a resource in our sex education programmes. We always pick people with particular counselling skills, whatever helping agency we use – and the project team have them...'

Some of the professionals found the teams useful as facilitators or in helping to start up or revive groups, as this community health worker explained in City and Hackney – 'It was (team member's) help which got our little group off the ground. We had access to resources, videos, etc. through her, and the girls could see that something was available. It's somewhere to refer girls to. We don't have to look around and wonder who can help...'

The contact was often thought to be useful in itself – 'Just to have a face to a name, so that when you're on the phone you know who you're speaking to. It's important because health visitors do a lot of referrals...' And this view was reinforced by a youth worker in Milton Keynes – 'It gave me a clearer idea of what they were doing and that they were there. It was useful because I get a lot of stuff through the post, and having a visit gave me a contact person who I knew I could get hold of. It helps me to feel confident about telling young people that the project is there...'

There were few critical comments from professionals about the teams who visited their place of work. These centred round doubts about the competence of one or two members of the teams in the classroom situation, and comments from family planning nurses about whether the teams had sufficient expertise in family planning techniques and methods. In City and Hackney a youth worker thought there were not enough black people and people from ethnic minorities in the team, and another youth worker who had had a good relationship with one team member was disappointed with her successors on a subsequent occasion – 'They let us down badly. When they discovered that all we wanted was a clinic visit and not a series of group sessions they cancelled at one day's notice. Our kids were let down...'

The lack of follow-up was commented on by a number of professionals, like this health visitor in City and Hackney – 'There hasn't been any feedback or progress report on what they're doing. We haven't heard from them since their visit. I thought at the time that they were duplicating family planning provision for young people because Brook was already there and still is. If Brook weren't meeting the needs of young people they should do something to improve Brook, instead of using DHSS money to fund a new project..' She, like many professionals interviewed in City and Hackney, appeared to be oblivious of the connection between CHYPP and Brook in this project.

Professionals' views of young people's reactions to project team at their own place of work

Fewer than half the professionals in City and Hackney and less than a quarter of the professionals in the other two areas had experience of seeing the teams work with young people at their place of work. On the whole the comments were favourable, and it was thought that the young people liked the opportunity to talk and ask questions, and that they found the team members informal, non-judgmental and easy to understand. The Milton Keynes team had particular success with schoolchildren, as this teacher explained – 'The You 2 project were not just giving out information for an examined Child Development course, but covering relationships and attitudes. The young people liked this. It's this tutorial area we haven't the resources to do. You 2 asked the teachers not to be there all the time so that there was a space for the young people to talk...'

In City and Hackney one team member was particularly popular in schools – 'They liked the fact that she was an outsider. I had wanted to involve a teacher, but then I realised that the girls preferred her as an outsider. They liked her manner generally. It became a family/cultural thing – they discussed these issues with her. We have a lot of ethnic minorities in the 6th form. The Bengali girls are only allowed to carry on with school if they stay in a girls' school. She got very drawn into discussions on family situations. Afterwards they opened up with me a bit – they were less inhibited. They really enjoyed their sessions and kept asking if it was their group's turn to have (team member) next...'

And the CHYPP team were also popular with YTS groups – 'The kids loved it – that people listened and weren't shocked – and to discover that some of their own feelings were quite normal. CHYPP handled sexuality very well. They were cautious – they gave the children a chance to enquire – CHYPP didn't push it...'

There were few criticisms reported by young people of the teams' input. One teacher thought that some were 'excited but also shocked' at seeing the Caesarean scar of one of the team members, but she commented that this showed the children that their bodies were not things to be ashamed of. There were one or two comments that the young people found it difficult to open up with members of the opposite sex or to discuss certain topics, but these were thought to have been overcome by the teams.

Effect of contact with project teams on work of professionals

Around 90 per cent of the professionals interviewed in City and Hackney and South Sefton had had contact of some kind with the project teams, compared with two-thirds of those interviewed in Milton Keynes. This was mainly because of the low level of contact between family planning staff and particularly health visitors in Milton Keynes, and also because only one of the four BPAS counsellors had had contact with them. In general, family planning staff and health visitors were the professionals who had not had contact with the teams.

We asked professionals whether their contact with the projects had had any effect on the content or methods of their work with young people. Over half of those who had had contact with the teams in City and Hackney said it had had some effect, compared with 40 per cent in Milton Keynes and 20 per cent in South Sefton.

None of the family planning doctors or nurses in any area thought their contact with the teams had had any effect on their work, but more than half the City and Hackney health visitors thought it had. The main groups which felt that the teams had had some impact on their working methods were teachers and youth workers in City and Hackney and Milton Keynes, with over two-thirds of the teachers in both areas and over half the youth workers saying that the contact had helped their work.

The main effect of the teams on the work of professionals was the knowledge that there was an expert source for referral or training, often combined with a comment by teachers that the content or methods of the respondent's teaching and knowledge in this area had improved. A teacher in City and Hackney illustrated what she had learnt from one team member in particular – 'It's affected both the content and the methods of my work. I was very cagey and anxious before and (team member) tried to alleviate my fears and showed me that you need to know your groups to do this. Also the use of the 'grapevine' game – I was introduced to this through her. I've been able to widen the work successfully...'

Teachers in Milton Keynes felt they had learnt both from the resources of the teams but also from their techniques with young people – 'The training session did make me think about my own didacticism – what sort of teacher I am – to listen to the children and not finish off sentences for them – to leave space for them...'

Youth workers in all three areas often saw the projects as a useful referral source, rather than having affected the way they talked to or educated young people, while the teachers were more likely to mention the resources and training provided by the projects, like this City and Hackney teacher – 'It gives us more confidence in dealing with the issues – just knowing there was a resource back-up and knowing there is advice we can seek...' – and this view was echoed in South Sefton – 'In community work you can only be as effective as the people you employ. It's made life easier for me – it's a community resource...'

The professionals who said the contact with the project had had no effect on the way they worked with young people had often had fleeting contact with the project teams or regarded the teams as a resource to use when they needed them, as this youth worker in Milton Keynes explained – 'At the end of the session with the video the teachers had more understanding of the kids. It was helpful to get a trained professional in. We haven't invited them back, but that's not a bad thing. It's up to the young people to follow up if they want to...'

Family planning staff tended to remark that the contact with the teams had had no effect on their work because they thought they had enough training and could and did provide a good service to young people in any case.

We asked those who had had no contact with the teams whether the existence of the projects had had any effect on their work with young people. Not surprisingly, only one professional – a health visitor – thought it had had any effect, in that it had heightened her awareness of the needs of young people. All the other professionals with no contact said that they did not know enough about the projects to comment, while two family planning staff, one in Milton Keynes and one in City and Hackney, said they had not been aware of the existence of the projects in any case.

Professionals' overall assessment of the projects

How did the professionals rate the projects in general? We asked them a series of questions, which we also asked the project team members and their steering or management groups, about the strengths and weaknesses of the projects, the criteria they themselves would use for assessing the success or otherwise of the projects and how successful they thought the projects had been according to these criteria. We also wanted to know whether, looking back on the history of the project, they thought that anything should have been done differently, what they thought was the usefulness of setting up projects like these in three districts for a limited time period, and whether they thought the project as developed in their district could be transferred to other districts. We asked them what should happen to the projects after the Department of Health funding came to an end, and finally, we asked them what they themselves considered would be the best way of providing services for young people in their districts which would meet the aims of the Department of Health when they funded the projects.

Strengths of the projects

We introduced our questions on the strengths and weaknesses of the projects by saying that they were set up as 'model' projects to reduce the risk of unwanted pregnancy among young people and to encourage them to seek advice early if they suspected they were pregnant. We asked respondents what they thought were the strengths of the projects in meeting the aims of reducing unwanted pregnancy among young people.

Over one third of the professionals in both City and Hackney and Milton Keynes felt unable to comment on the projects' strengths, compared with just over one fifth in South Sefton. Again, the family planning staff and health visitors were the groups least able to comment, with over 80 per cent of the family planning nurses in City and Hackney and a similar proportion of health visitors in Milton Keynes saying that they did not know what the projects' strengths were. It was perhaps surprising that well over half the teachers in City and Hackney and half the youth workers in Milton Keynes and City and Hackney also felt unable to comment.

Among the professionals who were prepared to comment, the main strength of all three projects was thought to be the nature of the service provided for young people, with its informality, friendliness and accessibility, targeted specifically at young people. This comment was made by over 40 per cent of professionals in South Sefton and around one fifth in Milton Keynes and City and Hackney. Apart from this, there was little overall agreement among professionals. The City and Hackney and Milton Keynes projects were thought by some to have provided an extra service on top of what was there before. The teamwork and enthusiasm of the staff was praised in South Sefton by around one fifth of the professionals, as were the resources and training provided and the location of the project. The outreach work and work in schools was commended by nearly half the teachers in Milton Keynes, but by no teachers in the other two areas. There were mentions for the work the projects did in providing a pregnancy testing or pregnancy counselling service, and the South Sefton team were thought to have good aims and ideas.

The targeting of the projects on young people was thought to be a strength by this City and Hackney health visitor who said of Brook – 'It is separate from the perceived health care facilities. It is confidential and perceived by the young people as such – also it's not moralistic...' The non-judgmental nature of the projects appealed to a teacher in Milton Keynes – 'The positive way in which they approach the education to avoid unwanted pregnancy. It's not "thou shalt not" – but "look at the pros and cons and make your own decisions" – which is how we work in school...'

The informality of the projects was thought to be a particular strength by some, as this social worker in Milton Keynes said – 'It's taken out of the formal setting and is therefore more accessible to those who need it most...' And a health visitor in City and Hackney, talking of the CHYPP team, said – 'Its probable strength is that being lay people they would be less intimidating and therefore might be more helpful to young people...'

Few professionals understood the aims of the projects to be connected with reducing the risks of unwanted pregnancy among young people. The project teams themselves saw their aims as much broader, and an HIV/AIDS worker described the main strength of the City and Hackney project as he saw it – 'It integrates the aim of reducing unwanted pregnancy into much wider aims. It covers other things, such as general sex education, assertiveness and decision-making skills, which all work towards the aim of reducing unwanted pregnancy. The project is also very sensitive and receptive to the views and needs of young people. It has built up a good reputation among people working with young people...'

A YTS manager was sceptical of the success of any service in reducing the risk of unwanted pregnancy – 'Personally I don't think you can reduce unwanted pregnancies in this age group, but I do think the project can be a great help to pregnant girls. It doesn't matter what you say if there's a luscious fellow there and they think they're in love...'

Weaknesses of the projects

Again, over one third of the professionals in City and Hackney and Milton Keynes and one fifth in South Sefton said they could not comment on the weaknesses of the projects because they did not know enough about them. It was therefore perhaps not surprising that the main weaknesses of the projects by those who felt able to comment were said to be a lack of publicity and too little contact with other workers with young people. This was cited by over a fifth of the professionals in City and Hackney and Milton Keynes and as many as half the professionals in South Sefton.

The lack of publicity was mentioned by family planning staff and health visitors in all three areas, like this doctor in South Sefton – 'It is not widely known enough. They have the potential to do some smashing work, but it takes time for the word to get around...' – and this nurse in the same area – 'It's very difficult to pass an opinion about something I know nothing about. Probably the fact that nobody does know anything about it is a weakness. I've not even seen any posters or anything...'

The teams' lack of contact with other professionals and their failure to publicise themselves sufficiently to professionals with whom they might work was commented on in all three areas. This family planning doctor in City and Hackney thought the team should have been more persistent in their efforts to contact professionals – 'They're finding it difficult to get responses from other professionals. They wrote to the heads of all the schools and very few replied. They've got to overcome this. They've been here two years but they haven't got a big enough name yet so that people recognise them...'

Her view was echoed by a health visitor in the same area – 'I feel we haven't really had any contact with the project. None of the things they do are near enough to refer young people to or to get feedback from...' – and from a YTS worker in City and Hackney – 'We had to find them – they didn't come to us. And when we phoned CHYPP they said we were the first YTS to get in touch, so if we hadn't contacted them, how would we ever have known them? A few young people are aware of them, but many others don't know, especially those who are not on a scheme like YTS...'

In spite of the fact that all three teams stressed the success of their outreach work, particularly in schools, there were criticisms from teachers in all three areas, as this Milton Keynes teacher commented – 'I'm not sure the project team knew enough or have done enough to get into schools. They don't know who the people involved are...' – and a teacher in South Sefton where the team had less success in schools said – 'Perhaps they should have been more persistent in getting involved with the school...'

A family planning doctor in City and Hackney thought the project team was not sufficiently well enough linked in to clinics – 'Because teachers will still do sex education there won't be a direct link with clinics, so young people will still be wary of coming. In Norwich where I used to work we had loads of boys coming to the clinic. I think it was because our boss used to do a lot of school visits and show the boys how to use condoms. It got to be a kind of one-upmanship. You were in the club if you'd been to the clinic for your condoms...'

The projects' premises were thought to be rather inaccessible or unsuitable by a number of professionals in all three areas, like this special project worker in City and Hackney who thought the project base in a district health authority building was unsuitable – 'It has to be community-based if it's to be a community facility – for example in central Hackney...' The facilities in both Milton Keynes and South Sefton came in for criticism. This youth worker in South Sefton summarised the views of several workers who had visited the premises – 'I don't like those cubicles. The building provision isn't sufficient. They need a bigger room.

I felt threatened when I went into that little room with (team member) – it was like being in a toilet. Sometimes when you're discussing things you have to feel the space. They come close when they're ready...'

Criteria used for assessing success of projects

The main criterion cited by professionals in all three areas was the satisfaction or response of young people to the projects. This stress on consumer satisfaction was mentioned by over half the respondents in City and Hackney and South Sefton and one third in Milton Keynes. It was sometimes linked to the criterion of numbers attending the projects, particularly by family planning staff and health visitors. A family planning nurse in City and Hackney said she would assess the success of the projects by – '...attendance and repeat attendance, because if they don't come back then they must have been put off in some way...' – and her views were echoed in South Sefton – 'By the number of young people who attend, whether they have repeat visits and whether they encourage their friends to go...'

Considering that the original aims of the projects were to help reduce the risks of unwanted pregnancy there was surprisingly little reference to judging the success of the projects by reduced pregnancy or abortion rates, except by family planning staff and health visitors. Indeed, like the project teams, other professionals hardly mentioned these rates, except to say that they were irrelevant to the success of the projects, like this HIV/AIDS worker, who thought the criteria for judging the success of the projects should be – 'The general awareness of young people of the availability of services and of their own bodies and sexuality – and the ability to make decisions around those things. I certainly wouldn't see the fall in the rate of unwanted pregnancies as a good indicator. It's a long-term process – the aim is in itself quite short-sighted...'

Few other criteria were mentioned by more than one or two individuals apart from the criterion of whether professionals were prepared to refer or were satisfied with the services offered by the projects. A number of respondents simply thought that it was impossible to establish any criteria for success.

So how successful did the professionals think the projects had been, according to the criteria they had laid down? There were marked differences between the areas, with over one third of the City and Hackney and South Sefton professionals saying the projects had been very successful or successful, compared with only 15 per cent in Milton Keynes. One of the problems was that two-thirds of the Milton Keynes professionals felt unable to rate the success of the project, compared with about half the respondents in the other two areas. Around one-sixth of respondents in all three areas thought the projects had been fairly successful, but only a handful thought they had been unsuccessful.

Only one health authority staff member rated a project very successful, and the main response from these family planning staff and health visitors was that they could not judge the success of the projects. But some teachers, youth workers, project workers and YTS managers said they too could not rate them. It appeared that few of them felt sufficiently sure that they had an overview or any tangible measures by which to assess their success.

Others were not so inhibited, like this teacher in City and Hackney who judged the project by its impact on professional staff – 'It's very successful. We made contact and we're all delighted with what we've got. We've had so little training in how to deal with problems such as child abuse and so much has now been brought to our attention. It's nice to have someone to seek advice from...' – and a teacher from Milton Keynes – 'Very successful – we want them back. We could not do what they did. Even if we were trained we wouldn't have the same effect. We couldn't be that positive and relaxed...'

Essentially the professionals who felt able to comment on the success of the projects used their own personal experience of the project teams rather than any objective criteria to judge the success. They might have said that they would use attendance figures or consumer satisfaction as criteria for success, but then found it impossible to comment on whether the projects satisfied these criteria.

Should anything have been done differently?

We asked the professionals whether, looking back on the history of the projects, anything should have been done differently. Well over half the City and Hackney professionals and one third in the other two areas could not comment. Those who did comment usually thought that certain things should have been done differently.

There were marked differences between the views of the professionals and the views of the project teams and their steering groups on what should have been done differently. The professionals' comments centred round better publicity and marketing of the projects, mentioned especially in City and Hackney and South Sefton, and more or earlier involvement of other agencies involved with young people, both in the health authority and in schools, the youth service and other agencies.

The lack of publicity was mentioned particularly by health authority staff in all three areas, and it did appear that there had been a lack of liaison between the projects and these very important groups of professionals working with young people. In City and Hackney, family planning staff thought this had been a definite mistake, as this doctor explained – 'More effort should have been made to inform people about it. Nobody knew anything about it. If you don't know anything about it you're not likely to tell people to visit it. There always seems to be a dreadful communication problem between (the community health headquarters) and the staff who work in clinics...'

Her view was reinforced by a family planning nurse who was very unsure of what the project offered – 'It should been advertised more so we had a piece of paper we could give to the young people about CHYPP and tell them to go there if they or a friend ever had a problem...'

There was repeated evidence that professionals were not sure what kind of service CHYPP offered directly to young people, as this youth worker illustrated – 'There should have been better publicity on their part. There are lots more people in Hackney who could have made use of CHYPP but didn't know about them. So many referrals have to come about through other people knowing about you. Young people won't use the yellow pages to find out who to contact about their sex problems...' Few professionals made the direct link between CHYPP and Brook, as this health visitor indicated – 'They might have integrated the project with something that's already happening – like Brook – and expanded the service that's already there...'

This lack of a base to which young people could be referred, and the apparent reluctance of the CHYPP team to refer young people to Brook, was thought to be something which should have been done differently, as this YTS manager commented – 'When I was with them I wondered how successful they were at getting through to all kids. They went to institutions, but what about all the other kids who aren't attached to anything? What about the ones who have dropped out of school, are unemployed and maybe homeless? It takes a certain type of person to do outreach work. You have to have no qualms about asserting yourself and confronting issues with young people, and at the same time be prepared for the reactions from young people – aggression, rejection, frustration. You must be strategic and anticipate. CHYPP called themselves pioneers, but they weren't. They didn't tackle difficult areas which would take them beyond their own resources...'

The lack of publicity was commented on in both the other areas. In Milton Keynes, a youth worker thought that publicity was not perhaps properly targeted – 'All the information about the project has been directed at me – it should have been directed at the young people...' – and a South Sefton health visitor thought the publicity had been poor in general – 'It should have come out with a blaze of publicity. Every clinic should be filled with cards, leaflets and posters. I suppose it stands or falls on publicity at the beginning. I suppose they thought it would grow through word of mouth, but it certainly hasn't, because nobody has heard of it...'

Health visitors and family planning nurses in all areas felt that too little effort was made to inform them about the projects or to involve them in the ideas of the teams, like this nurse in South Sefton – 'There should have been more publicity definitely. And encouraging visits from other health services staff to see what is going on. You'd have more confidence in recommending them if you'd seen what they do...' A health visitor in Milton Keynes agreed – 'None of us are aware of the project. A visit by the project staff would have fixed it in our minds. With hindsight, I've had one girl I could have referred to You 2...'

There was no doubt that health authority managers could have done more in all three areas to facilitate communication between the project teams and the health authority staff we interviewed. Sometimes it appeared that there was more than a breakdown of communication preventing contact. This family planning nurse in Milton Keynes was puzzled that there had been so little information about the projects – 'I could have made an effort myself but it would been nice to have had a meeting to tell us about what they do that is different to us and how we could interact...' – and a health visitor in South Sefton had similar views – 'Perhaps if they want us to get involved they should have attended one of our staff meetings and told us their aims and objectives and how we could get involved...'

Some youth workers, like this one in South Sefton, thought the involvement of other agencies working with young people had also been poorly handled – 'They could have had much more involvement with the youth service and keep it up over time – every three months – and give us feedback on what kids' needs are...'

Health education workers in Milton Keynes and South Sefton were concerned about the conditions under which the project teams were expected to work and the lack of planning before they got off the ground – 'How much groundwork was done before the project was established? It's in the wrong place – the idea of sharing premises with an old people's club!

The physical space is ludicrously cramped. It doesn't facilitate privacy. Some work beforehand with schools would have been helpful to build up trust and rapport before the centre opened. There could have been much more referral. It's taken people a while to discover it...' The Milton Keynes project was also thought to have suffered from lack of foresight and unsuitable premises – 'The Department of Health should have looked to see what was there already and not reinvented the wheel. They really set people up to fail, with difficult locations, cramped premises etc. It needed better planning, more time and more thought...'

The usefulness of setting up projects like these

There were very mixed views on the usefulness of setting up projects like these in three districts for a limited time period. The most frequent comment, particularly in South Sefton, was that this kind of exercise tested whether there was a need for services or projects of this kind. It was also thought, particularly in City and Hackney, that this kind of project demonstrated that there was a need. This view was often linked to a comment that projects like this increased local awareness of issues, as this health education officer explained – 'Because the projects have developed differently it's given a variety of different approaches. It's given an indication of what can be achieved by focussing on sexuality and sex education. It's raised awareness of need within the community. It's raised awareness as to what should be done...'

Few professionals commented on the fact that the projects might be different in the three different areas. As we have seen, most of them knew little enough about the project in their own district, so perhaps it would have been unreasonable to expect them to know anything about the other areas.

The professionals who thought the usefulness of setting up projects of this kind was to test need sometimes appeared to assume that 'testing' need was fairly straightforward, like this family planning nurse in City and Hackney – 'It enables the Department of Health to find out whether there is a demand for such projects. When they've assessed the demand they'll know whether it's necessary to continue...' But others recognised the difficulties in carrying out such a major task as 'assessing demand' through the evaluation of such projects. A BPAS counsellor was less ambitious and thought the usefulness of such projects was in highlighting 'the problem areas where services are needed...'

Other professionals were not sure how far projects like this could contribute much to service provision, and this youth worker in City and

Hackney made a nice distinction – 'It's useful for researching needs, but in terms of meeting needs it's a waste of time...'

This view was often linked to the short-term nature of the projects, as this youth worker in South Sefton commented – 'Limited projects are of limited use – you can put so much in and then they finish...' Teachers and others in Milton Keynes were particularly concerned about the potential damage that could be done by starting short-term projects and then withdrawing them – 'The need doesn't go away after a year or two years...' This view was shared by other professionals who were doubtful about this kind of exercise, like this youth worker in City and Hackney – 'I don't think it's useful because by the time the young people get to know you you're packing up again. It's obvious there is a need for the service, but it's a waste of time and effort relying on word of mouth if time is limited...'

The limited time period was a source of great concern to the project teams who thought they had far too little time to demonstrate either that there was a need or that they could meet that need. It was regarded as useful as a 'pump-priming' exercise by some professionals in City and Hackney, in that it might stimulate awareness of the needs of young people so that services of this kind could be developed within mainstream services. This is, of course, one of the great potential values of 'demonstration' projects of this kind, but very few professionals mentioned it.

Transferability of projects as developed in the areas
Around 80 per cent of the professionals in all areas thought that the project as developed in their district could be transferred to other districts. Most of the rest felt they could not comment, and only a tiny number of professionals thought that it could not be transferred, mainly because they thought it had not worked well.

The main reason professionals thought it could be transferred to other areas was because they thought that young people everywhere had the same needs and that young people's services were needed everywhere. They often did not indicate that there was anything special about the project in their own area, but interpreted the need more generally. Some professionals were more positive about the projects in their districts which they thought had been successful, as this health visitor said – 'If you can make it work in Bootle then you can make it work anywhere...'

Others were more circumspect and thought there might be difficulties in transferring the methods used by the projects to areas which were not similar. This was mentioned by a number of professionals in City and Hackney in particular, who thought the networking attempts of the CHYPP team might not transfer so easily to all areas, as this special project worker explained – 'It might be more difficult in, say, Enfield, because I wonder how many other groups or voluntary organisations would get involved. There's a plethora of organisations working with young people in City and Hackney and CHYPP has been able to work with them...'

But it was more common for professionals to say that any good methods of working with young people could have universal application, as this health visitor in City and Hackney said – 'Everyone knows about Brook clinics. They could be opened in other districts and people would use them...'

Future of the projects

The projects were funded by the Department of Health from October 1987 to March 1989. At the time that we interviewed the majority of the professionals in the late spring and summer of 1989, the projects' funding had come to an end. We asked them whether they thought the project in their districts should continue in their present form.

Nearly 80 per cent of those interviewed in City and Hackney thought the project should continue, compared with two-thirds in South Sefton and under 50 per cent in Milton Keynes. But well over a third of the Milton Keynes professionals felt unable to comment. This meant that, in fact, only one fifth of the Milton Keynes professionals said the project should not continue, compared with over a quarter of respondents in South Sefton. Very few professionals in City and Hackney stated categorically that the project should not continue, but over one in ten could not comment.

The main reason the professionals in all areas thought the projects should continue was that they had done good work and had been successful. It was also felt that the projects had met a need among young people which was not met by other agencies. In South Sefton, some professionals thought the project was just starting to 'take off' and should be given a chance to develop, and in Milton Keynes there was a plea from teachers that the project should be continued because the education service was in particular need of the resource it offered.

There was concern about what would happen to users of the services if the projects were to close down, as a family planning nurse in City and Hackney said – 'They've already built up a relationship with the young people. You can't just drop them when the project ends...' – and her view was echoed by a YTS manager in South Sefton – 'It would be such a loss if it went. Organisations and young people are just getting to know about it – and it's really good – so it's an awful letdown if it disappears...'

Although family planning staff were the main group of professionals to think that the projects should not continue, some individual family planning staff in all areas strongly supported the continuation of the projects, like this doctor in Milton Keynes – 'It's serving a group of people who would probably not receive services, and it's beginning to take off. It's a pretty inexpensive project for the value it's giving – a few girls' lives may not have been wrecked by unwanted pregnancy...'

But not everyone thought the projects should be continued, and this view was by no means restricted to family planning staff. Some teachers, health education workers and youth workers were not so keen on them continuing. The main reasons given by professionals for winding up the projects were that they could be absorbed into existing services, that they were not well enough known or that the service should be more widely spread. There were comments that health authority funds were so tight at the moment that there was no justification for spending precious funds on a young people's clinic which was poorly attended. Some professionals thought that the clinic could be discontinued but that the health education work could be retained.

The best way of providing services for young people

Finally, we asked the professionals what they themselves considered would be the best way now of providing services for young people in their districts which would meet the aims of the Department of Health when they funded these projects.

The most frequent answer in all three areas was that there should be more sex education in schools and other places where young people were to be found, like youth clubs and youth training schemes. However, there were some differences between the districts, with over half the professionals in City and Hackney stressing that more sex education was the answer, compared with around 40 per cent in Milton Keynes and just over a third of respondents in South Sefton. One of the reasons for this difference was the enthusiasm for sex education shown by the family planning staff and health visitors in City and Hackney. This was shared by half of their counterparts in Milton Keynes, but only around one third in South Sefton. The special project workers in City and Hackney were unanimously in favour of more sex education as the way forward, and, perhaps not surprisingly, teachers in both Milton Keynes and South Sefton agreed, while teachers in City and Hackney laid greater stress on other aspects of service provision.

The City and Hackney family planning doctors all thought that more sex education was essential in providing services for young people, as this doctor said – 'To increase the availability of sex education by getting it as part of the core curriculum. I'm sure it's something which should be hit at school level...' Her view was shared by one of her colleagues – 'We've still got to keep plugging away at schools and youth clubs. How many school visits have been done? It's very important. With good school visits you're half way there...'

There has been some dispute about whether 'outsiders' should be brought into schools to take part in sex education programmes. Many of the professionals interviewed had no doubt that they should, like this family planning doctor in Milton Keynes – 'If teachers can't do sex education themselves they should bring in outsiders. "Catch them early" should be the slogan – "prevention and glasnost"...'

Health visitors and family planning nurses also thought they had a role to play in sex education in schools, and teachers interviewed in all three districts were keen to bring in outsiders, as long as they were 'the right type'. A teacher in South Sefton spoke of some of the problems:

> PACE should try to get more involved with schools and involved in our personal and social skills programmes. Perhaps young people will take this sort of information and advice from an outsider. I always have this great dilemma. I am an ogre to the kids, but have to wear another hat when I talk to them about relationships. It has to be the *right* outside person. I had someone from (another group) – it was awful – so laid back. I'm sure the kids would never go to them. There was no rapport at all...

This observation that not all teachers felt comfortable or secure in giving sex education was echoed in all areas. The need for help and support was stressed by several, including this City and Hackney teacher who explained what she thought was the best way forward – 'Getting into schools and colleges and youth centres. Giving information out early. Integrating sex education into other subjects such as health education. A lot of teachers don't see giving sex education as part of their role. Perhaps working more with doctors to help demystify things...'

Her view was shared by another teacher in City and Hackney who thought that there was a lot to be said for schools working closely with other professionals – 'Provide services that are easily available to young people where they feel welcome and where they know the workers. Get the family planning clinic staff into the schools – especially the doctors. There is an ethnic question here – doctors are all perceived to be Asian and male...'

A contact with the world outside school was thought to be a good idea by other professionals, like this City and Hackney health visitor – 'You've got to start before the clinic stage. You need some input into schools. If health visitors were involved in sex education in schools they could provide a link with the service – a drop-in, for example, where young people can ask any questions that weren't covered in class...It's very important to have the right staff – possibly younger staff – that young people can identify with...'

The emphasis on sex education was often linked with the recommendation that there should be a special clinic or special facilities for young people to go to for counselling, information, education and contraceptive services, either within the existing health services framework or in addition to them, as the young people's projects had been. In Milton Keynes, most of the family planning staff thought there should be the development of young people's services within the existing framework, but there was considerable support among other professionals in the area for the development of separate young people's facilities.

It was thought that these special young people's services should be easily accessible and separate from other facilities. This was stressed particularly in City and Hackney where no drop-in centre had been established by CHYPP which was based in the community health headquarters. This youth worker was clear on what was needed – 'Bring it out of the hospital and have it literally at street level to give instant access to young people. CHYPP's geographical situation is a no-no. It's almost like going into hospital. Location is prime – you've got to be available to tap passing traffic. I believe in shop-fronts for accessibility. In the long run it may even be cheaper to buy or rent High Street premises than to hassle around with unsuitable accommodation...'

This view was shared by a YTS manager in the same area – 'They could set up a more accessible service, which might mean going out into the High Street, and market themselves in a different way. They could have been working more closely with youth clubs. One of the team could have been more available to the youth service...'

A BPAS counsellor thought the remit of the young people's services should be fairly wide – 'I think it would be very helpful to have a specialised unit or units to offer counselling and advice on sexual problems, contraception and pregnancy problems – something similar to how family planning clinics run but specifically for young people. I think I'd like to see a specialised but comprehensive service for young people – not just

205

medical but a mixture. I'm a bit reluctant to say it should be attached to health centres because of the medical connotation. It should be away from the medical model – more like a drop-in centre. It should give teenagers an opportunity to talk about their own fears and anxieties about sex and sexuality – fears about AIDS, rape, incest. I think, sadly, we will always see the people who think it isn't going to happen to them – the message is not getting over to young people. Doctors are not good at explaining how to use contraception, but they'll dish them out. It's amazing how many young people we see who have never heard of contraception. As adults we tend to assume far too much knowledge...'

Teachers in Milton Keynes were very keen on separate services for young people, and, like youth workers, said that they should be easily accessible. One teacher echoed the views of the young people about the need for the services to be both accessible and 'discreet' – 'The building should be sited where it can and will be used by young people. It's got to be accessible but not too public...' There is clearly a problem in combining these two needs which young people stressed so often in their interviews. The High Street site might be accessible, but it might be too open for some young people.

Some respondents thought there was a need for much more general counselling for young people, like this Milton Keynes teacher – 'The whole area of health education needs upgrading. If the health education department of Milton Keynes was functioning properly the programme should be coordinated much better so that a lot of little units for AIDS, for smoking, for contraception weren't necessary. It ought to be coordinated between agencies. There ought to be a big drop-in centre where young people could go and find out about health and get counselling...' A social worker in the same area agreed – 'The service should be a drop-in one – a special service with links to mainstream services which should be supportive...'

More outreach work or mobile services or home visiting were suggested by around a fifth of the professionals in Milton Keynes and South Sefton, like this health visitor in South Sefton – 'The best way is through schools, but I know a lot of schools won't allow sex education. A lot of young people won't talk to their parents, so maybe the project should knock on doors like us and try to talk to young people at home...' A teacher in Milton Keynes thought the You 2 formula was good but that they needed to get out and about more – 'To have a similar set-up and approach with the same sort of people – moving out into estates – a mobile service perhaps...' Not everyone had thought of this kind of service, but there was considerable support for outreach work in youth clubs and other places where young people congregate.

There were some comments that there was little that could be done for some young people, as this YTS manager in South Sefton commented – 'With this age group there's nothing you can do. They cannot relate what they do with what happens...' There was thought to be a cultural acceptance of pregnancies among young people in South Sefton which was not necessarily found in the other areas, as this teacher explained – 'I just don't believe that it is unwanted pregnancy, whatever the girls may later come to realise. At the time the girl just wants to get pregnant and it's accepted by the family...' A similar view was expressed by a family planning doctor in the same area – 'For so many girls in Bootle pregnancy is not a disaster and they cope. Their parents are not so pleased. If the girls had any other life expectations they might be more distressed by it, but quite a few of the 16-year-olds would not regret it. Their mothers followed the same pattern and almost expect it...'

The question of whether teenage pregnancies should be prevented was challenged by a youth worker in Milton Keynes – 'One of the assumptions is that teenage pregnancy is bad for people. You're working from an assumption that might not be true. I've seen so many young girls who've blossomed and grown up so much from having a baby. I don't know that we should stop them from having babies, but they should have more information...'

Essentially the stress among most of the professionals in the three areas was on the educational and counselling needs of young people, using as many outlets and professionals as possible. Coordination of effort and exchange of information and skills were thought to be important, and the young people's projects were thought by some to have started to facilitate this. A teacher in Milton Keynes thought there was a need for teachers and other professionals to be supported and encouraged and that the responsibility should not be shirked by those in authority – 'It needs to be made a lot more explicit that here is an opportunity for the Department of Health and the Department of Education to work together. Alternatively the project should be taken over by the DES because it is a service that schools in Milton Keynes have valued...'

Whatever kind of services people recommended there was a plea for them to be well-publicised – 'If they don't see any posters they don't know where to go...' was the comment of a family planning nurse in City and

207

Hackney whose view was endorsed by another in Milton Keynes – 'The idea of a counselling service with a doctor and a counsellor in attendance is excellent, but it needs to be publicised. We desperately need a counselling service where young people could go, but everyone needs to know about it...'

It was the question of publicity and knowledge which, above all, dominated the interviews with professionals in these three areas. Good, appropriate services for young people were thought to be needed, but a good service cannot flourish if no-one uses it. Young people will not use services if they do not know anything about them. Professionals will not suggest or refer to services if they are not aware of their existence. Constant efforts have to be made to publicise services on all levels to everyone who might use them or who might be in touch with young people who might be in need of them.

Chapter 12
Views of the project teams and their managers on the achievements of the projects

An important part of the evaluation of these projects was to see what the project teams and their managers and steering groups thought they had achieved. After all, they were the people who had taken up the challenge, who had designed the projects to satisfy the aims of the Department of Health and who had set the priorities. We had monitored the work of the projects and we had followed their progress. We had attended steering group meetings and had interviewed young people using their services. We had listened to what professionals in the areas had to say about their successes and failures. What did the teams and their advisers have to say about the achievements of the projects?

At the end of the monitoring period we interviewed the four health worker members of each of the teams in City and Hackney and Milton Keynes but did not interview the clerical staff. We interviewed two clinic doctors in Milton Keynes and two of the Brook doctors and a Brook counsellor in City and Hackney. In South Sefton, we interviewed the clerical staff member as well as the two health workers since she had been with the project from the beginning and was perhaps more closely involved in the work of the team than clerical staff in the other two areas, and we interviewed the clinic doctor.

It should be noted that only the South Sefton team had remained intact from the start of the project, with both health workers and the clerical staff member having been in post since September 1987, and the doctor having joined in November 1987. The You 2 team had lost two members of the health worker team and gained one, and had had a complete turnover of clerical staff. The original doctor had remained with the project until she had a baby when the second doctor interviewed took her place. The City and Hackney team had lost two health workers and gained two during the 18 months and had also had changes in the clerical staff. Shoreditch Brook had had a number of administrators over the monitoring period and had also had changes in doctors, although we interviewed two who had done regular sessions at the clinic from the beginning. The counsellor had been at Shoreditch Brook from November 1987. There had also been some changes in the Brook management in London.

The managers of the projects in all three areas were also members of the steering groups and included senior medical, nursing and health education or health promotion staff employed by the health authority. The Milton Keynes steering group included outside advisers in the same way as the City and Hackney steering group, but because these Milton Keynes outside advisers were more involved with the management of the project than those in City and Hackney we interviewed them as well. This meant that we interviewed five managers or advisers in City and Hackney and South Sefton and eight in Milton Keynes. In addition we interviewed two London Brook managers. All the managers or advisers had been involved with the projects from the start and had been interviewed at the beginning of the monitoring period, apart from one City and Hackney manager and the two Brook managers.

Aims and priorities

We were interested to see what the teams and their managers saw as the main aims of the projects at the end of the monitoring period and whether they thought the aims had changed in any way over the 18 month period. It must be remembered that the aim of the Department of Health in setting up these projects was to reduce the risk of unwanted pregnancy among young people and to encourage them to seek advice early if they suspected they were pregnant. Few of the professionals were aware of these main aims, and the project teams had not regarded them as central when we interviewed them at the beginning of the projects. What did they think now?

The only people to regard the reduction of unwanted pregnancies as one of the main aims of the projects were three managers and a team member in Milton Keynes and one manager in City and Hackney. The main aims as seen by most of the managers outside City and Hackney and by the Brook staff were to provide family planning or counselling services acceptable to young people which were user-friendly, sensitive and informal. This view was shared by few project staff, who were much more likely to say that the main aims of the projects were to educate young people in sex, contraception, relationships and decision-making skills, aims which Brook staff also mentioned. The aim of building links with schools was thought important in Milton Keynes by the managers and advisers, and the training and support of other professionals was mentioned by project team members in City and Hackney and South Sefton. The aim of reaching young people not reached by other services which had been central to managers' concerns at the beginning of the projects was still mentioned by three managers in Milton Keynes and South Sefton.

But had the aims changed over the period? This was certainly the view in Milton Keynes, where three-quarters of the managers and team members thought they had. In City and Hackney, half the team members and most of the Brook workers thought the aims had changed, but in South Sefton only one manager and one member of the team thought they had.

One of the Milton Keynes team members summed up what she thought had happened to the aims of the project – 'It changed from directly working with pupils to working with teachers – to enable and train teachers to feel more comfortable with the subject themselves. We had to leave something behind after the project ended so that others would carry on the work. This had not initially been considered. We had to get the teachers to do it themselves...'

A Milton Keynes manager indicated how the aims had changed to concentrate on particular groups of young people – 'They started off very broadly and gradually focussed on something practicable. Initially they took all the under-25s, but in practical terms it became mainly for the under-18s and school age young people and some youth work...' We were interested to know why the aims had changed and the same manager summarised the views of a number of people in Milton Keynes – 'That's where the need is felt to be greatest. We feel this is where the need is and we felt this before the project started, but the project was said to be for under-25s. I would have been happy with an under-18 project...'

But others in Milton Keynes thought the aims had changed for a number of reasons, including the fact that the You 2 team felt happier with this type of work, that they had had difficulty in getting the clinic off the ground for a variety of reasons including locum cover, and that the demand from the schools was there. It was also thought that the team leader had influenced the direction in which the project developed. Essentially what many of them were talking about was a change in priorities and methods of working rather than a direct change in aims, but it was sometimes difficult for respondents to decide what had influenced what.

In City and Hackney, there had always been a reluctance in the team to subscribe too closely to the aims of the projects as laid down by the Department of Health. A team member summarised what she saw as the

211

aims of the projects – 'I'd reword them now. I'd change the emphasis to health promotion and choice rather than prevention of unwanted pregnancies. That's what we'll do in future. The aims were written with a preset agenda that it's desirable to stop people having unintended and unwanted pregnancies. I think the implication of that is that we are trying to change people's behaviour. I don't think that reflects the way that we work. We're not about telling people not to have unwanted babies. We're into offering people choices...'

The priorities set by CHYPP were first, the reduction of first unintended pregnancies, and to help them in achieving this they funded out of the CHYPP budget a review of pregnancy testing services in the district. Their second priority was a reduction of subsequent unintended pregnancies and problems associated with teenage motherhood. The setting of this as a priority led to considerable input from the team into a teenage antenatal clinic run by the health authority which had been foundering. The third priority was the reduction of late abortion. But the way in which the CHYPP team went about implementing their priorities and working only in very specific areas without involving the Brook clinics was central to the disagreement and rift with Brook which ensued.

The Brook team felt that the CHYPP team had departed from the original aims of the project. One member of the Brook team said:

> The aims at the beginning were quite general as a way of consciousness-raising. Within six months they became more specific and targeted, with more emphasis on sexual education and with more theory. The publicity became less of a priority, contact with the NHS became less of a priority. They seemed to become more campaigning – not towards clients or GPs - but towards public opinion. There was more theory, more politicising, more "research". There seemed to be an agenda to test a hypothesis which I didn't understand. It was never disclosed. I called it empire-building...The aim was to reduce unwanted and repeated unwanted pregnancies. The difficulty was how to do it. CHYPP seemed to target other services and institutions. Brook seemed to target the client...

These different approaches and philosophies, combined with an almost complete lack of consultation or collaboration between CHYPP and Brook on priorities or strategy, are discussed in more detail later in this chapter, but they had a major effect on the City and Hackney project, which, as we have seen from interviews with professionals in the area, was rarely recognised as having a link with Brook at all.

In South Sefton, few people saw the aims as having changed although the priorities were thought to have shifted slightly. A team member said -

'We've stuck very strictly to what the aims were, but we've been responsive to what the local community actually wants. We are aware of women wanting special services – friendly and welcoming – women of all ages. Men too respond to this type of service and they shouldn't be left out when considering community facilities...'

Unlike the Milton Keynes project and to a lesser extent CHYPP, the South Sefton team had had very little contact with schools, and one of the team members thought that their priorities had been right – 'It was a good thing we didn't attempt to go into schools. All the health professionals kept saying, "Go into schools," but it was evident that we didn't have the resources to do it. The team was not big enough and we didn't have a proper programme, but it was appropriate to help teachers with resources as we did...'

The priorities set in all three areas by the management and the teams themselves changed and evolved 'organically', as one manager put it. There was little doubt that the teams felt they had to be opportunistic and respond to what arose or came their way, particularly given the short-term nature of the projects. This led, for example, to the development of the work in schools in Milton Keynes and the work with older women and young boys in South Sefton.

The question arose throughout these interviews of whether it was feasible for a certain set of priorities to be laid down at the beginning of projects of this nature and to be strictly adhered to in any case. On the whole the project teams and their managers felt that the right priorities had been chosen and developed in attempting to fulfil the brief given by the Department of Health, but there was certainly no real agreement, even within the districts themselves, of exactly what these priorities were.

Effect of projects on services for young people

We asked the teams and their managers whether they thought that the services offered by the project had improved the family planning and pregnancy counselling services for young people in the district. The respondents were much more sure that they had than the professionals we interviewed. Most of the project team members thought they had improved the services for young people a lot, and so did most of the managers in City and Hackney and South Sefton and the Brook respondents. The managers and advisers in Milton Keynes were more likely to think the project had made some difference to services, although there was some doubt about how much.

The availability of an extra service which was accessible to young people was thought to have been the main improvement in the areas. In City and Hackney, many people commented that the project must have improved the service simply by providing three Brook clinic sessions instead of one, while in the other two areas it was felt that the provision of a clinic and drop-in facility where there had been none before must have improved the service provision to young people. In South Sefton there was an assumption that PACE was being used by young people who had never used other services, and team members thought it was being used by young people who would not use other services. Some of the Milton Keynes respondents were quite sure that the service was being used by people who did not or would not use other services, often misinterpreting data collected by the teams and the family planning clinics for the purposes of the PSI evaluation. There was an assumption that the almost complete lack of knowledge of You 2 on the part of young people using family planning clinics or BPAS meant that You 2 was supplying a service to people who would not use family planning clinics. It is possible that they were, but this could not be deduced from the information gathered in the family planning clinics and BPAS which was collated by PSI for the evaluation (see Appendix IV).

In City and Hackney the CHYPP team members stressed the development of the teenage antenatal clinic and the support they had given to a young mothers' group as being evidence of an improvement in family planning and pregnancy counselling services in the district. In addition they said that the pregnancy testing service was now more widely available in the district because of the review paid for by CHYPP funding.

Effects of projects on sex education

The project teams in both City and Hackney and Milton Keynes were almost unanimous in thinking that the projects had brought about a lot of improvement in the provision of education for young people about sex, contraception and pregnancy in the district. This judgment was shared by most of the City and Hackney managers, but by fewer than half the Milton Keynes managers and advisers. In South Sefton, only one manager and one team member thought the project had improved the provision a lot. Almost all the other respondents in all three areas thought that the projects had made some difference, however.

Why did the teams think they had made so much difference to sex education in the areas? One team member in Milton Keynes had no doubts at all – 'When we went to the schools they didn't have anyone in charge of sex education. Some didn't have any sex education at all. Now all seven have a statement in accordance with the law. All seven have a programme of sex education. In five out of the seven we're on the working parties they have established on how to implement sex education...' This view was endorsed both by team members and by managers, many of whom had experience of what had been going on in the schools in the areas. Another team member thought the team had achieved a lot – 'We've got the schools to integrate sex education into their curriculum properly – not just getting in a speaker but a proper policy. Some of the schools were doing it anyway but some weren't...'

Steering group members commended the way in which the You 2 team had approached the question of sex education in schools – 'Their approach to people in education was clearly thought out. They knew where they were going. They went in at the administrative level too, which was good...' It was thought that the success of You 2 in schools had led to an expansion of the health education staff in the district, and managers pointed out that when the central government funding for the projects was coming to an end, letters from headteachers were received by the health authority saying how much they had appreciated the work of the project.

A steering group member had had very positive feedback about You 2's work in schools – 'I suspect it focussed everybody's concern about this subject and provided a forum for discussion. It makes them think very carefully about what they're doing...' And a team member agreed that their main contribution had been to give teachers the confidence to initiate and run sex education programmes themselves – 'We've stimulated the teachers to do quite a lot with their curriculum... I feel now the work should be done with teachers, not pupils. The workers should team up with the teachers...'

In City and Hackney, team members stressed their outreach work with professionals working with young people outside schools as well as with teachers and schoolchildren. A team member said that the district health authority had not been doing this before. CHYPP had been working not only with pupils in primary and secondary schools and further education colleges, but with teachers, youth workers, residential social workers, YTS schemes and health authority staff with a view to 'training the trainers'. Another team member thought that they had been very successful – 'Teachers are aware that we can work with them. Their doubts and fears go when they meet us and see we can work with them. It sets off a chain reaction and then they're more confident about how to approach these subjects...'

A member of the steering group thought that CHYPP had achieved a lot in the time they had been operating. 'CHYPP has been very important in this process. When schools have approached me about sex education I've been able to say, "Contact CHYPP." Right from the start CHYPP have consulted me and what they've done is very consistent with the general development of health education...'

It was thought by some respondents that one of the team members who had left the project some months before the end of the monitoring period had made a particularly big contribution to CHYPP's work in sex education, a view endorsed by the professionals we interviewed in the area. The Brook respondents felt that no attempt had been made to integrate Brook into any sex education programmes and found this surprising considering the extensive educational work carried out by Brook in other areas.

In many ways, considering how much emphasis CHYPP put on their outreach and educational activities, their managers knew surprisingly little about what they had achieved.

In South Sefton, with its much smaller team, educational outreach work had been much more limited, and the team members were aware that their impact on sex education had not been as great as they would have liked – 'In the time we've had we've improved things, but there's a lot more to do. Where we've been able to lay our hands on young people things were greatly improved, but there are a lot of young people left to get in touch with...'

One manager commented on the difficulties facing the PACE team in improving sex education facilities in schools and other organisations. She thought they had made a lot of difference – 'You've got to paint it against the background of a very Catholic society and a very matriarchal society. It's still like that. Men don't go to sea now, but they go down south and come back at weekends or they go on oil rigs. There's still the pattern of the men away and the women running the family. The Catholic influence is still prevalent and the society is still very family orientated. They don't see babies as a major problem. There are a lot of single mothers supported by their families. They're not a problem. It's the unsupported girls we're concerned about...'

Other managers thought that the team had done as well as they could under the circumstances, but thought that schools in the area had a long way to go in developing a health education policy. There were said to be signs that such a policy was being developed and that PACE had made some contribution. Other managers thought that some of the other work with professionals had helped to develop sex education programmes, but that sex education in schools in South Sefton presented a particularly tough challenge.

Work with other professionals and agencies

One of the main intentions of all three projects had been to work with other professionals. There were hopes that one of the achievements of the projects would be to help train other professionals in working with young people in the areas of sex, contraception and unwanted pregnancy. It was understood that the projects were to have a relatively short life, although when they were first proposed it was thought they would have central government funding for three years. It was therefore in the interests of the health authorities concerned that the projects could make an input into the work of other staff and agencies concerned with young people and that the teams could also establish methods of working which could be used as models for others to use.

We therefore asked a series of questions about how much respondents felt that the project teams had contributed to the work of other professionals and agencies. We were interested in establishing how this contribution had been achieved or what factors had prevented any contribution. Throughout these interviews we wanted to record for others the opportunities and problems which had been encountered by the projects, which had been set up as potential models.

We compared the evidence from this series of questions with the analysis of the team's activities summarised in the activities analysis tables in Appendix II. It must be stressed that these activities were documented on a weekly basis by the teams themselves, and that any omissions were their responsibility.

Family planning clinic staff

It might have been assumed that liaison with family planning clinic staff in the areas would have been one of the top priorities of the project teams. After all, the family planning clinic staff were usually closely involved with providing services to young people on the same topics as the projects. If one of the main aims of these projects was to provide good and appropriate services to young people, it might have been thought that cooperation with existing services, which would continue to exist after the projects had finished, would be high on their agenda. This was not the case in any of the three areas. The activities analysis shows very little contact between family planning clinic staff and the project teams in all three areas.

There were a number of reasons for this, some of which could have been foreseen when the bids for funding of the projects were put in by the health authorities. It is clear that any management would have been aware that making a bid for extra central funding which involved the setting up of new projects with new staff would need careful handling so that existing staff did not feel bypassed, criticised or overlooked. In the event, however carefully the situation was handled, there was evidence of ill-feeling among some family planning clinic staff in all three areas, and, perhaps more important, there was evidence of an almost complete lack of contact and collaboration between the projects and the family planning staff, in spite of the fact that in all three areas the management and advisers of the project teams included senior nursing managers and managers responsible for the family planning clinics.

Only two respondents thought that the project teams had contributed a lot to the work of family planning staff. They were both senior nursing managers who had had little ongoing contact with the work of the teams, but thought that the teams had been involved in training family planning nurses. Only six respondents – a manager and a team member in each area – thought the team had made 'some' contribution to the work of family planning clinic staff. The majority of team members and management in all three areas thought the team had made little or no contribution to the work of family planning clinic staff or they felt unable to comment.

We had been aware from our interviews with family planning clinic staff in the areas that there was some hostility and a great deal of ignorance on their part about what the project teams were doing. Why had this happened and what did the teams feel about it?

In City and Hackney, a team member thought they had made little contribution to the work of family planning clinic staff – 'It hasn't been a priority, because we decided that the service side was providing two extra clinics. We had existing young people's clinics and it didn't seem appropriate to spend our time working with family planning clinic staff, given our limited time...'

Other team members mentioned having done some training courses with family planning nurses and having sent information about CHYPP to all family planning staff, but one of the team members, who had only been with the project for the last seven months, had had no contact with clinic staff.

The Brook team were hazy about the work done by the CHYPP team. They themselves had had some contact with family planning staff, mainly with those who worked in the Shoreditch health centre, but it was felt that CHYPP was very detached. Brook had thought that CHYPP and Brook would run training courses together for family planning staff in counselling and reception work, but had been told by CHYPP that this 'had got lost on the agenda'.

A manager had been surprised at how little the family planning nurses knew of the CHYPP work, or of the Brook clinic for that matter, and this view was certainly borne out by the comments of most of the family planning staff interviewed.

In Milton Keynes there was evidence from the interviews with family planning staff of even less knowledge of the You 2 project, often combined with a lack of interest or even of hostility to the project. The majority of respondents in Milton Keynes thought the projects had contributed little or nothing at all to the work of family planning staff. One team member thought they had made some contribution by working with family planning student nurses and meeting senior doctors and nurses, but wondered whether the team had had unrealistic hopes of achieving things too quickly. Other team members thought there had been little or no liaison and attributed this to a lack of consultation with the family planning staff before the project started, a sense of competition for funds and clients and an unwillingness on the part of family planning staff to 'get a dialogue going'. Another project team member said – 'I believe they felt they provided an adequate service and were really quite offended that it was thought that a service was needed. We were helpful by taking on some of their clients. We got all the ones that wouldn't have gone there and the ones that they refused because they were too young...'

Managers and advisers spoke of 'a bit of friction' and 'not too much interaction' and 'no input there at all'. One manager said – 'All along the family planning service felt suspicious about this. They felt the set-up wasn't professional enough. They didn't like their approach and thought they were a bit trendy...'

It was thought that the aloofness of the family planning service from the You 2 project had made it more difficult for the young people's service to be integrated into the mainstream family planning service at the end of the central funding. This was undoubtedly true, and it must be seen as a potential danger for demonstration projects of this kind. If the ongoing mainstream services are not prepared to adapt and are not involved in any way in the planning and the process of 'model' projects, their ability or willingness to continue with the work of these projects must be in doubt.

The potential waste of time, effort and money in such a result cannot be underestimated.

In South Sefton one member of the project team thought there had been some contribution – 'They know we're here and we are getting referrals from them now and some of them know us. Certainly (team member) has had a lot of contact with them, but lack of time has prevented us from contacting everyone. We did do group work with some of them in the beginning...'

But another team member said – 'We haven't had much to do with them at all except to refer the occasional client to them who needed an urgent service like the morning after pill...' Again team members stressed that they were thought to be doing little for clinics 'because we're reaching a different market' – a theme which recurred both in Milton Keynes and South Sefton without any evidence to back it up.

There was thought to have been a lack of publicity to family planning clinics, and it was regretted that PACE posters had not been put up in clinics in the area. Managers in the area again knew surprisingly little about the contact, or lack of contact, between the project and a mainstream service functioning in the same field.

Other health authority staff
The projects could clearly have been used as a resource by other health authority staff such as health visitors or school nurses. However, the interviews with professionals indicated that there was little close contact between the project teams and health visitors. The majority of managers and team members in all three areas thought that the projects had made little or no contribution to the work of health authority staff, although nearly half the South Sefton respondents thought they had made at least some contribution. It was thought that the fact that one of the PACE team was a health visitor herself had helped, although none of the health visitors interviewed mentioned this. Some respondents in South Sefton thought there had been informal contact with individual health visitors, while some managers thought there had been more formal input. It was suggested that PACE had made some contribution to the work of school nurses, but the team members did not mention this.

The limited extent of the contact with other health authority staff in Milton Keynes and South Sefton is clearly shown in the activities analysis. In City and Hackney more contact was indicated, but it appears that much of this was with one or two managers rather than with staff in the field.

In Milton Keynes only one respondent thought the team had made even some contribution to the work of other health authority staff. The lack of contact noted in interviews with health authority professionals was borne out by the comments of the team and managers. A team member said the team had given talks or made contact with all the health visitors and community nurses, explaining their role and how they could work together. It was suggested by both managers and team members that health visitors had very little contact with the age-group the projects were aiming at, although this seemed a rather surprising comment considering that the projects were set up for people under the age of 25. It was thought that there might have been some contact with school nurses, but respondents were rather vague about this.

In City and Hackney, the team generally thought they had made a little contribution to the work of health authority staff, mainly health visitors, school nurses and community medical officers, but the contact had either been with individuals or at particular meetings. Time constraints were given as the reason for not doing more. Managers knew little of what the team had done, but said that the health visitors and other community staff had access to the project team. Brook staff thought the CHYPP team had made little or no impact on the work of health authority staff.

Health education staff

The three projects all had close links with the health education or health promotion departments of the health authority. Indeed in both Milton Keynes and South Sefton the health education or health promotion managers had the line management responsibility for the projects. The projects teams all stressed the importance of their educational role, but how much had they contributed to the work of the health education staff?

The activities analysis clearly under-reports the extent to which the teams had ongoing contact with their managers in the health education or health promotion departments, and it is possible that informal contact with health education colleagues may also have been under-reported.

The greatest impact was thought to have been achieved in South Sefton where most of the managers and project team members thought the projects had contributed a lot to the health education staff, mainly through working closely with them in creating a good mutual resource. There was close cooperation between the team and the health promotion staff in trying to build up relationships with schools, and the team had good links with the AIDS coordinator. The project team was based in the health promotion department for the first few months of the monitoring period since the project premises were not ready, and this had clearly forged links with the department which might not otherwise have been there. One of the health promotion staff commented – 'We got to know them on a personal level. We could see the way they were working and the resources they were using...'

There can be little doubt that ongoing personal contact between the team and other professionals played a crucial role in building up close relationships. In City and Hackney, where the health education department was in the same building as the CHYPP team, the project staff had worked with the health education officer and with the HIV/AIDS officer and had done joint training sessions. The project team and managers stressed the importance of linking AIDS and issues surrounding sexuality, and thought the link provided a useful mutual resource.

In Milton Keynes, although the team had done a great deal of work in schools, there was some hesitation in saying that the project had contributed a lot to the work of the health education staff, which had undergone some reorganisation during the monitoring period. There was some evidence that the project team and health education staff had worked alongside each other initially, rather than providing a mutual resource, but that there had been closer liaison towards the end of the monitoring period.

GPs

GP family planning services are, of course, well established and used by large numbers of women, including large numbers of young women. There is some evidence that teenagers may not always feel comfortable in seeking family planning or pregnancy counselling services from their GPs, and the survey we conducted of project users in the three areas suggested that young people often had unfavourable perceptions of the services they received or might receive from GPs. There is a possibility that GPs might have something to learn from services which are geared to the needs of young people. To what extent had the project teams achieved any links with GPs in their areas and had they contributed to the work of GPs in any way?

The activities analysis indicates little contact with GPs in any of the areas, and, indeed, in South Sefton, only one contact of any kind was recorded with GPs.

Only two respondents – a team member and a doctor in Milton Keynes – thought that the projects had contributed a lot to the work of GPs. The Milton Keynes project was generally thought to have contributed more to the work of GPs than the other two projects, mainly, it should be noted, because GPs were said to have referred a lot of women for pregnancy tests.

GPs had certainly referred women for pregnancy tests, thus indicating that they knew that You 2 offered a pregnancy testing service, but whether this could be construed as the project contributing much to the work of GPs with young people is a matter for debate. As we have seen, many women used the You 2 service as a free pregnancy testing service to confirm a wanted pregnancy.

Not all the Milton Keynes team thought they had contributed much to the work of GPs and one team member thought they had contributed nothing at all. The health authority had been worried about relationships with GPs at the beginning of the project, and publicity to GPs had been minimal. Ongoing contact with individual GPs or GP practices was limited during the monitoring period, and another team member thought the project team had made little contribution to the work of GPs – 'They refer to us because we're there, but we've had no influence on their practice...'

The same feeling was apparent in City and Hackney, and managers were not sure that working with GPs would have been a suitable priority for the project team – 'I'm well aware that it's good using GPs for health promotion. But good ones are good but overwhelmed, while bad ones are useless...'

CHYPP team members agreed that contact with GPs had been limited. It was thought that the teenage ante-natal clinic was a resource to GPs, although there was little evidence that publicity about the Brook clinic had been widespread. One team member thought that there was little more that could have been done – 'We've made ourselves available to them. If they'd asked for our help in doing anything we'd have helped. We didn't go out of our way to look for it. We weren't proactive. If they wanted training in sex education we're available but they haven't asked...'

None of the respondents in South Sefton thought the project had had much effect on the work of GPs. There had been some referrals from GPs, often for smears, but in general there was little contact. It was suggested that liaison with local GPs could have been more sensitively handled by the health authority at the beginning of the project when the clinic was being set up.

There was evidence in all three areas that the projects had sent out some initial publicity to GPs but had done little to follow this up. There had been some meetings with some GP practices or at postgraduate centres, but the overall impression of the activities of all three projects with GPs was that it had been a low priority, and had achieved little.

BPAS

In Milton Keynes, terminations of pregnancy were carried out on an agency basis by the British Pregnancy Advisory Service (BPAS). A member of the BPAS staff was on the steering group for the You 2 project and was also involved in the training programme given to the project team staff at the beginning of the monitoring period.

Few contacts were reported by the project team with BPAS. Respondents in Milton Keynes were fairly evenly divided in their views on how much the project had contributed to the work of BPAS, with several managers unable to comment. It was thought that You 2 had helped BPAS by taking over a high proportion of the educational and training work which BPAS had little time for but considered a high priority. It was also thought helpful that You 2 was open every day to provide pregnancy testing, that the clinic doctor's referral for an NHS termination of pregnancy could be accepted by BPAS under the terms of the agency agreement with the health authority, and that women referred to BPAS by You 2 would have had pregnancy counselling of a high standard.

There was some feeling that the BPAS staff had contributed more to the work of You 2 than the other way round, but, in general, it was thought that the presence on the steering group of a very experienced BPAS staff manager with a strong commitment to education and training had helped to forge important links between the two organisations, even if most BPAS staff had had little contact with the You 2 team members.

Schoolteachers

The City and Hackney and Milton Keynes teams were generally thought by both managers and team members to have made a significant contribution to the work of schoolteachers, but South Sefton respondents were more doubtful about the impact made by the PACE project. Team members thought it was likely to be a slow process in South Sefton – 'We're starting at the top because that seems to be the only way to do it, but it's going to take a long time. There are problems here with the Catholic community...'

The activities analysis shows the extent to which the Milton Keynes project had far more contacts of all types with schools and schoolteachers than the other two projects (see Appendix II). The CHYPP team were more active with schoolteachers than with other professionals, but, even so, they were much less likely than the You 2 team to have been involved in sessions with young people at the schools, which could only have come about through the contact and planning with teachers. In South Sefton, there was little contact with teachers, both in absolute terms and relatively to the activities of the other two projects.

The main contributions of the CHYPP and You 2 teams to the work of school teachers were said to be in establishing a good rapport with them and in offering support and training. In both areas the teams were said to have given a high priority to offering resources to teachers and to providing informal training. It was thought that the teams helped teachers by providing specialist help on sex education, a subject with which many teachers were said to feel uncomfortable. A conference held by You 2 was said to have been particularly useful for teachers.

Youth service workers
Most of the South Sefton respondents thought the PACE team had made a significant contribution to the work of the youth service workers, while most team members and managers in both City and Hackney and Milton Keynes thought their projects had made little or no contribution to the youth service or felt they had insufficient information to comment.

The PACE team reported more activities with youth service workers than with most other workers, but the level of contacts with youth service workers was rather less than that of the other two projects, who, of course, had more staff to develop such contacts. The CHYPP team had had a number of contacts of all types, but clearly felt they had not made much headway.

In South Sefton, the PACE project was based in a community centre which had a number of youth clubs on the premises, which naturally gave it easier access to youth workers, although there had been problems in keeping the youth clubs running in the centre. In addition, one of the team members had made contact with youth workers in the district a priority, and had been to a number of meetings to publicise the project's services. The build-up of work had been slow and there had been no work directly with young people at youth clubs, although it was said that youth workers were keen to get sessions going.

The CHYPP team felt they had had limited success with youth workers, partly because of the fragmented nature of the youth service in the area and partly because so many youth workers worked only part-time, often in the evenings, which made contact difficult. A team member thought that it might have been easier to work from the top down – through the Youth Office – rather than taking the 'bottom up' approach which had worked in schools. There was thought to be a problem of working only with girls in youth clubs, which the CHYPP team thought was sometimes a necessary approach. The informality of youth clubs was also thought to make it difficult for CHYPP to plan a programme for the young people since it was never certain who would come to the club on a particular night – 'The composition of the group changes and so your plan or programme doesn't reach everyone...' One team member was disappointed with the lack of contact – 'The youth leaders don't seem to value the importance of sex education. They don't see it as a priority...'

In Milton Keynes there was a general consensus of opinion that work with youth clubs had not 'caught on'. There was some disagreement in the team about the extent to which youth work should have been made a priority. Some team members thought that it was a bit of a waste of time since so many youth clubs were 'activity' orientated, while other team members had been keen to develop the work more. A manager was disappointed in the response of the youth service to the You 2 project – 'They saw it as a very fringe thing to their main priorities...' You 2 had run one session a week at a youth centre in Central Milton Keynes, but it had had very few clients there, and nobody could give a satisfactory explanation for its almost complete lack of success.

It did appear from interviews with youth workers that project team members in all three areas had not always understood the ways in which youth workers worked with young people, and there certainly seemed to be a need for more mutual understanding. The youth service by its very nature is bound to be fragmented and informal, but it should not have been beyond the capacity of flexible services, which stressed their informality, to find some way of meeting the needs of both the youth workers and the young people. The youth service in all three areas was in touch with the age-groups the projects were trying to attract, and had particular contacts with the vulnerable age-groups who had left school.

Other voluntary and community organisations

Work with other voluntary and community organisations had been developed on an ad hoc basis and was thought to have been most successful in South Sefton, although nearly half the respondents in City and Hackney and Milton Keynes were unaware that the projects had had this kind of contact.

The activities analysis suggests that the CHYPP and PACE teams had made a number of initial contacts with such groups which had not been followed up. In Milton Keynes, rather fewer such contacts had been made and little further activity had taken place.

In South Sefton and Milton Keynes there had been some work with organisations which shared premises with the project, like the Women's Health Group in Milton Keynes and the Look After Your Health workers in South Sefton. In City and Hackney and South Sefton there had been contact with young mothers' groups and the PACE team had developed contacts with local playgroups and nurseries. The main impression of this kind of work was that it had developed almost as a fringe activity and that there had been few systematic attempts to develop community links of this kind.

Youth Training Schemes

All three projects had made contact with youth training schemes (as they were called at the time), and in general the project team members thought they had contributed a lot to the work of trainers. Managers and advisers in City and Hackney and Milton Keynes knew little about this part of the work of the teams, but managers in South Sefton thought the team had made an important contribution.

The work of the teams with YTS trainers might have been under-reported by team members, but it did not figure very much in the activities analysis of the work of either the CHYPP or the PACE teams' work. In Milton Keynes, there were a number of contacts leading to quite a heavy programme of work with young people (see Appendix II).

One of the PACE team members stressed the importance of working with youth training schemes – 'The young people have not had the opportunities to discuss contraception and relationships in the kind of atmosphere we provide before and they seem to feel that their sex education was pretty perfunctory and came too late...'

There were thought to be some problems in Milton Keynes because the group of young people attending the sessions changed so that it was difficult to develop programmes for them. It was also suggested that YTS trainers wanted to 'tell You 2 how they wanted them to work...' The team members felt very positive about their contribution to the work of YTS trainers on the whole, although it appeared that they did rather more work with trainees than with the trainers.

CHYPP had done very little work either with YTS trainers or trainees although they were beginning to develop this work at the end of the project. A team member commented – 'It's quite hard to find them, so we didn't try that hard...' It was not regarded as a priority either by the team or by the managers in City and Hackney.

Social services staff

Work with social services department staff had been very limited in Milton Keynes and South Sefton. The majority of respondents who knew anything about it said that the project had made little or no contribution to the work of social services staff in Milton Keynes, while most respondents who could comment in South Sefton thought the project had made some contribution.

The You 2 and PACE teams appeared to have made a number of initial contacts with social services staff, according to the activities analysis, but there was little further contact with them, and virtually no contact at all as far as young people were concerned, either on an individual or group basis. In City and Hackney, on the other hand, there had been a small number of initial contacts which had led to a relatively high number of sessions planning work with young people and a fairly high number of sessions training social services staff, mostly staff working in residential establishments with young people.

In City and Hackney, most of the team and managers who could comment thought CHYPP had contributed a lot to social services staff, mainly because they had worked closely with residential social workers and with the training department of the local social services department. Both the team and managers thought this was a considerable achievement. The social services staff were said to have welcomed the training sessions because they felt they had not had any training in what they considered to be a very important area of their work. They were mainly working with young people who were 'at risk', many of whom were said to have been sexually abused.

The South Sefton team thought they were a useful resource for social workers who did not know where else to send clients, particularly for pregnancy counselling. One of the team was said to be offering a lot of support to young girls who did not have a social worker. She said she liaised closely with individual social workers, particularly the hospital social worker in a local maternity unit. This work did not appear to have been reported on the activity sheets kept by the team members.

The liaison between the You 2 project and social services staff had been very limited and one of the managers professed great disappointment in the lack of contact that social services staff had with other services in general, particularly in the case of pregnant schoolgirls – 'A lot of them are actually *in care*. You would have thought that social services would have taken on the contraceptive needs of 14-year-old girls...'

The local social services department had been undergoing considerable reorganisation during the monitoring period, and this was thought to have accounted for some of the lack of liaison and contact with the You 2 project. A member of social services staff had been on the steering group but she had left the district some months before the end of the project and had not been replaced on the steering group.

Contact had been made with local social workers and residential homes at the beginning of the project but there had been virtually no response. A team member thought that social workers might be worried about the 'left-wing' or 'fringe' reputation of the Bakehouse where the You 2 project was based, and might be reluctant to refer young people to it. There had been work with the IT (Intermediate Treatment) team at the beginning of the project, but this had foundered for a variety of reasons although a team member regretted this since she thought that You 2 could make a valuable contribution with a 'vulnerable group of young people' like those involved in the IT groups.

Other professionals or workers with young people

The teams and their managers mentioned a variety of other professionals or workers with young people with whom they had had at least some contact, ranging from maternity services in Milton Keynes and South Sefton, drugs centres and the probation services in South Sefton, and school governors and educational welfare officers in City and Hackney. The CHYPP team said that in spite of determined efforts to talk to school governors they had had no success in making real contact.

The CHYPP team had organised a day's sex education conference which was attended by a number of representatives of Hackney community groups and was said by one of the advisers to have been 'magnificently well organised'. The South Sefton team were said to have had good contact with drugs centre workers. No referrals to the project had been recorded as having come through drugs workers, but drugs were said to be a big problem in the Bootle area. A manager said that young people taking drugs would know about PACE through the drugs outreach workers, but it was impossible to establish how many young people, if any, came to PACE through this route.

Few contacts were reported on the activity sheets with other professionals or agencies, and there was little indication on the PACE team's sheets of a high incidence of work with drugs workers (see Appendix II).

Contribution of Brook to the work of professionals and others

We asked the City and Hackney respondents whether Brook had contributed to the work of any of the professionals or workers with young people in the area as part of the project. There were mixed views on this, although the Brook staff all thought they had made some contribution. In general, the non-Brook staff thought that Brook was well recognised as a resource for young people in the area, although one team member thought that Brook had simply provided the clinic service for the project and passed any other outreach work to the CHYPP team. Brook staff thought they had good links with local GPs and the local hospital, and had done some work with one of the Youth Training Schemes.

The relationship between CHYPP and Brook

The projects were set up to demonstrate different ways of providing services to young people, and a deliberate decision to select different types of structure and organisation was taken by the Department of Health when selecting districts in which to fund the projects. One of the obvious models for young people's services was clearly the Brook Advisory Centres with its long experience in this field. This was one of the attractions of the City and Hackney proposal, which offered an educational and outreach service provided by a team based in the health authority combined with a clinic service provided by Brook.

There was every indication that the model outlined by City and Hackney might prove to be a powerful combination which could offer most of the services young people needed, with the added bonus of not having to start from scratch, a factor which was to prove so difficult for the other projects. However, there were potential problems of liaison and coordination, particularly with the separate lines of management of the two parts of the project, and the fact that the Brook staff were employed on a sessional basis on two evenings and a Saturday morning in a clinic which was used for other purposes when they were not there, while the CHYPP team were employed in normal working hours on a full-time or part-time basis in their own offices within the health authority headquarters.

We were interested to know how the liaison between Brook and CHYPP was carried out in practice and how they managed to coordinate the services they were being funded by the Department of Health to provide as part of the City and Hackney project. We were particularly interested in the views of respondents on the advantages and disadvantages in organising services for young people in this kind of way.

How the liaison between Brook and CHYPP worked in practice

It was clear from the interviews with project staff and managers in City and Hackney that liaison between CHYPP and Brook staff had been limited, particularly after the first few months of the project. Indeed, it would be fair to say that the relationship between the CHYPP team and the Brook staff in the latter part of the project's life had reached a point where there was virtually no contact between them at all. We wished to establish whether there were any structural reasons for the lack of liaison so that lessons could be learnt by others.

CHYPP project team members thought the liaison between CHYPP and Brook had varied. The main responsibility for liaising with Brook at an administrative level was said to rest with the coordinator of the CHYPP team who had had contact with the London Brook office and with the Director of the Brook Advisory Centre. She had also had contact on an ongoing basis with the Shoreditch Brook counsellor who had been present from the beginning of the project. This contact had initially been arranged on a monthly basis, but this arrangement had lapsed, and in the last six months of the project there had been 'much less' contact. Two other members of the CHYPP team had had little or no contact with Brook since they had joined seven months before the end of the project, while the other member of the team had had little contact with the Brook team after the first few months of the project during which she had helped to get the clinic refurbished. She thought this lack of contact was mainly because she worked on a half-time basis.

The Brook doctors knew little of how the liaison between CHYPP and Brook was carried out. The Brook staff reported that the ongoing contact with the counsellor had petered out after the first few months in which meetings had been sporadic. There had been an agreement to hold monthly meetings, but months went by without any contact other than occasional telephone calls. There had been very little contact between CHYPP staff and Brook managers. In the last five months of the project Brook reported no meetings at all between the CHYPP staff and Brook staff or managers.

There had been changes in the London and national management of Brook over the period of the project, but it was clear that liaison with Brook was not high on the list of CHYPP's priorities and Brook staff had difficulty in liaising with CHYPP.

The health authority managers and advisers of the CHYPP project did not know how the liaison between Brook and CHYPP had been carried out in practice.

Coordination by CHYPP and Brook on services for young people
Given the division of tasks between CHYPP and Brook outlined in the City
and Hackney proposal, there was clearly a need for the two teams to
coordinate their services to young people. After all, the funding was for a
single project offering services to young people provided by two agencies
working together in close collaboration.

The expertise of Brook in providing services for young people was
clearly a valuable resource for the CHYPP team. Similarly, because the
CHYPP team had been set up with the funding from the Department of
Health, Brook could expect that their Shoreditch clinic and counselling
service would be made more widely known in the area through the work of
the CHYPP team. The model in City and Hackney of dividing the responsibilities for clinic work and outreach and educational work meant that the
CHYPP team could concentrate on the outreach and development work to
a much greater extent than the Milton Keynes and South Sefton teams
could, and that the Brook clinic could concentrate on the task they already
did well. This should have provided the City and Hackney project with
considerable advantages over the other two projects. But how much did
CHYPP and Brook coordinate the services they offered to young people?

None of the respondents thought there had been a lot of coordination,
a CHYPP manager and a project team member thought there had been some
coordination, two of the Brook staff and two of the CHYPP team thought
there had been little coordination, while three of the Brook staff thought
there had been no coordination at all. Most of the other managers and one
of the project team staff did not know how much Brook and CHYPP had
coordinated their services.

We were interested to know how this apparent lack of coordination had
affected the project. It appeared curious that a project which was being
supported by public money as a model of service provision should
demonstrate such little coordination in the organisation of the two strands
of its operation.

The coordinator of the CHYPP team said there had never been any
intention to coordinate the different parts of the project – 'They're not
overlapping services really. We would refer to them if we got young girls,
and if they had talks to do they'd ask us. We organised the Open Day
together and did joint publicity, but in terms of day-to-day work we did
very little... We're offering very different bits of the service. It's very
different from South Sefton and Milton Keynes where both bits are from
the same place. It's a different model. It would have been a different project
if we'd done it differently...'

Another CHYPP team member agreed – 'We weren't aiming to do the same things. It's like asking how the garage and the supermarket coordinate. They're not doing the same things. On the level of publicising the issues we have coordinated a lot. But in terms of delivering the services we haven't been doing the same services. If we had coordinated at that level we would not have been doing our job. Brook contributed to the overall strategy...'

Another CHYPP member thought there had been little coordination – '...apart from making sure we publicise Brook when we do a session – taking literature – Brook leaflets and our own...'

How did the Brook staff and managers think the lack of coordination had affected the project? Some Brook staff thought there had been no common approach, with the possible result that the increased clinic service might not have been taken up by local people as much as it should have been. There was some difficulty in assessing how much demand was generated locally since the booking for the Shoreditch Brook clinic was done centrally at the Tottenham Court Road office, following the general Brook policy to have someone available to take bookings for all their clinics at all times and not only when clinics were open.

Brook staff thought it was difficult to know whether CHYPP were referring young people to the Brook clinic – 'I'd like to have known whether they were telling other people about us and getting more people to come to us, but I don't really know...' Other Brook staff members thought there was no coordination in promoting young people's services to the community. The lack of coordination meant that Brook staff did not know what the CHYPP team were doing in the community and therefore felt they missed an opportunity to contribute to this work. A manager commented – 'It's been a waste of resources...We could have shared resources, knowledge, expertise and teamed up to have achieved more...' Another manager said, 'It's been a struggle to do anything together which might have been mutually beneficial...'

Brook/CHYPP liaison – a model of service delivery?
The Brook/CHYPP liaison was clearly a potentially strong combination, but there was little evidence of close collaboration. In practice, what did the respondents think were the main advantages of the Brook/CHYPP structure as a model of service delivery and what were the main disadvantages?

The CHYPP team members and managers thought that one of the main advantages was that Brook was a well-known name, with well-established expertise, and that they had had the advantage of being able to set up new

233

clinic sessions very quickly. They had linked CHYPP into a larger network of provision of service to young people. The young people's clinic could have been provided within the health authority, but it was thought that an outside agency could 'create change in services which have existed for a long time' more easily. One manager said, 'Bringing in other models of practice is another way of stimulating change in a non-threatening way...' Another manager thought the main advantage of this form of service delivery was that 'CHYPP could buy in off-the-shelf knowledge. This freed them up to concentrate on outreach work...'

Brook staff saw few, if any, advantages to the Brook/CHYPP model as it had evolved in practice. One doctor said – 'My impression of the sessions is that it is an ordinary Brook centre...' – while another said – 'I don't know. I don't know what they did for us. Maybe it was considerable. I just don't know...'

Another Brook respondent thought the only advantage of the link had been the improvement of the clinic premises at the beginning of the project, but the general feeling among Brook staff and managers was that the Brook clinic ran in the same way as other Brook clinics. They found it difficult to see any advantages in the CHYPP/Brook liaison as a model of service delivery, since they could see little evidence of any input from CHYPP into their work. As one Brook respondent said – 'I don't think they publicised Brook at all. Why not? The only answer I can get is that they didn't see it as part of their brief...'

What were the disadvantages of having different agencies and teams supplying the project services? Health authority managers did not see any disadvantages on the whole, but the CHYPP team and the Brook staff did. Some CHYPP team members thought that the fact that Brook was not part of the health authority was a disadvantage in that they might not necessarily 'fall in line' with any policy CHYPP would want to develop for family planning clinics. It was also thought that it was difficult to involve Brook into training for health authority staff since the Brook staff worked on a sessional basis and would have to be paid for their training input.

The Brook staff felt strongly that there were several disadvantages in the type of liaison between the two agencies which had evolved in this project. One Brook respondent put it tersely – 'Just lack of cohesion, lack of confidence, lack of communication, lack of collaboration, lack of control and lack of direction...'

Brook has long experience of collaboration with health authorities, and usually provides young people's clinics alongside health authority family planning clinics with few problems. What was different about this structure was that a project had been set up with central government funding in which the bulk of the money had gone to financing the CHYPP project team and the Brook service had received funding only for providing three clinic sessions. Any other work in which Brook might have been involved was not funded. Communication with the health authority, which was usually done on a direct basis by Brook, was channelled through the CHYPP project coordinator.

It could have been seen from the beginning that there was a potential problem in Brook losing some of its autonomy in a project of this nature without really gaining any advantages. It could be argued, and indeed it was argued, that they gained two extra clinic sessions through being part of a project with central government money. However, they clearly expected that their expertise in providing services for young people would be called upon in helping to develop the outreach and educational work which CHYPP embarked upon. This did not happen, and, far from involving Brook in the planning and development of a coherent strategy for reaching young people, it appeared that CHYPP decided at a very early stage to keep Brook at arm's length.

There were clear differences in philosophy between Brook and CHYPP, illustrated by several respondents throughout these interviews, but summarised by a Brook manager – 'Brook sees itself as providing a service for young people. A lot of our work is crisis counselling and practical help. This takes a long time with young people. I don't feel that CHYPP was particularly interested in getting involved with young people's problems. They were interested in the *theory* of it all. I've never met such a group of theoretical people...'

It was perhaps not surprising that the relationship between Brook and CHYPP deteriorated over the monitoring period to the point of no contact by the end of the eighteen months. There were certainly many lessons to be drawn from the experience which will be discussed in more detail in Chapter 14.

Chapter 13
Assessment of the projects by the project teams and their managers

All three projects set out to work with other professionals and agencies who were closely linked to young people. They adopted a variety of ways of working with them, and, as the last chapter showed, they met with varying degrees of success. Similarly, they developed a variety of ways of working with young people, either on an outreach basis or through direct service provision, again with varying degrees of success. This chapter sets out to examine what the teams and their managers thought were their main successes and failures in their work both with professionals and young people. It concludes by looking at the assessment they made of the achievements of the projects and their recommendations for the future.

The projects' work with professionals and other agencies
We were interested to see which aspects of their work with other professionals and agencies the teams and their managers thought had been the most and the least successful and to explore in some detail why this had happened. We wanted to identify the main ingredients of successful collaboration and the ways in which problems could have been avoided where collaboration was less successful.

Most successful aspects of projects' work with professionals
In both City and Hackney and Milton Keynes the work with teachers in schools and colleges was thought to be the most successful by a majority of respondents. In Milton Keynes, all the managers and advisers thought this was the most successful part of the project's work, but this view, perhaps surprisingly, was shared by only two of the team members. The other two team members thought the YTS work was the most successful and one of them also cited the liaison with BPAS.

In City and Hackney, three of the team members mentioned work with teachers or lecturers as the most successful aspect of their work with other professionals, two of them mentioned work with social services staff, one cited YTS work and one mentioned the work with the ante-natal clinic staff and the young mothers' group. The majority of the managers thought the work with teachers and lecturers had been the most successful, but work with health education staff and social services staff was also mentioned. The Brook staff found it difficult to comment on the most successful aspect of the project's work with other professionals. They thought that Brook worked with other professionals in the way they always did, but had not been involved in any liaison with CHYPP on work with professionals.

In South Sefton, one of the team members mentioned work with YTS trainers, one mentioned the youth service and one thought the work with a particular group of young mothers had been the most successful. The managers were divided, with three citing the YTS work, two mentioning work with schools and colleges, which had in fact been one of the most limited parts of the project's work, and one mentioning work with social services.

Ingredients of success
The work in schools and colleges was thought to have been successful for a number of reasons. There was thought to have been a need for help to teachers in designing sex education programmes, particularly because of the new legislation, but also because not all teachers found it easy to handle sex education. A team member in Milton Keynes said – 'We made them feel comfortable. We were not a threat to their professionalism. We said that we all want one thing – shall we work together?'

The team members in all three areas were thought to have been skilled at putting teachers at their ease, and they were praised by managers for being willing to take advice and to discuss fully with the schools exactly what was needed and how best to deliver it. This was found especially noteworthy in Milton Keynes, where one manager commented - 'They worked at all layers – the governors, the headteachers and the teachers...'

An important ingredient of success in schools was thought to be the demonstration by the teams that they were well prepared and had good resources. This was said to be a key factor in establishing a good relationship with teachers. One of the CHYPP team who had left before the end of the project was described by a Brook worker as 'very systematic, very professional. She stuck to the point and had a clear plan. It seemed when everything else went into the fog, the sex education was a little beacon, blinking on and off...'

The work with YTS trainers was thought to have been successful, particularly in South Sefton, because the young people on such schemes were the 'right age' and the YTS trainers were thought to have needed the kind of input the project staff could give to their training programme, which included life skills and social skills. The health promotion unit in South Sefton had been active with YTS schemes for many years and it was thought that PACE had benefited from the credibility the unit had built up.

In general, the main ingredients of success in working with professionals and other agencies were thought to be a combination of informality and commitment on the part of the project teams, backed up by a structured programme offering the use of good resources. A willingness to work in close cooperation with professionals, fitting in with their needs and structures, was said to be an important ingredient of successful collaboration.

Least successful aspect of projects' work with other professionals
There were differences among the projects in assessing the least successful aspect of their work with other professionals. In Milton Keynes, family planning staff were most frequently mentioned by team members and management, although one team member mentioned work with GPs and another mentioned work with the youth service. Two of the managers and advisers thought the least successful aspect had been work with social services.

In South Sefton, work with schoolteachers was thought to have been the least successful part of the work with professionals by two of the team members and two managers. Others mentioned work with GPs, family planning staff and other health authority staff.

In City and Hackney, the most frequently mentioned professionals by both project team members and managers were youth service workers, although two of the CHYPP project team thought the collaboration with Brook had been the least successful aspect of their work with professionals, and the Brook workers thought collaboration with GPs, the youth services and other voluntary bodies had been the least successful aspect of the project's work.

Reasons for lack of success
What had brought about the lack of success and how could the problems have been avoided? As might have been expected, the answers to these

questions sometimes uncovered simmering feuds and personality clashes. We were more interested in the structural issues which others planning services for young people would do well to take into account, but there can be little doubt that lack of attention to the sensitivity of professionals defending their territories can lead to spectacularly unsuccessful collaboration.

The lack of liaison with the family planning service in Milton Keynes was thought by some respondents to have been inevitable, given the way in which the projects had been set up and given the personalities involved. There was thought to have been a certain rigidity on the part of some family planning staff which had led to a clash of philosophies, as one team member said – 'They didn't seem to want to bend their rules at all. They didn't seem to want a service for young people. They felt their ways were right and they were going to continue. They said the kids should accept what is there...'

But some respondents thought that it had been a mistake not to involve the family planning staff from the beginning – 'I think all these things need to be approached with tact and diplomacy. I think if I'd been running the family planning clinics I'd have felt it was a slap in the face...'

Managers pointed out that many attempts had been made at liaison with the family planning service staff but the result had been 'non-collaboration and non-cooperation'. Some thought that the speed with which the projects had been set up had affected good liaison, but essentially it appeared that ill-feeling persisted because the family planning staff were not involved in providing a service which had received special central funding. One manager commented – 'I think that is going to be true where family planning staff are not involved in setting up young people's services...'

An adviser thought that the tension could not have been avoided – 'It was handled as well as it might have been. It's the same in any new project. On the one hand there is far too much work for everybody, but on the other hand everybody is worried about their territory being invaded...'

But a manager thought that conflict could have been avoided by more meetings and communication, particularly at grass-roots level – 'At no stage was a meeting called for the different teams to meet each other and say, "This is what we're hoping to do". Communications was a big factor. The people at management level were involved in committee meetings but there was no meeting with the real people who worked in the clinics. Management had the wrong perception and we took our cue from them, and I'm not sure that was at all helpful for the project. You 2 was seen as a threat to the existing services and they resented the unprofessionalism of some of the people involved initially...'

Another adviser thought that one of the main reasons for You 2's lack of success with some professional groups was a lack of public relations skills, particularly in the initial stages – 'A lot of toes were trodden on. If I were setting up a new venture I would spend 90 per cent of my time on public relations and 10 per cent on the clinic. They seemed unaware of the importance of PR and of their image. Their image has improved. They were very cavalier at first... Was it that they didn't see it as important as long as the young people got the service? Is it me being pedantic?'

Two of the Milton Keynes steering group thought that work with social services had been the least successful aspect of the team's efforts. It was said that the reorganisation of the local social services had led to some lack of continuity of staff. Social services staff were said to have other priorities, but steering group members thought that not enough attention was paid to the contraceptive and counselling needs of young people in care, and particularly of those leaving care.

The contacts with the youth service were thought not to have been successful by two of the Milton Keynes team members and by some managers and team members in City and Hackney. One of the Milton Keynes team members pointed to disagreement in the team on priorities as far as the youth service was concerned – 'We could have had counselling sessions in the youth clubs at no extra cost. I think the youth workers would have set it up for us – rooms, appointments...We had a lot of arguments about this...'

But in City and Hackney, team members thought the problem lay in the way that youth workers worked with young people – 'Youth workers' work is much more unstructured, so that for them to bring in people like us with a structure and needs – like one hour sessions, a quiet room – many youth clubs are not geared to that. We also need small groups, so we need other staff to offer something "good" to the others. For example, if we're working with the girls we need something for the boys... It is very different from working in schools, because schools are structured...'

A manager thought there had been a possible problem because CHYPP had not had a male worker – 'If we'd had a male worker in CHYPP we might have got a better foothold in the clubs. Girls will come to Brook, but it's the boys you want to hook at the youth club. They won't talk about these things to a woman...' Brook staff also felt that more input could have been made into youth clubs, particularly in working with youth workers to attract young men into the Brook clinic to discuss relationships and responsibilities.

Another manager thought there were certain local issues which had affected the work in youth clubs – 'The one resource you need to get anywhere is time, especially in Hackney. Even when the money is available you need a long time, and if you're going to do participative work you've got to get the communities involved. They have an over-elaborate committee structure in voluntary organisations. A lot of time is needed in groundwork so that blocks don't come up later...'

There were comments that CHYPP had not established much contact with the gynaecologists in the district, and Brook staff thought this was one of the least successful aspects of the project's work. It was clear both in City and Hackney and South Sefton that little contact or collaboration had been established with gynaecologists. In Milton Keynes, because of the agency agreement with BPAS, the situation was rather different.

Some Brook staff thought the liaison between CHYPP and Brook was the least successful aspect of the project's work with other professionals and agencies, and one Brook staff member thought there were messages to be drawn from this – 'They didn't have any supervision. They didn't answer to anyone. There was no critique. It could have been avoided by having a proper legitimate steering group. There was nobody in charge – no leadership...'

The lack of success with schools in South Sefton was illustrated by one of the PACE team members – 'We invited every headteacher to our Open Day and sent out information packs and no-one came – we got no response at all... It's the Catholic population. We have to tread so carefully... It couldn't have been avoided. It means that we've had to be so discreet about our publicity. The kids themselves need us to be discreet from a family point of view...'

An adviser thought there were more reasons for the lack of success with teachers – 'They're not antagonistic – just careful to keep themselves covered at all times... It will take time. Schools are under a lot of pressure. It might be important to us, but if you're a head of a school who's going to take on financial responsibility it's not a priority. I can imagine that PACE may have found it disheartening, but given my experience – you have to accept it and use the system...'

Other South Sefton staff and managers thought that contact with the family planning and health authority staff had been the least successful aspect, mainly because there had been so few referrals and lack of liaison.

A team member thought that the problems might have been avoided by more direct contact and invitations to visit, but there was a feeling among the team that the health authority staff could have done more themselves to establish contact. There were also thought to be differences in approach and attitudes. One manager commented – 'They were on a different wavelength really. PACE was an informal drop-in service, and they were available most of the time, whereas the family planning clinic staff have a number of different roles, working as health visitors, school nurses and only doing sessions in family planning clinics...'

Liaison with GPs was thought to be difficult in all three areas, but none of those who mentioned it as being the least successful aspect of the projects' work had any concrete suggestions about how the liaison might have been made more successful. It was clear that contact with GPs who represented such a wide spectrum of interests was found to be particularly hard to set up and maintain, and, given the difficulties, the teams found other priorities.

Some of the lack of successful collaboration with family planning staff and GPs, as well as health authority staff, was thought to be a result of the different approach of the project teams to providing a contraceptive and pregnancy counselling service for young people. The projects were said to offer an informal, non-judgmental service which was said to be different from that offered by GPs and family planning clinics. It was suggested that this difference in philosophy and practice led to some misunderstanding of the projects on the part of some groups of professionals, particularly those who were involved in direct service provision to young people.

There was an underlying feeling in all three areas that the projects saw different kinds of people from those who went to GPs and family planning clinics, and that therefore the latter should not have felt threatened by the projects and should have collaborated more. One South Sefton manager said – 'The patients who go to PACE are the type who wouldn't go near a GP anyway...' This assumption was not borne out either by the statistics or by the interviews with young people, but it was very much entrenched in the thinking of both managers and projects teams in all three areas. It is discussed in some detail in Chapter 14 since the nature of the actual and potential clientele is of considerable importance in assessing the ways in which services for young people should be designed.

Particular contribution of the projects to the work of professionals
We asked the teams and managers whether the projects offered professionals or other agencies anything that they could not get elsewhere.

The vast majority of respondents in City and Hackney and Milton Keynes and all the respondents in South Sefton thought the projects in their areas had done so.

But what had they offered that was so special? There were interesting differences in response among the three areas. In City and Hackney the most frequently mentioned unique feature offered by the project to professionals was training, while in Milton Keynes and South Sefton it was said to be expertise in dealing with the contraceptive, counselling and sex education needs of young people. Milton Keynes respondents mentioned the provision of resources more than those in the other two areas, while more respondents in South Sefton spoke of the provision of an acceptable service to which professionals could refer young people.

The provision of training and resources as a unique contribution by the projects to the needs of professionals offers an interesting commentary on the existing provision of these facilities, both within the districts and on a national level. In all three areas there was thought to be a need for training and helping professionals to deal with young people's contraceptive and counselling needs. Training courses and resources were said to be available, for example, from the FPA and other national agencies, but these were said to be expensive by both project team members and managers.

What exactly did the teams offer and what were the long-term implications of offering such facilities? In City and Hackney a project team member explained – 'It's the sort of training we've been offering – for example to the residential social workers – in their own setting, in their own time and tailored to their needs. The FPA courses are not free. We offered free and tailor-made training and agreed it with them. We asked them what they wanted. Similarly with the schools. We could do it after school. And we've been able to offer one to one back-up and support. We've been available. We've been more flexible than, for example, a central body offering a three day training course. We're local – and we've quite often worked with young people in the same school...'

The stress on offering something which was 'local' came up again in comments by a steering group member in City and Hackney – 'People would not have gone to the FPA education service because it's not local. We're a little more flexible and it was something we offered which was linked to services, so immediate referral was possible. And there's a range of possible services, family planning, pregnancy testing and health education... CHYPP has been able to influence a lot of levels. Young people don't like the existing services anyway. We've got to work on where we see people...'

Local provision of resources and support, with instant access, was also a point made in both Milton Keynes and South Sefton. One of the Milton Keynes team summarised their special contribution – 'We provided easy access to the resources on our topic and information on speakers, the law and all the aspects surrounding sexuality and young people. They could get all this on the end of a phone from Brook or the FPA, but with us they could drop in, discuss it and see resources. We gave them support on the spot. They could get support elsewhere but not so easily. *We* went to *them*. We took the services to them – touted for business. The teachers were really keen but they're so busy. They said on the teachers' day that they wanted "to be spoon-fed"...'

Two questions which must arise are whether this instant and intensive help and support was really necessary and whether this kind of help could have come from health education or health promotion departments, either through their own staff or in acting as facilitators. In all three areas it was thought that such resources could not have been provided within existing health education or health promotion departments, and it was generally agreed that the professionals who were offered the training and resources found it useful and beneficial. However, there are clearly important questions around the provision of such facilities which are said to be needed and appreciated by professionals, and they are discussed in Chapter 14.

One of the managers in South Sefton thought that the particular contribution of the project to professionals was that they could influence mainstream services with their way of working – 'Sometimes you need projects for others to watch – and then you can transfer them into the mainstream...' It remains to be seen how transferable such projects are, and the extent to which their unique contribution can be safeguarded when subsumed into the 'mainstream'.

The projects' work with young people
Most successful aspects of projects' work with young people
There were clear differences between the areas in the assessment by the project teams and their managers and advisers of the most successful aspects of their work with young people. In all three areas, the single most frequently mentioned successful aspect was the counselling given to young people, but there were marked differences between the projects and within the projects on the importance attached to it. It was mentioned by two thirds of the team and managers in South Sefton. In Milton Keynes it was cited

by half the managers and advisers, but only one of the team members and one of the doctors. In City and Hackney it was mentioned by all the Brook staff and doctors, but by only one manager and none of the project team members.

All the team members and two of the managers in South Sefton added that group work was also the most successful aspect of PACE's work with young people. None of the respondents in the other two areas mentioned group work. Three of the South Sefton managers thought the work with young men was the most successful aspect of the project's work.

In Milton Keynes, two of the project team and a doctor thought the work with young people in schools had been the most successful aspect of their work with young people, a view held by half the managers and advisers. Three of the CHYPP project team and one of the managers and advisers cited work with young people in schools, but it was not mentioned at all in South Sefton.

It was interesting that only three respondents – two managers in Milton Keynes and a project team member in South Sefton – thought that the young people's *clinic* had been the most successful aspect of their projects' work with young people.

Few other aspects were cited, but there were mentions of the work with young people in residential care in City and Hackney, the provision of a local service in both Milton Keynes and South Sefton, service developments in general in City and Hackney and work with drug users in South Sefton.

The differences between the projects and within the projects clearly reflected the personal interests of the respondents. The fact that none of the CHYPP team rated the direct provision by Brook of the counselling and clinic service to young people as the most successful aspect of the project's service to young people was perhaps not surprising, but it helps to explain some of the problems in collaboration and communication between the two parts of the project. It could be argued that the Brook counselling and clinic service to young people was demonstrably much more successful than those in the other two areas, if only simply in terms of numbers seen. It could also be argued that it was more successful than other parts of the CHYPP project, again in terms of numbers of young people seen.

The message from this type of success rating is that people tend to measure success in very subjective terms, and it underlines the fact that objective measures of success are difficult to establish. Numbers alone are not enough, but subjective ratings are no basis on which to build policy in the absence of other criteria. They can give important clues to success and can indicate problem areas, but should not be taken in isolation.

Ingredients of success

Why were these aspects of the services thought to be the most successful? In general the quality and appropriateness of the service offered were thought to have been the crucial factors. A Milton Keynes team member summarised the views of respondents in the district who thought the counselling had been the most successful aspect of their work – 'We made it a service where they would feel comfortable. We gave them the answers. We never patronised anyone and we never sent them away...'

The work in schools was also thought to be of a high quality and appropriate to the needs of young people in both Milton Keynes and City and Hackney. A CHYPP team member gave her reasons for thinking this work successful – 'We were using methods which engaged young people in discussion in a way different from most of their school work. Presented in that way it will engage anyone's interest. And people want to know...'

What were the ingredients of success? The quality of staff was the most frequently mentioned factor in City and Hackney and Milton Keynes while the informality of the project and the team was mentioned most often in South Sefton.

In City and Hackney, many comments on the quality of staff were related to the expertise and experience the Brook staff brought to the work with young people. A Brook staff member summarised the special qualities she thought Brook staff had offered – 'We've got experience in running a service. We've got our standards. We know what young people accept and feel comfortable with. It's our style of work as much as anything. We trade on our reputation... A lot of youngsters think of Brook as a place they can go and are welcome. I think it's that we provide a service that they use on their terms. It's medical – but they *choose* to come to us. The things they value – it's the friendliness, the informality and the confidentiality...'

These words were echoed about the project team staff in the other areas. In South Sefton a team member summarised the ingredients of their success with young people as she saw them – 'Confidentiality, respect and patience...' And in Milton Keynes too, the informality and friendliness of the staff, combined with 'trustworthiness' and expertise were mentioned by both team members and managers.

The location and informality of the service setting was thought to be important in both Milton Keynes and South Sefton. A non-clinical setting for services for young people had been high on the agenda when these projects were being planned in these areas, and managers and staff alike thought it an important ingredient of success. The availability of a drop-in service was also thought important by some respondents in these two areas.

In South Sefton the work with young men was thought to be the most successful part of the PACE service by some managers, who thought the project had helped young male drug users, some of whom might be at risk of HIV through sharing needles, and others of whom needed other help which PACE team members could provide. It was said that drug workers sent young drug users to PACE where they could be given condoms. There was no substantive evidence to back this claim, although, as the statistics show, approximately half the clients of the PACE project during the monitoring period were young men or boys, most of whom came for condoms. The PACE staff were thought to be very good at working with the young men, and the quality of the staff was cited as the main factor in attracting them to the project.

Least successful aspects of the projects' work with young people
Nearly half the team members and managers in Milton Keynes and South Sefton could not think of any particular aspect of the work with young people which had been particularly unsuccessful. One third of the South Sefton respondents thought that work with young people in schools had been the least successful aspect of their work, mainly because of the problems of access to schools outlined in the previous section. One of the PACE project team thought that their publicity to young people had been unsuccessful. She thought this was related to the amount of time they had been able to put into 'getting round to enough people...' These were the only two unsuccessful aspects of work with young people mentioned in South Sefton.

In City and Hackney, two members of the team and a manager thought there had been a lack of success in working with young people in youth clubs, a view shared by a team member in Milton Keynes. In both areas, team members thought 'one-off sessions', wherever they were held, were the least successful part of their work with young people, and in both areas, managers mentioned the clinics as having been the least successful part of the projects' work.

In Milton Keynes there were criticisms by both managers and team members of the two bases other than the Bakehouse from which the project had tried to operate a counselling service. One was in a neighbourhood centre and one was in the Barnhouse, a youth centre in the city centre. There had been virtually no clients at either location. The main criticism in City and Hackney came from the Brook staff, who thought that the lack of liaison between Brook and CHYPP had been the least successful aspect of the project's work with young people.

Reasons for lack of success

In Milton Keynes, it was thought that the lack of success in the two bases other than the Bakehouse could have been avoided by choosing more suitable locations. An adviser thought one of the locations had been totally inappropriate from the start – 'It's not a place where young people want to go. It's considered a shady and criminal area – a very downmarket area. If you want to flog stolen goods that's where you go...'

There was some doubt about whether the venue in a youth centre was very suitable either, partly because there was little 'passing trade'. It was pointed out many times in Milton Keynes that there was little travel by young people between the various 'villages' or neighbourhoods which make up the city, and many respondents, both professionals and project team members and managers, thought that a central location would have been helpful for a young people's project. The question of location was also brought up by respondents who thought the clinic had not been successful in Milton Keynes. There was a feeling that the premises in the Bakehouse were too cramped and might not have attracted young people who wanted a clinic service rather than a counselling service, possibly because the premises were so informal.

The lack of success with young people in youth clubs in Milton Keynes and City and Hackney was thought to be due partly to the nature of the dispersed organisation of the youth service, which meant that a lot of individual contacts with youth workers had to be made and continually followed up, and partly due to the differences between the views of the youth workers and the project team members of what was important in working with young people. One of the CHYPP team members commented – 'It's the way the youth service is geared. They see youth provision as related to leisure and sports facilities – no in-depth thinking about anything...'

One of the Milton Keynes team members thought the team could have been more persistent in trying to get through to youth clubs, and it did appear that in both areas the difficulties of access, combined with differences in philosophy, discouraged the teams from trying to establish ongoing contacts with groups of young people in the relevant age-group who could well have been in need of their services.

The question of the lack of success of 'one-off' sessions was mentioned in both Milton Keynes and City and Hackney. A You 2 team member summarised the views of respondents in both areas – 'I don't think one-off sessions with young people are useful. You can't cover contraception and relationships in one session. You can only introduce it – certainly with the under-16s... You've got to make the point and say you can't do one-offs with teachers. They must look to themselves to provide proper sex education from within the curriculum...' A City and Hackney team member agreed – 'You need to do a lot more groundwork – training the trainers. It should be built into teachers' training courses and youth workers' and residential social workers' training. It is qualitatively different from other health education...'

The Brook/CHYPP liaison was thought to have been the least successful aspect of the City and Hackney project's work with young people by most of the Brook staff. We asked how the problems could have been avoided. The need for structured systems of contact and collaboration from the start were stressed. It was also felt that there should have been more collaboration on the actual delivery of services to young people. Brook would have liked to have had a drop-in centre for young people and more contact with young men, which they had developed in other centres. There was said to be no evidence of CHYPP having referred young people to the Brook clinic. One staff member said – 'The ideal would have been them ringing up several times a week to refer young people to us. They haven't asked us for help, information, leaflets. I would have imagined them having regular orders for Brook leaflets and using them... These problems could have been avoided if we had agreed on a common aim and worked together to achieve it...'

Another Brook staff member thought that one of the problems in lack of collaboration between Brook and CHYPP had arisen through CHYPP deciding not to work with boys because they did not have a male worker. Boys were unlikely to come to a clinic unless they were encouraged to do so. Brook staff felt that CHYPP staff had not encouraged any young people to come to Brook.

Particular groups of young people helped by project
In assessing the success of the projects we were interested to know whether the team members and managers thought there were any particular groups of young people whom the project had been able to help. We knew that there were certain groups at whom they had aimed, like the young people

who did not or would not use other services, but we wanted to know whether they thought they had been successful in reaching them.

Most of those interviewed thought that the project had helped particular groups of young people, but there were interesting differences between the three projects and among the staff and managers. Few groups were mentioned by more than three or four respondents in any area. In City and Hackney it was thought that the project had helped young people in care and young mothers using pregnancy as a way out of their problems. In Milton Keynes young people with unsympathetic GPs, sexually active teenagers, young people on YTS schemes and schoolchildren were mentioned by more than one respondent. In South Sefton, the project was thought to have helped unemployed girls who became pregnant, drug users and young men. Young people from ethnic minorities were mentioned by only one respondent – a manager in City and Hackney who thought the project staff had been able to understand their problems. Young people from Catholic communities were also mentioned by only one respondent – a manager in South Sefton who thought that the siting of the project in a general community centre helped those who would not wish to be seen entering a clinic.

Respondents found it difficult to say why they thought particular groups of young people had been helped. The general impression was that no particular groups had been targeted, but that some groups had been more exposed to the project team's attentions than others. It was perhaps surprising that there was so little agreement on which groups had been most helped by the projects in any of the areas.

Whether project offered young people anything they could not get elsewhere

There was almost universal agreement that the projects offered young people something they could not get elsewhere. An accessible service and counselling were the two most commonly mentioned aspects of the projects' services in Milton Keynes and South Sefton. There were clear differences between the assessment of the CHYPP team and managers and the Brook staff about what was unique in the City and Hackney project. The Brook staff thought the counselling they offered was something the young people could not get elsewhere in the district, while the project team members thought the sex education and support for young women who were continuing with pregnancies were unique features of the CHYPP project.

Overall assessment of the projects

In seeking to establish an overall assessment of the projects, we asked the project team members and their managers the same series of questions we had asked the professionals, reported in Chapter 11. We added a few extra questions which gave the teams and their managers an opportunity to explore in more detail the reasons for things working well or not working well. Our aim, as always in this evaluation, was to provide others planning young people's services with insights and information into the problems and opportunities involved in exercises of this kind.

Strengths of the projects

There was no general consensus in any area on the main strengths of the projects in meeting the Department of Health's aims of reducing unwanted pregnancy among young people, although the most frequently mentioned strength in both Milton Keynes and South Sefton was said to be the informality of the project. This factor was hardly mentioned in City and Hackney. The quality of the staff was also thought to be an important strength in Milton Keynes and to a lesser extent in South Sefton, but was not mentioned at all in City and Hackney. There was very little agreement in City and Hackney on the strengths of the project, and most possible strengths were each mentioned by only one or two respondents. Outreach work and the provision of extra services for young people were the only factors which were mentioned by more than two respondents in City and Hackney.

The CHYPP project team laid emphasis on the developmental nature of their work and the way in which they had worked with young women who had become pregnant. They cited in particular their work in the ante-natal or post-natal clinics or in the 'young mums' group. One team member described what she thought the team had provided – 'The more you have young mums together, discussing the responsibility of actually bringing up a young child, the more they will think about their future fertility...'

The provision of extra services was thought to be important by Brook staff. The use of 'dedicated' short-term funding was thought important by a manager – 'A short timetable forces your mind to get on with things quickly. You've got to achieve some things quickly...' This view was not shared with respondents in any of the areas, the majority of whom thought the short-term funding was a distinct disadvantage, and thought that insufficient time had been given to the projects to achieve anything.

An adviser in City and Hackney explained what she saw as the difficulties, and the strengths of CHYPP in attempting to overcome them

– 'It's a very slow process to build up a network of trust. We've done it here. Changes take such a long time and many factors contribute to the process. You need services and communities who can respond when it's needed. There is no way in an inner-city area but to work slowly like CHYPP has... Their strength is their process of trying to work with community groups outside the NHS...'

The informality of the approach of the project teams was thought important in both Milton Keynes and South Sefton by both team members and managers, who often linked this view to praise for the quality of the staff and the availability of a drop-in service with instant pregnancy testing. Some of the respondents thought the much- criticised project premises in each area also helped ·add to the informality which they thought was attractive to young people.

A manager in South Sefton summarised the strengths of the project as she saw them – 'Availability – they're there all the time – commitment and enthusiasm...' And this perceived commitment and enthusiasm of both the You 2 and PACE teams communicated itself to managers and advisers in both areas. Neither team was thought to have had an easy ride, and a Milton Keynes adviser thought one of the main strengths of the You 2 team was their perseverance – 'They worked hard and they learned hard. They were tremendously energetic and enterprising. They didn't let themselves be too depressed by inevitable setbacks. Considering how many people came and left they were amazing...'

Weaknesses of the projects

As we saw in Chapter 11, the main weaknesses of the projects according to the professionals were centred round lack of publicity and contact with other professionals like themselves who were also working with young people. Some of them also criticised the premises in which the projects were based. The project teams and their managers had rather different views of the main weaknesses of the projects in meeting the aims of the Department of Health.

The most frequently mentioned weakness was said to be a lack of resources. This was cited by most of the team members and managers in City and Hackney, and by most of the managers in South Sefton. In Milton Keynes there was more concern that the aims of the Department of Health in setting up the projects had been too narrow, a view shared by project team members in City and Hackney, while in both Milton Keynes and South Sefton the project premises were thought to be a weakness by some managers and team members. The short-term nature of the project funding was thought a problem by some respondents in all three areas.

It was striking that few respondents, apart from clinic doctors and Brook staff, commented on lack of publicity as being a weakness of the projects – the main perceived weakness cited by professionals. Other weaknesses mentioned by team members and managers included starting from scratch, staff changes and conflicts, lack of staff experience, management problems, the unsympathetic attitude of other professionals and lack of clinic facilities. There were individual comments on the projects not being innovative enough, having no baseline information on teenage behaviour, experiencing difficulty in getting NHS abortions for their clients, deviating from the original concept of the projects, and of having made no impact on teenage pregnancies. One project team member, in a sideways swipe at the evaluation, thought that one of the weaknesses of the project had been the need to record too many details about clients.

There was clearly little consensus about the weaknesses of the projects in the above catalogue, apart from the insistence on lack of resources. Considering that these projects had had special 'dedicated' funding of a not inconsiderable amount, it was interesting to explore the reasons given for seeing lack of resources as a weakness.

In spite of the fact that the CHYPP team had four members as well as clerical support, and had had the benefit of a separate clinic team in the Brook staff, three out of four project team members thought there were too few of them to do the job they had been given, particularly in training other professionals. The training of those working in sexual abuse, special needs, HIV and AIDS was mentioned and it must be questioned whether this was really part of the remit of the project team. The perceived lack of resources, combined with the short-term nature of the funding was thought by some managers in City and Hackney to have affected the security of the team members. There was a feeling that it was difficult to recruit and retain team members who had no security of employment at the end of the funding period, and that this factor had led to two of the original team members leaving some months before the end of the monitoring period.

In Milton Keynes, too, project team members thought there had been insufficient resources to do all they wanted to do, including involving young people's families. Managers were also concerned about the perceived lack of resources, which some related to the short-term nature of the funding. One manager thought the resources had not allowed for the need for training of the project team – 'We underestimated the amount of time we had to put

253

into training. We hadn't considered the training needs of the staff and the role of the trainers. We should have had more time for training before we started the service provision. It's difficult to do both together...'

The small size of the team was thought to be a weakness in South Sefton by some managers who thought that with more resources more could have been achieved in outreach work in particular.

It was interesting that relatively few of the respondents thought lack of publicity was a problem and that these critics were restricted largely to the clinic doctors, who saw fewer young people in their sessions than they had expected. Lack of publicity was also thought to be a weakness by the Brook staff who were similarly engaged in providing a clinic service, but, in addition, had very little contact with the project team. The Brook staff were worried that the CHYPP team were not mentioning the Brook facilities to those with whom they had contact in their outreach work, and there was a general criticism of lack of posters or publicity locally.

The criticism of the premises in both Milton Keynes and South Sefton was sharp among team members and doctors as well as some advisers. In Milton Keynes a team member thought that insufficient thought had been given to the problems which might ensue from locating the project in a building which had a plethora of 'fringe groups' – 'That was the biggest mistake ever. The health authority knew about its reputation because they told us...' Doctors in both areas were concerned about the medical facilities and commented on potential lack of confidentiality as well as inadequate facilities and access, and other managers and advisers thought it a weakness that the facilities did not allow for IUD fitting. Although some respondents were keen on the siting of the PACE project in a community centre, others thought the actual centre was unsuitable – 'The impression is that it's full of old people doing dancing...'

The question of whether the original Department of Health aims had been too narrow exercised many respondents throughout these interviews. Some thought they had been not only too narrow but misguided, as this CHYPP team member explained – 'There was a weakness in how the projects were conceived. There were lots of assumptions that unwanted pregnancy was a problem. It was set up very much around pregnancy counselling which seemed to be too late when they were already pregnant. Clearly there are young women who get pregnant who don't want to be but need knowledge and skills to use the pregnancy. Approaching it in that way is different from preventing unwanted pregnancy. It's a service response and I think that we've shifted the emphasis back along the implicit causal chain...'

It is perhaps difficult to discuss the relative strengths and weaknesses of projects of this kind in meeting certain objectives when some of the leading players think the game ought to have been played according to a different set of rules, or even that a different game altogether should have been underway.

Success of the projects in meeting DOH criteria

We knew that not all team members and managers were enthusiastic about the aims of the projects as laid down by the Department, but we asked them how successful they thought the projects had been in meeting those aims. There was a reluctance to comment by project team members in particular, with most of the CHYPP and PACE teams saying they could not say how successful they had been. Some managers and advisers in all three areas agreed with them that it was impossible to judge the success of the projects at that stage according to those criteria, particularly in the absence of easily accessible statistics. One adviser in City and Hackney summarised her position which reflected that of others:

> It's impossible to evaluate short-term programmes with long-term measures. It's not like that. Measuring changes in attitude and behaviour is very different. You end up describing and counting services. Do long-term indicators help us make choices about service provision? Health education is getting a bit stronger about saying this...

A manager in City and Hackney went further – 'I think they were very unrealistic aims of the Department. Would numbers have been worse or better without the project? We were assuming that greater knowledge and understanding of sexuality would reduce the risk of pregnancy. If we've reduced pregnancies it's impossible in an area like this to see whether it's due to us or whether it's national or whether it's because of what they've seen on "Eastenders". It's very difficult to get a control district...'

A Brook respondent thought the question was impossible to quantify – 'Are we asking by how much percentage we've reduced pregnancy? We've been asking that question for years. I honestly believe that if there weren't a Brook, the unwanted pregnancy rate would be higher, but I can't say by how much. The more sessions there are available the more the rate will go down. But no matter how good the service is, there's a proportion of people who don't want help. You can't behave like the thought police...'

Very few respondents thought the projects had been very successful or even successful by the criteria implicit in the aims of the project as laid

255

down by the Department of Health, and, even then, most qualified their comments by restricting them to the people they saw – 'We managed to get however many hundreds of clients who presumably would have got pregnant otherwise. But it's terribly difficult to evaluate. One can only speculate...'

The majority of respondents who felt able to comment thought the projects had been fairly successful. Most stressed the limited time period available, the relatively modest attendance figures and the difficulty of measuring the impact in terms of prevented pregnancies. Respondents stressed that perhaps anything was better than nothing, as this clinic doctor explained – 'We just touched the tip of the iceberg. If you look at the figures I don't think we had a big impact on unwanted pregnancy. You've got to think that anything you do must be worth it. But one clinic in Bootle is not going to make much difference...' Her view was echoed by a team member in Milton Keynes – 'You can't tell in eighteen months. The project would have to be here a lot longer. It was a drop in the ocean...'

Success according to criteria used by team members and managers
Since the team members and managers were so reluctant to measure the projects according to the criteria laid down by the Department of Health, and indeed had often rejected the criteria as being unrealistic or difficult to use as measurements of achievement, we asked them what criteria they themselves would use for assessing the success or otherwise of the project in their area.

Relatively few respondents thought that movements in pregnancy or abortion rates were relevant criteria for measuring the achievements of the projects, and some managers thought they were irrelevant to their success or failure.

The project teams and doctors in Milton Keynes and South Sefton were almost unanimous in saying that they would measure the success by the numbers of young people attending and returning to the projects. Most of the Brook staff agreed, but this view was held by only one of the CHYPP team. Management and advisers in all three areas rarely mentioned numbers of attenders.

Client satisfaction was thought to be important by management in City and Hackney and Milton Keynes and by individual team members in all three areas. Other professional satisfaction was a criterion mentioned by most of the team members and managers in City and Hackney, and by managers in South Sefton and Milton Keynes.

Apart from these main criteria of client attendance figures, client satisfaction and professional satisfaction, few other criteria of success were mentioned and these were usually cited by only one respondent. They included the commitment by the steering group to the project, the number of schools wishing to continue the sex education programme initiated by the project, the integration of sex education with education on AIDS, the extent of the project's input into the health authority's policy, the continued funding by the health authority of at least part of the project at the end of the central funding period and changes in client behaviour.

The agreement that numbers of attenders were relevant criteria of success was often linked to an observation that the projects had done well according to these criteria. Team members who felt this way sometimes added that people were satisfied and returned time and again, as this South Sefton team member commented – 'Big numbers have used the project and I'd measure it by the general response of people who've come here and said they liked it and come back again...' Some respondents thought it was more important to explore the type of attenders in addition to the numbers of attenders.

How successful did the respondents think the projects had been according to their own criteria? The project team members were much more prepared to comment on this question and indeed all but one thought their projects had been successful or very successful according to their own criteria. A member of the CHYPP team, who had selected a number of criteria relating to professional use, sex education work, input into health authority policy and work in the ante-natal and post-natal clinics, commented that the project had been very successful – 'I've picked the criteria I think would look good. There's no way in which we will be able to relate the work of a project like CHYPP to the pregnancy rate of under-25s...'

And the selection of criteria by the project teams was not surprising. They could not look at the longer-term because the statistics on pregnancies or abortions were not yet available. They had to look at what they had got, and most of them thought it was very good, like this Milton Keynes team member – 'You have to look at the numbers – 600 people, 180 visits to clinics, contact with 3,000 students...'

Most respondents who commented on numbers of attendances were often speaking in ignorance of what had happened, and in any case had no control group, as some pointed out. Some Brook staff, who could put the figures into the context of other districts, were rather disappointed that the project had not attracted more under-18-year-olds to the clinic and also commented on the high proportion of clinic attenders who came from other areas – 'We didn't see tremendous numbers of very young people, local people or socially deprived people. We didn't see many local people. This is where CHYPP could have played a role...'

Some respondents were reluctant to play 'the numbers game', even though they recognised the need for objective criteria. A Brook staff member said – 'No researcher can quantify the success. For every woman that's come to us for help – that may have stopped another unwanted pregnancy...'

In selecting client satisfaction as a criterion of success, most respondents could not give a reason for their rating other than citing the numbers of people who returned to the project. Professional satisfaction was measured by the teams saying they had been asked to return or to provide more sessions, while managers had sometimes had feedback from professionals and sometimes relied on the feedback from the team members.

Many respondents qualified their remarks about the success of the project according to their criteria with the proviso that the projects had achieved a lot in a short time period. This stress on the limited time available to build up new services was a recurrent theme in these interviews, and clearly dominated the thoughts of team members and managers alike.

Problems or difficulties affecting success
All the respondents in Milton Keynes and South Sefton thought that the projects in their areas had had particular problems or difficulties which had made them less successful than they could have been. In City and Hackney, this view was shared by all the Brook respondents, by three out of four CHYPP team members, but by less than two-thirds of the managers.

The problems which were thought to have affected the success of the projects varied from project to project. In City and Hackney, the main problems were thought to relate to staff changes, the short-term funding leading to insecurity among staff and to the lack of liaison between CHYPP and Brook. In Milton Keynes and South Sefton, the project premises in each area were thought to have caused problems, particularly in the view of the team members, and there were also thought to have been managerial problems in both areas. The short-term nature of the funding was thought a problem by managers in both areas, but was not mentioned in this context by team members. In Milton Keynes there was said to have been a problem in getting locum cover for the clinic doctor when she was not able to attend, and in all three areas there had been problems with supplies and equipment.

The problem of getting and keeping good staff on short-term projects is not unique to these projects, but it should be kept firmly in mind when 'demonstration' projects are set up. There can be no doubt that some of the problems encountered by these teams related to the fact that most staff had to be recruited on a short-term basis with no guarantee of a job at the end of the eighteen-month period. A CHYPP team member explained some of the drawbacks – 'Health authority rates are less than if you did this work anywhere else. People have to be very committed. That and the short-term project make it difficult to develop staff and a team and career progression. On the other hand the project wouldn't have existed if it hadn't been set up as a short-term project...'

The loss of two staff members after less than a year had undoubtedly affected CHYPP's work in the view of one of the new members – 'You lose consistency. They had begun to network with different groups, and new staff have to begin the process of acquainting themselves with the work before you can get down to the business...'

An adviser in Milton Keynes thought that staffing problems of this kind were endemic in education, social services and the health authority – 'It's about recruiting at the appropriate level. We always want more than we will pay for. Only good pay gets continuity of staff. Otherwise you get people looking for better opportunities two months after the project has started...'

The problem of the lack of liaison between Brook and CHYPP was a theme running through the interviews in City and Hackney. There was no doubt in the minds of Brook staff that CHYPP's perceived lack of support for Brook had made the project less successful than it could have been, although none of the CHYPP team mentioned it as a problem. Perhaps this was not surprising, as one of the Brook staff commented – 'I think CHYPP has had very little impact on the work of Brook. CHYPP might just as well not have existed as far as Brook was concerned...'

Both the Milton Keynes and South Sefton teams felt there should have been clearer management guidelines and support. As one Milton Keynes team member commented – 'We had to make the priorities but we didn't have the expertise...' And in South Sefton there was a general feeling of lack of support 'from the higher echelons'. One of the messages for others who might plan services was summarised by a team member – 'There should have been more attempt in the beginning to make sure everyone knew and accepted PACE as a very important part of what was happening in the community under the auspices of the health authority. We've constantly had to prove ourselves...'

The long delay in getting the PACE project premises ready was also thought to have been a management problem and to have affected the success of the project. There were criticisms of endless bureaucracy in getting supplies and equipment, which were echoed in the other projects but appeared to have been particularly acute in South Sefton.

There were also thought to have been some problems in that the staff members each had different line managers in South Sefton. An adviser thought this made it difficult for the team members to work as a team. This problem arose in the projects set up by the Department of Health to provide health care for single homeless people, (Williams and Allen, 1989). It does seem to be important for short-term projects of this kind, staffed by a multidisciplinary team, to have clear lines of accountability to one manager or set of managers who can take quick decisions and can cut through the bureaucracy. Interdisciplinary management in situations like this only seems to get in the way of operational efficiency. Problems arose in the simplest of matters, for example, in the release of funding or in the sanctioning of activities. One adviser thought it very time-consuming for the team to have deal with three very busy managers individually on relatively straightforward matters. It could be argued that some of the problems the team encountered were due to what they described as 'a total lack of urgency'. There was a general feeling in both Milton Keynes and South Sefton that no one manager was supporting the team and presenting their views at a higher level.

There were problems in both areas about the 'holding of the budget', and there were continuing problems about gaining access to money for the day-to-day running of the projects or for expenditure which was thought necessary but had not been foreseen in the budgets prepared for the Department of Health. Health authority finance departments are not geared to the needs of short-term projects which need, by their very nature, to be flexible in their response to demands on them. This fact appeared not to have been anticipated by those managing the staff and budgets.

Problems with the location and physical characteristics of the premises were certainly thought to have affected the success of the projects in Milton Keynes and South Sefton. The South Sefton project had also suffered from break-ins, lack of security and the physical fabric of the building. In Milton Keynes there had been problems with the steep outside stairs leading to the project base and with the fact that toilet facilities were not part of the project premises.

What should have been done differently?

Given the problems described above, it was perhaps surprising that there was not an overwhelming consensus that some things should have been done differently. But most of the managers and advisers and one of the team members in City and Hackney did not think that anything should have been done differently. This view was shared by two managers in Milton Keynes and a manager and team member in South Sefton.

Looking back on the history of the projects, there were three main areas in which respondents recommended change: better planning of policies and staff roles, a better management structure, and more resources. There were also recommendations from Milton Keynes and South Sefton that there should have been better premises and location for the projects, from Milton Keynes that there should have been different staff training, from South Sefton that there should have been fewer and different priorities, from Milton Keynes that there should have been more contact with schools and health authority staff, and from Brook staff that there should have been more Brook/CHYPP contact and collaboration.

But how would the teams and their managers have gone about the task of better planning of policies and roles? A CHYPP team member thought the short-term nature of the project had made it very difficult:

> Eighteen months was too short. If we'd had a longer time-scale we'd have spent more time on groundwork with youth workers. We'd have taken more time to train ourselves more and to plan more. We'd have found out what people wanted. We might have gone round more. We just launched in. It would have been more possible to evaluate it in terms of counting pregnancies. It's not possible to show change in numbers. We'd have done some survey of schools and what they were doing – get some kind of baseline. That kind of thing would have been useful, not only in planning but in evaluating the project. It might have been worth trying to make the steering group more effective. We could have brought in people from education and social services at an earlier stage. But it was difficult for them to have a role, and at the beginning there wasn't time for them to have a role. We had to get on with it. We should have done that, and then we'd have had people who knew what we were doing and the difficulties. They would have been involved. The steering group didn't meet in the last year of the project...

This response is quoted in full since it encapsulated in a number of ways the problems faced by all three projects. In Milton Keynes, the steering group met frequently, even if not all the meetings were comfortable for the project team, but in South Sefton, the steering group, made up only of health authority staff, was said to have had a number of meetings cancelled, which left the team without a clear 'steer'.

Clarity of purpose and setting of priorities was felt to be lacking in both Milton Keynes and South Sefton, and even in City and Hackney, where the project coordinator had been party to the original bid to the Department of Health, there was a feeling that more preparation time should have been budgeted for. The problem was particularly acute in Milton Keynes and South Sefton where the majority of staff were appointed only weeks before the project started. There was felt to be precious little time for planning, let alone training, and, in the absence of very firm management guidelines, it was not surprising that team members felt themselves undersupported.

The Department of Health itself came in for criticism, not only for restricting the funding to eighteen months after it had been understood originally that the funding would be for three years, but also for failing to give more resources, as one CHYPP team member commented – 'It should have been set up with long-term funding and access to resources which would have given it higher status – space, money and workers...' The Department was also criticised for taking the project bids too much on trust and not involving itself closely enough with the question of whether the projects could deliver what they promised. A City and Hackney manager said – 'They should have said what processes they wanted evaluated. We probably should have focussed on fewer areas and concentrated hard on them. We tried to spread too thinly...'

One of the projects had wished to evaluate itself from the beginning and there were clear misgivings about the independent evaluators all the way through the projects in all three areas. In South Sefton, one of the team members was concerned that the constraints of the evaluation had affected the delivery of the services and the development of the project – 'Before the money was accepted from the Department there should have been a clear negotiating structure set up between whoever was doing the evaluating, the health authority and the project staff. There's been very little room for negotiating once the money was accepted. We felt under conditions – the staff of the project, who knew their clients and the area and were in touch with grass-roots feeling, couldn't change the set-up of the research...'

There was criticism in all three areas about the narrowness of the group within the health authority who set the projects up, and it was felt that better planning and more consultation with other professionals could have led to greater success. This was strongly felt in Milton Keynes, with particular reference to the family planning staff with whom there were such poor relations, but it also arose in City and Hackney, where it was thought that health visitors and school nurses, as well as family planning staff, could have been involved in the planning of the project to the benefit of both staff and clients. In all three areas there was concern about the lack of groundwork which had been done with GPs. It could be added that no groundwork appeared to have been done with the gynaecologists, but this, strangely, was only commented on by one respondent in the three areas – one of the clinic doctors.

The funding of the Brook sessions came in for criticism by Brook staff who felt that they had not received adequate funding for running the clinics and taking part in the project. The view was expressed that it would have been better if Brook had been given the funding and responsibility for running the project in City and Hackney. It was felt that there should have been much more activity with professionals and voluntary groups in informing them about the Brook clinics and counselling service, and in organising visits by individuals or groups of young people. There was also a strong feeling among Brook respondents that the steering group should have been more actively involved in the project and that the CHYPP team should have been more clearly accountable to management.

The question of better planning of policies and roles merged frequently with the question of better management, and comments on this came from team members and managers and advisers alike. There can be little doubt that the management of short-term demonstration projects of this kind is particularly difficult to incorporate into existing management structures where people may already have too much to do. None of the health authorities appeared to have solved this problem. In one area, the management appeared to have been devolved to project team level, while in the other two areas, there appeared to have been a number of people with some kind of management responsibility, which led to some confusion among the workers as well as feelings of lack of support.

The usefulness of setting up projects like these
What did the team members and managers think was the usefulness of setting up projects like these in three districts for a limited time period? There was no consensus of opinion on this. The most common view was that it was a useful exercise in developing a service model and stimulating innovation, but this view was held only by a third of all respondents, with

roughly equal proportions from each district. It was thought by one fifth of respondents to be useful in evaluating need.

Other factors were mentioned by less than a handful of respondents each, although some views were forcefully put. These included the feeling that such projects demonstrated need, that they increased local awareness of the issues, and that they had been valuable for the staff and managers taking part. Respondents often added a rider to their comments that the projects had been of only limited use because of the short time period and that their usefulness had been adversely affected by the threatened withdrawing of the service at the end of the central government funding period.

Although it was thought that the projects could stimulate innovation, few respondents mentioned their potential impact at a local level. A manager in South Sefton thought this was their main usefulness – 'I think in terms of innovation – if you are trying to show there are different ways of doing things to different disciplines. I'm a great believer in a research-based approach. Then it starts to challenge their assumptions about their way of doing things. It opens up minds. It starts the conversation...'

Managers in Milton Keynes agreed. One manager said, 'It demonstrates what can be done. It's an opportunity for people to try out new ideas...' And another from the same area thought that the fact that the projects were funded by the Department of Health and were to be evaluated by an outsider and written up for others to see would give them added status. There was support for central funding of such innovative schemes from a Milton Keynes manager who thought that it had given them freedom from the 'bureaucracy' of negotiating the planning and the funding with the health authority.

In City and Hackney an adviser thought that there were great advantages in projects of this kind – 'It gave us a chance to put into practice ways of working and to focus on certain issues. It's a demonstration project. Things will be written up more rigorously. We don't normally have time to do all this...'

A City and Hackney manager thought there was usefulness in learning from the experience of three different models, but queried the usefulness for the projects locally – 'It's a pity it's not for a longer period. By the time you get going and have learnt from your mistakes the project is finished. You have no time to put into practice the good things you've learnt...'

Another City and Hackney manager took a more cynical view, which was shared by others – 'It makes the Department of Health feel it's doing something. Three districts have got money they otherwise wouldn't have got. But it's no use unless someone learns something. Its use is in providing some way of disseminating the project. Learning the problems so that others can avoid making mistakes – that's the most useful thing...'

The managers tended to put some emphasis on 'learning from mistakes', which could be interpreted as not particularly comforting for the project team members, most of whom were very committed to the projects. Most commented on the short timescale to which they had been working – 'To take the services away at the end of the period seems quite contradictory. With one hand you give the community something and with the other you take it away...'

Transferability of projects as developed in the areas
Nearly 90 per cent of the project team members and managers thought the project as developed in their area could be transferred to other districts. Almost the same proportion of professionals interviewed had thought the same, but for different reasons. The team members and managers mostly thought that the projects offered good models and that the methods used would be applicable anywhere or at least in similar areas, whereas the professionals tended to turn the question round and say that young people had the same needs everywhere, a view expressed by few of the team members and managers.

It was perhaps not surprising that the team members and managers wanted to be positive about the transferability of the projects they had developed. All the South Sefton team members thought they had developed a good model, as one member summarised – 'It's easy to set up if it's done properly. It's not expensive to run, but it needs to be handled well – to get the informality...' In Milton Keynes too there was enthusiasm for the potential transferability of the model – 'Because it's something cheap to run, useful and much needed. The model is fantastic – a multidisciplinary team dealing with the problems of young people...' Another Milton Keynes member thought it was easy to set up and could train staff members very quickly – 'Anybody could learn to do the teaching side. I sat in with (team member) for a couple of sessions at (school). There was a bit of in-house discussion at the Bakehouse, but that's all you need...'

City and Hackney team members were a little more circumspect in their agreement that the project they had developed could be transferred, and there were comments that projects were different according to the different personalities staffing them. One team member thought the clinical side should be more firmly integrated with the project than had happened in the

CHYPP/Brook relationship, while another thought there might not be a need in other areas for the concentration on the ante-natal and post-natal clinic work which CHYPP had developed.

The Brook staff were divided on whether the model could be transferred. On the one hand some Brook staff thought the principle was good in that Brook needed 'an outreach department and if the project were designed properly there should be one in every district in the country...' On the other hand, some Brook staff thought the model as developed in City and Hackney was 'flawed' – 'It was two models. The Brook model was coopted and attached on to the CHYPP agenda. It was not a good idea...' Another Brook staff member elaborated on this view – 'I don't think it was as successful a model as it should have been because of the split between the service provision and the education. My belief is that if your aim is to prevent young people from starting sexual relationships prematurely they have to have information. The place is in the schools – thinking about relationships and responsibility and choices...'

Most significant achievement of project
The project teams and their manager and advisers had given a full assessment of the strengths and weaknesses, successes and failures of their projects. We wanted to end on an upbeat note and to give them a chance to summarise what they thought had been the single most significant achievement of the project in their district.

It was not surprising that there was variation between the projects, but again, there was considerable disagreement on the most significant achievement within individual projects. There were only two examples of any real consensus within projects. For example, all three members of the South Sefton team thought that providing a family planning service acceptable to young people had been their main achievement, and three-quarters of the managers and advisers in Milton Keynes thought the schools programme had been the main achievement of You 2, a view shared by two of the team members. The only other example of any consensus of view was the fact that two team members and two managers in City and Hackney thought that the involvement of a variety of local professionals in the CHYPP project had been their most important achievement.

The work in schools was only mentioned by one member of the CHYPP team and no other respondent in City and Hackney or South Sefton. The provision of a family planning service acceptable to young people was mentioned by only a handful of respondents in Milton Keynes and City and

Hackney, and the PACE's team views on this were supported by only one manager in South Sefton.

Apart from these three examples, no single achievement was supported by more than one or two respondents in each area. These included the gradual building up of attendance figures, mentioned mainly by clinic doctors; getting the Brook clinic funding extended and accepted by the health authority in City and Hackney; the survival of the projects after the central funding had ended; the demonstration that there was a need for services of this kind; and the building up of local credibility. There were also individual mentions for the work of CHYPP in dealing specifically with teenage pregnancy, particularly through the building up of the post-natal clinic and the 'young mums support group', and the perceived success of PACE with male clients.

A telling comment came from one of the managers in South Sefton who thought the main achievement of the PACE project had been to demonstrate a need and try to provide a targeted service to satisfy that need – 'It's actually answered what we thought was a problem. Whether it's been a success or not, it has highlighted the fact that it's been needed. You have a hypothesis and say this is what we need in Bootle. We said, "Right, we'll try it." I think it might have been a better success if we'd had more time...'

A common theme in these interviews was summarised by another manager in South Sefton, looking at the single most significant achievement of the project – 'If we got one kid who wouldn't have gone somewhere else and we've saved an unwanted pregnancy, it has been a success. And if we've improved the quality of life for any of those kids by removing their fears then it's been a success...' This idea of success and achievement might be too limited for some, but it represented a widely-held view, reflecting the crusading nature of many of those working in and supporting projects of this kind.

Future of the projects

The majority of project team members and their managers and advisers were interviewed in the three months after the end of March 1989 when the central funding by the Department of Health had come to an end. However, it was not completely clear what was going to happen to the projects and their staff at the time that we interviewed. We asked respondents whether they thought the projects should continue in their present form.

The respondents were almost unanimous in the view that the projects should continue as they were. The only dissenting voices came from some Brook staff and from two managers in Milton Keynes. The team members

267

and managers were more enthusiastic about the continuation of the projects in their present form than the professionals interviewed had been. Around a quarter of the professionals in South Sefton and a fifth in Milton Keynes had thought the projects should not continue in their present form, although few of the City and Hackney professionals had agreed.

The main reason the respondents thought the projects should continue was that they were held to have been successful, with the added comment in some instances that they were just beginning to take off and needed a chance to develop. Other comments included the views that the projects met the needs of the locality and filled a gap, that they were a good resource for the education service, that they should build on the lessons learnt, that they provided a developmental service which should continue indefinitely and that they were in the position now to expand into AIDS and HIV prevention work.

Success was thought to breed success, and team members in particular thought their efforts should not go unrecognised. In City and Hackney, funding had been achieved for two whole-time equivalent development workers and for the continuation of the three Brook clinics. In Milton Keynes there had been an agreement to fund a reduced service through the Healthy Cities project, the young people's clinic service was to be taken over by the family planning services and there were negotiations underway with Brook to provide a clinic and counselling service in the city centre. In South Sefton other money had been used to secure continuation of the service. There was to be tripartite funding from the Health Promotion Unit, the Drug Education Unit and the Community Nurses budget.

It was doubtful whether the projects would continue in their present form even though they were so strongly supported by the team members and influential managers. There was a clear shift in the thinking in South Sefton, where the funding coming from the Drugs Unit was designed to increase the work done with drug users and in the prevention of HIV and AIDS. It was said that the project had worked with many drug users during the eighteen months monitoring period, although no hard evidence was available to support this claim.

It was by no means uncommon for much of the work of all three projects to have been judged successful without any internal assessment of whether it had actually had been. In City and Hackney, for example, the CHYPP support of the ante-natal clinic, the post-natal clinic and the 'young mums group' had all been judged very successful by the CHYPP team members.

One of the Brook staff members challenged this view, and gave her reasons for thinking that the project should not continue in its present form:
'The whole thing should be reassessed. Who is in charge? Where did the money go? Why did the setting up of the ante-natal clinic have the money? What was the ethos of setting up the ante-natal clinic under the CHYPP banner? I can't see that it would help the abortion rates. I don't think it would be good for the project to go on without analysing where the money went or whether it was good value for money. Brook cost £16,000 and the other parts cost a lot more...'

But the way forward was clearly not going to be a continuation of the projects as such. A decision had to be taken by the health authorities about what to do. Although funding was available from various sources for the continuation of some of the work of the projects, there was no likelihood of the funding which had been provided by the Department of Health being matched in future years.

The best way of providing services for young people
And so, finally, we asked team members and their managers and advisers what they considered would be the best way now of providing services for young people in the district which would meet the aims of the Department of Health when they funded these projects. There was no doubt that most respondents wanted a continuation and development of counselling and contraceptive services for young people, but there was a split between those who thought these services should be separate from the mainstream and those who thought they should be integrated into the mainstream, if not actually provided within existing facilities. A small group of respondents thought the young people's services should ideally be provided by existing mainstream services. One third of the respondents thought the best way forward was to continue the projects as they were.

The professionals interviewed had agreed that there was a need for more services for young people, either within the mainstream or separate from it, but their main recommendation for the future had been the provision of more sex education for young people. In view of the stress the projects had laid on outreach work and the development of sex education programmes, it was perhaps surprising that only a minority of team members and managers mentioned these as priorities for the future. Perhaps they thought they were implicit in their recommended continuation of the projects.

The professionals, in recommending the development of services for young people, had also stressed the need for good publicity and well-advertised services. Again, the team members and managers hardly mentioned these aspects when looking to the future. But it was clear throughout these interviews that none of them had been as aware as the professionals of the lack of publicity attached to these projects.

The question of providing special and separate services for young people or of integrating them into mainstream services dominated some of the arguments before and during the monitoring period. There was an assumption by some people that separate services, run by people outside the mainstream, were the only way of achieving the break with the old, outmoded types of services for young people which were not thought to have been successful. On the other hand, some respondents thought that innovative thinking could take place within mainstream services.

One of the CHYPP team members thought that the CHYPP project had managed the best of all worlds, and in this respect was a model for the future – 'I think it's a good and successful way of working, particularly given the constraints of working in the health services at this time. We're value for money. And also it's a recognition of "development" work, which doesn't usually exist in the health authority. By being established as a developmental project, it gives that concept, and the work that's been done, a legitimate process...'

There was support in City and Hackney, as in the other areas, for 'dedicated staff to tackle a specific problem', but the question of what 'dedicated' meant in these terms was clearly open to interpretation. This respondent saw it as meaning staff with specific responsibilities, used only for that purpose, but throughout these interviews there was a strong undercurrent of support for the view that staff working in young people's services should have a very strong commitment to this type of work and should be 'dedicated' in that respect. The question was whether this 'dedication' could or should be achieved by professionals already providing contraceptive and counselling services, or whether there was a need for a separate service which brought fresh ideas and a new approach.

The project team members were divided on this point. One Milton Keynes member thought it was best to spread the work as widely as possible – 'I'd make sure there was enough counselling available in different agencies – to do pregnancy testing, tell people about other agencies that can help. It could be done at the CAB. There are tribunal specialists, employment specialists. People like it – they don't mind being passed on. If kids get the right reaction in the first place, they will come back and know that there is someone there who will help them in the same agency... And

Brook should do the clinics because they're very well known nationally and much rspected. I hope they will run a mini You 2...'

The hope that Brook would come to Milton Keynes was echoed by several respondents, some of whom retained their resentment of the family planning service in the area, who were thought to have lost credibility by their hostiity to the project. On the other hand, some respondents thought the family planning service had learnt from the You 2 project that young people needed special provision. It was said that their planned new young people's session, with its drop-in facility, showed that they could be flexible. Other respondents were more sceptical and did not think that the family planning service had really understood the messages from You 2, which were that young people needed informality and a non-medical, non-judgmental service. Old wounds were slow to heal in Milton Keynes.

Some respondents in all areas thought that it did not much matter who provided the services for young people as long as they were provided in an informal and friendly way, with the opportunity to talk to non-medical personnel and with the medical services provided in a non-judgmental manner. There was a stress on the need for drop-in services, and for premises which were both discreet and central, a combination which it was thought difficult to achieve. There were pleas for 'dedicated' funding for the purchase of resource material, and pleas for more 'reliable' funding in South Sefton.

The question of the development of more general counselling services for young people which could provide specific counselling in connection with unwanted pregnancies and contraception was mentioned by few team members or managers, although it had been suggested by a number of professionals. Like the team member in Milton Keynes quoted above, a South Sefton adviser thought there was scope for more agencies to provide counselling to young people on a variety of topics:

'There should be a young people's advisory service – a bit like a young person's CAB – because it's very difficult to separate sex problems from other health problems or housing or educational problems. It should be in community centres, shopping centres. By limiting it to pregnancy advice or contraception, young people might not think it's "the place for me to go and talk about my problems". Take someone with several problems, for example drugs and pregnancy. Where would you go first?'

The difficulty of demonstrating the success of health education programmes was a constant theme in these interviews. A South Sefton manager thought that more and better health education facilities were the best way forward:

> We should bomb it at these children and get them before they are 16. The church and all those moral institutions should recognise the world we're living in today. Some of the schools would not allow us in. We get so many single parents...We can't show people the end product in health education. You can't demonstrate it. If a boy says, " I will use this form of contraception and I will have a responsible attitude," he's not going to come back and say he's using it. No way are you going to know about that until later on...

The future of PACE, with some funding from the Drugs Unit and an increased responsibility for HIV and AIDS counselling, was thought to be a logical step by some managers. HIV and drugs had been identified as major problems in the area, and it was thought 'logical and sensible' that the skills of the PACE health workers should be used to help tackle the problem – 'They have already established a community-based approach, which is the same philosophy we are trying to develop in the drugs thing. Also the informal contact at the community centre makes it more normal for drug abusers. They don't want to put a label on saying, "We are drug users..."'

Finally the Brook respondents saw the way forward in a development of the Brook clinics, with a Brook service running virtually all day and every day, providing counselling and a clinic service. There was support among Brook staff for an increase in outreach and sex education work, which few Brook clinics had the funding to do, but for which Brook staff felt well-suited. There was thought to be a need for increased counselling for young people on a variety of anxieties, as this Brook staff member said – 'It's not just about contraception. It's to give young people the opportunity to talk through where they are in their lives now, what they want, what are the difficulties and what are the options...'

The three projects all struggled to provide a good service for young people and all thought they had succeeded to a greater or lesser extent. This report has looked at their activities, their successes and failures, the reactions of their clients and other professionals to them and has ended by looking at their own assessment of their achievements. Other people have a great deal to learn from their experience and Chapter 14 assesses the value of these three projects.

Chapter 14
Discussion of findings

The three young people's projects were set up in response to the Department of Health's invitations to health authorities to submit proposals for projects to provide a family planning and pregnancy counselling service specifically for young people under 25. The aim of the projects, as laid down by the Department of Health, was to reduce the risk of unwanted pregnancy among young people and to encourage them to seek advice early if they suspected they were pregnant. The original intention was for the projects to be funded centrally for a three year period starting in the financial year 1986-7. In the event, the funding covered an eighteen-month period from October 1987 to March 1989. The work of the projects was evaluated by Policy Studies Institute, and this chapter draws together the findings of the research and discusses the key issues.

It is important for the government's aim and purpose in setting up these projects to be kept in mind when the projects are assessed. This report has presented a great deal of evidence which suggests that the project staff and their managers and advisers were not always completely in tune with the aims of the projects as laid down by the Department. There were also strong indications that professionals in the areas who had experience of working with young people were not always fully aware of the Department's aims.

Criteria for evaluation

In evaluating the projects, it is necessary to establish by what criteria they should be evaluated. One of the main criteria must obviously be the extent to which they achieved success in meeting the aims laid down by the Department of Health. There are other criteria by which the projects may be evaluated, and, indeed we went to some lengths to explore the criteria by which the project was assessed by the staff of the project teams, their managers and advisers, as well as other professionals working in the field.

The question of whether the projects could have a measurable effect on key indicators such as birth rates, conception rates and abortion rates was discussed in Chapter 1. These may be important criteria in the long term, but, given the very short-term nature of the projects and the evaluation, little firm evidence can be put forward. We can only speculate on what might happen in future as a result of what was essentially a short-term intervention. The usefulness of such an exercise is limited, and therefore, we have concentrated mostly on other criteria by which the achievements of these projects may be measured. This approach was agreed with the Department of Health before the evaluation began.

This discussion of findings examines the ways in which the projects tried to meet the aims of the Department, and assesses the extent to which they met their own aims and the expectations of others working with young people in the same areas. It explores in some detail the views of the consumers – the young people for whom the projects were designed – and it draws together the lessons which can be learned by others who wish to provide services for young people. It must be stressed again that this evaluation presents a snapshot of a time period – the eighteen months during which the projects were monitored. The project teams themselves learned a lot in this time and have been able to build on the experience. Our aim throughout this evaluation has been to be constructive and to use the experience of those running and managing the projects to help others achieve positive results.

It is probable that when services are under scrutiny for cutting, services which have relatively low attendance rates may be the first to go. Young people's services often fall into this category for a variety of reasons. It is therefore all the more important that the evaluation of these three projects concentrates firmly on the lessons for other providers which could be learned from the experience of projects which had the benefit of guaranteed central funding, if only for a limited period of time.

However, before we discuss the findings in detail, we should draw attention to some of the differences between special projects like these and services which might be set up by health authorities as part of their mainstream provision. It should be borne in mind that the experience of 'demonstration projects', although packed with important lessons, may not always be directly relevant to mainstream health authority services or even to innovatory services started up within health authorities or by other agencies.

Problems of special projects
Special projects of this kind, set up for limited time periods with special funding, always face special problems. They are often set up from scratch,

with the problems of having to recruit and train new staff, who may not have been members of the employing authority's staff. They may then find difficulties in retaining staff to whom they can only offer a short-term contract with no guarantee of further employment at the end of the period. They often have problems in finding, furnishing and equipping suitable premises, particularly on a short lease.

They are often seen as 'outsiders' in that their funding is 'extra' funding, whether provided by the health authority or by central government. Whoever provides the money, there are often problems with others working in the same field who might reasonably think that any extra cash should have come their way to develop services. If the funding comes from central government, there may be resentment at a local level from agencies or professionals who think that their own efforts and achievement should have been rewarded with extra money for innovatory projects, and that special funding should not go to unproven, untried newcomers with no track record.

Special projects are seen as 'demonstration' projects and are expected to demonstrate something. They are usually evaluated, although the evaluation may be internal, rather than, as in this case, carried out by independent external evaluators. Evaluation by an outsider means that staff are working under the close scrutiny of people who are monitoring what they do, and expecting them to keep very detailed records, both of their own activities and of those using the services they offer. Independent evaluators, who are not involved in an 'action research' project, do not have the role of feeding back information to the project staff or of giving advice to staff. They are not part of the project team or management, and project staff may find this difficult to handle.

At the same time, special projects are usually under scrutiny from management and steering groups, since special funding brings special responsibilities at a management level. Managers too are accountable for these projects. But the problem often arises that the management of these projects is not clearly worked out before they are set up. There can be problems when the staffing is multidisciplinary and there are different professional managers for different staff. There can be problems when the management of the project is simply tacked on to the work of an already overburdened manager. And there can be problems when the management of the project is put at such a high level that the bulk of the management remains at project team leader level, if there is a team leader, and that person is not really capable of taking a strategic view because of the day-to-day demands of running the project.

The staffing of special projects brings other problems in terms of determining priorities and organising the work. The agenda has usually been set, partly by the need to meet the aims of the funding body and partly by the response of the managers who designed the proposal or bid which secured the funding. This often leaves little room for manoeuvre, certainly in the initial stages of the project's life. This can cause considerable problems, particularly since the staff have often not been involved in the design of the proposal. The realities of running projects of this kind may bear little relation to the ideals exemplified in proposals designed to get hold of money.

There can be no doubt that all three projects suffered from at least some of these problems. Indeed, it would be fair to say that the Milton Keynes and South Sefton projects, which were both completely new services, with new staff and premises and no existing customers, suffered from most of these problems. The City and Hackney project had the advantage of starting with a team leader who had helped to design the proposal, with existing premises in the community health headquarters, and with an existing Brook clinic which could be expanded. The City and Hackney project had other problems in working as a special project, not least the fact that it operated with two separate teams – the CHYPP team and the Brook team – which became more separated as the project developed, so that by the end of the monitoring period they had virtually no contact with one another.

It cannot be stressed too often that even in special projects of this kind, time must be allotted for careful preparation of the roles and tasks of the various players in the projects, and that overall strategic management roles should be made explicit. If the preparation time is cut to the minimum, as it was in the case of these three projects, and if the management of the projects is not clearly formulated, it should come as no surprise that things may go wrong. Health authorities which may not be under the same constraints of working to so tight a timetable should learn from the experience of these special projects.

Initial problems and challenges
The lack of preparation time for the projects was a key factor in the extent to which the staff could operate efficiently from the beginning of the eighteen-month period. Very few of the staff in any of the projects were appointed until the month before the monitoring period started, and, indeed, City and Hackney and Brook staff were still being appointed after the projects began. The two extra Brook clinics in City and Hackney did not start until the project had been running for a month. The doctor in South

Sefton did not start work until five months after the project started, not only because it was found difficult to find anyone suitable for the post, but also because the South Sefton project had no premises of its own until four months into the monitoring period.

The forming of a team which can work together smoothly to achieve common objectives takes time. In all three projects, the teams were made up of people from different backgrounds and disciplines, most of whom had never worked together before. This in itself might not be a problem if enough time had been available to develop team working and to allot roles and responsibilities in a relaxed manner. The three projects developed team working in rather different ways, but all faced problems which others developing such services might find instructive. It should be noted that the South Sefton team was the only one which had the same staff members and doctor at the end of the eighteen-month monitoring period as it had at the beginning. Staff turnover in the other two project teams and in the Brook clinic was extensive.

In Milton Keynes, the management embarked on an intensive training programme for the staff during the first two months of the project, while expecting the team members to provide a service to young people at the same time. The effects of the training programme, which was seen as very rigorous by participants and providers alike, were double-edged. Although it was undoubtedly useful in providing team members with expertise and counselling skills which they had mostly lacked at the beginning of the project, it had a serious effect on inter-personal relationships within the team and on the interface with management, exacerbated by the fact that no team leader had been appointed initially and that two of the team had been 'inherited' from an existing project providing women's health care in a much more informal way than the trainers thought suitable for a health authority based project. One of the members of staff resigned at the end of the training period, and the rest of the team took some time to recover from the experience.

At the same time as undergoing a training programme and providing a drop-in and clinic service for young people, the Milton Keynes team were also trying to develop links with schools, professionals and other agencies working with young people.

The main problem in South Sefton for the team initially was that they had no premises of their own for the first four months of the monitoring period, but had to use a room in the health promotion department. This had certain advantages in that they could build up their expertise in the subject without having to provide a service, and at the same time could learn a great deal from the health promotion unit about resources and approach. However, the uncertainty of their position, combined with constant administrative problems in trying to get into their premises, certainly inhibited the extent to which they could function efficiently. The staff found it difficult to build up contacts with professionals, since they had no base from which to offer a service and found it virtually impossible to contact young people for the same reason.

In City and Hackney, CHYPP started with a number of advantages over their counterparts in Milton Keynes and South Sefton. They had a much more limited role than the other two project teams, in that they were not attempting to run any kind of direct service for young people, either in the form of a drop-in service or a young people's clinic. Their aim from the beginning was to provide only an outreach service, with no drop-in service for young people and with the clinic service being provided by Brook. They also had more money than the other two projects, and had more staff than South Sefton. In terms of staff for outreach work only, of course, they had more staff than either of the other projects.

They also had advantages in the nature of their staffing. Most of the CHYPP team were rather more experienced in the type of work envisaged than staff in the other two areas. They had a team coordinator who had not only been involved in designing the proposal to the Department of Health, but had also been working for the health authority for some time. There can be no doubt that a certain familiarity with the workings of large bureaucracies can be very helpful when launching innovatory projects.

CHYPP spent their first months conducting a review of the pregnancy testing service in the district (Fleissig, Jessopp, Griffiths, 1989), approaching professionals and schools in the district, trying to build up the teenage ante-natal clinic run by City and Hackney health authority, and starting to develop links with young mothers' groups.

During the same period, Brook was setting up two additional clinic sessions, starting in November 1987. They had considerable problems in recruiting and retaining administrators for the three Shoreditch clinic sessions, had some problems in providing medical and nursing staff at the clinics, while, at the same time, the Brook national and London organisations were undergoing management changes. Difficulties in retaining administrators at the Shoreditch Brook clinic continued throughout the monitoring period.

What lessons can be learnt from this brief account of the first months of the projects? It is difficult enough to develop a programme of work for a new project to be completed within an eighteen-month period even if the project is run by a brilliant organiser with vision and drive who has had time for preparation, knows exactly what is wanted and has a clear plan of action with excellent management support and a fully trained and experienced team of workers. None of the projects had these advantages, although City and Hackney, for reasons outlined above, had a headstart on the other two.

The main problem faced by Milton Keynes and South Sefton was that the clinic service provided to the young people was a completely new service. The experience of Brook in other areas has shown that, even with the well-known Brook name and reputation, a new clinic service takes time to build up. The Milton Keynes and South Sefton projects did not have the advantage of the Brook name, and had to build up a young people's clinic service from no base whatsoever. In other areas, young people's clinic services have often been inspired by a dedicated clinic doctor who sees a need for special services for young people and drives the idea through to fruition. It is unusual for services like those in Milton Keynes and South Sefton to be set up without this kind of medical clinical backing. Indeed, in both areas, there was evidence that existing family planning clinic staff were less than enthusiastic about the young people's projects. Both projects experienced difficulty in recruiting doctors of the right calibre for the clinic, and this should have been foreseen.

A further problem for both Milton Keynes and South Sefton was the setting up of the drop-in service. In South Sefton this was also set up in premises where there were no existing clients and no history of any service provision of a related kind to young people, whereas the Milton Keynes team were operating in premises which had been used by the Women's Health Group mainly for pregnancy testing. Two of the original team were former Women's Health Group members and it is clear that many of the clients who used the drop-in service, at least initially, were unaware of the difference between the Women's Health Group pregnancy testing service and that offered by You 2. In this respect, the Milton Keynes project inherited a reputation as a provider of pregnancy tests. This was undoubtedly a very important factor in determining the type of service sought by those who used the drop-in service in Milton Keynes, and must largely account for the extent to which the Milton Keynes drop-in service was overwhelmingly used as a pregnancy testing service throughout the monitoring period.

The main messages for health authorities from the experience of the first few months of these projects is that careful planning should take place before a young people's service is launched. A plan of action should be drawn up, with roles and responsibilities clearly delineated. Any necessary basic training should take place before any kind of service is offered to young people or to other professionals, schools or other agencies. Activities should be restricted to those which are feasible, and priorities should be established before the project starts. In all three areas there was an impression of the projects shooting off in all directions without a clear strategy. There was evidence that publicity material was prepared without sufficient professional advice and that contacts were made which were not followed up, particularly if the initial encounter was in any way interpreted as negative by team members or the team leader.

In all three areas there was evidence from interviews with professionals working with young people that none of the projects were widely known in their areas, and that even among those professionals and agencies nominated by the project teams as those with whom they had had good and close relationships, there was considerable lack of understanding of the aims and activities of the projects. In some cases, what the team described as a close relationship was not regarded by those interviewed as anything other than passing contact. We will return to the impact of the projects on other professionals and agencies, but the lesson for those undertaking young people's projects of this kind is that it is important to focus efforts initially and to follow up contacts systematically. It should also be made very clear to professional contacts and agencies exactly what it is that the projects can offer which is not being offered elsewhere.

Direct services for young people

One of the indicators of success suggested by the Department of Health when setting up these projects was the number of the target population reached by the projects. The target population was defined as those under the age of 25. Mid-year population estimates for 1989 supplied by the Office of Population Censuses and Surveys (OPCS) show 18,001 women aged 15-24 in the City and Hackney DHA, 15,544 women aged 15-24 in the Milton Keynes DHA and 13,031 women aged 15-24 in the South Sefton DHA.

The number of the target population reached was the only indicator of the type suggested by the Department which was readily open to measurement during the life of the projects, but it should be stressed that it was only possible to measure with any accuracy the number of individuals who attended to services provided directly to young people, ie those attending the clinic and drop-in services provided at the project base or clinic. Close monitoring took place of the attenders at these services. Chapters 2, 3 and 4 of this report describe the numbers and characteristics of these attenders in great detail, and this discussion draws together the main conclusions from this analysis.

It was not possible to make a count of the number of young people or other individuals who had contact with the project team during their outreach activities. The teams themselves did not keep a record, and it would have been very difficult for them to do so. There would have been problems with multi-counting of individuals, for example in schools or YTS schemes where more than one session was held with the same group of young people. It would also have been difficult to analyse the material, since the nature of the outreach contacts with young people varied considerably, from intensive sex education sessions to casual brief encounters with individuals. The teams did keep records of the number of sessions they held with young people (see Appendix II), and this gives some indication of the extent of their outreach activities directly with young people, although it can give no accurate indication of the actual number of the target population reached.

The following discussion looks first at the service provided directly to young people at the project or clinic base and then looks at the views of the young people using these services. It then examines the services provided on an outreach basis to young people and looks at the views of professionals workers towards the outreach services which were aimed both at young people and professionals.

Who used the direct services to young people

There were striking differences between the projects in the numbers of people and type of clientele they attracted. This was not necessarily because of the different types of service offered, since Milton Keynes and South Sefton offered essentially the same type of service directly to young people – a drop-in service open all day every weekday, and a clinic service with a doctor present once a week in the early afternoon. The drop-in service in both areas offered pregnancy testing, counselling and non-medical contraception at the project base, as well as telephone advice and counselling.

The major difference between the City and Hackney project and the other two projects in terms of direct services to young people was that the City and Hackney project offered only a clinic service. This was provided by Brook at the Shoreditch clinic on two evenings a week and on a Saturday morning. Although it was also available for pregnancy testing and non-medical counselling, it was essentially run as a young people's clinic with doctors and nurses present. There was no drop-in non-appointment service as such. CHYPP did not provide any facilities for young people to visit their project base and did not set out to offer any telephone counselling or advice service directly to young people.

One other important factor which must be taken into account when looking at the target population reached is the fact that the South Sefton project did not open its doors to clients until the project had been running for four months, so the possible time period for visits was restricted to 14 months. Two of the Brook clinic sessions opened in November 1987, restricting their potential attendances to 17 months, but, on the other hand, most of the attendances at their Monday clinic session were inherited from the Brook clinic which had been running there for some time.

In terms of population reached, the figures show that 883 people (876 women and 7 men) made at least one visit to the City and Hackney project at the Shoreditch Brook clinic in the 18-month period from October 1987 to March 1989. The comparable figures for Milton Keynes were 711 people (701 women and 10 men), and for South Sefton 360 people (210 women and 150 men). But these bald statistics conceal a wide variation in types of visit, service received and age of attender which are detailed in earlier chapters.

All the City and Hackney project attenders visited the clinic only. The vast majority of project attenders in Milton Keynes (82 per cent) made visits to the drop-in service only, and 94 per cent used the drop-in service at all. Only 18 per cent of the total women clients (129) made any visits to the Milton Keynes clinic in the 18-month period. (124 were under the age of 25).

In South Sefton, 50 per cent of the women and over 80 per cent of the men made visits to the drop-in service only, while 79 per cent of women and 94 per cent of men used the drop-in service at all. 50 per cent of women (104) and 19 per cent of men (29) made any visits to the clinic service. (61 of the women clinic attenders were under the age of 25.)

Most people in Milton Keynes and South Sefton attended the projects once only whereas in City and Hackney, 45 per cent visited the clinic once and 24 per cent attended twice.

There were striking differences between the projects in terms of the age of the clients of the services. This, of course, had significant implications in terms of the target population reached. In City and Hackney, 20 per cent of the female attenders were over the age of 25, in Milton Keynes, 12 per cent were over 25, while in South Sefton, as many as 36 per cent of women using the project services were over 25. In other words, in 14 months of direct service operation, the South Sefton project reached 134 young women under the age of 25. This was, of course, only a tiny proportion of the potential target population.

Very few of the male attenders were over 25, although 5 per cent of the South Sefton male attenders were over 40. 80 per cent of the South Sefton male attenders were teenagers, and over a fifth were schoolboys under 16.

The age profile of women *clinic* attenders differed considerably between the projects. In Milton Keynes, 4 per cent of those attending the clinic were over 25, but the comparable figure for City and Hackney was 20 per cent and in South Sefton over 40 per cent of the clinic attenders were over 25, with one-sixth being over 40. It is very doubtful whether this clinic could really be classified as a young people's clinic.

Looking at the other end of the age-scale, only 4 per cent of the City and Hackney clinic attenders were under 16, compared with 19 per cent in Milton Keynes and 13 per cent in South Sefton.

The age groups which it might have been thought would have been targeted as potential clinic attenders were the 16-19 year-olds and the 20-24 year-olds. Again there were differences between the projects. Just over a quarter of the clinic attenders in both South Sefton and City and Hackney were between 16 and 19, compared with 52 per cent in Milton Keynes. On the other hand, nearly 50 per cent of the City and Hackney clinic attenders were aged between 20 and 24, compared with a quarter in Milton Keynes and just over one fifth in South Sefton.

Given the age profile of project attenders as a whole, it was not surprising to find that nearly a third of the South Sefton drop-in women attenders were over 25, compared with 12 per cent in Milton Keynes. Nearly half the Milton Keynes women drop-in users were between 20 and 24, while one third of women drop-in users in both Milton Keynes and South Sefton were between 16 and 19.

Most users in City and Hackney were single women with no children. A higher proportion of women in Milton Keynes and South Sefton were married or living as married and around 40 per cent in each area had children. The vast majority of women in Milton Keynes and South Sefton were of white British ethnic origin, whereas in City and Hackney 55 per cent of women fell into this category. Nearly one fifth in City and Hackney regarded themselves of West Indian or Black British ethnic origin.

The biggest difference between the projects lay in the type of service received. Nearly 90 per cent of women attending the Milton Keynes drop-in service came for a pregnancy test, whether on their first visit or on repeat visits, while the comparable proportion for South Sefton was 25 per cent, where around one fifth of women came in connection with general health advice or counselling. A high proportion of those attending the Milton Keynes drop-in service for pregnancy testing came to confirm a wanted pregnancy.

Around half those attending the City and Hackney Brook clinic came in connection with a pregnancy test or counselling on their first visit, usually requesting a termination of pregnancy. Comparable figures in Milton Keynes were 35 per cent and in South Sefton 14 per cent. But most of those requesting termination of pregnancy at the Milton Keynes clinic had previously had a pregnancy test at the drop-in service. In South Sefton, over one third of the women attending the young people's clinic came only for a smear or for a general women's health problem or for advice and counselling only. As we have seen, a high proportion were over 25.

The majority of the young men attending the projects' services were given sheaths or condoms on their visits. In South Sefton they were encouraged to visit the clinic.

There were big differences between the projects in the extent to which they were used as pregnancy counselling and pregnancy testing services. Nearly half the City and Hackney women had pregnancy tests at their first visit. Most of these were positive and the majority sought a referral for termination of pregnancy. In Milton Keynes, nearly 90 per cent of the women attending the drop-in service had a pregnancy test at their first visit. Nearly half of these had positive results, of whom the majority intended to continue with their pregnancy. A further 10 per cent had negative results but wanted to be pregnant. In South Sefton, over two-thirds of those tested had negative tests, of whom some wanted to be pregnant. Only 16 per cent had positive tests about which they were undecided or unhappy.

Nearly one third of those attending the City and Hackney Brook clinic had had previous terminations of pregnancy compared with around 10 per cent in the other two areas. Having had a previous termination of pregnancy did not necessarily prevent the risk of further unwanted pregnancies since similar proportions of those having pregnancy tests had had previous TOPs.

The majority of users of the clinic and drop-in services in Milton Keynes and South Sefton came for the first time to the project through a friend, relative or other user of the project. In South Sefton, the presence of project staff in a community centre helped to bring people into the project. In Milton Keynes, around a fifth of those coming to the drop-in service came because their GP had told them about the service, but the majority of these came for a free pregnancy test, often in connection with a wanted pregnancy. Referrals from other professionals were very limited in all three projects.

Publicity about the projects had helped to attract some clients in both Milton Keynes and South Sefton, but hardly at all in City and Hackney. One fifth of the City and Hackney clinic users were already using the Brook clinic before the project started, and a further fifth came through the central Brook clinic office.

Lessons about direct service provision for young people

There are two main factors which affect the extent to which young people are attracted initially to use services of the kind provided by these projects – the nature and extent of any local 'inherited' factors and the extent to which the projects are successful in their efforts to attract users. After the initial phases of a project of this kind, the third important factor is the extent to which the projects can build up a clientele through the reputation they build up both among young people who might use the services and among professionals who might refer or recommend young people to use them.

The City and Hackney Brook clinic inherited a relatively high proportion of clinic users from the existing Brook clinic and from the health authority young people's clinic which had been running at the Shoreditch health centre. It also undoubtedly benefited greatly from being part of the general Brook umbrella, and, through this, attracted a relatively high number of people who did not live in the area but found the Shoreditch Brook clinic convenient for a number of other reasons, for example, because they needed a quick appointment or because they lived or worked within easy travelling distance of Shoreditch.

The most disconcerting thing about the Shoreditch Brook clientele was that such a high proportion came with unwanted pregnancies and that such a high proportion were over 20. The City and Hackney project was not getting through in large numbers, it appeared, to teenagers living in the district who were motivated to use a young people's service for contraceptive help and advice.

The Milton Keynes project had clearly inherited the reputation of the Women's Health Group which had provided pregnancy testing. The fact that the pregnancy testing offered by You 2 was free and quick undoubtedly attracted a large number of people who wanted to continue with their pregnancy as well as those who were unsure or unhappy with a pregnancy. It also, of course, attracted a lot of people who were 'just testing'. There can be no doubt at all that the Milton Keynes drop-in service was used essentially as a pregnancy testing service. Pregnancy counselling took place, and young people were referred to the young people's clinic and to their GPs, but, in terms of target population reached, it is doubtful whether the numbers seen really justify the amount of staffing and effort put into the direct drop-in service for young people when it was mainly being used as a pregnancy testing service, often by people who wanted to be pregnant.

The South Sefton service was used to a fairly large extent as a women's health service by older women who could not get the kind of service they wanted elsewhere. Nearly 40 per cent of the female clients were 25 or over, and much of the service offered was concerned with general women's health problems or smears rather than contraception or pregnancy counselling. Again, it must be asked whether this was the best way of using central funding for a young people's pregnancy counselling and contraceptive project.

How did the projects try to build up a clientele and how successful were they in their efforts? The main complaint by professionals interviewed, both those who had had contact with the projects and those who had not, was that the publicity for all three projects was inadequate. They were not only talking about publicity to professionals but also about publicity to young people. The young people interviewed, whether they had used the projects or not, had seen little or no publicity about the projects, and, in City and Hackney, none of those interviewed had ever heard of the CHYPP project, let alone seen any publicity about it.

The first rule for any project of this kind, and for any young people's service, is to make sure that publicity is of a high professional standard, that sufficient funds are devoted to it, that it is made available on a large scale wherever young people are to be found and to as many professionals and agencies as possible. As one of the professionals interviewed said – 'If they don't see any posters they don't know where to go...' Good appropriate services for young people are needed, but a good service cannot flourish if nobody uses it. One big initial mailing or distribution of posters is insufficient. Constant efforts have to made to publicise services on all levels to everyone who might use them or who might be in touch with young people who might be in need of them.

The same message holds true if a clientele is inherited in any way. In some cases, as in Milton Keynes, the 'inherited' factor was not so much a regular clientele as a reputation – for being a free pregnancy testing service with sympathetic staff. This might not necessarily have been a poor base from which to build up a service to young people, but the evidence suggests that You 2 found it difficult to shake off the image it inherited. Better and more consistent publicity could have helped to get over the message to young people that a more broadly-based service was available from the project.

Young people's views

One of the most important ways of building up a clientele is to provide services that young people like and want to use. Word of mouth recommendation is one of the most important methods of publicising services and encouraging others to use them. This is true of most services, but has been shown to be particularly true of services for young people.

We interviewed users of the projects towards the end of the monitoring period. The majority of those interviewed were under the age of 25, but a substantial minority of those interviewed in South Sefton were over 25, reflecting the profile of the clientele of that project, if not the targeted age-group. In addition to the users of the projects, we also interviewed a small number of young women who had not used the projects. These were mainly young women who had had unwanted pregnancies or had become pregnant while teenagers, who might have been helped by services aimed specifically at young people.

Young people's views of the projects' services

We found that few young people had come to the projects because of publicity or through the recommendation of a professional. There was every indication that professionals could do a lot more to tell young people about projects of this kind, but, as this report has shown, professionals in touch with young people in the areas often knew little themselves about the projects.

Young people often came to the project because they had heard about it from a friend, and there was some evidence of a 'snowball effect' starting in the last few months of the projects among schoolgirls using the clinic services in Milton Keynes and South Sefton. There has been a lot of experience in the past among professionals and others in feeding information into the 'grapevine', and it should not be necessary to 'reinvent the wheel' every time a new project is set up. Much can be learnt from the experience of others. There was little evidence of the projects trying to tap into this experience.

It should also be noted that many users of the services had a very functional view of the projects' services. They came because the projects were local and convenient and open when they needed them. This was undoubtedly one of the reasons why older women used the South Sefton project. Young people also used the projects if they provided a free service which usually cost money elsewhere, such as pregnancy testing. It is interesting how lack of publicity may not be a hindrance to uptake of services when people are highly motivated and need a free service quickly.

On the other hand, the fact that the only clinic session both in Milton Keynes and South Sefton was in the early afternoon was very inconvenient for many young people, particularly for those still at school who had to miss school to attend the clinic. This kind of timing is clearly inappropriate for a teenage clientele, whether they are students or working, and no-one planning services for young people should provide only an early afternoon clinic session.

The projects were undoubtedly much appreciated by the young people who used them. The clinic doctors were particularly praised by young people, mainly for their friendliness, approachability and willingness to listen and help. Many of the young people interviewed had rather curious images of doctors, whom they described as being formal, unfriendly, stern, wearing white coats and sitting behind desks. They constantly used phrases such as 'comfortable' and 'friendly' to describe the clinic doctors, and were surprised and pleased that 'she never shouted at me'. They liked the projects' clinic services because they were not 'told off' and not 'interrogated'. Nurses at the Brook clinic were appreciated because they 'treat you as a person' or 'as an individual' or 'not just another person in the queue...' There was evidence that young people's experience of health services had not always been totally happy.

Young people's use and views of other services

The young people's projects were often said by team members and their managers to be getting through to young people who would never use any other kind of service. This was not true. Nearly half of those interviewed who were under 25 had used their GPs' services in connection with contraception or pregnancy, although few had used family planning clinics. Some of the project users had not stopped using their doctors' services but were using the project for a specific purpose such as a pregnancy test.

There was, however, some evidence that they did not always find their GPs sympathetic towards them, and there were comments that doctors were disapproving and did not have the time or the patience to explain things to them. GPs were also said to have no interest in methods other than the pill. One of the most common worries of the young people, whether they had used their GPs' services or not, was the question of confidentiality. Many of the teenagers were worried that their doctor would tell their parents if they asked for help with contraception, and there were doubts about how confidential doctors' surgeries or health centres were. Nearly one third of those interviewed in the projects outside London said that what appealed to them most about project's services was the confidentiality.

It is frequently asserted that women prefer women doctors and that this is particularly true of teenagers. The interviews suggested that the situation is more complicated than this. There is a small group of young women who much prefer a woman doctor and feel very strongly about this preference. There is another group of young women who prefer a woman doctor for intimate discussions and examinations, while there is another group who do not mind what sex the doctor is, as long as they are kind and friendly and have the necessary expertise. As other studies have shown, kindness and friendliness go a long way towards convincing people that they are getting a good service.

Few of the young people interviewed had used family planning clinics, and, again, their experience was mixed, with complaints about waiting times and unfriendliness. There was evidence of refusal to discuss unwanted pregnancy or to see girls under 16. Many young people who had not been to clinics had images of the clinics which were even more curious than the pictures they painted of their GPs. Family planning clinics were seen as 'adult' places where 'older people' went, often meaning people over the age of 20. They were seen as places for young mothers with babies, lacking confidentiality and insisting on internal examinations. The name itself was a source of puzzlement to some young people who thought such clinics were inappropriate for their needs because they were not planning a family.

Those who had not used the projects, like the users of the projects, were not always enthusiastic about GP and family planning clinic services, and their images of these services were similar to those of the project users. There were, in fact, many similarities between them and the project users. It must be remembered that a fairly high proportion of project users either came to the projects in connection with an unwanted pregnancy or had had unwanted pregnancies in the past.

There was some evidence that teenage mothers and those seeking termination of pregnancy had approached GPs for help with contraception and had been turned away or refused contraceptive advice or help. Equally, some young women did not approach their GPs in connection with an unwanted pregnancy until it was too late because they thought they would not be treated sympathetically. Those who had not used the projects had very similar worries to the project users about lack of confidentiality at their doctors' surgeries and had similar stories of unsympathetic and unfriendly treatment by GPs.

Those who had not used the projects' services were more likely to have used family planning clinics than the project users, and, on the whole, had a much more positive attitude towards them. It does look as though family planning clinics could go out of their way more to encourage young people to attend. When they do go they often appear to be pleasantly surprised and some are particularly appreciative of seeing a woman doctor.

What can be learnt from the young people?

Those providing services for young people can learn a great deal from these interviews, both with the users of the project services and those who had not used them. There is an enormous reservoir of shyness and diffidence about approaching doctors or clinics in connection with sex, contraception or pregnancy. Young people were worried about being rebuked or reprimanded, and there was considerable evidence that they were not always treated with sensitivity and understanding by professionals who clearly found difficulty in dealing both with inarticulate teenagers and those whom they found demanding.

It must be a matter of great concern that we found evidence of teenagers feeling discouraged from using contraception by doctors and clinics. These girls were motivated enough to seek help, and were trying to behave in a responsible manner. If they felt rebuffed, it is perhaps not surprising that those with less courage and motivation were reluctant even to consider approaching doctors or clinics.

If unwanted pregnancies among young people are to be prevented, there should be as many points of access to contraceptive and counselling services as possible. This must include mainstream services such as those provided by GPs and family planning clinics as well as any young people's services. It looks as though GPs and family planning clinics could learn much from the approach of special young people's services like those described in this study and develop a welcoming, friendly and non-judgmental attitude towards young people.

But to what extent is the problem one of image rather than reality? Doctors working in young people's clinics, like those in these projects, are often GPs themselves. It seems unlikely that they change their behaviour when they leave their own surgeries. It does look as though GPs in general could brush up their image and convince young girls – and boys – that they are not the grumpy, gruff, formal, forbidding people described so often in these interviews. Most important, they should make it absolutely clear that confidentiality is the cornerstone of medical practice.

Family planning clinics, too, could do much to change their image as far as young people are concerned. Although they are used by many teenagers and young people, they still appear to have found it difficult to convince some, possibly those most at risk of an unwanted pregnancy, that they will provide a confidential and sympathetic service to everyone. If they are not prepared to discuss termination of pregnancy or to see under-16-year-olds they should make it absolutely clear where, when and how such clients can find immediate help. The same is true of GPs. No young woman should be refused help by any service or professional without being told where such help is available.

Sex education
There have been many assertions about the effect of sex education on the behaviour of young people. All three of these projects saw sex education as an important part of their role, and aimed to provide it both on an outreach basis and within their direct services to young people. It is important to put their efforts into the context of the experience of the young people we interviewed, since it has an important bearing on the best way of delivering services of this kind to young people. We will return to this theme at the end of this discussion.

There was evidence from interviews in all three areas that young people had received variable amounts and types of education about sex, contraception and personal relationships. The young women interviewed in South Sefton, many of whom had attended Catholic schools in the district, appeared to have received less education on these topics than those in other areas.

Most of those interviewed, whether they had used the projects' services or not, thought they had received too little education both at home and school on sex, contraception and personal relationships. There was evidence of some people having received too little too late, while others had received too much too early, with the result that they had not understood the relevance of certain aspects of their education. It appeared to be much too easy to 'miss' a crucial lesson on contraception by being away for the day, moving schools, or being male. It was clearly difficult for schools to get sex education 'right'. Some of those interviewed had been to the same schools and were in the same year as others interviewed, but their interpretation of the sex education they had received varied enormously. Some of them appeared to have received a great deal of valuable information and discussion, while others seem to have received little or none. It seemed that sex education simply passed some young people by, while making a significant impact on others.

There was a general demand from the young people interviewed in all areas for more lessons in more depth on more topics more often. It was thought important that boys should have as much education in sex and personal relationships as girls. There was a general scepticism about gaining information from friends – 'the usual whispers' and 'snippets' were thought by young people to be inadequate. It was also thought essential for schools to give more advice and help on where young people could go to discuss personal problems and to gain access to contraceptive and pregnancy counselling services of a confidential nature.

There was also a desire for more extensive sex education from parents. Although many young people described close and full discussions with parents about sex and contraception, there was a certain embarrassment on the part of young people in talking to their parents about their developing sex lives. Indeed, as the Policy Studies Institute research on sex education showed (Allen, 1987), parents and teenagers alike often find it difficult to talk about sex to each other. As one of the young people interviewed for this study remarked – 'I think the school should do more because you get embarrassed with your mum and dad...'

Half of those interviewed who had used the projects' services said they had learnt something new from the project staff or doctor. There is clearly a need for more information, help and advice for young people from people who have expertise. The big question is how this can best be delivered. It has always been clear that information alone is not enough, as was underlined by the fact that the young mothers and pregnant teenagers who were interviewed, many of whom had had unwanted pregnancies, often rated their sex education from home and school more highly than those using the projects' services did.

Outreach work and liaison by projects with other professionals and agencies

All three projects laid great stress on developing outreach work with other professionals and agencies, with the twin aims of providing services to young people on an outreach basis and of providing professionals with help, advice, training and resources in their work with young people. An important purpose of this outreach work in all three areas was to demonstrate to other professionals and agencies ways of working with young people which could be continued by others after the short-term projects had come to an end.

As the report has shown, the projects met with varying degrees of success in their attempts to develop outreach work and contacts with key professionals and other agencies. In some instances, for example in the work with schools developed by Milton Keynes, the outreach work appeared to have been very successful, according to several criteria. The activity sheets show a high number of contacts and sessions achieved, both with teachers and with young people (see Appendix II). Interviews with teachers and others involved in education indicated a high level of satisfaction with the services received from the project, both in supporting teachers with resources, discussion and training, and in the nature and content of the sex education sessions which took place with young people in schools.

Similarly, the work in schools in City and Hackney, particularly when carried out by one of the team members who left before the end of the project, was also found to be successful according to the same criteria. The work by CHYPP with residential social workers also appeared well-targeted, carefully developed, and of considerable use to the workers involved.

On the other hand, there was evidence of unsatisfactory liaison and collaboration between all three projects and other professionals and agencies, when measured either by the number of contacts, the type of liaison or by the reaction of the professionals involved. There was also evidence that many good contacts were based on chance or proximity rather than on a systematic approach to communicating with professionals. What lessons can be learnt from the experience of the project teams in attempting to develop outreach work, both with young people and with other professionals and agencies? It must be recognised that professionals and other agencies are usually the 'gatekeepers' controlling access to groups of young people, and that outreach work can usually only be developed through these gatekeepers. It is therefore essential for any project of this type to establish credibility with professionals and agencies working with young people.

Lessons about liaison with other professionals and agencies
Perhaps the main lesson to be learnt about the development of outreach work through the involvement of other professionals and agencies is the necessity to prepare the ground very carefully indeed. Sending out blanket letters announcing the arrival of a special service for young people has very little impact, especially if it is not followed up with a personal contact, as can be seen by the almost complete lack of liaison between the projects and GPs. There were obviously other reasons for the lack of contact with GPs, but the main one must have been that none of the projects made any real attempt to inform GPs in any detail about what they were doing or to involve them in the projects. Similarly, the complete lack of reaction by the governors of the schools in City and Hackney to a letter sent out by CHYPP can be attributed not only to a lack of interest on the part of the governors but also to a lack of follow-up by the CHYPP team. There were other instances where professionals and other agencies interviewed at the end of the monitoring period said that they had had only one contact with the projects which had not been followed up.

If other professionals and agencies are to be involved in outreach work in any way, and this includes the question of their referring young people to the projects' services, they must feel confident in the type of services being offered by the projects and confident that the project staff can deliver these services. They must also know something about the services and staff. Many of the professionals interviewed were vague and ill-informed about something as central to the projects as the times and location of the young people's clinic provision, and some key professionals knew nothing at all about the clinic provision. It is not perhaps surprising that so few direct referrals to the projects were made by professionals and other agencies.

The lack of liaison between the health authority family planning clinic staff and the project teams was marked in all three areas. Similarly, there was a considerable lack of knowledge of these projects by other health authority staff such as health visitors and other community nurses in all three areas. They had had little contact with the project teams, and some of them had never even heard of the projects until we interviewed them at the end of the monitoring period.

It is probable that steps should have been taken at management level to improve the contact and liaison between the projects and family planning clinic staff. It is absurd to have disputes or lack of contact within a health authority between professionals who are all supposed to be supplying services to an important group of people, particularly when they are under close scrutiny to see to what extent they can act as 'model' services. There was evidence that close contact at a management level was not enough. This was often not translated into contact at the 'grass roots' level, and it is at this level that collaboration can make its impact on improved services to young people, which was one of the main aims of the projects.

All health authorities thinking of setting up new services to a client group should be aware that lack of attention to the sensitivities of existing professionals and agencies defending their territories can lead to spectacularly unsuccessful liaison and cooperation between the old and the new, which can only be detrimental to developing services designed to meet the needs of the public.

The projects also demonstrated an important lesson for those who may be thinking of setting up short-term projects. It should be made clear to existing providers that innovatory projects may have important messages for them, in terms of developing new approaches to service provision tailored to the needs of particular groups of people. Short-term projects of this kind should not be set up if the health authority is not prepared to continue to develop the successful aspects of their work. It is a tremendous waste of time, money and effort if the mainstream services take no notice whatever of the achievements of projects of this kind and continue as though they had never existed.

One of the managers in South Sefton thought that innovatory services of this kind were good for other services – 'It starts to challenge their assumptions about their way of doing things. It opens up minds. It starts the conversation...' Sadly, there was little evidence of anything like this happening in any of the areas. Too many minds appeared to have been closed before the projects got off the ground, and others knew too little about the projects to have their assumptions challenged. Not too many conversations had been started on changing attitudes and delivery of existing services.

There are undoubtedly a number of problems in involving existing mainstream services in innovatory and 'demonstration' projects. The project teams were, on the one hand, trying to develop close links with other professionals and agencies both in order to gain access to young people and in order to help to train, advise and resource the professionals. At the same time, they were trying to create a climate of change in which existing agencies could take on their mantle after they were gone in the hope that others would continue to develop services in an imaginative and innovative way. There was clearly a tension, both within the teams and with other agencies, in trying to achieve all these objectives at once.

Some of the other agencies and professionals were sceptical about the ability and expertise of the project team staff. They did not consider that they had anything to learn from people with no track record. What the teams demonstrated was how quickly it is possible to develop expertise and a useful model of service, given the right training, resources and backup. Nowhere was this more apparent than in the Milton Keynes team, who managed to capitalise in a very short period of time on the disparate talents they brought to the project and to provide a service to schools which was highly regarded by teachers and other educationists and, apparently, by schoolchildren.

On the other hand, the lack of success of all three project teams in developing close links with youth workers demonstrated that flexibility is all-important, and that one type of approach which might be successful in one arena might well be inappropriate in another. The CHYPP and You 2 teams managed to put together packages which were needed and appreciated by schools. They did not manage this with other agencies like youth workers. PACE had some difficulty in developing outreach work, particularly in schools, for other reasons, which included local factors such as a high Catholic population, but it was also related to the small size of the team in which most of the outreach development rested on the shoulders of only one person.

There can be no doubt that not enough thought was given in the preparatory stages of these projects to the potential problems there would be in developing liaison and good working relationships with other professionals and agencies. There was a very strong impression that the project teams were thrown in the deep end and told to get on with it, without enough strategic planning beforehand.

It could be argued that it would have been better to have targeted certain key professionals and agencies, for example schools or youth clubs, and concentrated on these from the beginning. Given the short-term nature of projects, there is a lot to be said for this argument, particularly in using limited resources. However, this approach would have meant that certain successful liaison with some individual agencies might not have been possible. Longer-term projects have a greater opportunity to spread the net more widely.

There was evidence that the teams gave up on certain contacts at too early a stage, being discouraged by individual responses or by finding the work involved in developing the contacts too time-consuming or onerous. There was certainly evidence of some lack of organisation in the division of tasks among team members at times in all three projects.

What happened in practice was that each team found congenial and fruitful relationships with a limited number of professionals and agencies and worked hard to develop these links. The results could be deemed successful in that they were usually much appreciated by the professionals or agencies, but there were certain drawbacks, not only in that the projects' resources were concentrated on relatively few agencies.

There was evidence that the provision of resources and staff by the CHYPP and Milton Keynes projects to schools work was greater than the schools could have obtained from any other source, without paying very large sums of money. Individual programmes were drawn up, tailor-made to the requirements of the schools concerned. Sessions were conducted by the teams with young people in the schools, and a great deal of help was given to teachers.

In the same way, the CHYPP team put a lot of effort into developing the teenage ante-natal clinic, which had been a relatively unsuccessful venture run by the City and Hackney health authority, and in supporting a post-natal clinic and a young mothers' group. These clinics and groups were attended by few young people, but appeared to take up a disproportionate amount of the project team's work and funding. None of the young people interviewed at these clinics or groups had ever heard of CHYPP, in spite of the close involvement of the team. This in itself might not be important, but there was no additional evidence that the concentration of effort by CHYPP staff had any demonstrable result.

The main message is that a strategy should be drawn up from the beginning of projects of this kind, whether short-term or long-term, with clearly defined priorities. Opportunities should be taken to develop certain avenues if they appear fruitful, but each development should be part of a wider plan for using resources to the best effect.

Models of working

What lessons can be learnt from the models of organisation demonstrated by these three projects? We have drawn attention to the problems encountered by the projects in relation to their management structure and we have noted the difficulties the projects had in recruiting and retaining staff on short-term contracts of this kind. The question remains of whether the staff recruited was of the right level and from the most appropriate disciplines.

Milton Keynes and South Sefton

There was criticism, particularly in Milton Keynes, that no nurse had been appointed to support the clinic doctor. It did not seem to make a lot of difference in either area that there was no clinic nurse as such. There were a number of reasons for this, including the lack of space in which a nurse might work, but, probably most important was the fact that there were too few clients at the clinic sessions in Milton Keynes and South Sefton for a nurse to have had much to do.

In both Milton Keynes and South Sefton, the statistical evidence shows that the clinics were poorly attended, and, in South Sefton, as we have seen, the attendances would have been virtually halved if the clinic had been restricted to young people under the age of 25. As a model of service, there were clearly problems with having a clinic session only once a week in the early afternoon. We have seen that it was very inconvenient for many people, particularly teenagers who were still at school or working. The clinic clients were particularly appreciative of the clinic doctors and found the service good, but the takeup was very low, and showed few signs of increasing over the eighteen-month period. It is recognised that young people's clinics take time to get established, but there can be no doubt that the timing of the clinic sessions in these two projects was unsuitable and not to be recommended. In addition, there must be some questionmarks over the facilities and location of the clinics. The use of the premises of these two projects for clinic sessions was thought unsuitable by many professionals. Those setting up the projects thought the informality was important, but it is likely that informality can be built into much better premises. It is possible that some young people were deterred from using the clinics because of the premises in which they were located and the facilities they had available.

The premises did not seem to matter as much in connection with drop-in clients, although many professionals found them far from ideal, mainly because they were so cramped and small. The question of their location was also much discussed, with many professionals thinking that they were not in the most suitable places. The young people had views on this and they will be discussed at the end of this chapter when looking at the best ways of providing services for young people.

There did seem to be a lot to be said for having a drop-in service open five days a week, but the use made of this service in Milton Keynes and Sefton must raise the question of whether it was properly publicised, staffed or targeted. As we have seen, the Milton Keynes drop-in service was predominantly used as a pregnancy testing service, to a large extent by people who were confirming wanted pregnancies and only wanted a quick, free pregnancy test. The South Sefton drop-in service was used by many women over the age of 25 as a well-woman service. It was also used as a source of free condoms by male teenagers, many of whom were still at school. After the project period was over they were said to include a large number of drug addicts, but we could find no hard evidence for this assertion, which was not mentioned by any project team members or professionals during the monitoring period (and see Appendix II for an analysis of the activity sheets completed by the project teams).

The drop-in service staff were appreciated by the young people interviewed, although they did not attract the warmth of comment reserved for the clinic doctors. There was some evidence that the presence of a number of staff in such a small space could be off-putting for some clients. Anyone visiting the projects when all the staff were present, particularly on a clinic afternoon when one of the rooms was used by the doctor, could only be aware of the extremely crowded nature of the service, which appeared intimidating to some users.

On the other hand, there were long periods when few people came to the drop-in service, and looking at the daily figures, particularly in South Sefton, there were days on which there were no attendances at all. Even in Milton Keynes with its greater number of attendances for pregnancy testing, there were many times, particularly in the first few months, when staff were sitting around waiting for clients.

As a model of service, it is clear that any drop-in service must go out of its way to attract young people in a much more targeted way than the Milton Keynes and South Sefton projects were able to demonstrate. A rota of work should be designed so that staff are available in the drop-in service, but the flow of work should be closely monitored to see what staff are needed and how they are best deployed. There is a need, which will be discussed at the end of this chapter for more services to be available on a drop-in basis, for example, medical help and more counselling help of a general kind.

City and Hackney

The model of service which, on the face of it, looked the strongest, was that proposed by the City and Hackney health authority. This consisted of a clinic service provided by the Brook Advisory Centres three times a week and an outreach service provided by the CHYPP team of four. The Brook clinic service could capitalise on the Brook reputation and could build on an existing Brook clinic session by providing two more sessions, one of which was on a Saturday morning, which is generally recognised to be a good time for attracting young people. The other two sessions took place in the early evening.

There was every indication that this model would prove to be a powerful combination and one which might well be replicated by other health authorities. In the event, it turned out to be unsuccessful as a combined effort, although the two component parts of the project could demonstrate success for various aspects of their own work. The evidence suggests that collaboration between CHYPP and Brook was limited to begin with and had faded away completely towards the end of the monitoring period.

What are the lessons which can be learnt from this experience? After all, Brook has a long track record of working closely with health authorities, and indeed, has provided young people's clinic and counselling services on an agency basis to a number of health authorities for a number of years. What kind of model of service is offered by a collaborative venture which ended up with no collaboration at all?

There were problems surrounding the different approach and style of the two teams. The Brook team were operating from a base which was already established and they felt it important to continue to provide the kind of services for which they were well-known, both in the district and in the London area in general. The Brook staff at a national and London level were excited by the idea of being able to expand their operations to collaborate on outreach work with the CHYPP team. The development of outreach work has been an aim of Brook for some years, but funding has rarely been available for them to pursue this aim, although some outreach work has taken place in some areas.

The CHYPP team saw the Brook involvement in quite a different light, a fact which was apparent in the interviews with team members both at the beginning and the end of the project. They regarded Brook essentially as the provider of the direct clinic and counselling service to young people, and saw little point in collaborating with Brook staff on outreach or developmental work, which they saw very much as the role of the CHYPP team.

There was evidence of a fundamental difference in philosophy as well as approach between the CHYPP and Brook teams. The Brook team found CHYPP 'theoretical', while CHYPP appeared to regard Brook as service deliverers within a limited context. The fact that Brook has, over the years, developed a reputable and innovative service, based on a philosophy which has emerged through listening carefully to the needs of young people, seemed often to have been completely overlooked by CHYPP.

The decision by CHYPP to keep Brook at arm's length was not conducive to the development of a coherent policy towards the provision of services to young people in the district. The management upheavals within Brook during the monitoring period did not help to foster close cooperation with CHYPP. It can only be concluded that a valuable opportunity was missed.

The future for young people's services
This study has highlighted many problems involved in providing services for young people in connection with contraception and pregnancy counselling. The projects were set up with certain aims laid down by the Department of Health. Each project developed other aims, fixed different priorities and achieved success in some areas but not in others. One of the great challenges for service providers and those working with young people is to design services which meet young people's needs and are attractive enough for them to use them regularly and consistently.

The three projects concentrated on providing direct services to young people and seeking to develop outreach work with them through working with professionals and other agencies. The question to be asked at the end of a report of this nature is what kind of services for young people should be provided in future in the light of the lessons learnt from these projects?

The young people interviewed gave clear indications of the type of direct services they wanted to help them. They wanted a lot of local centres, which were discreet and inconspicuous, but easy to find and well-publicised. They wanted them to be open at convenient times, to be informal and non-clinical, staffed by friendly, non-judgmental, well-qualified staff who made them feel comfortable and did not tell them off. They wanted doctors who were kind and friendly, explained things well, gave them time and were not 'stern'. They did not want the staff to be 'grumpy old bags who think you're too young...' They expressed a need for services offering general counselling on problems which might affect all teenagers.

Above all, they wanted the services to be confidential at all levels. This stress on the need for a confidential service permeated the interviews with young people. It was also found in interviews with young people carried out in the Policy Studies Institute research on sex education (Allen 1987). It is the single most important factor in designing services for young people, and it is sad that some young people have such little faith in the extent to which they can rely on confidentiality in their dealings with professionals and other agencies.

Professionals and the project team staff and managers agreed on the nature of services needed for young people in terms of informality and accessibility. There was support among professionals who worked with young people in non-medical settings, like teachers and youth workers, for a counselling service which was not geared solely to contraception and pregnancy. There was thought to be a general need for more local services. The point that 'young people don't travel' and do not venture far from their home territory came through time and again in the interviews with professionals. Therefore, although there was considerable support for special and separate services for young people, there was also support for existing services and agencies to tailor their services to meet the needs of young people in a more sympathetic way.

The main feature singled out by professionals as being important in the provision of services for young people was good and continuing publicity, both to the young people themselves and to the professionals and other agencies who might refer young people to the services.

The three projects were set up specifically to provide services for young people under the age of 25 with the aim of helping to avoid unwanted pregnancies. In the event, they demonstrated the need for other services, such as a convenient family planning and well woman's clinic in South Sefton, and a free, quick pregnancy testing service for all-comers in Milton Keynes. The provision of friendly, informal and easily accessible services, open every day in convenient locations, is clearly a model which might be followed for other client groups.

Education in sex and personal relationships was a central aim in the work of the projects. Professionals and young people alike stressed the importance of the provision of good sex education in helping young people develop into responsible and happy adults. The provision of sex education in the districts where the projects were based was said to be patchy and inadequate, and the projects uncovered an unmet need for more support and resources on the part of schools.

There is clearly a considerable need for such support, provided in a structured and continuing programme. The projects did very little work in connection with AIDS, either directly with young people or in educational terms. The future provision of education in sex and personal relationships must be closely linked with the AIDS education programme. There was evidence that separate programmes were running in many areas, and that collaboration between the AIDS programme and other health education programmes was not always close. It is extraordinary that the two programmes are not completely integrated in every area. Those planning the future development of any services for young people should make it a priority to ensure no duplication of effort or confusion of purpose.

There is every indication that outreach work with young people should be provided both by those who are providing the direct service and by health education and health promotion departments of health authorities or local education authorities. The experience in City and Hackney of split services in one project with little or no collaboration between the two parts of the service was not a model of good practice. The outreach work provided by direct agencies should be backed up by health education and health promotion departments. Educational work in sex and personal relationships should be well-integrated into health education and health promotion departments, which should provide and develop expertise and resources in this important area of work to support schools and other agencies which have ongoing contact with young people.

The need for good programmes of education in sex and personal relationships to be integrated in AIDS prevention work cannot be underestimated, and it is recommended that the Department of Health and the Department of Education and Science make this a priority. The present patchiness and variability of services and education for young people examined in this study underline the need for joint action.

Chapter 15
Conclusions and recommendations

There are many lessons which can be learned from the experience of the three projects set up with Department of Health funding to provide a family planning and pregnancy counselling service for young people under the age of 25. The evidence presented in this report suggests that there are a number of issues surrounding the provision of such services for young people which must be examined carefully by health authorities thinking of setting up young people's services, by those who already have such services and by those who do not intend to set up special services for young people.

This study was concerned with evaluating services specifically designed for young people. No ideal model of family planning and pregnancy counselling service provision for young people emerges from the experience of the three projects which were evaluated. It was not the remit of the evaluation to compare designated and mainstream provision of family planning services for young people. However, many areas have no designated services for young people but provide services for them within their mainstream family planning services. The conclusions and recommendations of this report are concerned mainly with designated services, because of the nature of the evaluation, but the report contains many messages for those providing services for young people, whether through special and separate provision or through other mainstream services.

Need for young people's family planning and counselling services
1. All health authorities should give a high priority to the particular needs of young people in commissioning family planning services. The report confirms the view that young people under the age of 20 need special attention, but the extent to which separate services should be offered to them may be determined by local circumstances. There is no one single prescription which will meet the needs of all districts. The following recommendations are based on an assumption of some kind of designated

young people's service, but the main recommendation is that young people's services should be an integral part of mainstream family planning provision, however they are delivered.

Aims and objectives
2. A young people's service should have clear aims and objectives in terms of reaching the target group. These aims and objectives should be focussed on what is achievable and should not be couched in terms which are too general to be meaningful. The key issues are clarity about which groups to target in terms of age and sex, and a recognition of particular local needs.

3. The aims and objectives should be laid down, understood and agreed by all staff working for the service. Service providers and commissioners alike should be informed of the aims and objectives. All professionals and other agencies likely to wish to use or refer to the services should also be informed of the aims and objectives.

Type of services to be offered
4. Careful consideration should be given to the scope of the young people's service and the type of services to be offered. There are two main types of service which can be offered to young people: 'direct services', offering services at a defined base directly to young people who come to this base, and 'outreach services' which go out from this base to young people or those who are working with young people.

Direct services
5. It is recommended that all services of this type should offer direct services to young people, and that these should include:
a) a clinic service with a doctor present, offering contraceptive advice and supplies, post-coital contraception, pregnancy testing, pregnancy counselling, referral for termination of pregnancy, AIDS counselling, etc. Consideration should be given to the extent to which health education of a more general nature should be offered by doctors in these clinics. The opportunity to influence a group of people who tend to visit a GP infrequently should not be overlooked;

b) a 'drop-in' service offering a wider range of health-related services than those offered by the projects studied in this report. They should include advice on contraception and pregnancy counselling, but should also offer counselling and information of a more general nature, more closely geared to helping young people with health-related problems

305

which may arise. They should include counselling in personal relationships and should offer health education. They should offer on-the-spot pregnancy testing services as a matter of course, but care should be taken that they do not become pregnancy testing centres to the exclusion of other services. The general and the specific nature of the services offered should be widely publicised.

6. The frequency and timing of these direct services should be related to local circumstances. This study indicates the need for clinic sessions to take place in the late afternoon or early evening. Morning or early afternoon sessions are not suitable for young people, particularly for those who may still be at school. A Saturday morning session is to be recommended. Drop-in services do not necessarily have to be open all day and every day. They should be available in the late afternoon and early evening for the reasons outlined above. Opening hours should be strictly adhered to and the drop-in service should always have a trained counsellor present.

7. The location of the direct services is important. Young people themselves want discreet premises which are easy to find. A central location is essential since young people do not travel easily. The clinic and 'drop-in' services should be offered on the same premises for ease of quick referral and effective coordination of service provision. Young people prefer 'one door to knock on', and it is important not to risk losing them by asking them to visit a different place for related services.

8. The atmosphere in the premises should be informal and friendly but should not imply a lack of professionalism. There should be comfortable chairs, an informal reception area and unintimidating reception staff, with not too many staff present as individuals enter the reception area to be booked in or to make an enquiry. The initial reception is of crucial importance in sustaining attendance and should be as 'user-friendly' as possible.

9. Staffing of the services should be carefully considered. This study found that choice of professional staff is a crucial factor in the success of young people's services. Suitable young people's clinic doctors may be hard to find, as experience in the study areas indicated. No young people's clinic should be set up until a suitable doctor has been recruited. The question of whether a clinic nurse is necessary should be assessed. Clinics should employ counsellors with sufficient training, whose expertise should not be confined only to contraception and pregnancy. These counsellors should

preferably be available for the 'drop-in' sessions as well as the clinic sessions to provide continuity.

10. The question of whether women staff are preferable to men staff should be examined. Although some young people express a strong desire to see a woman doctor, the evidence suggests that friendliness and listening skills are more important than the sex of the doctor.

11. The most important characteristic of the service offered should be an awareness of the key issue of confidentiality. This is of paramount importance to young people.

'Outreach' work

12. There is much to be said for at least some outreach work taking place from the premises in which the young people's direct service is based.

13. The staff undertaking or responsible for the outreach work should be the same staff as those engaged in providing a direct service. A key lesson from this study is that there should be no division of responsibilities for the direct and outreach services between two agencies with different staff on different premises unless the liaison between the two agencies is very close and there is a monitoring and management mechanism to ensure unity of purpose and function. It is very important that any outreach work of an educational nature is carried out in close collaboration with the health education or health promotion department of the health authority, with the local education authority and with AIDS education officers or coordinators.

14. If outreach work is to be undertaken, there should be a clear understanding of what the different strands of outreach work may be. Distinctions should be made between the various categories, and an early decision should be taken about which type or types of outreach work can or should be undertaken. The following categories of work should be considered:
a) outreach work informing professional and other agencies of the direct service to young people so that they may refer young people to a known service;
b) outreach work offering training or resources to professionals, schools or other agencies wishing to develop programmes or packages of education in sex and personal relationships;

c) outreach work offering tailor-made programmes and packages of education in sex and personal relationships which may be adopted and delivered by schools or other agencies to young people;

d) outreach work offering programmes or packages of education in sex and personal relationships to be implemented or delivered to groups of young people on their own premises, eg school or youth club, by staff from the young people's service;

e) outreach work designed to reach young people who are not in touch with an institution or agency.

Planning and management

15. No young people's service should be set up without the close involvement and cooperation of family planning staff who work in related areas. The need for such a service should be clearly demonstrated to such staff, and the reasons for setting up a young people's service, particularly if new staff are to be employed, should be made explicit.

16. No young people's service should be set up for a time-limited period on short-term funding. Such projects are rarely taken seriously by other health authority staff, take too long to prove themselves, find it difficult to recruit and retain suitable staff, and may raise unrealistic expectations among users or potential users which cannot be fulfilled.

17. The young people's service should be an integral part of the mainstream family planning service provision, and very close liaison with all other staff delivering services of similar nature is essential.

18. A management structure should be in place before the young people's service starts. One person should have management responsibility for the service. This person should not be at a level too far removed from the day-to-day running of the service. If the staff come from different disciplines, there should not be a situation in which different members of staff have different line managers in addition to the manager of the service. A clear definition of staff roles, responsibilities and lines of accountability should be drawn up before staff are appointed. All members of staff should be appointed at the same time and all members should be in post before any attempt is made to deliver services.

19. It should be made explicit where responsibility for the budget lies. There should be a young people's service coordinator who is responsible for all aspects of the day-to-day running of the service.

20. One of the main aims should be to facilitate liaison with other agencies involved with young people. One way of doing this would be to set up a multi-disciplinary advisory group, with representatives from relevant professional groups and other agencies working with young people, for example GPs, family planning doctors and nurses, education services, social services, youth service etc.. This group should operate purely in an advisory capacity and should not have management or steering functions. If such functions are thought necessary, a different structure should be established. The advisory group should have a clear remit, should meet regularly and should be attended by all relevant staff of the service. The importance of its role should be recognised, and a two-way flow of information and development of thinking about the best ways of providing services for young people should be encouraged. The value of such an arrangement is that professionals are aware of and have an interest in the success of a young people's service.

21. All staff should be fully trained for their functions before any direct or outreach service is provided. In-service training may be necessary at a later stage, but should not involve most members of staff at one time.

22. Locum cover for doctors should be arranged before the service starts.

23. All necessary resources, equipment and back-up services should be in place before the service starts.

Publicity
24. A coherent plan of publicity arrangements should be drawn up before the service is launched. All publicity material should be of a highly professional standard. It should be aimed at and designed for both young people and professionals. Ongoing and updated publicity is essential. Publicity about the services should be sustained, regular and incremental. There is no point in sending out material to professionals and other agencies which is not followed up. All means of publicising the services should be employed.

Monitoring and evaluation
25. Services should be closely monitored. Good and accurate record-keeping is essential. Services should be monitored and evaluated at two levels. Staff and local management should monitor their own performance and assess whether they are meeting their own objectives. Districts should monitor and evaluate the services to ensure that they are

being provided according to specifications and to monitor the outcomes. Districts should ensure that the services are meeting the needs of young people.

Targeting of the services
26. The services should be targeted at young people under the age of 20. The greatest need for such services appears to be among teenagers, although young women in their early twenties use young people's services such as Brook in relatively large numbers. Older women should be encouraged to use other mainstream services, which should be developed to meet their specific needs. Every effort should be made to bring boys and young men into the clientele of young people's services.

Liaison with other professionals and agencies
27. One of the most important messages which came through in this report was the need for young people's services of this kind to liaise and collaborate with other professionals and agencies providing services for young people. This liaison should be a continuing priority for those running young people's services.

28. Two of the most important links which should be developed are with GPs and with consultant obstetricians and gynaecologists. None of the projects studied had made any real attempt to forge such links, which may be difficult to develop, but are essential if effective and relevant services are to be developed for young people.

Implications of this report for professionals and other agencies
29. Professionals and other agencies providing services for young people should take careful note of the images held of their services by many of the young people interviewed in this study. Most young people use and will continue to use services offered by GPs and other professionals and agencies, but many doctors and professionals could learn much from the approach and content of the work of doctors and others working in young people's services of this kind.

30. Family planning clinics have much to learn from the experience of the three young people's projects and the young people using them. There is a need for family planning clinics to make clear to young people that they will welcome them, that they are not only for 'older' people over the age of 20, and that they are not only for people 'planning families'. They should also make clear that they will offer pregnancy counselling.

Education in sex and personal relationships

31. The need for improved and extended education in sex and personal relationships was amply demonstrated in this study. The expertise and resources of all possible sources should be tapped by the staff of the young people's service and the aim should be to build up a well-serviced resource centre in the young people's service. Although schools and other agencies may well be the best deliverers of education in sex and personal relationships, many need and welcome help, support and resources of a specialist nature. Young people's services are in a particularly good position to provide this, if they have sufficiently well-trained staff and enough resources themselves.

32. There is a crucial need for education about HIV and AIDS to be integrated with education in sex and personal relationships. The impact of education about HIV and AIDS has yet to be measured, but there are indications that unless the two types of education go together, the value of one or the other is diminished. They should not exist as two parallel programmes but there should be unified management and delivery of such programmes. There is a need for joint action by the Department of Health and the Department of Education and Science to promote a rational approach to the provision of such health education.

A health authority strategy for young people

33. Each health authority should aim to develop a strategy for commissioning services which meet the specific needs of young people. The process should involve all relevant professional groups and other agencies, both inside and outside the health authority, and should be given management support at the highest level. Specific initiatives need to be placed within an overall strategic framework. Without such a framework, there is a risk that innovative services for young people may be marginalised and the lessons from this report may be lost.

Appendix I

Trends in abortion and fertility rates in the 1980s in England and Wales, City and Hackney, Milton Keynes and South Sefton

England and Wales
Abortions
There has been a general increase in the number of abortions performed in England and Wales during the 1980s, rising from 128,581 in 1981 to 170,463 in 1989. This increase in the number of abortions has mainly taken place on non-NHS premises, resulting in a decreasing proportion of abortions being performed on NHS premises. At the beginning of the 1980s, 48 per cent of abortions occurred on NHS premises, but this had fallen to 42 per cent by the end of the decade. Very few abortions on NHS premises occur outside the Regional Health Authority where a woman resides (Table I.1).

We can control for changes in the number of women in the different age groups by examining the rate of abortions. Table I.2 shows the rate of abortions per 1000 women for the age groups of women of interest to this study. It also shows the rate for all women in the childbearing ages for comparative purposes. The rate of abortions for all women aged 15-44 in England and Wales was stable in the early 1980s at just over 12 per 1000 women, but rose steadily in the latter part of the decade to 15.5 per 1000 women in 1989. There was therefore a real increase in the abortion rate in the late 1980s. This increase was even more noticeable for teenagers and women in their early twenties (Table I.2).

Live births
The birth rates* have shown less change than the abortion rates. The overall birth rate for women in the childbearing ages showed a slight increase in the second half of the 1980s, as did the fertility rate* for teenage girls. However, the fertility rate for women in their early twenties fell until 1986 and then rose slightly in 1987 and 1988 before falling again in 1989 (Table I.3). It should be noted that any changes in the age-specific fertility rates are a complex result of changes in cohort and period childbearing patterns and do not necessarily indicate any change in eventual childbearing intentions or completed family size.

* The terms 'birth rate' and 'fertility rate' are used throughout to refer only to live births.

312

Appendix 1

City and Hackney
Abortions

A much larger number of abortions occur for women resident in City and Hackney than for those in the other two districts in this study: roughly three times the number. This is not merely a product of a higher number of resident women in this district, since the abortion rate is likewise much higher. The rate for women in their early twenties, in particular, is much higher than that in the other areas and is also very much higher than the overall rate for this age group in England and Wales. It should be remembered, however, that City and Hackney is an Inner London area with a highly mobile, young population with many attendant social problems. Other districts of a similar type have similarly high abortion rates in this age group.

The overall abortion rate in City and Hackney increased from 27.0 per 1000 women in 1981 to 42.3 in 1989, while the rate for women aged 20-24 rose from 39.9 to 73.9 over the same period, peaking in 1988 at 77.7. The increase in the abortion rate in this age group was most noticeable between 1985 and 1986, when it rose from 58.6 to 70.0 per 1000 women. The teenage abortion rate rose steadily between 1981 and 1987, from 29.0 to 37.9 per 1000 women, but then declined to 32.4 per 1000 women in 1989 (Table I.2).

There was a general increase over the decade in the proportion of abortions taking place in NHS premises in the home Regional Health Authority: North East Thames RHA. It rose from 41 per cent in 1981 to a high of 63 per cent in 1985, but fell to 56 per cent in 1989. However, this was still higher than the national NHS average. There was a corresponding decrease between 1981 and 1984 in the proportion of abortions taking place on non-NHS premises outside the RHA, but the proportion then started rising again and by 1989 30 per cent of abortions took place on such premises (Table I.1).

Live births

The overall fertility rate for women in the childbearing ages in City and Hackney is also much higher than the national average and is the highest of the three District Health Authorities in this study. However, the difference is not as striking as the difference in the abortion rates between City and Hackney and the other areas and England and Wales. The overall fertility rate in City and Hackney, in contrast to that of England and Wales, fell slightly from 1982 to 1986, but then rose in 1987 before resuming a decreasing trend.

The pattern of the age-specific fertility rate for women aged 20-24 followed this same trend, showing an overall fall between 1982 and 1989 from 115.5 to 102.0 per 1000 women. It showed the same increase as the overall fertility rate in City and Hackney in 1987. This increase was not countered by a fall in the abortion rates for this year, as these also showed a large increase in this age group in 1986 and a continuing increase until 1989.

313

The fertility rate for teenagers in City and Hackney was very high in the early 1980s, at 50.2 per 1000 women in 1981, when compared with the national average and the other two areas in this study. The teenage fertility rate, however, fell steadily over the period, which is at odds with the patterns shown by the national figures and those in the other two districts. In 1989, the fertility rate for teenagers in City and Hackney reached 36.1, which is similar to the national average and the rates in the other two areas (Table I.3). This fall in the teenage birth rate in City and Hackney has not been countered by an increase in the abortion rate, which suggests a decrease in the conception rate of teenagers in this area.

Milton Keynes
This District Health Authority was constituted in 1983. Consequently some figures are only available after this date.

Abortions
Milton Keynes had the lowest number of abortions of the three District Health Authorities in this study until 1986. After 1986 there was a dramatic change in the pattern of abortions taking place on NHS and non-NHS premises. There was a fall in the proportion of abortions occurring on NHS premises within the local RHA, from 57 per cent in 1986 to 30 per cent in 1987 to only 2 per cent in 1988 and 1 per cent in 1989. There was a corresponding increase in the proportion of abortions occurring on non-NHS premises outside the local RHA, from 42 per cent in 1986 to 69 per cent in 1987 and 97 per cent in 1988 and 1989. (This was due to a change in policy whereby it was arranged for abortions to be provided on behalf of the NHS by a non-NHS body under an agency arrangement.)

The abortion rate for all women aged 15-44 was also the lowest of the three areas in the early 1980s, but rose in 1986 from 10.3 per 1000 women in 1985 to 12.8 in 1986, and continued to rise steadily to reach 14.8 in 1989. It should be noted that the increase occurred a year before the policy change on premises was implemented, so there was a real increase in the abortion rate before any obvious change in access arrangements. The rise in abortion rates is particularly noticeable for teenagers, among whom the abortion rate increased from 16.4 per 1000 women to 20.2 in 1986 and reached 25.4 in 1989. It is puzzling as to why the abortion rate for women in their early twenties showed this large increase a year later, the same year as the implementation of the agency arrangement, with a rise in the rate from 14.9 in 1986 to 20.7 in 1987. The rate increased again in 1988 but showed a slight decrease in 1989, to 21 per 1000 women in the 20-24 age group.

Live births
The fertility rate for all women in the childbearing age group was fairly stable in Milton Keynes until 1986, at around 71-72 per 1000 women. In 1986 the rate

fell to 66.5 and has remained stable since. This fall corresponds with the timing in the rise in the overall abortion rate but is of a larger dimension. It should be noted that the overall fertility rate in Milton Keynes DHA does not show the general increase apparent in the national figures, but shows a steady decrease over the period 1982-89.

In the early 1980s, the fertility rate in Milton Keynes for women aged 20-24 was very high, compared with the national average and the other two areas in this study. It was 132 per 1000 women in 1982, compared with a national figure of 101.6. It fell steadily over the period, particularly in 1984, from 130.7 in 1983 to 117.6 per 1000 women in 1984. This decreasing trend continued but slowed in pace in the final two years of the decade, reaching 86.5 in 1989, so that now the women aged 20-24 in Milton Keynes have the lowest fertility rates of women of these ages in any of the areas in this study, being even lower that the national average for this age group of 92.1. The trends in birth and abortion rates in this DHA are probably affected by the migration of people into the recently expanded New Town. Certainly there is evidence that the number of women in their early twenties grew from 1983 onwards.

The teenage fertility rate in this district was fairly stable during the 1980s, compared with the trends in the other two districts. It did not follow the rising trend of the national figures, and, in fact, it fluctuated from a low of 32.6 in 1984 to a high of 35.8 in 1985 before falling again in 1986 to 32.9. It rose in 1987 and 1988 before falling to 34.7 in the last year of the decade, which is virtually the same as the rate of 34.9 in the first year of the decade. The fall in the birth rate in 1986 coincided with the rise in the abortion rate for this age group of women in Milton Keynes.

South Sefton
This District Health Authority was constituted in 1983. Consequently some figures are only available from this date.

Abortions
South Sefton has had the lowest number of abortions of the three districts in this study since 1986. The pattern of abortions taking place on NHS and non-NHS premises is the most similar among the three districts to the national average, but, even so, the proportion of abortions taking place on NHS premises has been consistently below the national average. In 1983, 43 per cent of abortions occurred on NHS premises in the home Regional Health Authority but this had fallen to 33 per cent in 1989. Most of the abortions on non-NHS premises also occur within the home RHA, unlike the other two districts and the national pattern. These abortions on home RHA non-NHS premises increased from 44 per cent of the total in 1983 to 50 per cent in 1989.

The abortion rate for all women in the childbearing ages showed a general increase during the 1980s, but was somewhat smaller than the rise demonstrated by the national figures and those of the other two areas. The teenage abortion rate shows the same fluctuating pattern over the period as the overall abortion rate for women in South Sefton, but the general pattern has been to increase, with rises in 1984 and 1986, the same years as the overall rate increased. The abortion rate of women in their early twenties, on the other hand, has shown a steady increase throughout the 1980s, from 18.4 per 1000 women in 1983 to 25.1 in 1989.

Live births
The birth rate in South Sefton DHA showed more fluctuation over the period than was found in the national pattern and in the other two DHAs. While the fertility rate for all women aged 15-44 showed a general increase over the 1980s, it varied from 59.7 per 1000 women in 1982 to 64.9 in 1983 and then fell to 61.2 in 1984 before rising for the rest of the period. The fertility rates for the youngest two age groups showed similar fluctuations. The general trend, however, was for the teenage rates to increase, from 29.8 in 1982 to 37.9 in 1989, and for the rates for women aged 20-24 to decrease, from 104.5 to 94.6 over the same period. The birth rates for all of these women were lower than those in the other two areas in 1982, but were comparable to the national averages. By 1989 the rates of the other two areas had converged to show broadly comparable levels of fertility.

It should be noted that the 1985 birth rates appear to be inconsistent with the general trends, in that the teenage and overall fertility rates show a decrease while that of the women aged 20-24 shows an increase. These figures have been checked and the Fertility Statistics Unit at OPCS confirms that they are correct.

Conclusions
It is very difficult to draw many general conclusions about the fertility and abortion trends in the three areas of this study since they show many different patterns. This is understandable, given that they have differing demographic profiles and social characteristics.

We drew attention in Chapter 1 of this report to the difficulty of drawing any conclusions about the impact of any projects or services for young people on the basis of the birth or abortion rates for one or two years. The fluctuations in rates on a year by year basis throughout the 1980s in all three areas and at a national level have been clearly demonstrated in the tables and commentary in this Appendix. This makes it particularly difficult to draw any conclusions about the rates in 1988 and 1989, the only two years which might have been affected by the setting up of the three young people's projects. Any fall or rise in the rates in those two years might be countered in the next few years by further rises and falls. The figures for the three areas have to be looked at against the trends in the national figures, and must be examined in relation to trends in areas with similar demographic, economic and social characteristics. This is a long-term exercise. In any case, it is not possible, given the type of fluctuations observed, to attribute any changes in rates to any particular factor. Most changes, as we have noted, are due to a combination of factors at a national and local level.

The main points which have emerged in the tables and the analysis are summarised below:

Abortions

1. The number of abortions to residents of all three areas increased throughout the 1980s, reflecting the trend in the country as a whole.
2. The proportion of abortions performed on NHS premises fell over the period in all three areas, although City and Hackney DHA did show an increased proportion in the mid-1980s. This decline in the proportion of NHS abortions also reflected the national trend.
3. Abortion rates among the 15-44 age group rose generally over the period in all three areas, particularly in the latter half of the 1980s. In Milton Keynes and South Sefton they rose in line with the national trend. In City and Hackney they increased at a faster rate.
4. City and Hackney DHA had much higher abortion rates than the other two DHAs throughout the decade, both for teenage girls and for women in their early twenties. The teenage abortion rate, however, rose and then fell over the period in contrast to the other two areas and the national trend. On the other hand, the increase in the abortion rate for women in their early twenties in City and Hackney was notable over the period, reaching a peak of 73.9 per 1000 in 1989.
5. Milton Keynes DHA had a dramatic change in policy in 1987 in its provision of abortions on NHS premises. There was a rise in the overall abortion rate around this time, but for teenage girls the increase predated this change in access. The increase in the teenage abortion rate over the period was marked.
6. South Sefton DHA had the lowest provision of abortions on NHS premises of the three DHAs until the change in policy in Milton Keynes. Its provision of NHS abortions is still below the national average. The rise in the abortion rate was noticeable for both age groups of women but in line with the national trend.

Live births

1. Birth rates showed less change than abortion rates over the 1980s.
2. The patterns in the three areas show wide disparities, with City and Hackney DHA and Milton Keynes DHA not reflecting the national rise in teenage fertility.
3. City and Hackney teenage fertility rates showed a steady decline and those of women aged 20-24 showed a general decline over the period, apart from a sudden rise in 1987.

4. Milton Keynes DHA teenage fertility rates were fairly constant during the 1980s at a rate rather above the national average. The fertility rates for women in their early twenties showed a dramatic decrease over the period at a much faster rate than was found nationally.

5. South Sefton teenage fertility rates followed the trend shown by the national figures of a steady increase in the 1980s. The fertility rates among women in the 20-24 age group also followed the national trend, which was of a steady decrease over the period, in contrast to the teenage rates.

Table I.1   Legal abortions – total numbers and percentage by regional health authority of operation and category of premises 1981-89

District Health Authority		Year							
	1981	1982	1983	1984	1985	1986	1987	1988	1989
	%	%	%	%	%	%	%	%	%
City and Hackney									
Home RHA - NHS	41	43	58	61	63	62	61	61	56
- non-NHS	15	19	16	17	15	13	12	13	14
Other RHA - NHS	2	2	*	1	1	*	*	1	*
- non-NHS	42	36	26	20	21	25	27	26	30
Total number (base)	1156	1143	1267	1408	1566	1749	1913	2014	2089
Milton Keynes									
Home RHA - NHS	n/a	n/a	55	61	52	57	30	2	1
- non-NHS			nil	nil	nil	nil	nil	nil	nil
Other RHA - NHS			4	1	3	1	1	1	1
- non-NHS			41	38	45	42	69	97	97
Total number (base)			396	380	396	527	598	654	690
South Sefton									
Home RHA - NHS	n/a	n/a	43	38	35	39	38	33	33
- non-NHS			44	47	49	47	43	51	50
Other RHA - NHS			2	2	4	3	2	3	3
- non-NHS			11	13	12	12	16	14	14
Total number (base)			444	494	450	493	490	500	543
England and Wales (total)									
Home RHA - NHS	45	46	47	45	44	44	42	39	40
- non-NHS	24	24	25	26	27	27	28	31	31
Other RHA - NHS	3	3	2	2	2	2	2	2	2
- non-NHS	29	27	26	26	27	27	27	28	28
Total number (base)	128581	128553	127375	136388	141101	147619	156191	168298	170463

* Less than 0.5%

Table I.2   Abortion rates (per 1,000 women) by age groups of women 1981-89

District Health Authority	1981	1982	1983	1984	1985	1986	1987	1988	1989
City and Hackney									
15-19*	29.0	29.7	34.0	34.8	36.3	34.4	37.9	32.1	32.4
20-24	39.9	42.0	45.9	51.3	58.6	70.0	74.2	77.7	73.9
15-44**	27.0	27.0	29.2	31.6	34.6	38.0	40.8	42.0	42.3
Milton Keynes									
15-19*	n/a	n/a	14.3	17.1	16.4	20.2	24.3	25.9	25.4
20-24			15.6	14.2	13.7	14.9	20.7	22.3	21.0
15-44**			11.7	10.4	10.3	12.8	13.6	14.3	14.8
South Sefton									
15-19*	n/a	n/a	15.8	18.3	17.1	18.6	17.1	22.0	23.9
20-24			18.4	20.2	21.0	23.3	25.1	24.0	25.1
15-44**			11.5	12.7	11.7	12.7	12.8	13.0	14.2
England and Wales (total)									
15-19*	17.3	17.4	17.6	19.0	19.8	19.8	20.9	22.9	22.7
20-24	18.6	18.5	18.0	19.5	20.4	21.9	23.8	26.5	27.3
15-44**	12.4	12.3	12.0	12.8	13.1	13.5	14.2	15.2	15.5

* Assumes all abortions to girls under 16 are to 15 year-old girls
** Includes any abortions where age of woman is not stated

Table I.3   Live birth rates (per 1,000 women) by age groups of women 1982-89

District Health Authority	82	83	84	85	86	87	88	89
City and Hackney								
15-19*	50.2	47.9	47.8	42.5	42.1	41.7	39.4	36.1
20-24	115.5	118.8	109.7	108.8	106.6	112.7	110.5	102.0
15-44*	76.3	75.2	75.7	74.0	73.9	80.3	79.0	77.0
Milton Keynes								
15-19*	34.9	33.4	32.6	35.8	32.9	35.0	36.6	34.7
20-24	132.0	130.7	117.6	109.3	101.5	93.5	91.2	86.5
15-44*	76.2	71.4	71.7	71.3	66.5	65.9	66.4	62.5
South Sefton								
15-19*	29.8	32.2	31.5	29.1	32.9	33.1	35.7	37.9
20-24	104.5	104.4	95.6	100.8	92.9	97.1	97.3	94.6
15-44*	59.7	64.9	61.2	63.7	63.1	63.3	65.2	66.1
England and Wales (total)								
15-19*	27.4	26.9	27.6	29.5	30.1	30.9	32.4	31.9
20-24	101.6	98.5	95.5	94.5	92.7	93.4	94.9	92.1
15-44*	59.9	59.6	59.7	60.9	60.6	62.0	62.9	62.5

* Assumes any births to girls aged under 15 are to girls aged 15.

Appendix II

Analysis of 'outreach' and training activities of project teams

The project team members recorded their activities on 'activity' sheets which were devised in conjunction with the team members who were in post at the beginning of the projects. They were designed to show the meetings or contacts that team members had with professionals, agencies and other organisations outside the projects. They were not designed to indicate the team members' contact with *individual* young people, but were intended to show their contact with *groups* of young people, for example at schools or youth clubs. In addition, the team members recorded the training activities in which they took part, in which they themselves were receiving training.

The activities of the project team members were analysed in two ways: first, according to the *categories of organisation* with whom they had contact and by the *type of activity* they recorded with this organisation. These activities were divided into the number of 'sessions' held and the number of 'people sessions' held (ie the number of project staff at each session, see Section 4 below.) Secondly, the training activities in which the team members themselves received training were analysed.

Two sets of tables follow. The first set of tables (A) analyse the 'outreach' activities of the project team members. The second set of tables (B) analyse the 'training' of the project team members. Keys to interpreting the tables follow the tables. A short commentary on the findings of the tables follows the 'keys'.

It should be noted that telephone enquiries to the projects were designed to be recorded and analysed separately. This analysis follows in Appendix III. However, some of the project team members recorded at least some telephone contacts on their activity sheets. These were not double counted – ie if they were recorded as activities they were counted as activities and if they were recorded as telephone enquiries they were counted as such.

A. Key to Activities Analysis
1. Categories of organisation
These are given in the tables on the left-hand side. They are mainly self-explanatory, but two categories need further details:

Table 14.1 CHYPP Activities Analysis

S = Sessions
PS = People sessions

Contact	Intro (phone)		Intro (meeting)		Session planning		YP sessions		Professional training sessions		Advice/ lending resources		Other		Devpt. joint initiatives		Referral/ liaison re individuals		Routine contact	
	S	PS	S	PS	S	PS	S	PS	S	PS	S	PS	S	PS	S	PS	S	PS	S	PS
FPC staff	-	-	2	3	5	5	-	-	4	5	-	-	-	-	1	1	-	-	-	-
Other HA staff	2	2	22	26	1	1	3	6	2	2	11	11	-	-	16	17	1	1	-	-
Health Ed/Promotion staff	-	-	4	4	15	20	-	-	-	-	3	4	-	-	5	5	-	-	-	-
Brook	-	-	4	6	1	1	-	-	-	-	-	-	-	-	3	5	-	-	11	13
GPs	1	1	6	9	-	-	-	-	-	-	-	-	-	-	2	2	1	1	-	-
BPAS	-	-	-	-	-	-	-	-	-	-	-	-	-	-	-	-	-	-	-	-
Schools	3	3	9	11	19	21	21	24	15	18	10	10	4	4	1	2	-	-	-	-
Youth service	9	9	10	12	15	18	16	20	2	2	12	12	-	-	2	2	-	-	-	-
Other vol. and community staff	5	5	26	27	6	7	7	7	-	-	1	1	-	-	2	3	1	1	-	-
Youth Training Schemes	1	1	1	1	3	4	5	5	-	-	1	1	-	-	-	-	-	-	-	-
Social services	-	-	5	6	17	26	4	6	7	13	4	4	-	-	2	3	-	-	-	-
Teenage ante-natal clinic (CHYPP only)	-	-	2	2	-	-	1	1	-	-	1	1	-	-	7	7	-	-	34	34
Young Mothers Group (CHYPP only)	-	-	-	-	-	-	2	2	-	-	-	-	-	-	12	12	-	-	7	7
Baby clinic (CHYPP only)	-	-	-	-	-	-	-	-	-	-	-	-	-	-	1	1	-	-	1	1
Other authority (eg police, probation, local authority, careers service)	-	-	3	3	2	2	-	-	-	-	1	1	-	-	4	4	-	-	2	2

Table II.2 Milton Keynes (You 2) – Activities Analysis
S = Sessions
PS = People sessions

Contact	Intro (phone)		Intro (meeting)		Session planning		YP sessions		Professional training sessions		Advice/ lending resources		Other		Devpt. joint initiatives		Referral/ liaison re individuals		Routine contact	
	S	PS	S	PS	S	PS	S	PS	S	PS	S	PS	S	PS	S	PS	S	PS	S	PS
FPC staff	-	-	1	1	2	2	-	-	1	1	-	-	-	-	2	2	-	-	-	-
Other HA staff	-	-	9	9	-	-	-	-	-	-	2	3	-	-	24*	37*	2	2	-	-
Health Ed/Promotion staff	-	-	4	4	-	-	-	-	1	1	6	6	-	-	4	4	-	-	-	-
Brook	-	-	-	-	-	-	-	-	-	-	-	-	-	-	9*	9*	1	1	-	-
GPs	-	-	8	8	-	-	-	-	-	-	-	-	-	-	-	-	1	1	-	-
BPAS	-	-	1	3	-	-	-	-	-	-	-	-	-	-	-	-	1	1	-	-
Schools	13	13	13	16	24	29	102	203	16	29	4	4	19	21	1	1	-	-	-	-
Youth service	13	13	15	15	-	-	1	1	-	-	2	2	1	1	3	3	-	-	-	-
Other vol. and community staff	5	5	7	9	-	-	-	-	-	-	-	-	-	-	6	6	3	3	-	-
Youth Training Schemes	9	9	7	7	10	11	34	52	3	5	2	2	1	1	-	-	-	-	-	-
Social services	10	10	4	4	-	-	2	2	-	-	-	-	1	1	-	-	1	1	-	-
Other authority	7	7	5	8	-	-	-	-	-	-	1	1	-	-	7	7	-	-	-	-

* mostly in connection with Sex Education Questionnaire and trying to set up MK Brook clinic for post-March 89.

Table II.3 South Sefton (PACE) – Activities Analysis

S = Sessions
PS = People sessions

Contact	Intro (phone)		Intro (meeting)		Session planning		YP sessions		Professional training sessions		Advice/ lending resources		Other		Devpt. joint initiatives		Referral/ liaison re individuals		Routine contact	
	S	PS	S	PS	S	PS	S	PS	S	PS	S	PS	S	PS	S	PS	S	PS	S	PS
FPC staff	-	-	2	2	-	-	-	-	-	-	-	-	-	-	-	-	-	-	-	-
Other HA staff	-	-	8	11	-	-	-	-	1	1	4	6	-	-	2	2	3	3	-	-
Health Ed/Promotion staff	-	-	6	7	1	2	-	-	-	-	-	-	-	-	14	17	-	-	-	-
Brook	-	-	3	3	-	-	-	-	-	-	-	-	-	-	-	-	-	-	-	-
GPs	-	-	1	1	-	-	-	-	-	-	-	-	-	-	-	-	-	-	-	-
BPAS	-	-	-	-	-	-	-	-	-	-	-	-	-	-	-	-	2	2	-	-
Schools	-	-	5	5	-	-	13	18	-	-	2	2	4	4	-	-	-	-	-	-
Youth service	-	-	15	17	2	2	2	3	-	-	-	-	-	-	1	1	-	-	-	-
Other vol. and community staff	-	-	15	17	1	1	1	2	-	-	-	-	-	-	3	3	1	1	-	-
Youth Training Schemes	-	-	1	1	1	1	9	10	-	-	-	-	-	-	-	-	1	1	-	-
Social services	-	-	7	11	-	-	-	-	-	-	-	-	-	-	-	-	3	3	-	-
Other authority	2	2	2	3	-	-	2	2	1	2	-	-	-	-	5	5	-	-	-	-
Home visits by HV member of staff	-	-	-	-	-	-	25	25	-	-	-	-	-	-	-	-	-	-	-	-

(i)   'Other health authority staff' includes health visitors, school nurses, community management doctors and nurses.

(ii)   'Other voluntary and community staff' includes the Family Welfare Association, NSPCC, Samaritans, CAB, Marriage Guidance, drug advisory or other drugs workers, local churches, other community centres and other local organisations.

(iii)   'Other authority staff' includes staff employed by another authority (not elsewhere covered) as indicated, eg. police, probation, local authority, careers service etc.

2.   *Type of activity*

The type of activity was categorised into ten main types which are given across the top of each table. In addition, the home visits by the PACE member of staff who was a health visitor by training are indicated separately on the PACE table.

The following types of activity were analysed:

(i)   introducing the project by telephone.

(ii)   introducing the project by personal contact, eg. at a meeting at the project base or at the professional's/organisation's base.

(iii)   session planning: sessions held with a contact or with other professionals (eg. AIDS workers, youth workers, teachers) to plan sessions for young people or for professionals.

(iv)   young people sessions: sessions given to young people by the project team or by the project team with other professionals.

(v)   training other professionals: sessions given by the project team, or by the project team with other professionals, to train professionals or to help them with curriculum/programme development in sex education.

(vi)   advice/lending resources: contacts where the project gave information about resources or lent resources.

(vii)   other: was used mainly for schools contacts, and were miscellaneous meetings or contacts with schools which did not fall easily into the other categories.

(viii) development of joint initiatives: contacts where the purpose was to develop a service initiative jointly with another organisation or agency, eg. meetings about developing the use of other bases in Milton Keynes, a sex education questionnaire for schoolchildren in Milton Keynes, sex education conferences, future funding, the use of the South Sefton health bus for PACE work, a girls' night for the King George VI Centre etc.

(ix)   referral/liaison with another organisation or professional about a particular individual client.

(x)   routine contact: this category related *only* to CHYPP and covered (a) all routine contact between CHYPP and Brook and (b) all routine attendance by project team members at projects developed by CHYPP, eg. the Teenage Ante-natal Clinic and the Young Mothers' Group.

3. *Types of activities included and not included*
(i) *Types of activities included*

The types of activities include *all* the developmental and promotional work of the project team staff, and *all* their activities involved in working with professionals, agencies or young people to further the aims of the projects.

They include contacts with staff in the same departments as the project staff, or those sharing the same premises or facilities, where these were directly related to or connected with the projects or where they were related to developing mutual interests.

(ii) *Types of activities not included*

The types of activities not included were

*   *routine* contacts or meetings with staff in the same departments as the project staff, or those sharing the same premises or facilities;

*   *routine* attendance at other professional/related interest groups;

*   *routine* publicity of projects by advertisement, contact with newspapers, radio, mailings, listings, etc;

*   attendance at events where the project itself was not the main focus or the project staff were not included in the organisation of the event;

*   *routine* contacts involved principally in making arrangements of times, places, dates, etc;

*   contacts for training project staff or contacts for staff to acquire information or resources. These were analysed separately (see next section).

4. *'Sessions' and 'people sessions'*

The number of 'sessions' of a type of activity held with a particular organisation is counted in two ways:

(i)   by a particular event on a particular day – 'session'.
(ii) by the number of project staff recording attendance at each event – 'people session'.

For example, if there are 2 'sessions' recorded and 2 'people sessions' recorded, this means that there were 2 separate sessions, each taken or attended by *one* project team worker. In other instances, 3 'sessions' may have been recorded with 5 'people sessions', in which case there were 3 separate sessions, one taken by one project team worker and two others by two project team workers.

This method of presenting the data was found to be the only fair way of representing the workload of the teams. Giving the number of sessions or contacts alone would not have given a full picture of the work of the team, who sometimes attended the same event, as the tables show. However, simply presenting the number of 'people sessions', i.e. the sessions/contacts/events reported by each team member could have given an inflated impression of the number of activities undertaken.

It can be seen from the tables that most meetings were attended by only one project team member, but that professional training sessions or sessions with young people were rather more likely to be attended by more than one team member in City and Hackney and very much more likely to be attended by more than one team member in Milton Keynes.

Problems

There were some problems in interpreting the data provided by the teams on their activity sheets, particularly as far as the activities in schools were concerned:

(i)   For example, there was clearly considerable variation in the length of a 'session', which could range from one minute on the telephone to a full day at a school.

(ii) We did not always know how many project team staff took each group of students, so, if four staff were involved, we did not always know whether there were four 'parallel sessions' or two 'sessions' each taken by two members of staff.

These problems led to some discrepancy between the data assembled by the project teams themselves for their own purposes and the data provided to us by individual team members on their activity sheets.

B.   Training of Project Team Members

	Formal training events or sessions[1]		Less formal events[2]		Contacts to acquire information etc[3]	
	S	PS	S	PS	S	PS
CHYPP	11	11	22	29	4	4
MK (You 2)	33	75	17	20	10	10
SS (PACE)	7	8	4	5	1	1

S = Sessions
PS = People sessions

Key to training of project team members tables

1   Formal training events or sessions were arranged specifically for the project workers and were directly related to the project needs.

2   The less formal training events or sessions included

a)   meetings or contacts for project workers to find out about the skills, expertise or services of other organisations or professionals working in related fields (eg. AIDS, rape, child and sexual abuse, drugs, alcohol, other addiction, STD, Brook clinics).

b)   workshop or participatory events where project workers were participants as well as recipients of training.

c)   training days run by specific organisations for all those working in certain fields or with certain problems (eg. RHA training events etc).

This table does *not* include individual training courses embarked upon by project team members while working on the projects, eg. Certificate in Health Education, 'Training the Trainers', etc.

C.   Notes on the findings of the activities analysis

The analysis of the activities recorded by the project team members on their activity sheets confirms to a large extent the pattern of activities described by the team members and professionals in their interviews.

All three project teams made a wide range of introductory contacts by telephone or at meetings. It can be seen from the tables that some of these were followed up with less success than others, viz the social services and youth service contacts of You 2 and PACE. CHYPP, on the other hand, built a strong programme of work with social services through a limited number of initial contacts.

Neither CHYPP nor PACE appeared to capitalise to a great extent on the considerable number of introductory meetings they had with other voluntary and community staff, a mixed group with whom You 2 had relatively little contact at any stage. There was little or no evidence of the close contact with drugs workers reported by PACE in interviews at the end of the project monitoring period, and it can only be assumed that the extent of this activity was not recorded by the project team members on the activity sheets.

The most strikingly successful activity, in terms of numbers, was the You 2 contact with schools, which led to over 100 sessions with young people in schools, at which more than one member of the project team staff was usually present. The work of both CHYPP and PACE with young people in schools was also notable. The professional training sessions with teachers conducted by CHYPP and You 2 were well developed, as were CHYPP's professional training sessions with social services staff. You 2's success in developing young people's sessions with Youth Training Schemes was clear from the activity sheets, as was the relative success of PACE with the same group.

PACE's development of joint initiatives with health education/ health promotion staff was notable. CHYPP's concentration on the Teenage Ante-natal Clinic was clearly shown, as was its work with the Young Mothers' Group. The work of the PACE health visitor in making home visits to young women was also shown.

CHYPP staff recorded more activities in giving advice and lending resources than the other two projects.

The recorded contact with GPs and family planning clinic staff was conspicuously low in all three projects, reinforcing the comments made by the team members and others in their interviews. The contact with health authority staff, other than FPC staff, was more developed in City and Hackney than in the other two projects. (The figures in Milton Keynes were partly affected by the concentration of contacts with health authority staff on unsuccessful attempts to develop an ambitious sex education questionnaire initiated by health authority staff for use in schools and partly by their successful efforts to set up a Brook clinic in Milton Keynes for the period after the funding from the Department of Health had finished.)

Appendix III

Telephone enquiries

We designed forms in conjunction with the project teams to monitor telephone enquiries to the projects from professionals, other agencies and young people. The forms included details of the age of young people, the job or status of the professionals or other enquirers, and the nature and topic of the telephone call or enquiry. The forms also included information on whether the call was from a *new* client or professional contact or whether it was a *repeat* call.

Table III.1 shows the total number of calls which were recorded by the three project teams in the period from October 1987 to March 1989.

Table III. 1 Telephone enquiries received by project teams

	Total no of calls	Type of contact			From whom	
		New contact	Repeat contact	Not recorded	Young person/ client	Prof./ other agency
CHYPP	96	72	24	-	8	88
You 2	520	425	77	18	381	139
PACE	287	158	123	6	88	199

It can be seen that CHYPP recorded fewer telephone calls on the telephone enquiry forms than the other two projects. This was partly because they received very few calls directly from young people (8 in all were recorded), and partly because they recorded many, although not all, of their telephone contacts with professionals and other agencies on the activity sheets (analysed in Appendix II). There was a minimal amount of duplicate recording of telephone calls on the activity sheets and on the telephone enquiry forms.

It should be noted that in all three projects the majority of repeat contact calls were with professionals. Young people who telephoned more than once were usually telephoning again about the same topic or event, eg. to change appointments, to speak to a different member of staff about the same topic.

Table III. 2 Age of young people telephoning You 2 and PACE

| | You 2 | | PACE | |
	Nos	%	Nos	%
Under 16	14	4	6	7
16-19	100	26	11	12
20-24	115	30	31	35
25 and over	100	26	21	24
Unspecified	52	14	19	22
Total young people	(381)		(88)	

It can be seen from Table III.2 that around a quarter of the telephone enquirers were over 25 in both areas. However, the age of the young person was not recorded in over one-fifth of cases in South Sefton and in 14 per cent of cases in Milton Keynes. The majority of the enquiries were of a routine nature asking about available services, as will be seen below, and it is understandable that staff did not necessarily want to ask the enquirer's age in such circumstances.

Table III. 3 Nature of telephone enquiries from young people

| | You 2 | | PACE | |
	Nos	%	Nos	%
Service enquiry	102	27	11	13
Enquiry re times	98	26	3	3
Counselling appointment	35	9	20	23
Clinic appointment	31	8	8	9
Telephone counselling	25	6	25	28
Information re other services	11	3	7	8
Other advice/information	9	2	14	16
Referral to Women's Health Group (over-25s using same premises)	72	19	–	–
Total enquiries	(381)		(88)	

It can be seen that few of the telephone enquiries from young people in Milton Keynes were other than routine calls seeking appointments or information. In South Sefton, however, over a quarter of telephone enquiries resulted in some counselling being given on the telephone.

Table III. 4 Topic of telephone enquiries from young people

	You 2		PACE	
	Nos	%	Nos	%
Pregnancy test	235	62	6	7
Pregnancy	35	9	5	6
Contraception	35	9	25	28
TOP/post-TOP	25	7	8	9
Other women's health*	20	5	27	31
Post-coital advice	13	3	6	7
AIDS/STD	2	<1	2	2
Rape	2	<1	1	1
Not recorded	14	4	8	9
Total	(381)		(88)	

* includes other women's health matters, gynae problems, menopause, smear tests, menstruation, etc.

As Table III.4 shows, the majority of telephone enquiries to You 2 (62 per cent) were about pregnancy testing, which was not surprising, given the use made of the project's services by young people. Nearly one-third of the telephone enquiries to PACE were to do with general women's health matters, which, again, reflects the use made of the project by people seeking help on topics which were not strictly within the remit of the original aims of the projects.

Table III. 5 Enquiries by type of professional or other agency

	CHYPP		You 2		PACE	
	Nos	%	Nos	%	Nos	%
Health professional	25	28	19	14	53	27
Teacher/other educational	21	24	25	18	29	15
Social worker	12	14	13	9	39	20
Voluntary org.	10	11	17	12	4	2
Youth workers	9	10	8	6	13	7
MSC/YTS trainer	2	2	24	17	11	5
Other PAS	2	2	7	5	7	4
Parent	1	1	9	6	5	3
Student	1	1	7	5	2	1
Probation/police	–	–	1	<1	5	3
GP/GP receptionist	–	–	–	–	1	<1
Unspecified	1	1	9	6	22	11
Other	4	5	10	7	8	4
Total professionals	(88)		(139)		(199)	

Family planning and counselling projects for young people

Table III.5 shows that over a quarter of the telephone calls from professionals in both CHYPP and PACE were from health professionals. One quarter of the calls to CHYPP were from teachers, compared with less than one-fifth to You 2 and one-sixth to PACE. One-fifth of calls to PACE were from social workers, compared with less than one in ten of the You 2 calls. On the other hand, nearly one-fifth of the You 2 calls were from YTS trainers.

Table III. 6 Nature of telephone enquiries from professionals

	CHYPP		You 2		PACE	
	Nos	%	Nos	%	Nos	%
Resources	25	24	24	16	28	14
Help with teaching	23	22	35	23	25	13
General info re project	19	18	25	17	26	13
Client referral	10	9	35	23	47	24
Clinic information	9	8	7	5	4	2
Request for speaker	8	8	5	3	3	1
Liaison	8	8	–	–	19	10
Referral agencies	3	3	4	3	1	<1
Information re other services	1	1	10	7	10	5
Follow-up on mutual client	–	–	1	<1	22	11
Unspecified	–	–	–	–	14	8
Number of enquiries	(106*)		(149*)		(199)	

* More than one enquiry covered in some telephone calls.

Table III.6 shows that the most frequent enquiries to CHYPP from professionals were to do with resources or help with teaching. Help with teaching was also important with You 2, but in both PACE and You 2, nearly a quarter of professional enquiries were concerned with referring a client to the project, and in PACE, over 10 per cent of enquiries were concerned with following up a mutual client.

The topics covered in the telephone enquiries from professionals or other agencies ranged widely, but sex education accounted for nearly 40 per cent of the professional telephone enquiries to CHYPP, 25 per cent to You 2 and 17 per cent to PACE.

As was found with the enquiries from young people, repeat telephone calls from professionals were often about the same topic and referred to the same incident or episode.

Appendix IV

Analysis of self-completion forms filled in by women under-25 using family planning clinics and BPAS

Short forms were designed for self-completion by women under 25 who attended family planning clinics in Milton Keynes and South Sefton for the first time during the monitoring period. The forms were intended to be distributed by the clinic staff to women on their first attendance at all six of the Milton Keynes family planning clinics and the eight South Sefton family planning clinics within the vicinity of Bootle. (Two of the South Sefton clinics only held monthly clinics and did not return any information.) In addition, forms were distributed to young women under 25 attending BPAS in Milton Keynes for counselling in connection with a termination of pregnancy. City and Hackney family planning clinics did not take part in the exercise because the health authority considered that it would be too onerous a duty for the staff of the clinics.

The purpose of the forms was to establish how these young people had heard of the family planning clinic or BPAS, the extent and source of their knowledge of the three young people's projects, and to see to what extent any knowledge of the existence of the three young people's projects had influenced these under-25-year-olds to attend these other family planning clinics or BPAS.

Although we received considerable cooperation from the family planning clinic staff in the areas, there were some problems, particularly initially, in ensuring that forms were completed by all eligible women. We carried out checks on the numbers of women in the relevant age-group on the family planning clinic returns, and found some discrepancies between the numbers of new attenders aged under 25 and the numbers of forms we had received. However, given these limitations, we present the figures with the proviso that a small proportion of under-25s attending some of the family planning clinics were missed. The BPAS figures were an accurate representation of eligible women.

We received completed forms from 448 women under 25 attending BPAS during the monitoring period, 356 women under 25 attending the Milton Keynes family planning clinics and 398 women under 25 attending the South Sefton family planning clinics. Table IV.1 gives the breakdown by age.

Table IV. 1   Age of clients under 25 filling in self-completion forms

	Milton Keynes BPAS		Milton Keynes FPCs		South Sefton FPCs	
	Nos	%	Nos	%	Nos	%
19 and under	207	47	171	48	198	50
20-24	235	53	170	48	200	50
Not known	–	–	15	4	–	–
Base: total clients under 25 completing forms	(448)	(100)	(356)	(100)	(398)	(100)

The figures for first attendance at family planning clinics in Milton Keynes and South Sefton both show an exact 50:50 split between the under 20s and the 20-24 age-group (when the figure for those who did not state their age is removed from the Milton Keynes total). Among those attending BPAS, the split was 53 per cent over 20 and 47 per cent under 20.

There were some interesting differences between the clinics in the ways in which women had found out about the service, as Table IV.2 shows.

Nearly three-quarters of the women attending BPAS had been referred by their GPs. Since BPAS was operating under an agency agreement with the Milton Keynes health authority to perform NHS abortions, it was likely that a high proportion of new clients would have been referred by their GPs. It was interesting to note that 7 per cent of clients had heard of BPAS through You 2, and these women accounted for the second single largest group in terms of referral source.

The young women attending family planning clinics were more likely to have come to the clinic through an informal contact, but there were some differences between Milton Keynes and South Sefton, with 62 per cent of the South Sefton women mentioning a friend, relative or other informal source, compared with 47 per cent in Milton Keynes. Friends accounted for 44 per cent of the South Sefton referrals, compared with 28 per cent in Milton Keynes.

Over 10 per cent of Milton Keynes clinic attenders heard of the family planning clinic through their GPs, compared with 6 per cent in South Sefton. 14 per cent in Milton Keynes found the family planning clinic in the telephone book, compared with 6 per cent in South Sefton. Eight per cent in South Sefton came through a community health professional, mainly health visitors, compared with 2 per cent in Milton Keynes.

Apart from these sources of information or referral, young women came to the clinics through a variety of sources. It was interesting, and perhaps indicative, that very few came through publicity of any kind, reinforcing the finding in the

Table IV. 2 How clients under 25 had found out about BPAS/FPC

	Milton Keynes BPAS		Milton Keynes FPCs		South Sefton FPCs	
	Nos	%	Nos	%	Nos	%
Friend	21	5	101	28	175	44
Mother	4	<1	23	6	16	4
Sister	2	<1	15	4	24	6
Other relative	1	<1	9	3	19	5
Other informal	1	<1	21	6	13	3
Leaflets/posters/ newspapers	6	1	0	0	4	1
Telephone book	9	2	49	14	25	6
GP/GP surgery	324	72	41	12	25	6
Other FP Clinic	5	1	7	2	6	2
Health centre/other clinic	10	2	10	3	16	4
Hospital	5	1	2	<1	5	1
Community health professional	1	<1	7	2	32	8
Social worker	0	0	1	<1	2	<1
FPC answerphone	0	0	13	4	0	0
You 2/PACE	30	7	4	1	0	0
Bakehouse/WHG	8	2	1	<1	0	0
CAB/other vol. org	5	1	3	<1	0	0
School	1	<1	3	<1	2	<1
Been before/just knew	6	1	13	4	31	8
DK/n.a.	13	3	33	9	9	2
Total clients under 25	(448)	(100)	(356)	(100)	(398)	(100)
(Total sources given)	(452)		(356)		(404)	

main report of the lack of publicity surrounding family planning services or abortion services.

The young women were asked to record whether they had seen or heard anything about the You 2 or PACE projects for young people in Milton Keynes or South Sefton.

Table IV. 3 Whether clients under 25 had heard of You 2/PACE

	Milton Keynes BPAS		Milton Keynes FPCs		South Sefton FPCs	
	Nos	%	Nos	%	Nos	%
Yes	69	15	17	5	25	6
No	379	85	339	95	373	94
Base: total clients under 25 completing forms	(448)	(100)	(356)	(100)	(398)	(100)

Table IV.3 shows that 15 per cent of the women under 25 attending BPAS in Milton Keynes and 5 per cent of those attending the Milton Keynes family planning clinics had heard of You 2, and 6 per cent of those attending the South Sefton clinics had heard of PACE. It cannot be said that these young people's projects had had much impact on these under-25-year-olds.

A distinction should be made between those attending BPAS and those attending family planning clinics for the first time. Those attending BPAS were pregnant, and the vast majority were seeking a termination of pregnancy. The fact that 15 per cent had heard of You 2 has to be treated with caution. Seven per cent of the total said that they had come to BPAS through You 2, and it is likely that the majority of these had been referred directly by You 2. For the rest of the BPAS under-25s who had heard of You 2, this knowledge had not prevented an unwanted pregnancy, but it is not possible to say at what point they had first heard of it. They may only have heard of the project after they had become pregnant through its reputation as a pregnancy testing service.

The staff of the young people's projects, particularly in Milton Keynes, interpreted the low level of knowledge of their services among young women attending family planning clinics as indicating that they were attracting a different type of clientele from the family planning clinics and that they were getting through to young people who would not use family planning clinics. It is, of course, impossible to deduce this from the evidence available on these self-completion forms. All that can be said is that small proportions of young women under the age of 25 who were attending family planning clinics in the two areas for the first time had heard of young people's projects set up specifically to attract them.

Those who had heard of You 2 or PACE were asked whether this had influenced their decision to attend BPAS or the family planning clinic. We were interested to know whether the publicity surrounding the projects, or their outreach work, or any other work they had carried out in raising the level of consciousness about contraception or pregnancy counselling, had had any influence on young people.

Table IV. 4 Whether clients under 25 had been influenced in their decision to attend BPAS/FPCs by what they had heard about You 2/ PACE

	Milton Keynes BPAS		Milton Keynes FPCs		South Sefton FPCs	
	Nos	%	Nos	%	Nos	%
Yes	25	6	5	1	2	<1
Partly	17	4	3	1	6	2
No	24	5	8	2	17	4
n.a.	3	<1	1	<1	0	0
Not heard of You 2/ PACE	379	85	339	95	373	94
Base: total clients under 25 completing forms	(448)	(100)	(356)	(100)	(398)	(100)

Table IV.4 shows that 10 per cent of those attending BPAS had been influenced, at least partly, by what they had heard about You 2. However, only 2 per cent of those attending the Milton Keynes family planning clinics had been influenced by what they had heard about You 2 and 3 per cent of those attending South Sefton clinics had been influenced by what they had heard about PACE.

These findings are perhaps not surprising. The greater influence on the BPAS clients is to be expected in that more were directly referred by You 2. It could be argued that people who were influenced by You 2 or PACE to use contraception or seek pregnancy counselling would have tended to use the services offered by You 2 or PACE. On the other hand it is notable that so few young women who had actually attended the family planning clinics had heard of the projects. It might have been hoped that the existence of projects for young people would have raised consciousness and encouraged young people to use existing services as well as services specially designed for their needs.

Appendix V

Interview sampling and selection methods

Personal interviews were carried out with respondents from the following four groups. All interviews were carried out by members of PSI staff or by two experienced interviewers, using a series of semi-structured questionnaires, which are available on request from PSI. All respondents in each group were asked the same questions in the same order, but a number of questions were 'open-ended', allowing for full answers to be recorded verbatim. Code-frames were constructed for the analysis of these answers. This technique allows for the extensive use of quotations from interviews used in this report.

(i) The project teams, their managers and advisers

All members of the project teams and their principal managers and advisers were interviewed when the projects had been running for about three months or when they joined the team, and again immediately after the end of the 18-month monitoring period.

Table V.1   Interviews with project teams, their managers and advisers at beginning of monitoring period (or when team members joined)

	City & Hackney Nos	Milton Keynes Nos	South Sefton Nos
Health workers	6	6	2
Clerical/admin staff	1	2	1
FPC doctors	–	1	1
Brook FP doctors	2	–	–
Brook nurses	2	–	–
Other Brook staff	2	–.	–
Managers and steering group advisers	5	11	5

Table V. 2   Interviews with project teams, their managers and advisers at end of monitoring period

	City & Hackney Nos	Milton Keynes Nos	South Sefton Nos
Health workers*	4	4	2
Clerical/admin staff	–	–	1
FPC doctors	–	2	1
Brook FP doctors	2	–	–
Other Brook staff	3	–	–
Managers and steering group advisers	5	8	5

*   In addition, informal interviews took place with 2 CHYPP team members and 1 You 2 team member when they left the projects before the end of the monitoring period.

Table V.1 gives details of the interviews carried out at the beginning of the monitoring period (or when team members joined the projects) and Table V.2 gives details of the interviews carried out at the end of the monitoring period. Changes in the team membership and in the doctors and Brook staff are noted in Chapters 1 and 12. Chapter 12 gives some details of the managers and advisers interviewed, who were all members of the steering groups in the three areas and included senior medical, nursing and health education or health promotion staff employed by the health authority. In Milton Keynes, outside advisers from the education service, social services and BPAS who were on the steering group were interviewed in addition to health authority staff. All managers and advisers were interviewed both at the beginning and end of the monitoring period, apart from one City and Hackney manager and two Brook managers who were interviewed only at the end of the monitoring period and three Milton Keynes advisers who were interviewed only at the beginning of the monitoring period.

(ii) Professionals
Interviews were carried out towards the end of the monitoring period with a variety of professionals working with young people in the districts. Family planning clinic doctors, family planning clinic nurses and health visitors were selected at random from lists supplied by the health authorities. The AIDS coordinators in each district and four staff from BPAS in Milton Keynes were interviewed because of their special relevance to the projects. The other professionals were selected from the contacts made by the project teams, and were usually those with whom the teams had had most contact. 37 professionals

were interviewed in City and Hackney, 41 in Milton Keynes and 32 in South Sefton. Table V.3 gives a breakdown by profession.

Table V. 3   Professionals interviewed at end of monitoring period

	City & Hackney Nos	Milton Keynes Nos	South Sefton Nos
Family planning doctors	4	6	5
Family planning nurses	6	6	6
Health visitors	6	6	6
Midwives	1	–	–
AIDS coordinators	1	1	1
BPAS counsellors	–	4	–
Teachers/FE lecturers	7	9	5
Social workers	2	1	1
Ed. Welfare Officer	1	–	–
Youth workers	4	5	4
YTS managers	2	3	3
Special youth project workers	3	–	1
Total all professionals	37	41	32

(iii) Young people using the projects' services
Interviews took place at the project premises in Milton Keynes and South Sefton and at the Shoreditch Brook clinic in City and Hackney with 142 young people using the projects' services. Interviewing started at the beginning of November 1988, five months before the end of the monitoring period. We aimed to interview 50 young people in each district, but only achieved 42 interviews in South Sefton by the end of the monitoring period. In City and Hackney, all 50 interviews were with women, 49 women and 1 man were interviewed in Milton Keynes and 37 women and 5 men in South Sefton.

Our interviewing was restricted to days on which clinics were held in Milton Keynes and South Sefton, because we could not afford to spend days achieving one or no interviews, which might have happened on other days, according to the daily returns of numbers of people attending the drop-in services. (See Chapter 5 for a discussion of this.)

Young people were asked if they would be prepared to be interviewed after they had seen the doctor or a member of staff. Everyone attending the Milton Keynes and South Sefton projects on the selected days was asked if they would be interviewed, but this was not possible in City and Hackney, even with two interviewers present, because of the greater numbers of clients at the clinic

340

sessions. Interviewers asked the next client as soon as they had finished an interview, so that no pre-selection took place. No-one who had been interviewed on a previous occasion was eligible. The refusal rate was very low.

Personal characteristics of those interviewed are given in Tables 5.1 to 5.5 of the report.

(iv) Young people who had not used the projects' services

Interviews took place with 31 young women, the majority of whom had had unwanted pregnancies or who had become pregnant while teenagers. In City and Hackney we interviewed young women attending the teenage ante-natal clinic (6) and attending a young mothers' group (3); in Milton Keynes we interviewed young women from a centre providing support for schoolgirl mothers (5) and from those attending BPAS seeking termination of pregnancy (6); in South Sefton we interviewed young women from a young mothers' group (11). The respondents were not selected on a random basis, but were simply present at the projects concerned on the days the interviewer was there. The ages of those interviewed are given in Chapter 8.

References

Alberman, E. and Dennis, K.J. (eds), *Late Abortions in England and Wales*, Royal College of Obstetricians and Gynaecologists, London, 1984

Allen, I., *Family Planning, Sterilisation and Abortion Services*, Policy Studies Institute, 1981

Allen, I., *Counselling Services for Sterilisation, Vasectomy and Termination of Pregnancy*, Policy Studies Institute, 1985

Allen, I., *Education in Sex and Personal Relationships*, Policy Studies Institute, 1987

Bury, J., *Teenage Pregnancy in Britain*, Birth Control Trust, 1984

Clarke, L., Farrell, C. and Beaumont, B., *Camden Abortion Study: the views and experiences of women having NHS and private treatment*, British Pregnancy Advisory Service, 1983

Family Planning Association, *District Health Authority Family Planning Services in England and Wales*, FPA, 1985

Farrell, C., *My Mother said ... the way young people learned about sex and birth control*, Routledge and Kegan Paul, 1978

Fleissig, A., Jessopp, L. and Griffiths, S., 'A walk-in pregnancy testing service', *Health Trends*, May 1989, Vol 21, No 2, pp.58-61

Simms, M. and Smith, C., *Teenage Mothers and their Partners*, Institute for Social Studies in Medical Care, HMSO, 1985

Williams, S. and Allen, I., *Health Care for Single Homeless People*, Policy Studies Institute, 1989